Teaching Modern Foreign Languages at Advanced Level

Modern foreign languages (mfl) at GCE Advanced/Advanced Subsidiary (A/AS) level represent a challenge for both learners and teachers. For learners the perceived difficulty of the subject and the gap between pre- and post-16, that is the hugely different demands made by GCSE and A/AS level qualifications, can become stumbling-blocks. For teachers the high levels of subject knowledge required, the difference in teaching approaches as well as the lack of guidance material on how best to teach learners at A/AS level can cause concern and uncertainty.

This book presents a framework for the teaching of mfl at A/AS level based on contributions from a number of experienced colleagues in the field. Chapters, which build on good practice pre-16 such as the importance of sequencing and grading as well as of multi-skill activities, address three broad themes: changing A/AS level courses, the transition from GCSE to A/AS level, as well as planning, teaching and assessment at A/AS level. The Epilogue provides an outlook to the learning and teaching of mfl in higher education. In recognition of the growing importance of vocational contexts, the book also features a discussion of vocational alternatives to A/AS level. Grammar, culture, learner independence, literature, translation and the use of new technologies are examined in relation to A/AS level requirements; their discussion offers principles which can be applied more generally to mfl teaching at intermediate and advanced levels.

Although the book is aimed at mfl teachers with little or no experience of A/AS level teaching, including newly qualified and student teachers, in view of the recent changes at 16–19 it will also be very useful to colleagues experienced at A/AS level mfl teaching. Chapters draw on relevant theoretical frameworks and research findings in a practical way. Numerous examples and reflection activities have been included to provide impulses for reflection on or preparation for personal practice.

Teaching Modern Foreign Languages at Advanced Level

Edited by
Norbert Pachler

London and New York

First published 1999
by Routledge
2 Park Square, Milton Park, Abingdon, Oxon, OX14 4RN

Simultaneously published in the USA and Canada
by Routledge
270 Madison Ave, New York NY 10016

Routledge is an imprint of the Taylor & Francis Group

Transferred to Digital Printing 2006

© 1999 selection and editorial matter Norbert Pachler
© the contributors for individual chapters

Typeset in Goudy by
J&L Composition Ltd, Filey, North Yorkshire

British Library Cataloguing in Publication Data
A catalogue record for this book is available
from the British Library

Library of Congress Cataloging in Publication Data
Pachler, Norbert.
    Teaching modern foreign languages at advanced level/Norbert
Pachler,
        p. cm.
    Includes bibliographical references (p.) and index.
    1. Languages, Modern–Study and teaching. I. Title.
PB35.P13 1999
418'.0071–dc21   99-22622
                    CIP

ISBN 0 415 20314 7

Publisher's Note
The publisher has gone to great lengths to ensure the quality of this reprint
but points out that some imperfections in the original may be apparent

Contents

List of figures

List of activities

List of contributors

Douglas Allford is Lecturer in Languages in Education at the Institute of Education, University of London, where he teaches on the MA in Modern Languages in Education. He holds a PhD and has many years' experience teaching German for commercial, economic and other applied purposes at most levels from *ab initio* to postgraduate. In this connection he became interested in translation not only as a skill but also as a pedagogic tool. His current research and writing interests include, as well as aspects of mfl teaching, independent language learning; literature and language teaching; discourse analysis; aspects of language and cognition.

Ann Barnes is subject co-ordinator for PGCE Modern Foreign Languages at the University of Warwick. Previously, she taught German and French in a comprehensive school, and was Head of German in a Sixth Form College. Her publications include work on developing advanced reading skills and teaching languages in the sixth form, as well as using ICT in language teaching and the professional development of trainee teachers.

Jo Bond studied at Oxford University, holds a Masters Degree in French and German and has been teaching modern foreign languages to a wide ability range at Key Stages 3 and 4 and to A level in West Midlands secondary schools since 1986. Amongst others Jo held the post of Modern Languages Co-ordinator. Jo created cartoons for several CILT Network publications, contributed to *Learning to teach modern foreign languages in the Secondary School* (Routledge 1997) and wrote a chapter on grammar for the CILT title *Aus eigener Erfahrung: von GCSE bis 'A' level*.

Jim Coleman spent fourteen years at the University of Glasgow, publishing three books and several articles on French Renaissance literature, including definitive critical editions of humanist poet and tragedian Jean de La Péruse, after graduating from Exeter University and researching in Paris. More recently, he has co-authored innovative language-learning materials, and concentrated on research into second-language acquisition, especially in the university context, with over forty published articles and nearly seventy conference papers/invited lectures, one-third of them outside the UK. He moved to the University of Portsmouth in 1988, becoming Professor of Foreign Language Learning in 1992. In 1993–5, he coordinated the largest ever survey of university language students, measuring the proficiency, background, motivation and attitudes of 25,000 European students. He is currently managing a three-year, government-funded project to define and disseminate best practice with regard to student residence abroad. He has also published on contemporary France.

Kit Field qualified as a teacher in 1982. Five years after his initial qualification he moved to the New Mills Comprehensive School in Derbyshire to take up the post of Head of Modern Languages Faculty. Here he taught French and German to the full age and ability range and became involved in the Technical and Vocational Education (TVEI) Initiative. Kit is presently Principal Lecturer of Education in the Centre for Educational Leadership and School Improvement and Canterbury Christ Church University College. This follows several years as the Deputy Course Director for the PGCE (Secondary) programme, for which Kit had particular responsibility for the modern foreign languages course. Kit co-authored the text entitled *Learning to Teach Modern Foreign Languages in the Secondary School* with Norbert Pachler and has written several chapters and articles on mentoring and the OFSTED inspection process. Currently he is editing a book to be published by Routledge entitled *Issues in Modern Foreign Languages* and is writing a book entitled *Effective Subject Leadership*.

Shirley Lawes has taught French in secondary, further and adult education as well as in industry. She has also been involved for many years in training tutors and teachers of modern foreign languages. Shirley, Senior Lecturer in Education, is currently course tutor for the PGCE/Maîtrise programme at Canterbury Christ Church University College in partnership with the *Université du Littoral* in France. Her writing and research are focused around aspects of teaching and learning modern foreign languages in post-compulsory education and a comparative study of young people's attitudes to vocational education in Kent and the Pas de Calais, France.

Lynne Meiring is a PGCE tutor at the University of Wales Swansea. She has been involved in Initial Teacher Education for seven years. She also contributes to the MEd programme and carries out higher degree supervision. Lynne graduated from UCNW Bangor in 1976 with a BA (Hons) followed by a PGCE in 1977 and gained her MEd degree from UW Swansea in 1995. She has taught French and German over a period of 15 years in schools and colleges in England and Wales. She has also designed and delivered language courses for industry. She was involved in the Welsh Office initiative to retrain non-specialist teachers for mfl teaching. Research interests have included measuring the quality and quantity of pupil use of target language and the feasibility of teaching mfl to SEN within the context of the National Curriculum.

Nigel Norman has been a Lecturer in Education with responsibility for the Secondary PGCE in Modern Foreign Languages at the University of Wales Swansea Department of Education since 1991. His research interests include the methodology of language teaching, grammar and literacy and information technology in languages. He also contributes to advanced courses for qualified teachers. Previously he was Advisory Teacher in Wiltshire, where he was involved in curriculum development, in-service training and resources management. Prior to that he spent seven years as Head of Modern Languages in a comprehensive school and ten years in a boys' grammar school, which included a year's exchange teaching in Germany. He has published course materials for German teaching and regularly reviews for the *Times Educational Supplement*.

Norbert Pachler works at the Institute of Education, University of London, as Lecturer in Languages in Education with responsibility for the Secondary PGCE in Modern Foreign Languages and the MA in Modern Languages in Education. He previously worked for De Montfort University Bedford as Senior Lecturer in Secondary Education. His research interests include modern foreign languages teaching and learning, comparative education as well as the application of new technologies in teaching and learning. He has published in these fields. In 1997 *Learning to Teach Modern Foreign Languages in the Secondary School*, which he wrote together with Kit Field, was published by Routledge. More recently, he was co-editor of *Learning to Teach Using ICT in the Secondary School* together with Marilyn Leask published by Routledge in 1999. He holds a Dr. phil. degree, has taught in secondary and further education and has worked for the inspectorate and advisory service of a local education authority on curriculum development and in-service training.

Bob Powell has been Director of the Language Centre at the University of Warwick since 1993. He began his teaching career in secondary schools in Wales and the Midlands before moving into higher education first as a Lecturer in Italian in Aberystwyth and then, for seventeen years as Lecturer in Education at the University of Bath. He holds a PhD and has published teaching materials in French and Italian as well as numerous articles on a range of language-teaching topics in academic and professional journals. He was President of the Association for Language Learning from 1991 to 1994.

Thomas Reimann studied Business Studies and Political Science at the University of Mannheim, Germany. He has considerable experience in industry and more recently in education where he worked in a modern languages department at an 11–18 school and as Deputy Head of Sixth Form with specific responsibilities for recruitment and marketing. In the last two years he has also become involved in modern foreign languages initial teacher education and run sessions at various conferences. He is currently self-employed and works as a consultant for different agencies and companies.

Karen Turner is Lecturer in Education (Modern Foreign Languages) at the Institute of Education, University of London, where she works with Postgraduate Certificate in Education and MA students. Her particular interests lie in teacher education, modern foreign language teaching methodology, reading in a foreign language and the role of foreign language learning in language development. She has taught in England and France and has considerable experience of teaching modern foreign languages in comprehensive and selective secondary schools. She was advisory teacher for modern foreign languages in the former Inner London Education Authority before joining the Institute of Education.

Foreword

by Trevor McDonald,
Chairman of the Nuffield Languages Inquiry

'Into the face of the young man who sat on the terrace of the Hotel Magnifique at Cannes there had crept a look of furtive shame, the shifty, hangdog look which announces that an Englishman is about to talk French.' This gem from P. G. Wodehouse (*The luck of the Bodkins*) has always made me smile, reminding me of the many occasions when I have felt every bit as awkward when travelling or working in countries where I did not speak the language.

Learning a language successfully lifts our confidence, and helps us even when we go on to encounter speakers of languages unfamiliar to us – as inevitably most will be. For those of us with a taste for exploration, learning a language can become a journey rich in challenge and in satisfaction: the challenge of a lifelong progress towards a horizon which we never quite reach but which always beckons, and at the same time the satisfaction of becoming increasingly familiar with new ways of thinking and communicating, and of entering a culture often accessible only through language.

Continuing the language learning of more of our young people beyond the basic requirements of our national curriculum is an aim to which we must all aspire. Too many sixteen year olds – including large numbers who have been successful in their language learning – abandon the study of languages after GCSE (or Standard Grade in Scotland). Numbers entering advanced courses in languages remain in decline. But the signs of a resurgence are there. There is very strong demand for languages as a supporting discipline among the 30% of students entering higher education. The market for languages in adult and continuing education remains buoyant. There has been a dearth of positive messages aimed at sixteen year olds about the importance of maintaining or progressing their language skills, but again there are positive signs of change.

Meanwhile, for those students entering advanced courses, this book reminds us that teachers and researchers are constantly seeking new insights into the teaching and learning process, and are applying ever more refinement to the design of courses and approaches. The future is in good hands.

Acknowledgements

This book owes a lot to a wide range of people who have influenced my thinking about the modern foreign languages teaching and learning process: students, colleagues, fellow educators with whom I have worked and whose work I have read over the years. It is impossible to thank them all individually, but I would like to take this opportunity to acknowledge their formative influence.

My particular thanks go to those colleagues who have been willing to take time out of their busy schedules to contribute to this book and to open themselves to external scrutiny.

Equally, without the continued support, encouragement and forbearance of those close to me this project would not have come to fruition.

I would also like to thank colleagues at the Institute of Education as well as Gill Watson for their constructive and perceptive comments on my own contributions to this book. I hope they find their suggestions have been taken on board.

Support from Helen Fairlie, Jude Bowen and Kate Oldfield at Routledge has allowed this book to materialise. Many thanks also to Ann Palmer for her work on the index of this book.

Thanks are due to Oxford University Press for permission to include some copyright material from Rod Ellis in the text (see Figure 6.2 in Chapter 6).

Prologue

Towards a methodology of modern foreign languages teaching at A/AS level

Norbert Pachler

The last decade or so has been a time of continuous change for those involved in the education system in the UK and in modern foreign languages (mfl) teaching in particular. The second half of the 1980s and the early 1990s saw the development and implementation of the National Curriculum as one important strand of the 1988 Education Reform Act. The National Curriculum brought with it, for the first time ever, the introduction of a statutory entitlement for all pupils aged 11 to 16 to study a modern foreign language. This was prompted partly by the hype around the Single European Market with its free movement of goods and people and the assumption that the ability to communicate in mfl was to become a basic skill and essential in the preparation of young people for adult life. Hopes were high to see the number of learners taking up a modern foreign language at post-16 rise.

Whilst mfl as subsidiary component of a vocational course, such as the General National Vocational Qualification (GNVQ), or as free-standing vocational qualification, such as FLIC or FLAW, etc. (see Chapter 15), have increased in popularity, the number of learners taking a modern foreign language at General Certificate of Education (GCE) Advanced (A) level examination in England, Wales and Northern Ireland has remained relatively stable (see Figure P.1). This at a time when the participation rate at post-16 in England increased from 51.5 per cent in 1998/9 to 71.5 per cent in 1994/5 (see Lucas 1997, p. 215) and when the number of pupils gaining A*–C grade GCSEs has risen significantly (see Figure P.2). In other words, whilst the number of pupils taking A/AS level has remained stable, in percentage terms of the number of learners staying on at post-16 it has actually declined. Therefore, by far not all pupils who have the pre-requisite linguistic qualifications, i.e. satisfactory mfl GCSE passes, choose to continue their study of a modern foreign language at A/AS level. The introduction of the Advanced Supplementary qualification can be said to have had very little impact in addressing this development. It remains to be seen whether the new Advanced Subsidiary level qualification will improve the situation (see Chapter 2). A/AS level mfl learners remain a rare and treasured species.

In Scotland, the situation is even worse where the number of learners studying a

Figure P.1 Number of candidates gaining grades A–C in GCE A Level French, German, Spanish and Italian from 1990 to 1995 (no statistics are available for years 1988 and 1989)

Year	French	German	Spanish	Italian
1990	27,116	9,446	3,799	722
1991	30,794	10,583	4,230	846
1992	31,261	11,338	4,720	876
1993	29,886	10,857	4,850	840
1994	28,942	10,832	4,740	802
1995	27,563	10,634	4,837	913

Source: Pachler and Field 1997, p. 333

Figure P.2 Number of pupils gaining grades A*–C in GCSE French, German, Spanish and Italian from 1988 to 1995 (Grade A* was introduced in 1994)

Year	French	German	Spanish	Italian
1988	269,033	76,320	19,125	2,890
1989	256,737	80,456	21,091	2,991
1990	280,890	84,306	24,870	3,901
1991	304,587	91,277	27,406	4,369
1992	322,653	101,388	29,468	4,937
1993	319,642	108,398	32,145	5,978
1994	328,306	118,985	36,335	5,479
1995	350,027	129,386	40,366	5,610

Source: Pachler and Field 1997, p. 6

modern foreign language at Higher Grade dropped from some 16,000 in 1975 to some 12,000 in 1985 and some 8,000 in 1995 (see Pachler and Field 1997, p. 21).

Whilst the increase in participation rates at post-16 has not translated into an increase in take-up at A/AS level, a change in *clientele* can, nevertheless, be discerned:

> [learners] who have opted to follow A/AS level courses have become more diverse in ability and interests. Their motivation and reasons for studying mfl have become more wide-ranging. [Learners] taking A/AS levels will not necessarily go on to study a modern foreign language at degree level. For many the mfl may be an additional A/AS level, supporting other scientific, technological or commercial subjects.
>
> (Pachler and Field 1997, p. 332)

One reason for young people to decide not to opt for the study of mfl at A/AS level and beyond is the perceived difficulty of the subject. The specialisation, if not over-specialisation, characteristic of the education system in England, Wales and Northern Ireland at post-16, together with the transactional nature of the National

Curriculum mfl Orders and the GCSE examination, lead to a situation where at the beginning of the A/AS level course hugely different demands are made on (mfl) learners than previously in their educational career (see also Pachler and Field 1997, Epilogue). This is often a considerable source of anxiety for learners and one reason why the participation rate at 17+ is on average some 15.5 per cent lower than at 16+ (see Lucas 1997, p. 215), i.e. there is a considerable dropout rate in the first year of post-compulsory education, although not only at A/AS level.

These are some of the contexts (prospective) teachers of mfl at A/AS level need to be aware of. A concerted effort seems necessary to ensure that an adequate mfl base post-16 is retained. Since, without a steady flow of enthusiastic mfl learners at A/AS level moving on to study mfl at Higher Education and going into Initial Teacher Education, the future of mfl in compulsory secondary education is at risk.

In the wake of the introduction of the National Curriculum Orders for mfl a lot of attention has been paid to the question of *how* to teach and assess mfl at 11 to 16 and numerous exemplification and guidance documents have emanated from government bodies. Also, with the increase in mfl being offered in secondary schools, requisite commercial publications have mushroomed. In the meantime, very little has been written and published about methodological questions at A/AS level. Whilst in recent years ample attention has been paid to post-16 qualifications, debates have tended to centre around ideological and socio-political questions, i.e. what types of qualifications are right for the twenty-first century, academic or vocational or a mixture of both, not so much methodological considerations, i.e. how best to teach mfl to 16–19 year olds (see Chapter 15). It is the stated aim of this publication to address this shortfall which is somewhat surprising as the A/AS examination remains a high-stake examination, fondly labelled as 'gold standard' in certain quarters, deciding, amongst other things, on university entrance and attracting enormous media attention every August when results are published.

This book attempts to delineate a methodological framework for mfl teachers at A/AS level. It is a logical progression of my earlier work with Kit Field (see Pachler and Field 1997). There obviously is a need for building on good practice at 11 to 16, for instance in order to ensure a smooth transition for learners, through e.g.:

- target language use for the instruction of and for interacting with learners;
- graded questioning;
- structuring and sequencing to ensure transfer and progression;
- use of multi-skill activities (i.e. combination of listening, speaking, reading and writing);
- a variety of interaction modes (i.e. teacher-centred work, pair work, group work, independent study, etc);
- differentiation; or
- the provision of models (repeat → choose from a selection → give open ended answers) etc.

At the same time, mfl teaching at A/AS level features fundamental differences such as the increased importance of explicit grammar teaching (see Chapter 6) or the necessity to increasingly draw on general knowledge, particularly in relation to target-culture teaching (see Chapter 5). These differences are not least due to the increased intellectual and cognitive capacities of learners, the learning outcomes expected by examinations as well as, of course, the much higher degree of learner independence required and the subsequent need for awareness and appropriate use of learning strategies. (see Chapters 4 and 13).

The chapters of this book, whilst contributed by a number of different authors, aim to go beyond the fragmentary treatment of isolated aspects of A/AS level mfl teaching. The book attempts to offer a coherent whole drawing on the expertise of colleagues nationally who have experience in the teaching of A/AS level mfl courses. All contributions were specially commissioned and written for this book following a detailed conceptual framework which I developed in consultation with numerous colleagues in the field.

At the same time, the book is, of course, in no way intended to constrain the imagination and creativity of the reader but merely aims to provide impulses for reflection on or, in the case of colleagues new to A/AS level mfl teaching, preparation for personal practice. Contributions draw to a varying degree on theoretical frameworks and research findings.

Where possible, the book attempts to acknowledge the existence of a varied mfl provision at post-16 outside the A/AS level framework (see Chapter 15). Given the fundamental ideological differences of these mostly vocational qualifications in their rootedness in a competence-based model of education, geared towards the description of educational achievements in terms of observable and assessable behaviours, I thought it best that, in order to ensure methodological cohesion, the focus of this book be confined, by and large, to A/AS level qualifications.

References

Lucas, N. (1997) 'The changing sixth form: the growth of pre-vocational education'. In Capel, S., Leask, M. and Turner, T. (eds) *Starting to Teach in the Secondary School*. London: Routledge, pp. 211–31.

Pachler, N. and Field, K. (1997) *Learning to Teach Modern Foreign Languages in the Secondary School*. London: Routledge.

Part I

Changing A/AS level courses

Chapter 1

The relevance of A/AS level courses to post-16 learners

Kit Field and Shirley Lawes

Introduction

GCE Advanced (A) levels have represented the 'gold standard' for the British education system since their introduction in the early 1950s. Specialisation through the selection of three and occasionally four subject areas has led to many discussions over what they actually prepare learners for. Access to A levels has tended to be restricted to the more academically able learners.

Socio-political developments have led to an increase in staying-on rates at post-16. In particular, the economic recession of the 1980s reduced the number of apprenticeships available to school leavers. Moreover, as Lucas points out (see 1997, p. 214), studies throughout the 1980s demonstrate that the proportion of Continental European youngsters continuing their education after the age of 16 has been significantly higher than in Britain. The trend across Europe is that the burden of vocational training has shifted from the world of work to educational institutions with Britain lagging behind. Comprehensivisation has increased access to post-16 and consequently post-19 study for learners.

For many years there has now been a focus of attention on post-16 study. In 1988, Gordon Higginson, chairing a committee appointed by the then Secretary of State for Education and Science and the Secretary of State for Wales, recommended a diversification of the content for A level study (see DES 1988). This theme has continued to run. National Vocational Qualifications (NVQs) and General National Vocational Qualifications (GNVQs) were created providing a qualification framework for vocational education and training supposedly of equivalence to academic qualifications. Discussions amongst commentators have not only concentrated on the academic/vocational divide, but also on the issue of breadth and depth (see Chapter 15). The International Baccalauréat examination, emanating from France, in contrast, encourages the continued study of up to eight subject disciplines, thereby making it an excellent route for the 'non-specialist' linguist (see Neather 1991).

A recent article in the *Times Educational Supplement* concerning the subject popularity amongst learners in secondary schools compared preferences expressed in 1971 with those in 1996 (see Judd 1997). In the early survey only

27 per cent of learners rated modern foreign languages (mfl) as their favourite subject and it ranked tenth out of eleven subjects. In 1996, mfl were still at number 10 but with only a 19 per cent popularity score.

The study of mfl is by far not the only choice learners have at post-16 and A/AS levels are not the only examinations available.

Objectives

By the end of this chapter you should:

- be aware of the range of study options available to post-16 mfl learners
- be able to recognise the relevance of different mfl study routes for a range of learner types
- understand the role of mfl in the post-16 curriculum
- be aware of the aims and objectives for the different study routes, and
- appreciate learners' motivations for following post-16 mfl courses

Modern foreign languages at post-16

Recent developments in the post-16 curriculum have led to several issues coming to the fore for mfl learners. They are compelled to make choices regarding further study at a young age. The basis for these choices is their own experience of learning a modern foreign language up to GCSE level. Figure 1.1 is a crude representation of these choices.

Ron Dearing's *Review of Qualifications for 16–19 Year Olds* (1996) considers these issues closely. The need to provide full post-16 programmes covering the key skills of Communication, Application of number and Information Technology is central

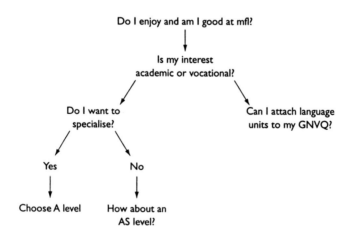

Figure 1.1 Choosing a post-16 mfl study route

to the recommendations made because they are expected by employers and Higher Education Institutions of learners completing a post-16 programme of study, regardless of the subjects actually studied. Also of concern is the popularity and appeal of subjects selected for study, their vocational viability, the academic rigour and lastly the potential for personal development. What follows is an analysis of mfl as a post-16 subject with these points in mind.

Popularity and appeal

It is too early to assess the impact of the new syllabuses and how successful they will be in attracting learners. It is possible to say, however, that, while we might celebrate the expansion of mfl provision at GCSE level, we still need to look very carefully at how we nurture potential A/AS level candidates throughout Key Stage 4 and how we motivate a greater number and wider variety of learners towards continuing to study a modern foreign language post-16. Is it possible that the 'languages for all' policy pursued in recent years at 11 to 16 has led to a situation where *most* pupils have achieved a basic level of communicative competence, but that in some situations, the most able linguists are not achieving their full potential if they are not sufficiently motivated to go on to A/AS level study?

One of the first things it is useful to check before the start of a post-16 mfl programme is exactly what motivates learners. This information, in turn, will provide an indication of learners' future goals and ambitions. In the past, when a smaller proportion of learners stayed on at post-16, it might have been more safely assumed that mfl study to A level was mostly in preparation for further mfl study at degree level. This is now less likely to be true partly because of the vastly increased number of young people who are going on to university to study a wider variety of degrees, often joint degrees, in which a modern foreign language may feature to a greater or lesser extent (see e.g. Coleman 1996). We should not assume therefore that *all* learners at A/AS level are budding linguists; we need to cater for a variety of motives and purposes. Indeed, even the 'specialists' continue to have 'non-specialist' language needs. So what might the range of motives and purposes within a learning group be? If the teacher is clear at the outset what motivates learners individually, then it is possible to help them identify and achieve longer-term goals.

___CTION

Activity 1.1 Why study mfl at post-16?

(a) Look at the following list of possible reasons for studying a modern foreign language at A/AS level and add any others you can think of.

(b) Ask your learners to respond to the questions individually.

1. Because you like the language
2. To travel to different countries
3. Because you are good at it
4. To become a better-educated person
5. Because you like the teacher
6. For your future career
7. Because your friends are doing it
8. Because your parents want you to do it
9. To get to know people who speak it
10. To have a better understanding of the way of life in the country where it is spoken
11.
12
13.
14.

(c) In order to assist you with your planning, analyse the outcomes and answer the following questions:

• what are the reasons for your learners opting for mfl?
• how can you use this information to inform your teaching style?

Activity 1.1 has been adapted from a survey carried out in the early 1990s by Jim Coleman (1995) into the motives of university learners for learning French. It is interesting to note that 'for your future career' was selected by 85.6 per cent of learners during year one, but this reduced to 73.5 per cent by year three, and that 'because you like the language' increased from 80.1 per cent in year one to 84.3 per cent in year three. The proportion of learners who wanted to become a better-educated person – just over one third – hardly changed over the three-year period. The most significant change was 'getting to know the people who speak it' which increased from 24.3 per cent to 33.3 per cent from years one to three. By the time learners enter university, the vocational motive is high. It is likely that, at the beginning of the first year of study at post-16, learners, on the whole, have more mixed motives for their choice of mfl. At that stage of their lives, learners embark on a period where longer-term decisions are made, where they have to begin to make choices about their future and to start to take on adult responsibilities. If the teacher is clear at the outset what motivates learners individually, then it is possible to help them identify and achieve long-term goals.

GCSE mfl courses encourage active communication. Successful GCSE learners are able to comprehend and communicate essentially factual messages. The appeal of mfl for many at post-16 is to develop this functional approach beyond the basic level attained at GCSE. The context of GCSE is essentially what might be called 'touristic' and 'domestic'. For many learners, post-16 study represents an opportunity to build upon this for vocational and more adult social purposes. David Phillips (1981) identified five different learner types embarking on post-16 study. The challenge for teachers and learners is to identify a programme which matches up to their aspirations.

Phillips's first category is best described as 'specialists', by which is meant those wishing to continue the study of mfl at university and for whom the traditional A level route has not been problematic. It is on this group of learners that teachers have traditionally concentrated their efforts. In order to be able to prepare such learners for university study, there has traditionally been little objection to the inclusion of literature in A level syllabuses. Literature tended to constitute a major part of undergraduate courses (see Epilogue). The Dearing Report remarks (see 1996, p. 9) that mfl undergraduates, according to university tutors and admissions officers, require a sound grounding in syntax and grammar. The traditional A level route has tended to offer opportunities for focused study including the demonstration of grammatical and syntactic accuracy. It is clear, however, that this focus on the literary register of language and a concentration on accuracy has not always been appreciated by the full range of learners. Dwindling numbers of learners opting for A level study (see Prologue) suggest that the approach required to learning in this way is holding less and less of an appeal.

Phillips's second type consists of learners intending to enter higher education, but for whom a modern foreign language is not the chosen subject of study. A/AS level subject specifications, formerly syllabuses, provide relevant learning opportunities here too. The emergence of course work and the study of regions and social aspects has led to a wide range of choice. A/AS level subject specifications include in their aims the fostering of cultural awareness or an understanding of culture and civilisation. It is not difficult to see how mfl can provide support and can integrate with other subject disciplines. Furthermore, language competence, the Dearing Report states (see 1996, p. 66), should be of functional value. Subject specification objectives encourage the development of study and personal skills, which can be seen as relevant to any other A/AS level programme. Some subject specifications make explicit mention of the need to develop skills appropriate to making a coherent argument, to classifying new points and to expanding on factual stimuli. This need to contribute to the development of key skills is another theme running through the Dearing recommendations. Communication is crucial to all post-16 learners. Mfl learning and communication cannot be separated from one another. Communication appears as a primary aim in all A/AS level subject specifications and successful learners of mfl tend to be perceived as good all round communicators.

For Phillips a third category, those learners wanting to begin work at 18+ and who (feel they) need a modern foreign language, also benefits from a communicative methodology. They might benefit from a GNVQ programme which provides the necessary vocational emphasis. Mfl units are not compulsory in GNVQ courses and they can be attached to many different vocational disciplines. Learners can treat the units as additional study but can acquire accreditation. Competence in a modern foreign language is seen as a transferable skill, usable in any vocational area. Learners are assessed against specific competence-based criteria which emphasise what they 'can do' in practical terms (see Chapter 15). A vocational 'slant' for Dearing means that communication can be seen in terms of giving presentations, developing team skills such as working in a group and of computer skills (see Dearing 1996, p. 51).

Phillips's fourth category is more complicated. He includes in it those who wish to continue the study of a modern foreign language out of interest as well as learners who had no other choice. The grouping of those who have made a positive choice with some who had no other choice is the root of many problems for teachers of mfl at post-16. For learners who lack intrinsic motivation it is often not so important what is taught, but how it is taught. A Baccalauréat programme, a combination of A and AS levels offering a broad base for study, might be the right choice for those learners. The opportunity to emphasise through the notion of weighting some subjects within a whole range without rejecting others is at the heart of the Baccalauréat. Consequently, a literary or vocational emphasis or an artistic or scientific emphasis does not mean specialisation. Learners are not required to make definitive choices, but will continue to study a broader range of subjects. Learners who make a positive choice are, therefore, able to concentrate time and effort on mfl, for example, and those who had no other choice are able to develop their foreign language skills along with other areas of interest.

Finally, Phillips refers to a group of dynamic and motivated learners, aspiring to the achievement of A level standard in a new language within two years. This rare group of learners cannot be integrated into a standard A/AS level group without difficulty and will need to learn at a very fast pace. Although such groups are unlikely to exist in many schools, it is interesting to analyse the needs of these learners given their ability. Teachers will need to ascertain their purpose of learning in order to accommodate them and to cater for their needs as, evidently, there is little time for induction. Such learners are likely to have had positive mfl learning experiences at Key Stage 4.

Vocational viability

The thrust of most curriculum developments in mfl learning in recent years has been its perceived importance to the British economy. The argument that fluency in a foreign language is an important vocational skill has become somewhat clichéd. Indeed, as Reeves points out (1996, p. 35), young people and even business and industry 'continue to be unimpressed by research data, reports and statistics which emphasise the need for a knowledge of foreign languages in industry and commerce'. Why is this the case? Is the continuing apathy towards the learning of mfl simply a result of Britain's imperial past or the consequence of sharing a language with the world's most powerful nation?

There has been an assumption, throughout the 1980s and 1990s, that as Europe unites commercially and economically, there is a need to provide young learners with appropriate mfl skills. This assumption has, at least in part, been one of the forces driving a more functional approach to teaching and learning mfl. However, what appears clear from statistics is that the message has not got through to potential learners. An alternative explanation is, however, that the need for able language users in the world of work is not as urgent as many would claim. The Dearing Report notes (1996, p. 8) that only a minority of employers actually felt that mfl were necessary. Speaking a foreign language is a useful 'extra', but for many the assumption that foreigners speak English does hold true.

> English is the mother tongue of 300 million people, a further 300 million use English as a second language and another 100 million can speak it fluently as a foreign language. Two-thirds of the world's scientists write in English and 80 per cent of information stored in electronic databases is in English.
>
> (Hagen 1998, p. 70)

The value of mfl in some vocational areas, however, is unquestionable. Stephen Hagen also points out (1998, p. 68) that in Western Europe and the Far East, English as a second language is little used. He goes on to cite a 1980s study which discovered that, while global companies were likely to use English as the standard language of formal communication such as for faxes, letters, e-mail and reports, when it came to using the telephone, social interaction and meetings, a mixture of languages was used. At the level of communication between individuals, therefore, fluency in one or more foreign languages might be seen as even more important now than ever before. The opportunity to choose Optional mfl units or attach Additional mfl units to a GNVQ programme, to get credit for mfl learning, viewed in this light, seems sensible.

The viability of mfl in a vocational context is far more obvious if one approaches the question from a skills point of view as opposed to trying to relate the course content to possible future needs. Mfl learning aims to lead learners to develop good communication skills. Whatever the route of learning and whatever the language, mfl learning demands high levels of organisation and structure with limited amounts of language available. Mfl learners need to make efficient use of language and to express difficult concepts coherently. A/AS level subject specifications increasingly incorporate a focus on study skills and strategies into their broad aims. An important aspect of mfl learning is also a critical understanding of different cultures and civilisations and an ability to make contact with target language (TL) speakers.

REFLECTION

Activity 1.2 Matching skills to professional needs

- Read through some A/AS level subject specifications. Make a note of the skills which are developed and/or encouraged (e.g. communication, organisation of ideas).
- By cross-referring to Activity 1.3 below, ascertain which occupations are well served by learning mfl (e.g. journalists, international bankers, marketing personnel, sales personnel, bilingual secretaries).
- Note which subject specifications demands relate most closely to which occupation type.
- You could map out the usefulness of mfl by drawing up a table with occupations across the top and skills developed listed below.

Even more traditional aspects to A/AS level study can provide opportunities to develop transferable skills. For example, the study of literature can develop skills applicable to a range of careers. Understanding a text in all its subtlety and then being able to present that analysis in a concise and meaningful way is a valuable skill which can easily be transferred, for instance, to the world of business management, government, administration and law.

REFELCTION

Activity 1.3 Vocational considerations

Talk to a careers adviser/teacher (at your institution). Find out which careers/occupations have potential for mfl use.

If long-term career decisions are made at 16, we do need to be sure that A/AS level and other post-16 study routes are different from GCSE and, indeed, from each other. What is distinctive about A/AS level is that it presents interesting intellectual challenges as well as functional application of language. A/AS level study of mfl provides not just the opportunity to develop language skills, but to develop critical thinking through the acquisition of knowledge about social and political issues, the culture and society of the target countries and literature in the TL. The level of fluency it is possible to achieve at A/AS level enables the learner to some extent to use the TL as a tool for other learning and is not just an end in itself. Herein lies a difficulty, however, in that when a learner's knowledge of the target culture and, indeed, of his or her own culture, society, politics and institutions is limited, the problem is not just *how* to express ideas, but *what* to say.

Academic rigour

Throughout the history of mfl teaching and learning, concerns have been expressed about the academic rigour surrounding the subject. Criticisms of and resistance to the so called Direct Method a whole century ago are oft repeated as mfl teachers argue in favour of a more functional approach. The consultation carried out by Dearing revealed some dissatisfaction within universities. New undergraduates were seen to be lacking a grounding in syntax and grammar (see Dearing 1996, p. 9).

At the time of writing, references to grammatical competence and academic rigour are detectable in the aims of some pre-1998 draft Subject Criteria A/AS level syllabuses only. (For the new Subject Criteria see QCA et al. 1999.) There appears to exist a problematic approach towards grammar and syntax at A/AS level. The lack of emphasis on grammar could be seen to deny the academic value of key aspects of linguistic competence. One syllabus for 1999 contains as aims reference to growing appreciation of language forms and registers as well as to the spoken word including 'to handle competently the necessary grammar and syntax'. Another couches the skills and competence in terms of learning outcomes and hence language use, as opposed to the constituent parts of language itself. This is not so far removed from the syllabus aims at GCSE level. Some find such a functional approach to mfl teaching at A/AS level problematic. A common defence of a more functional approach is that it is of greater relevance and interest to today's learners. The declining numbers of learners opting to follow A/AS level courses, however, make this doubtful. With subject specifications based on the new A/AS level Subject Criteria coming on stream at the time of writing, all A/AS level subject specifications can be expected to feature explicit references to grammar (see Chapters 2 and 6).

Mfl are in danger of being perceived as a service subject, one which supports the study of other disciplines and one which might be useful for the world of work. This low academic profile does little to attract academically able learners. The recommendations of many commentators for some time now have been to devise courses to meet the needs of non-specialists (see e.g. Wringe 1976).

REFLECTION

Activity 1.4 Linking mfl to other subjects
- Which subjects combine well with mfl?
- Talk with the Head of Sixth Form/the appropriate Curriculum Manager. Can mfl be studied in combination with any subject or are there some impossible subject combinations? Which ones? Give reasons for your answers.
- How many of your reasons give consideration to the place of mfl as a first A/AS level choice?
- Now consider which subjects can support the learning of mfl?
- Survey a group of mfl learners. Which other subjects do they study? What are the respective advantages and disadvantages of their subject combinations?

The notion of mfl as a service subject, we would argue, has had a negative effect on the perception of mfl as an academic subject. The overcrowded National Curriculum continues to squeeze a second modern foreign language out of mainstream study. There can only be a demotivating effect in terms of the academic profile of mfl when national bodies such as the Qualifications and Curriculum Authority (QCA) recommend the consideration of '[what] opportunities are there for using flexible approaches, such as twilight sessions, to make available a second language?' (1998, p. 14).

As has been noted already, the appeal of mfl as an academic post-16 subject is dwindling. Attention has been given to make the subject more appealing to a wider range of learners. This approach may have been at the expense of more academic learners. In an attempt to provide society with more linguists, it could be argued that we have cut off our noses to spite our faces.

Potential for personal development

One assumption one might safely make is that the majority of learners choose to continue studying a modern foreign language post-16 because they like it.

Here we arrive at the heart of the matter: the vital importance of the teacher's own enthusiasm for and love of the language and his or her ability to transmit them to learners. This, of course, should be a process which starts on day one in Year 7 and continues throughout the learner's experience. It might be argued that the 'battle' is lost or won in the first six weeks of mfl learning! Nevertheless, Year 10 is a crucial time in developing learner motivation towards continuing with mfl study beyond Year 11. While GCSE is an important milestone, it is possible for the teacher to encourage the view that it is not the only goal that learners might be aiming for (see also Pachler and Field 1997, ch. 1). The transition between GCSE and A/AS Level comes long before the actual start of the A/AS level course. As Pachler and Field (1997, p. 339) point out:

> it is very important for A/AS level mfl teachers to build on the tenets of mfl teaching pre-16, namely of providing enjoyment and stimulation to learners, promoting an ability to communicate and developing confidence and proficiency within a foreign cultural context.

Effective teaching and learning at Key Stage 4 is perhaps more important now than it has ever been given the increasing pressures for schools to produce good examination results. Equally, now that a much higher proportion of young people (75 per cent in 1997) remain in full-time education beyond the age of 16, learners who have opted to follow A/AS level courses have become more diverse in ability and interests and their motivation and reasons for studying mfl have become more wide ranging.

One thing we are sure of: to choose to study a modern foreign language at A/AS level rarely is a bad decision for a young person. Mfl is an area of study which can accompany any other combination of A/AS level subjects.

In addition to enabling learners to develop key skills, A/AS level mfl courses *can* provide a further dimension: that of moral, aesthetic and social development (see also the Central Advisory Council for England's Crowther Report 1959).

There is also the potential of supporting learners in their development of personal and interpersonal skills and also to provide them with the wherewithal to manage their own learning (see Chapter 4).

A recent curriculum update from the Assessment and Qualifications Alliance (AQA) (1998, p. 8) suggests that if a learner's main course of study does not cover the full range of skills, there will be a need to supplement it with additional units. In addition to meeting the requirements defined in the Subject Criteria (see QCA *et al.* 1999), certain subjects do provide a greater range of benefits to learners. For learners of mfl, many of the interpersonal, personal, moral, social and cultural elements are embedded in subject specification aims. Others are assumed.

REFLECTION
Activity 1.5 The contribution of mfl to whole school aims
- Look at the institution's mission statement and aims. Cross-reference these to the aims and objectives contained within mfl subject specifications used by the institution and also the 'hidden' curriculum underpinning the study of mfl.
- To what extent does studying mfl contribute to broad, whole institutional aims?
- Similarly, consider to what extent the aims and objectives of the pastoral curriculum are addressed by mfl study.

The study of mfl at post-16 requires learners to explore cultures beyond the immediate through communication with others. The content of programmes inevitably serves to open the mind; the recommended strategies and methods demand the development and use of interpersonal skills.

There is a case to be argued that learners of mfl are able at least to touch upon most aspects of the wider post-16 curriculum. It is no wonder that those who continue mfl study beyond A/AS level become highly attractive to employers for these reasons.

The transition from GCSE to A/AS level is considered in detail elsewhere (see Part II, in particular Chapter 3), but it is useful here to emphasise the different *content* of A/AS level subject specifications insofar as the learner is required to move on from largely functional language topics in which the transmission of facts is paramount. A/AS level requires learners to express *personal* opinions about a range of topics often related to their personal experience and then to work on more abstract topics which require them to express *informed* opinions on the basis of knowledge.

This shift or development in the content of learning to be undertaken clearly places different demands on the learner *and* the teacher. It is essential at the outset that the teacher is clear about what those demands are.

In addition to being aware of the reasons learners have for choosing A/AS level mfl and an understanding of what study skills learners will need, an audit of individual learning needs is essential. These three components will enable the teacher to plan for effective learning, striking the right balance between possible vocational application and academic study drawing on the strengths and addressing the weaknesses of the learner. A learning needs audit should take place at the start of a course. It could be repeated at appropriate points, partly as a self-review exercise for the learner. One would hope that learners have been encouraged throughout the secondary phase, indeed throughout their schooling, to be self-aware as learners. However, during A/AS level study it is essential that learners should be developing their autonomy, be conscious of their strengths and weaknesses and be able to devise, with support, their own learning strategies and targets. This is an ongoing process which the teacher needs to be conscious of throughout an A/AS level course.

REFLECTION
Activity 1.6 Planning to develop study skills
Look through some past A/AS level papers and note what study skills you would deploy to tackle the questions in different papers. Categorise the skills below under the appropriate headings. Add any other types of study skills and feel free to invent new headings:

independent reading skill	reading for gist
reading for detail	listening for gist
listening for detail	guessing the meanings of words from the context
using grammar to guess meaning	using clues in the text to guess meaning
improvisation	circumlocution
note taking	planning
drafting and re-drafting	use of the dictionary
general knowledge	cultural awareness

You may, for example, conclude that for 'Using clues to guess meaning' you need to develop the skills of: using pictures and graphics to interpret meaning, using headlines to predict meaning, using proper nouns to piece together meaning, noting punctuation to clarify meaning and analysing style and register to inform meaning.
• Consider what study skills the learner needs to develop during the A/AS level course.
• From a teacher's perspective, how is A/AS level different from GCSE?

The first step in developing learner independence is for the teacher to enable the learner to consider what his or her learning needs are and how they can be met. In practical terms, the teacher might survey individual learners. She might also draw on her knowledge of the learners, discussions with colleagues, profiles, records of achievement, school reports and, of course, GCSE results. Collectively, this information constitutes a *learner profile*, which will enable the teacher to plan the initial stages of the course effectively (see also Chapter 4).

REFLECTION

Activity 1.7 Developing learner profiles

Which of the following information about learners would you find useful to help you develop a profile of learners at post-16 level?

Consider how you might find out the following:

ability in each language skill	attitude to learning
cultural awareness interests	interpersonal skills
experience of the target culture	study skills
(visits and exchanges)	
confidence	other subjects being studied
future aspirations	extra curricular involvement

- Are there any other types of information you would like to add to the list?
- Use the methods of enquiry identified to build up a profile of different learners in a group.
- How will knowing this information help you adapt your teaching to suit individuals?

It may well be that learners need support in identifying aspects of their 'profile' as suggested in Activity 1.7 as they cannot be expected to know all they need to know or even be entirely aware of what they *do* know! An initial step would be to discuss in general terms with a group of learners what their concerns, expectations and aspirations are, to raise their awareness about their approaches to learning and to consider how they will respond to the demands of A/AS level and other post-16 mfl study. This should be followed by a written survey of individuals which might take the form of a questionnaire, an invitation to write down their own thoughts or to respond to some statements about aspects of the course, their future and their learning. This information, once collated should serve as an ongoing record with regular opportunities for the learner and the teacher to reflect on and update. In this way, both the learner and teacher 'track' progress from an attitudinal perspective and develop the learner's ability to self-evaluate and work towards independence. The learner profile obviously relates to the ongoing completion of a learner diary (see Chapter 3).

Summary

Studying mfl at post-16 level is beneficial to many different types of learners for many different reasons. There is a choice available between vocational programmes (GNVQ), more academic routes (A/AS level) and a broader based programme of study incorporating foreign language study (Baccalauréat). Such a choice is rarely if ever available within a single institution.

Teachers have rightly 'sold' their subject to a new clientele, in order to appeal to as many learners as possible. However, in the race to attract learners, mfl learning has lost out as an academic subject. Numbers opting for a language at this level are dwindling. Teachers must be aware of the demands of post-16 mfl study and make learners fully aware of the demands they face. Evidently, learners opt for their subjects for different reasons. It is still important to assert that mfl are an area of academic study worthy in their own right. It would be regrettable to lose the traditional academic language learner in a vain attempt to appeal to those who have more vocational reasons and motivations.

Consequently, our message is that the new post-16 curriculum lends itself to flexible application. Teachers must design courses to accommodate different learner types, their needs and aspirations and, in order to do so, must engage in enquiry work in the form of needs analysis prior to deciding on the exact format of mfl provision.

References

Assessment and Qualifications Alliance (1998) *Curriculum Update: Current Developments in GCE, GCSE, GNVQ Entry Level and Other Qualifications.*

Central Advisory Council for England (1959) *15 to 18: The Crowther Report.* London: HMSO.

Coleman, J. (1995) 'The evolution of language learner motivation in British universities, with some international comparisons'. In Wakely, R. *et al.* (eds) *Language Teaching and Learning in Higher Education: Issues and Perspectives.* London: CILT, pp. 1–16.

Coleman, J. (1996) *Studying Languages: A Survey of British and European Students: The Proficiency, Background, Attitudes and Motivations of Students in the UK and Europe.* London: CILT.

Dearing, R. (1996) *Review of Qualifications for 16–19 Year Olds.* London: DfEE.

DES (1988) *Advancing A Levels.* Report of a committee appointed by the Secretary of State for Education and Science and the Secretary of State for Wales. London: HMSO.

Hagen, S. (1998) 'Exporting today: policy implications'. In *The Linguist* 37, 3, pp. 66–71.

Judd, J. (1997) 'Familiar favourites.' In *Times Educational Supplement*, 24, April.

Lucas, N. (1997) 'The changing sixth form: the growth of pre-vocational education'. In Capel, S., Leask, M. and Turner, T. (eds) *Starting to Teach in the Secondary School.* London: Routledge, pp. 211–31.

Neather, T. (1991) 'A Level and Baccalauréat'. In *Language Learning Journal* 4. Rugby: Association of Language Learning, pp. 10–11.

Pachler, N. and Field, K. (1997) *Learning to Teach Modern Foreign Languages in the Secondary School.* London: Routledge.

Phillips, D. (1981) 'Innovations in curricula and examinations 16–18+: catering for the non specialist linguist in the sixth form'. In *Modern Languages* 62, 3, pp. 127–34.

QCA (1998) *A Discussion Document for Secondary Schools*. London.

QCA, ACCAC and CCEA (1999) *Subject Criteria for Modern Foreign Languages: GCE Advanced Subsidiary and Advanced Level Specifications*. London.

Reeves, N. (1996) 'Does Britain need linguists?' In Hawkins, E. (ed) *30 Years of Language Teaching*. London: CILT, pp. 35–48.

Wringe, C. (1976) *Developments in Modern Language Teaching*. London: Open Books Publishing.

The new A/AS level

Norbert Pachler[1]

Introduction

GCE Advanced (A) level examinations have become accepted as the 'gold standard' of educational achievement for learners at post-16. Governments past and present have been adamant that any change made to the curriculum and examinations post-16 should not compromise the standards of A level examinations. Yet, at the time of writing, changes are being implemented; they are discussed and commented upon in this chapter.[2]

Objectives

By the end of this chapter, you should have an awareness of:

- the context governing the 1996 Dearing Report into qualifications at 16–19 and its part in the so-called 'standards' debate
- recent changes to advanced level examinations including the 1999 A/AS Level Subject Criteria for Modern Foreign Languages (see QCA *et al.* 1999), and
- issues concerning the choice of modern foreign languages specifications (formerly syllabuses) for A/AS level learners.

The 'standards' debate

Soon after assuming office, the Labour government instigated its own consultation on the Dearing proposals for post-16 qualifications. Baroness Blackstone, Minister of State for Education in the Labour government, in responding to a letter from the Chairman of the Qualifications and Curriculum Authority (QCA)[3] giving advice following the consultation, stated:

> I look to the Authority to keep my officials informed of any significant issues arising from the revision of the GCE AS/A level subject cores in the light of the Government's decisions. We shall for instance want to be satisfied with the

specific steps the Authority will be taking in developing the new Advanced Subsidiary (AS) qualification to ensure that standards are maintained in all A level syllabuses . . .

In recent years A level results have been published in the national press. There has been an increase in the percentage of candidates achieving a pass grade (grades A–E) across all subjects, including modern foreign languages (mfl), year on year. This has fuelled speculation that the standard required to pass A level must have dropped. In the light of these concerns a study was commissioned by the then Schools Curriculum and Assessment Authority (SCAA) and the Office for Standards in Education (OFSTED) to investigate standards over time at both GCSE and GCE A level in three subjects: maths, English and chemistry (see SCAA and OFSTED 1996). Information supplied by the Awarding Bodies (formerly Examinations Boards) relating to four identified years over a twenty-year period provided the basis for comparisons to be made across Examinations Boards in any one year and over time both within and across boards. Syllabuses, examination papers, mark schemes and sample scripts from the A and E borderline were investigated by panels of subject experts. The panels included subject specialists from schools and colleges, higher education and OFSTED as well as experienced examiners. The report of the investigation revealed that expectations across Examinations Boards were similar over the twenty-year period of the study but that the syllabuses had changed markedly over that period and that, consequently, the assessment demands made of candidates were different. Other subjects, including German, have become part of a rolling programme of five-yearly reviews carried out by QCA (formerly SCAA). The findings have been similar; changes in syllabuses have been far reaching with consequent changes to the assessment requirements of candidates.

Changes in the syllabuses over time reflect developments in what is perceived by the subject community to be appropriate for A level study in the subject and to enable progression from examinations taken at the end of compulsory schooling. The study of mfl at A level underwent a considerable shift in emphasis in the 1970s and 1980s. The study of classic literary texts, read by candidates in the vernacular (albeit sometimes in edited versions) and discussed and assessed in English was replaced by the study of a wider range of contemporary foreign language texts, including articles from journals and newspapers. More recently even greater emphasis has been placed on the use of the target language (TL) at A level, bringing it into line with the requirements for the study of mfl in the secondary school curriculum at Key Stages 3 and 4. The new A/AS Level Subject Criteria for Modern Foreign Languages published in 1999 (QCA et al. 1999) require all specifications to give only 10 per cent weighting to examination components which are not specifically related to the use of the TL.

Changes to A level examinations to take account of the changing nature of the subject and of the needs of those sitting the examination invariably lead to questions about standards. Can standards over time be compared when criteria by which 'standards' can be judged as fundamental as syllabus content and candidature have changed substantially? The following may serve to illustrate the point:

Young teacher: Have you ever thought, headmaster, that your standards might perhaps be a little out of date?

Headmaster: Of course they are out of date. Standards are always out of date. That is what makes them standards.

A university tutor may well consider that A/AS level examinations in mfl are less demanding than they used to be. His or her main criterion for deciding this might be that current undergraduates are less well equipped at the start of their degree courses to study works of literature than undergraduates were thirty years ago. He or she may also find that today's undergraduates are less able to discuss the finer grammatical points than they were in the past. An employer in the City or in a major multi-national company, however, might be impressed by the greater confidence and competence of A/AS level entrants into the profession in conversing and negotiating in their chosen foreign language. One may consider, therefore, whether A/AS levels are now more closely meeting the needs of employers and that standards have actually risen. Perceptions of standards will differ depending on the basis of comparison used.

A more fruitful area of debate might be whether examinations should be dynamic and reflect changes in educational thinking and provision or whether, in the specious search for the maintenance of standards, they should remain the same to facilitate the provision of statistics that prove incontrovertibly whether standards have risen or declined. The search would be specious because, if examinations remained the same whilst society itself changed, the examination would not retain its original validity as an assessment of the course of study experienced by the candidates. A judgement about standard of achievement might more reasonably be based on the extent to which the candidates show knowledge, understanding and skills in the TL that represent appropriate progress after two years of study beyond what is required at GCSE Grades A*–C.

Standards across Awarding Bodies can be compared and action can be taken to reduce the likelihood of differing levels of demand. The introduction of A/AS Level Subject Cores in all major subjects including mfl in 1993–4 was an attempt to provide an agreed framework for all syllabuses in the subject and to identify criteria by which to judge the quality and rigour of the syllabus. Subject Cores were replaced by A/AS level Subject Criteria to take account of the recommendations of the Dearing Review of Qualifications 16–19. The number of Awarding Bodies providing qualifications post-16 and the number of what used to be called 'syllabuses' and are now called 'specifications' to be offered by each of them is being reduced in line with the Dearing recommendations. From the year 2000 centres will be able to select from a more restricted range of specifications offered by the three English unitary Awarding Bodies: the Assessment and Qualifications Alliance (AQA),[4] the EDEXCEL Foundation[5] and Oxford, Cambridge and RSA

Examinations (OCR).[6] The Welsh Joint Examinations Council (WJEC)[7] will either offer its own specifications (for some languages) or will produce them jointly with one of the English unitary Awarding Bodies. This will be the same in the case of the Northern Ireland Council for the Curriculum, Examinations and Assessment (CCEA).[8] Agreed criteria for the developing of specifications and fewer specifications provided by a reduced number of Awarding Bodies should enhance comparability in A/AS level examinations candidates take in mfl.

The new A/AS level examinations

Proposals for an alternative structure to A/AS level examinations have been debated for nearly thirty years. None of the proposals ever saw the light of day with the exception of the Advanced Supplementary examination; it was at the standard of the full A level but examined only half the content. The Advanced Supplementary examination did not achieve popularity. There was a tendency for candidates to perform less well in the Advanced Supplementary than in any full A level examinations they have taken. One reason is that the Advanced Supplementary level was taught in less time, providing candidates with less opportunity to acquire, develop and rehearse the knowledge, skills and understanding prior to the examination than those completing the full A level.

In response to the Dearing Report, the Advanced Supplementary examination was replaced by the Advanced Subsidiary (AS) which will also carry UCAS points equivalent to half a full A level. In other ways the new AS is very different. The AS examination is implemented from September 2000 and is, in effect, a new advanced level qualification. It is intended to recognise the progress achieved by candidates at a midway stage in their advanced level studies. For many candidates it will, therefore, become a 17+ examination. After achieving the AS, candidates will be able to choose to carry on to the second stage (the A2) of the A level course in the subject, decide to take other subjects at AS or terminate their studies after the AS.

In certain circumstances, learners will be able to study a broad curriculum at post-16. Those keen to add new languages to their portfolio could, for instance, start learning and achieve an AS qualification in Russian or Spanish, alongside French and/or German at advanced level, taking the AS examinations in the new languages either at the end of their first year of advanced level study or at the end of the second year. They might prefer to take AS qualifications in other subjects that interest them, a science, a humanities subject or information technology.

One of the greatest challenges for the Awarding Bodies is that the A/AS Level Subject Criteria for Modern Foreign Languages specify the same assessment objectives for both the AS and the A level. However, the weightings given to three of the objectives differ in the AS and the A2 (the second half of the A level, see Figure 2.1). A higher weighting is given in the A2 to the candidates' ability to 'demonstrate knowledge and understanding of aspects of the chosen society' and a different weighting than in the AS to the candidates' ability to understand and respond, in speech and writing, to spoken/written'. This greater emphasis on the study of the cultural background and heritage is reflected in the content to be studied as specified in the Subject Criteria. There are other additional requirements for candidates taking the full A level. For instance, they will be required to demonstrate their capacity for critical thinking and their ability to see relationships between different aspects of the subject. There will be expectations that assessment tasks and mark schemes will reflect the different expectations of candidates being assessed for the AS and those taking the A2 assessments.

A modular structure will be adopted for the majority of specifications. Candidates will be assessed on three units for the AS and three additional A2 units for the full A level award. A maximum weighting of 30 per cent can be given to internal assessment including course work. Awarding Bodies may offer assessment opportunities for candidates in both January and June. Candidates may be able to take units throughout the course (for example in January and June of the first year of advanced level study and in January and June of the second year). Alternatively, candidates for the AS may be able to take all unit assessments at the end of the AS course of study and A level candidates may be able to take all the AS and the A2 unit assessments at the end of the Advanced level course.

A feature of the subject criteria for all subjects is synoptic assessment in which candidates will be required to make links across aspects of the full A level course of study. Synoptic assessment has for a long time been a feature of some A level syllabuses but not a compulsory element to be tackled by all candidates. Synoptic assessment covers TL knowledge and the skills of TL use. It should take place at the end of the course of study and normally carry a weighting of 20 per cent of the A level. Candidates taking A level courses in mfl will be required to show their ability to use advanced level language skills in the TL to demonstrate their knowledge and understanding of the society and culture of at least one of the countries or communities they have studied as part of the course. This will draw on all of the assessment objectives. The use of dictionaries will not be permitted in any external assessment.

The draft A/AS level subject criteria for mfl

As I have noted above, a regulatory framework for A/AS level qualifications has been in existence since 1993 when the then School Examinations and Assessment Council (SEAC) drew up the A/AS Subject Core for Modern Foreign Languages (see SEAC 1993). This brief paper provided a basis for Examinations Boards to draw up syllabuses and sketched out aims, knowledge and understanding, concepts and skills as well as assessment objectives. The most recent edition (see QCA *et al.* 1999) is much more detailed. Its purpose, in line with the arguments of the standards debate rehearsed above, is to:

- 'help ensure consistent and comparable standards in the same subject across the awarding bodies
- define the relationship between the AS and A specifications, with the AS as a subset of the A level

- ensure that the rigour of A level is maintained
- help higher education institutions and employers know what has been studied and assessed' (QCA *et al.* 1999, p. 1).

The Subject Criteria build on good practice at GCSE, stressing the importance of the development of 'receptive' mfl skills in learners as well as confident and effective communication skills, sensitivity to language and language learning, cultural knowledge and competence and the development of positive attitudes towards mfl learning as a basis for further study and/or practical use.

As a pre-requisite for A/AS level mfl learning, the Subject Criteria suggest mfl competence at a level equivalent to higher-tier GCSE.

Whilst there is a clear transition from GCSE, e.g. in the requirement for learners to listen/read and respond to authentic sources, there are also a number of differences.

In methodological terms it is noteworthy that the Subject Criteria do not emphasise the TL 'imperative' in the way the 1995 National Curriculum does (see Pachler and Field 1997, Ch. 5); at AS level they talk about manipulating the TL 'accurately to organise facts and ideas, present explanations, opinions and information in both speech and writing' (QCA *et al.* 1999, p. 2) and at A level about using the TL 'to analyse, hypothesise, evaluate, argue a case, justify, persuade, rebut, develop arguments and present viewpoints, in speech and in writing' (QCA *et al.* 1999, p. 3). Whilst the TL can, therefore, be seen to be of great importance for instruction of and interaction with learners, there is also explicit mention in the Subject Criteria of transfer of meaning from English into the TL and/or vice versa (for translation see Chapter 12).

In a significant departure from practice at GCSE, the Subject Criteria specify a requirement for learners to 'understand and apply the grammatical system and a range of structures as detailed' followed by two lists of grammatical structures for French, German, Spanish and Urdu, one for AS and one for A level (see also Chapter 6).

The requirement to develop insights into and understanding of the cultural dimension of language learning on the one hand builds on requirements of the 1995 Programme of Study Part 1 at Key Stages 3 and 4 but at the same time requires much more recourse to learners' general knowledge and cognitive development (see also Chapter 5).

Interestingly and for the first time ever, the draft Subject Criteria feature grade descriptions for grades A, C and E for Speaking, Reading and Listening, Writing and a Cultural Component. These grade descriptors clearly build on good practice at Key Stages 3 and 4 and should prove helpful for mfl teachers in making grade predictions for their learners. It is interesting to note that the so-called 'receptive' skills of reading and listening (see Chapter 9) are 'bundled' as well as that cultural knowledge and competence has been identified as a separate component of assessment; its contribution to the mfl learning process has, thus, clearly been recognised (see also Chapter 5).

Another important innovation of the 1999 Subject Criteria is the introduction of the key skills of communication, Information Technology and improving own learning and performance and working with others as a part of A/AS level mfl specifications.

Choosing subject specifications

The new Subject Criteria will provide the basis for accreditation of subject specifications submitted by Awarding Bodies to the regulatory bodies. Given the requirement to comply with the Subject Criteria, subject specifications from different Awarding Bodies invariably feature a number of similarities and there is common ground. However, there are also areas of diversity; with it come opportunities to select what best meets the needs of learners. For this reason, mfl teachers should choose subject specifications very carefully and bear in mind the needs and strengths of their learners when they do so.

The Subject Criteria specify common aims, content (knowledge, understanding and skills) and assessment objectives which can be interpreted in different ways by Awarding Bodies. Therefore, amongst others, differences might occur in the following areas:

- choice of topics to be studied
- amount of literature included and scope for choice of individual texts
- types of assessment tasks used
- nature and extent of mother tongue use allowed and translation required

Assessment Objectives		Weighting	
		AS	A2
AO1	understand and respond, in speech and writing, to spoken language	25–35%	20–30%
AO2	understand and respond, in speech and writing, to written language	25–35%	20–30%
AO3	show knowledge of the grammar and syntax prescribed in the specification and the ability to apply this	25%	25%
AO4	demonstrate knowledge and understanding of aspects of the chosen society	10–20%	20–30%

Figure 2.1 Assessment objectives and their possible weighting
Source: QCA et al. 1999

- distribution and weighting of assessment components (see Figure 2.1)
- assessment criteria used for various assessment objectives: e.g. relative importance of communication, pronunciation, accuracy, fluency, range, appropriacy of register, spontaneity of TL use, quality of language or content (including cultural knowledge and awareness), etc.
- staged or end-of-course assessment
- nature of the assessment scheme: (a) balance of internal (e.g. course work) and external assessment; (b) amount of synoptic assessment required (i.e. the integration and application of knowledge, understanding and skills across different dimensions of the subject)
- integration of key skills of communication, Information Technology and improving of own learning and performance, or
- nature of the Special Paper for learners of high ability available (requiring higher level of independent thinking, creativity and critical insight)

Whilst choice and diversity are clearly desirable, the above list of criteria for the selection of subject specifications demonstrates how important it is for mfl teachers to make informed choices.

Summary

If the revisions to advanced level qualifications, including the introduction of the new AS level, are successful in achieving the goals intended by the Dearing Committee, a greater proportion of post-16 candidates will succeed in achieving an advanced qualification than is currently the case. A greater proportion of candidates should embark on post-GCSE courses in order to broaden their studies at post-16 and a higher percentage should complete their studies and achieve a pass grade. If these increases are achieved, there is little doubt that the standards debate will be fuelled once more. Evidence so far has suggested that the introduction of modular syllabuses has had the effect of raising the overall pass rate in the subjects concerned but that the number of candidates achieving the top grades has decreased. It will be interesting to see what the results of the first candidates awarded the new AS qualification in 2001 and for the first cohort taking the revised A level in 2002 reveal. Will they be perceived to provide evidence that the development of specifications against precise common criteria and the reductions in the number of specifications available ensure greater comparability and the maintenance of standards or that standards are in decline?

Notes

1 Substantial input to this chapter by Gill Watson is gratefully acknowledged.
2 The new Subject Criteria for Modern Foreign Languages, GCE AS and A Level specifications, were published in June 1999. Given the timing of their release, it has only just been possible to revise Chapter 2 of this book in line with any changes made to the Subject

Criteria as a result of consultation. The accuracy and validity of all other chapters in this book should not be affected, as they deal with general methodological issues of MFL teaching at advanced level.

3 Details available at: http://www.open.gov.uk/qca/
4 Details available at: http://www.aqa.org.uk
5 Details available at: http://www.edexel.org.uk
6 Details available at: http://www.ocr.org.uk
7 Details available at: http://www.wjec.co.uk
8 Details available at: http://ccea.org.uk

References

Dearing, R. (1996) *Review of Qualifications for 16–19 Year Olds.* London: DfEE.

Pachler, N. and Field, K. (1997) *Learning to Teach Modern Foreign Languages in the Secondary School.* London: Routledge

QCA, ACCAC and CCEA (1999) *Subject Criteria for Modern Foreign Languages: GCE Advanced Subsidiary and Advanced Level Specifications.* London.

SCAA and OFSTED (1996) *Standards in Public Examinations 1975 to 1995: A Report on English, Mathematics and Chemistry Examinations over Time.* London.

SEAC (1993) *A/AS Subject Core for Modern Foreign Languages.* London.

Part II

The transition from GCSE to A/AS level

Bridging the gap

Chapter 3

GCSE and A/AS level teaching and learning

Kit Field

Introduction

For many years now teachers have taken learner characteristics into account when planning post-16 courses. As long ago as 1976, Colin Wringe noted that learners studying French may well regard it as their 'third' subject. He concluded that teachers should not assume a high degree of motivation, in terms of a passion for the subject. On the other hand, many commentators (e.g. Graham 1997, Lonsdale 1996, Shaw and Anciaux 1996) note the need to take into account the positive attitudes and strengths of learners embarking on Advanced (A) and Advanced Subsidiary (AS) level courses. The assumption is that teachers should respect and build on these strengths, incorporating strategies with which learners are comfortable and gradually extend the learners' range of skills and knowledge to meet the demands of the subject specifications, formerly syllabuses, being followed. The demands of A/AS level courses are great and teachers recognise a need to 'bridge the gap' between General Certificate of Secondary Education (GCSE) study and A/AS level. This inevitably raises the question: what do learners bring with them to A/AS level courses from GCSE? And, in what ways are these qualities relevant to A/AS level study?

All of the writers referred to above mention commitment. Clearly, learners have opted to study a modern foreign language and have a degree of enthusiasm due to achieving a good grade at GCSE (usually at least a 'B'). This success implies, for instance, a readiness to communicate orally in structured tasks, pair work and role plays; an ability to read and listen for the purpose of extracting factual detail from short focused texts; or familiarity with basic letter writing.

At the same time, teachers and learners themselves have encountered difficulties bridging the gap between GCSE and A/AS level study. As far as learners are concerned, learning vocabulary which is not presented within a specified list (see Lonsdale 1996, p. 18), the manipulation of language and grammatical accuracy (see Graham 1997, p. 95), the close analysis of written texts and extensive reading in the target language (TL) all tend to be perceived as particular weaknesses by teachers. For teachers the lack of a 'defined syllabus' poses problems of task selection, although the subject specifications drawn up on the basis of the new

A/AS Level Subject Criteria for Modern Foreign Languages can be expected to provide more detailed guidance.

Teachers and learners are prepared to articulate these difficulties. Corless and Gaskell (see 1983, p. 76) noted the problems of the, then, traditional A level courses. The low profile of speaking, the dominant status of translation, the limited range of reading tasks and the high status of the literary register of language held little appeal to débutante post-16 learners. The recommendations contained within *French 16–19: A New Perspective* (DES 1981) to make A level modern foreign languages (mfl) learning more functional and practical in approach and content were welcomed. A clear focus on the use of language as opposed to the analysis of language was placed at the heart of syllabuses.

GCSE syllabus writers adopted a similar approach. Richard Johnstone's (1989) explanation of Basic Interpersonal and Communicative Skills (BICS) following Cummins (1980) can be seen to serve as a model for GCSE syllabuses. BICS, according to Johnstone, are a development of transactional language skills, enabling learners to ask for services and products, essentially in public situations. Indeed, for many learners the development of BICS is not an intellectual challenge. Graham's survey of learners suggests (see 1997, p. 18) that those following A level courses had not found GCSE particularly difficult. The very same learners, however, commented on the difficulty of A level study. Lid King notes (see 1996, p. 42) that beyond GCSE learners require lexical knowledge, strategic competence and discourse competence. By discourse competence, King means the ability to recognise and respond to different types of texts in an appropriate manner, taking into account the purpose, context and register deployed. None of these are highlighted as requirements at GCSE level. Despite the acceptance of a need for practical usage, it does appear that to attain A level standard, learners must move beyond BICS. Cognitive/Academic Language Proficiency (CALP), again outlined by Johnstone (1989) following Cummins (1980), is not an alternative to BICS, but is a progression. CALP is the competence associated with generating personal forms of language, enabling the expression of personal view points and opinions. Tove Skutnabb-Kangas argues (see 1984, pp. 111–12) that BICS and CALP do not develop hand in hand and that BICS are achievable independently. The reverse is clearly not feasible. Successful development of BICS is a prerequisite for success at CALP. In real terms, CALP requires a depth of study and degree of linguistic analysis to be associated with A/AS level study. It appeals to learner types, described by Hatch (see 1974, p. 16) as 'rule formers'. Successful GCSE learners may however be 'data gatherers'. 'Data gatherers' is a term applied to learners who choose to learn phrases off by heart and who apply these set phrases in relevant contexts. In effect, it is a term describing pure rote learners who do not proceed to personalising language forms.

Evidently, the content of A/AS level courses is a vast extension on what is expected at GCSE. Pachler and Field suggest a method by which topics can be broadened and deepened progressively and the teacher is invited to bridge the gap (see 1997, pp. 337–8). In planning more challenging topic areas, it is inevitable that the learner will be required to integrate the four language skills, which to date have, on the whole, been taught and learnt separately. S. Tebbut asserts (1996, p. 88) that 'our language skills of listening, reading, speaking and writing cannot be taught in isolation from each other'.

The problematic division between receptive and productive language skills has to be closed. GCSE learners are assessed in the separate skills and teachers inevitably teach to examination requirements. The issues of responding to texts, introducing texts through multi-sensory means and using detail contained within heard and written texts to inform writing are, in reality, hardly addressed at all at GCSE level.

The gap between GCSE and A/AS level is wide. Teachers ignore it at their peril. Ausubel's credo is key here: '[the] most important single factor influencing learning is what the learner already knows; ascertain this and teach him [sic] accordingly' (1968, p. 36). The psychologist Ausubel argued that teachers should find out what learners know and can do and build in a differentiated manner on this knowledge and skills base. Teachers of mfl, therefore, do need to ascertain what constitutes knowledge and skills.

Firstly, the enthusiasm and commitment of learners must be harnessed by ensuring that the content is interesting and stimulating. Secondly, opportunities to build on pre-existing learning strategies must be built into the course programme. Shaw and Anciaux intimate (see 1996, p. 8) that progression must be smooth. They assert that teachers' input must be just beyond what a learner can achieve; and yet not too far beyond. In this way learners are challenged, but not demoralised.

Objectives

By the end of this chapter you should:

- recognise the value of standard GCSE type activities in the process of developing language skills at A/AS level
- understand how to plan for progression of learner skills and language competence
- be able to plan for the integration of the four skills of speaking, listening, reading and writing, and
- appreciate the value of maximum TL use in the A/AS level classroom

Teaching and learning at A/AS level

One key feature of learning at A/AS level is the need to integrate the skills of speaking, listening, reading and writing. There is a tendency, at GCSE level, for teachers to teach these as discrete skills, particularly as the examination papers assess each skill separately. Examiners at A/AS level do expect learners to respond to spoken and written texts in the TL which requires comprehension skills in order to produce meaningful language. It is the intention in this chapter to examine the development of skills in isolation, yet also to demonstrate how each skill interacts with others. This is not to present a method of teaching which plans to focus on skills independently, but that teachers may choose to emphasise one aspect at a particular point in time. The process of language acquisition is holistic; in developing one area the learner will also develop others.

Speaking

A foreign language course founded upon communicative principles should equip an eighteen or nineteen year old student to do some quite ordinary things . . . to understand and comment on a radio or television news bulletin for example, to take notes during a discussion or conference, to pass information or decisions to another person in the foreign language or his own, to engage in a telephone conversation, to scan a document or manual for a specific purpose, to identify a point of view in the course of a conversation with a native speaker, to see what a salesman or an advertisement is up to, even to present a persuasive argument.

(Corless and Gaskell 1983, pp. 79–80)

This common-sense assertion is at first sight both challenging and achievable. The focus is on the practical and the need is to shift from transaction to interaction. By transactional I mean that the speaker requests a service or product. Interaction involves a degree of negotiation and empathy towards the interlocutor. The recipient of information in interaction is dynamic and not static as in transactional language use. The complexity of interaction lies in the subtlety of the illocutionary force, the larger meaning that determines whether the speaker is asserting, promising, persuading, requesting, guessing, etc. (see Searle 1969, p. 16). Searle identified this different layer of meaning, which is unrelated to the vocabulary used but which reflects the intention of a speaker. Corless and Gaskell's examples (see 1983, pp. 79–19) mirror the categories of language use listed in *French 16–19* (see DES 1981, pp. 10–11). These include note taking, passing on information, identifying and expressing points of view and disagreement and persuading. At A/AS level learners need to use language for narrative, informative, descriptive and persuasive purposes. At GCSE the use of language is usually informative only.

REFLECTION
Activity 3.1 Using prior learning experiences to bridge the gap
In the left-hand column below are 'GCSE-type' speaking activities drawn from Pachler and Field (1997, pp. 129–32). In the right-hand column are activities adapted from Corless and Gaskell (1983, pp. 79–80) which represent A/AS level standard speaking activities. Draw lines from the left-hand column to the right to demonstrate how the existing skills and experiences of 'new' A/AS level learners contribute to future goals and expectations.

GCSE	A/AS LEVEL
reserving and confirming	comment on radio/TV news bulletin
responding to visual aids	report on a discussion from notes
guessing	pass on information
structured role plays	engage in telephone conversation
information gap activities	explain how to use an appliance
acting out scripts and dialogues	participate in discussions
open ended role plays	respond to a salesperson
general conversation	present an argument
describing pictures	narrate an event
	provide detailed and creative description

However, the place of GCSE type pair work, role plays, question and answer and reading aloud is not redundant if only for motivational reasons: the content of A/AS level work involves learners in expressing opinions and drawing on their own knowledge. At GCSE level, the work is superficial by comparison and lends itself well to role plays (shopping, reserving tickets and hotel rooms, etc.). Graham, interestingly, reports on a learner's embarrassment when speaking at A level: 'her oral performance might somehow reflect on how she was viewed as a person, rather than merely on her linguistic performance' (1997, p. 106).

Role plays serve as a mask for the individual. The excitement of covering controversial, challenging topics and issues conflicts with adolescent self-consciousness. In the context of early A/AS level study (see Figure 3.1), being 'in role' is an excellent way for learners, for example, to present extreme views and ideas, to argue the pros and cons of a particular proposal and to respond to controversial suggestions.

At any level of language learning, and particularly at the beginning of a unit of work, the teacher needs to structure question-and-answer work carefully. Closed questions are suitable to elicit facts and information, which later form the basis of opinions and arguments. Graham (see 1997, p. 18) noticed the ease with which learners in their first year of A/AS level study could function with BICS type activities. These simple oral tasks facilitated the progression to higher level requirements such as discussions and presentations.

Learner 'A' receives eight cards, represented by the list on the left below. Each card represents an argument in support of the Channel Tunnel. Learner 'B' is given eight cards, each containing arguments against the Channel Tunnel. Learners are asked to conduct a discussion, adopting the viewpoints represented by their cards.

le tunnel rend plus facile la traversée de la Manche	*il y a un danger de terrorisme*
il nous faut pouvoir traverser la Manche plus vite	*le bateau offre un voyage reposant*
les commerçants peuvent travailler, même téléphoner en route	*la Grande Bretagne est un île, donc il est naturel de traverser la mer*
il ne faut passer par les douanes qu'une fois	*dans un âge d'ordinateurs le voyage n'est plus très nécessaire*
il n'est pas nécessaire de réserver une place	*on peut prendre l'avion si on aime la vitesse*
les trains roulent fréquemment	*le chemin de fer abîme le beau paysage*
les chauffeurs de camion peuvent se reposer en route	*n'importe quelle personne peut entrer dans le pays*
on peut continuer directement à Paris ou à Bruxelles	*il y a un risque de la rage*

Figure 3.1 Structuring discussions

REFLECTION
Activity 3.2 Examining question types
Observe a colleague in your institution teach an A/AS level mfl class. Note down every question he or she poses to individuals, groups and the whole class. After the lesson, place the questions in order, from closed to open. Consider why particular questions are asked at different stages of a lesson. Consider, too, why and when your colleague directed questions at individuals and/or groups. Discuss the outcomes with your colleague.

It is heartening that Gary Chambers (see 1991, p. 8) notes that teachers placed a greater emphasis on pair work, role play and drama techniques, when working with learners following newer post-1988 A/AS level courses.

T. Lonsdale proposes a step-by-step approach to developing language skills, including speaking. He recommends that the first step is to encourage learners to draw on existing skills to 'say something about topics' (1996, p. 20), rather than to engage in the detailed discussion of complex issues. He argues that the expectation of teachers is crucial to success. 'Brainstorming', allowing learners to say anything in the TL that they perceive to be relevant to a topic, is as motivating an activity at A/AS level as it is at GCSE. If performed in pairs or groups, the activity is also non-threatening as learners do not run the risk of being judged by the teacher. In fact, Graham (see 1997, p. 24) discovered an irrational fear of learners of the teacher. Responding to questions posed by the teacher, to which she knows the answers, can only serve to make obvious the gaps in learners' general knowledge. Much of learners' insecurity is founded on a perceived lack of knowledge and cultural awareness. Information-gap activities, as designed at GCSE level, provide an opportunity to 'kill two birds with one stone'. Firstly, learners practise interaction skills. Secondly, they can provide each other with essential facts, figures, information and knowledge. Figure 3.2 provides an example of how such an activity can be organised drawing on pre-existing skills and linguistic competence.

Essentially the topic in Figure 3.2 is familiar. The issue is realistic and controversial. Shaw and Anciaux recommend (see 1996, p. 12) that to stimulate oral activity, the topic must be related to personal experience. Personal experience includes that which has been previously learnt. The GCSE topic 'About Town' provides the security through familiarity and the structure of the activity resembles common information-gap tasks.

Regular practice of speaking the TL is often best achieved 'anonymously'. At the early stages of learning, group repetition prevents the individual from feeling under pressure. In a similar way, talking to a peer relieves the anxiety of speaking directly to the teacher. 'Buddy talk' is the regular narration of recent experiences to a

Objectives:	• to enable learners to locate essential services in a town
	• to provide the basis for discussion of the suitability of locating a site for a rubbish tip
Materials:	Two maps of a town, each consisting of details of where different buildings and services are located. The maps each contain different information.
Activity:	Without looking at each other's map, learners suggest a location for the rubbish tip. The partner responds, citing the location of another building/service as a reason for not locating the tip where suggested. As learners discuss, each notes information not contained on their own map – and eventually they negotiate a suitable site.

Figure 3.2 Planning an information-gap activity

friend. Recounting the day's news to a partner shifts the focus away from the self. Reporting the news events in the target country is a simple next step. Teachers can formalise these activities to allow for stress-free practice – until the irrational fear of the teacher has subsided.

Support for such 'free expression' resembles the type of activities designed to facilitate speaking at GCSE level. Piecing together newspaper headlines and pictures, narrating a story depicted by cartoons and pictures and the unjumbling of texts all enable the learner to use language realistically and to interact rather than simply to transact.

Evidently, at A/AS level embarrassment and anxiety are caused by a lack of knowledge rather than low levels of competence. Corless and Gaskell's research (see 1983, pp. 81–2) presents some principles which should underpin the teaching of speaking. These principles are applicable to both pre- and post-16 teaching. Speaking needs a purpose and should be achievable through cooperation rather than coercion in the classroom. Sample activities include problem solving, sharing ideas and experiences and discovery. Role plays lend themselves well to this type of purpose. One example is to ask a learner to simulate entering a shop and complain that an article is damaged and to demand repayment. The learner adopting the role of the shopkeeper should offer a range of alternative products in an attempt to avoid repaying any money. Both learners should adopt a persuasive stance and come to some agreement. The client is compelled to respond to the suggestions negatively and the shopkeeper has to present and describe goods in a positive manner. The open-ended nature of the task is deliberate and it allows for quality in discourse. Language use can be seen to serve a purpose. The content must also match the emotional and social stage of maturation of the learner. Finally, the teacher must accept that she is not always the best audience. The suggestion is that confidence and motivation are built upon security and that security can be provided through familiarity with content and activity type.

Certainly, active participation in oral work is reliant upon exciting stimuli. There is no reason to believe that visual (pictorial or graphic) aids do not have as big an impact at A/AS level as at GCSE level. Indeed, visual aids can assist with brain-storming activities as can listening to music, feeling objects, etc. A gradual shift from non-verbal to verbal stimuli in the form of texts, however, prompts an interaction with the written word.

REFLECTION
Activity 3.3 Selecting an audience for oral work
By observing A/AS level classes, decide which activity /
performing to the teacher and which to peers. Does this chang
learners develop?

responding to visual aids	reading aloud
structured role plays	information gap work
question/answer	open-ended role plays
giving a presentation	presenting an argument
passing on information	giving instructions and directions
negotiating and problem solving	

TL use

Well-taught learners will, of course, be accustomed to the teacher using the TL. Much of the classroom talk at this level should be in the TL (see also Chapter 12), yet the teacher should modify her level and register of TL use to accommodate learners' proficiency. Learners are used to simplified use of the TL and need to move on to spontaneous and fluent use. The teacher needs to monitor active and passive use by the learner and introduce new, recognisable alternatives to standard classroom language as learners manifest a readiness to move on. It would be false to assume, though, that learners' own reflections will always be in the TL. However, the teacher's contributions – if directly related to the learners' needs – can add realism and authenticity. Reservations of over-use of the TL in certain contexts (see Pachler and Field 1997, pp. 102–5) do not apply to the same extent at A/AS level (see Chapter 12). Increased contact time at A/AS level allows for more regular reinforcement. Smaller group sizes lead to increased opportunities for the individual to experiment. A greater emphasis on the individual's own learning needs gives the TL a more authentic context which, in turn, lends itself to more opportunities for language acquisition. The age, maturity and motivation of post-16 learners removes some of the problems associated with short attention spans and the relative similarity of starting points of learners embarking on A/AS level courses relieves some of the danger of alienation and frustration.

REFLECTION
Activity 3.4 When to use the TL
Discuss with learners, and consider yourself, when learners benefit more by using their mother tongue. When do teachers feel that English is more appropriate than the TL? How do the two viewpoints compare and contrast?

At A/AS level, the teacher needs to build on the sometimes contrived forms of TL use at GCSE and move towards a higher level of fluency and spontaneity.

Listening

The learners in Graham's research (see 1997, p. 94) identify 'authentic' types of 'text' used for listening as the principal difficulty of study at A/AS level. Most GCSE learners will have experienced listening comprehension as a task when they are required to extract information and record it in non-verbal or short answers. Indeed, it is the goal at GCSE level to act as the recipient of factually based messages. Corless and Gaskell (see 1983, p. 81) note that at a higher level, communication – which includes listening – is more than the conveyance of information; it

REFLECTION

Activity 3.5 Rating the difficulty factor in listening activities
Survey learners in their first year of A/AS level study. Ask them to rate 1–5 what they find difficult about listening:

speed		1	2	3	4	5
length		1	2	3	4	5
use of idiom		1	2	3	4	5
range of vocabulary		1	2	3	4	5
number of speakers		1	2	3	4	5
accents		1	2	3	4	5
type of text:	presentation of facts	1	2	3	4	5
	presentation of opinions	1	2	3	4	5
	discussions	1	2	3	4	5
	conversations	1	2	3	4	5
	arguments	1	2	3	4	5
	descriptions	1	2	3	4	5
	narratives	1	2	3	4	5

Ask colleagues how important they feel the above are in guiding their choice of texts. Compare the results of learners' perceptions of difficulty with your colleagues' criteria for text selection.

is also the conveyance, receipt and control of ideas. In order to control ideas, learners need to be informed of the range of bias before being exposed to texts which contain the expression of beliefs and opinions. Consequently, the recommendation is that learners should be familiar with the content of texts prior to listening in order that they can analyse and classify the content and recognise the implication(s) of the heard material. In this way, the process of listening differs little from that outlined in Pachler and Field (see 1997, pp. 121–4). The teacher's first priority needs to be the careful selection of texts for listening, taking into account the topicality, linguistic content, speed of delivery, register and use of regional accents. The measure of success, of course, is the level of response, and small-scale enquiry into the indicators of success can only serve to benefit teacher and learner.

The content of texts needs to stimulate interest. Again, Corless and Gaskell (see 1983, p. 84) identified four key aspects. Firstly, the content must engage learners' attention; importantly, teachers should not assume that learners have similar interests to themselves. Interest in the content by learners who are maturing (and who are not yet mature) can only derive from existing knowledge and cultural awareness. In order to provoke a response from the learner, the content should relate to an aspect of the target culture which is recognisable. This second aspect of motivation is worthy of further examination. A/AS level topics have an 'adult' orientation in content, e.g. politics, culture, etc. The identification of speakers' points of view is inevitably linked to the cultural content. In the early stages the teacher should, therefore, simplify the content of authentic texts. As Pachler and Field point out (see 1997, p. 337), the leap to questions associated with urbanism, for example, is enormous. However, to provide listening activities related to the topic 'About Town' ensures the first step of a phased process. By identifying facts and information from simplified texts, learners gain access to data necessary to sustain arguments and express opinions.

Corless and Gaskell, furthermore, point out (see 1983, p. 83) that the language contained within a listening text should be seen by learners as likely to be encountered outside the classroom or, indeed, that learners may wish to use the language forms themselves. These points lead on to the need for listening activities to have a purpose.

The GCSE examination assesses listening independently from other language skills. At A/AS level learners need to demonstrate comprehension skills, but listening is also a source of cultural information and provides examples of authentic language use. Indeed, learners are required to respond in the TL to spoken material. Given that listening contributes to the processes of acculturation and language development, it would be wrong to separate these two motivating factors.

Pre-listening activities assume a more important place at A/AS level than at GCSE level. One need is to ensure that learners are acquainted with key vocabulary in advance of listening to a text. Johnstone (1989) and Peck (1988) provide examples of activity types such as 'flashing headlines' which are intended to provide short, sensational clues to the plot of a narrative report (see Johnstone

1989, p. 149). Learners are required to complete the story in their own words before being exposed to the original. This provides the learner with clear expectations of the text, thereby facilitating comprehension. For example, the presentation of newspaper headlines, pictures and/or summaries of news items allows the learner to predict a sequence of events. Similarly, the silent viewing of a video snippet with carefully constructed questions provides the teacher and learner with the opportunity to exploit the language contained and to introduce key events in advance of listening. J. Eastman (see 1987, p. 132) offers more advice in the making explicit of the vocabulary from a text, thereby preventing an overly narrow focus on unknown words by the listener. He recommends running a pencil under a text as one reads, only removing the pencil at completely unfamiliar words. The impact, Eastman claims, is to bolster confidence, in that learners are often surprised at how much they do in fact know. Awaiting key words is another way of establishing a sense of expectation.

Effective and focused pre-listening activities provide the listener with a gist understanding prior to exposure to the text itself. This does not mean that the listener does not have to contextualise the material whilst listening. In a similar way to GCSE listening tasks, learners should be encouraged to listen to complete texts in order that the material can be centrally located. Figure 3.3 lists types of questions, which should be worded in the TL and which help the listener to decide whether texts are presentations, discussions, descriptions, broadcasts or dramatic events.

At pre-16, Pachler and Field (see 1997, p. 122) recommend to follow 'gist understanding' with a focus on detail. During the first weeks of an A/AS level course it is important that learners are not required to produce complex responses, which can be both distracting and demotivating. Non-verbal responses, in the form of true/false, multiple choice, tick boxes, mixing-and-matching, etc. have their place at A/AS level, too. Indeed, familiarity with activity types offers another form of security. Moreover, the link with pre-listening activities provides a greater degree of motivation. The confirmation of expectation through listening to the text as, indeed, to discover that one's preliminary predictions were wrong, is stimulating.

The use of listening to develop knowledge and discursive powers is a key

- How many speakers are there?
- What is the mood of each of the speakers?
- Which speaker asks questions?
- Are the sentences long/short?
- Are the sentences factual?
- Are the sentences descriptive?
- Do the speakers agree/disagree?
- Do the speakers know each other?
- Note five key words.

Figure 3.3 Listening for gist

difference between GCSE and A/AS level. Whether, for example, a train leaves from platform two or four tends to be of little importance at GCSE. The principle concern there is to recognise and be able to use certain structures to convey a message. At A/AS level the detail within texts increases in value in that it becomes an essential component of future language use. King (see 1996, p. 48) suggests physical responses, such as organising cards representing a sequence of events, to demonstrate comprehension. The activity generates a stimulus for language production and, therefore, both the linguistic and factual content are reinforced. The need to integrate receptive and productive language skills is made easier by the teacher planning to use the detail extracted from listening exercises as the basis for subsequent written or spoken word.

Ideas and information represented non-verbally in a grid or as letters representing multiple choice answers, can be very useful. The introduction of activities designed to use new language forms by verbalising responses is helpful in that language structures are drilled, but also because the learner is noting useful factual information for future reference. Appropriate activities include substitution exercises (see Pachler and Field 1997, p. 133). The use of synonyms, translations and retranslations also add the dimension of extending choice in terms of ways of expressing known information.

A further 'listening' to a text following this phase is also useful. It allows learners to correct and improve answers to questions. By this stage the learner should have developed a comprehensive set of TL notes. A final stage is to provide a TL summary, interpretation or response to the text. Figure 3.4 represents this process of listening activities.

It is not dissimilar from recommended methods for GCSE listening. Bridging the gap is easier if teachers and learners are able to recognise similarities in process and content. The shift to using listening as a means of gathering information to service productive skills should be a smooth transition.

Reading

As with listening, the main purpose of reading at GCSE level is to demonstrate an ability to comprehend. In the case of reading this involves what Patricia Rees calls an 'intensive approach' (1995, p. 45). By this she means that few learners will have

Pre-listening
↓ Gist understanding
↓ Extraction of detail
↓ Focus on language
↓ Correction
Summary

Figure 3.4 A process for listening activities

encountered texts more than two to three paragraphs in length at GCSE. Gary Chambers mirrors this view: '[if] we are lucky our learners may have encountered Lesekiste in their GCSE days' (1991, p. 5). *Lesekiste* – a collection of readers in cartoon form and containing simplified language forms – and similar readers apart, the source of most texts are those contained in textbooks, past papers and extracts of authentic texts supplied by the teacher. They tend to be contrived to suit a particular educational purpose. Rees notes (see 1995, pp. 30–1) that few learners have read complete magazines, newspapers, readers, books or poetry.

S. Tebbut (see 1996, p. 87) raises the question that learners need to develop beyond the reading of single pages, i.e. to cope with whole books, which requires a step-by-step shift from intensive to extensive reading. This change in focus entails a change in strategies for reading.

REFLECTION
Activity 3.6 Rating the difficulty factor in reading activities
Which of the following reading strategies do learners use most frequently? Ask a group of learners to rate them 1–5 in terms of difficulty. How can you support learners in the strategies that they find the hardest?

problem identification	1	2	3	4	5
substitution	1	2	3	4	5
resourcing	1	2	3	4	5
interpretation	1	2	3	4	5
reading aloud	1	2	3	4	5
translation	1	2	3	4	5
word analysis	1	2	3	4	5
sentence analysis	1	2	3	4	5
use of context	1	2	3	4	5
omission	1	2	3	4	5

The terminology of Activity 3.5 requires some clarification:

problem identification: the reader is able to spot difficulties as they are met. underlining idioms and structures as one reads is an example

substitution:	to cope with unknown words readers substitute alternatives which make sense
resourcing:	the use of dictionaries and reference material
interpretation:	the acceptance of approximate meaning
reading aloud:	using the sounds of words to provide a clue to meaning
translation:	the use of English translations
word analysis:	the close examination of the grammatical role and semantic relationship with other words
sentence analysis:	close analysis of an entire sentence to provide grammatical, semantic and contextual clues to meaning
use of content:	inspired guesses according to a gist understanding;
omission:	glossing over unknown words to maintain the flow of speed reading

Gary Chambers has the following recommendations regarding reading material:

> Why not create a homemade Lesekiste, containing short articles, poems and literary extracts which learners can read at their own pace without any enormous demands being made on them in terms of detailed response?
>
> (1991, p. 7)

Rees (see 1995, p. 43) notes learners' own concerns, which illustrate the principal differences between reading at GCSE and post-16 level. Her research indicates learners' worries with regard to reading: to break words down to make meaning more obvious, to use dictionaries to good effect, to have access to current affairs articles on a regular basis and to be exposed to a variety of subjects and writing styles. If one aim of reading at A/AS level is to help learners to read with fluency, understanding and enjoyment, teachers do need to interlace reading tasks with forms of strategy training. Corless and Gaskell (see 1983, p. 94) summarise the difference of approach as 'reading the lines' at the lower level and 'reading between the lines' at the higher level.

The arguments which apply to listening as a means of collecting data and information for the practice and development of productive language skills also apply to reading. The more permanent access to written texts leads to greater opportunities for interaction with the text. King (1996) notes that the basis for such an engagement with the written word is the learners' interest and prior knowledge. Consequently, the selection of texts must match the learners' interest, cultural awareness, intellectual and emotional maturity and linguistic capability. Reading for pleasure is an achievable goal, but the types of skills necessarily require training. Corless and Gaskell recognise (see 1983, p. 92) that the lower level skills of skimming and scanning need to be developed into 'reflective reading'.

Once again the gap between GCSE and A/AS level is wide and needs to be bridged. Based on Rees (see 1995, p. 47), the following components for a reading programme can be suggested:

- range and relevance
- text length and layout, and
- purposes and outcomes

Range

GCSE learners are used to reading short texts which contain factual information. As with listening, A/AS level learners can develop similar working patterns to GCSE to exploit the text and develop an ever-increasing knowledge base. Corless and Gaskell (see 1983, p. 85) commend the organisation of textbooks which present texts thematically. In such a way the exploitation of one text assists with the comprehension of the next. As confidence in the content increases, learners are able to examine the illocutionary force underpinning a text. Consequently the recommendation is to begin with factually based texts and to progress to texts which represent opinions or question established viewpoints.

Relevance

'Literature is, after all, the most authentic material one can have at one's disposal' (Chambers 1991, p. 3). Chambers's view can be defended easily. Literature is intended to communicate to the reader, without necessarily being designed for learning purposes. It represents culture and has been written deliberately with a clear purpose in mind. In this sense, literature is authentic and is therefore an ideal resource for the development of reading skills and cultural awareness (see also Chapter 11 and Pachler and Alford, forthcoming).

REFLECTION
Activity 3.7 Using literature to support language work
List topics covered in the A/AS level scheme of work. Beside each topic, note a literary text which contains passages relevant to the topic, e.g. racism – Albert Camus's *L'Etranger*.

The complex levels of meaning contained within literary texts renders them beyond the understanding of many débutante A/AS level learners. The term literature is used here in a traditional sense: novels, poems, plays and short stories. However, extracts related to general topics can provide a meaningful cultural context for study and serve as an introduction to more intensive study at a later date. The extracts provide the opportunity for pre-reading tasks and lend themselves to post-reading activities. The rewriting of poems, paragraphs and longer extracts in the form of newspaper articles, for example, can add to the experience. By rewriting, learners are able to implant their own ideas. Nigel Spack posits (see 1985) that pre-reading exercises can increase the sense of ownership of the content of a text; so can creative post-reading tasks.

Text length and layout

Reading lengthy texts can be daunting. GCSE learners expect short texts through habit. These are often accompanied by illustrations which can assist in the comprehension process. Letters, short magazine and newspaper articles contain many clues to meaning, which teachers at GCSE level recommend their learners to use. To ease the transition, texts can be altered in terms of presentation, offering a degree of continuity to learners. Chambers's suggestion (1991) to develop one's own Lesekiste makes sense.

REFLECTION
Activity 3.8 Familiarising learners with authentic texts
To familiarise learners with the layout of newspapers, ask them to identify five happy and five sad stories. Cut out the texts and separate pictures, headlines and texts. Ask learners from another group to reassemble the articles.

Purposes and outcomes

Gary Chambers articulates a goal of all mfl teachers:

> It is part of my aim to encourage [learners] to read, judge for themselves, express their opinions and feeling and respond to the reactions of class mates. Surely this is what reading is for. It does not involve the practice of a discrete skill, but the integration of all four commonly associated with language learning . . .
>
> (1991, p. 5).

Clearly good readers are active readers, not merely the passive recipients of information. The language contained within a text is not absorbed by a process of osmosis. Chambers's aim, then, is achievable only through planned intervention by the teacher. The process of strategy development is not automatic. The teacher needs to intervene and, in doing so, he or she cannot exclude the development of all language skills. The first stage of the process is discovery: the identification of the type and purpose of text. The second stage is to identify and practise the language structures used in the text to express appealing ideas. Thirdly, an active reader uses the structures to express related, but personalised views. This stage of performance is the most active of all.

REFLECTION

Activity 3.9 Developing a typology of reading activities

1.   Brainstorm with a colleague as many reading activities as you can think of, e.g. to identify happy and sad words in a text; create a gapped text; to translate and retranslate; prediction activities; unjumbling of texts.
2.   Using the categories described above, begin to develop a typology of reading activities.

An example has been provided for you:

Discovery	*Practice*	*Performance*
identify happy and sad words in a text	gapped text	translate and retranslate

---

These activities serve a purpose beyond comprehension alone. Teachers need to structure and sequence activities in order that they provide a model for 'private reading'.

The integration of reading with other language skills demands that the TL is the language of discussion. Responding in the TL to texts is a tall order but a realistic expectation at A/AS level. Closed questions allow even the weakest learner to respond. More open questions suit more able and experienced learners. A gradual shift is required from asking questions which demand one- or two-word answers to those which provoke discussion, and is an important teaching skill. Teachers do need to remember that, in order to answer, learners need something to say. It is in fact often through reading that learners develop the knowledge base which provides them with something to say.

Writing

The purposes of writing at A/AS level take on a new dimension. At GCSE level, learners write in order to convey factual information and to narrate events. The shift to analysis of language and the use of language to represent the abstract (ideas and opinions) is enormous. Clearly, writing is at the heart of the process of integrating language skills. Writing is the means by which learners record ideas, take notes, etc. It is also the means by which language structures are devised and practised. Often, comprehension is demonstrated by learners through writing responses.

REFLECTION
Activity 3.10 The purposes of writing
Note the purpose of writing activities you ask your learners to carry out over
a period of time (see list below). Do tasks and activities requiring writing
serve more than one purpose?
- recording facts
- expressing ideas
- describing
- narrating
- drilling structures
- demonstrating comprehension
- noting rules and patterns
- passing on information
- planning
- presenting
- demonstrating writing skills

The A/AS level learners in Graham's research (see 1997, p. 27) appreciate the value
of existing skills and express a sense of alienation by teachers' expectations being
too high. What Pachler and Field call 'targeted practice' (1997, p. 133) is an
appropriate point to begin the development of writing skills. 'Substitution' is
the replacement of words and phrases contained within a text by alternatives.
The use of synonyms, for example, serves to reinforce the structures contained
within the text and simultaneously to broaden the learners' active vocabulary.
Repetition exercises are traditionally the tasks used to practise and reinforce
grammatical structures; as such they are familiar to GCSE learners. Adapting a
model answer to suit individual needs is a common exercise at the lower level. The
extension of this type of activity to encourage the mastery of verbs and tenses, for
example, has the added benefit of encouraging the development of transferable
skills, enabling the learner to draw on existing knowledge and to generate language
forms to suit new contexts. For example, learners could use structures and phrases
to express disagreement with a point of view in respect to animal rights and apply
this in an argument criticising racist points of view. The grading of such activities in
terms of difficulty is explained by Pachler and Field (see 1997, p. 136); it is no less
relevant at A/AS level. Such activities need to be placed within a communicative
and topical context in order that the purposes of the activities are explicit and clear.

Listening and reading can be used to provide the learner with relevant facts,
figures and information. The recording of this information through writing
exercises serves to reinforce both the language and the cultural content. Gapped
texts requiring the learner to insert the correct forms of verbs and/or adjectives, for
instance, or the rewriting of a poem in the form of a newspaper article require the
learner to consider different registers of language. GCSE learners tend to be

particularly comfortable with letter writing and the encouragement to produce different forms of writing to express the same content does broaden the writer's appreciation.

Ann Clark suggests (see 1993, p. 35) that learners experimenting with new styles should work with familiar topics and vice versa. Learners grappling with complex social issues should not be challenged by abstract writing tasks at the same time. Clark's recommendation is that the learner should be able to relate the content to personal experience. Autobiographical accounts of events which are relevant to the topic provide the opportunity to draw on concrete examples. Narrative texts will contain descriptions and therefore the attainment of a higher level standard can be achieved step by step. The obvious link between the concrete and the abstract is the self; regular completion of a learner diary in the TL is an effective means of bridging the gap. To provide a structure for learners embarking on their A/AS level study, teachers can provide three simple questions in the TL:

- what did I do and learn today?
- how will I reinforce this?
- what will it enable me to do?

Writing is more than simply a way of 'servicing' other skill areas. Writing is one of the principal means by which learners' progress and attainment is assessed. It cannot be separated, therefore, from the development of appropriate learning strategies and study skills. The length of tasks and the complicated content demand degrees of concentration not often encountered by GCSE learners. A step-by-step approach to the production of written work is, therefore, sensible.

The planning of written work involves learners using skills developed at GCSE level. With reference to authentic texts, learners identify appropriate language structures. The production of single and simple sentences to represent a whole paragraph demands little more than has been developed earlier in their learning. The research skills required for writing involve the skills of reading and listening. At the early stages, it is for the teacher to direct learners to appropriate information. Drafting a text requires learners to adapt known language by using structures and correct grammatical forms. Lonsdale (see 1996, p. 22) suggests that structures, which provide precise meaning, e.g. *refuser de, avoir le temps de, être obligé de*, can be added to simple sentences, e.g. *le gouvernement n'aide pas les immigrés, les immigrés vivent dans les foyers*. By using such a process, the language is in context and the aim is that, eventually, sentences will 'sound right'. This approach can be supplemented by a further stage: that of monitoring one's own production of language. Writers need to develop a systematic means of checking. Figure 3.5 offers a possible method. Once a teacher corrects a first draft, learners should be encouraged to analyse their own mistakes. The completion of the checklist suggested meets this demand. To move learners on, they can be encouraged to read through the work of a peer and to note the errors contained. Lastly the grid can be used to check one's

(a) Read through your corrected work
(b) Read a friend's work
(c) Reread your own first draft
  - Do all the verbs agree with the subject?
  - Are the verbs in the correct tense, voice etc?
  - Do adjectives agree?
  - Is the word order correct?
  - Is the vocabulary broad and relevant?
  - Have I used idioms?
  - Are the sentences short?
  - Are sentences too long?
  - Is there a clear argument?
  - Have I used examples to illustrate?
  - Is the style of language appropriate?
  - Do I demonstrate adequate knowledge?
  - Is there a meaningful conclusion?

Figure 3.5 Developing a systematic checking method

own work, without the teacher being involved at this stage. The checklist also lends itself well to focusing on particular difficulties and target setting.

The questions in Figure 3.5 should, of course, be in the respective TL. The frequency and gravity of error should also be noted. One key difference with GCSE learning is the expansion of criteria from successful conveyance of the message to the quality of language and ideas.

There are always occasions when writers do not know sufficient vocabulary. At GCSE, the defined vocabulary list allows learners to work out for themselves what they should be able to write. At A/AS level, learners cannot predict in the same way. 'Avoidance strategies' need to be developed. Learners need to practise interpreting skills and circumlocution. Substitution exercises are of value here, as is the translation and explanation of idioms which are impossible to translate word for word (see Figure 3.6).

Translate into the TL, and explain the imagery contained in, the following idioms:
  - It is raining cats and dogs
  - To take the bull by the horns
  - To make hay while the sun shines
  - To open a can of worms
  - To be on a sticky wicket

Figure 3.6 Translation and circumlocution

Writing in the TL is not straightforward. Planning, drafting and checking are all paper exercises which can be facilitated by word-processing. Unjumbling texts, cutting and pasting paragraphs and placing them in a meaningful order removes the frustration of rewriting.

In order to write (as with speaking, listening and reading) learners need to be stimulated. It is the provision of support which can offer the learner security. Pachler and Field (see 1997, p. 135) provide examples of effective support such as visual stimuli, model answers and written stimuli. It is for the teacher to provide the support necessary and to assess appropriate moments for the gradual removal of such support. Only once the support is removed can learners begin to generate personalised language forms, rather than reproduce standardised examples.

Vocabulary

Gary Chambers (1990, p. 40) sums up the findings of many observers when he asserts: '[as] far as problems posed by A level are concerned post GCSE learners find the amount of new vocabulary to be learnt most difficult'.

At GCSE level, learners are usually provided with lots of vocabulary to learn, extracted from the defined vocabulary lists of GCSE syllabuses. The notional two thousand words can be achieved through a process of rote learning. Indeed, for many successful learners at GCSE level memorising the vocabulary topic by topic is a means by which they can measure their own progress. Graham's research indicates (see 1997, p. 72) that successful GCSE learners learnt from lists, asking members of the family to test them on a regular basis in preparation for vocabulary tests at school.

Walter Grauberg notes (see 1997, p. 6) that there is a tendency to focus on key words at GCSE, i.e. those words most commonly used and needed, drawing on *The Threshold Level for Modern Language Learning in Schools* (van Ek 1976). The methods of teaching and learning vocabulary at GCSE level are governed by the nature of syllabuses, which contain a defined list of lexical items at Foundation level, and the perceived needs of learners. The relationship between inflected forms are not always related to infinitives by GCSE learners. Topic-based learning has allowed teachers to provide a degree of cultural association in that learners do relate phrases and vocabulary to the context in which they were taught. At A/AS level, however, the range of vocabulary is vast and the lack of a defined list of lexical items renders a topic-based approach less effective. Grauberg is concerned, first of all, with how vocabulary is learnt. Learning a single infinitive and certain grammatical rules, can relieve the learner of learning seventy-seven different forms of the verb independently (see Grauberg 1997, p. 8). Grammatical analysis is not the only method recommended. 'Word formation' assists with the deciphering of compound nouns or verbs with prefixes and suffixes. 'Cultural associations' help the learner by providing contextual clues to meaning and further semantic clues can be provided by word association. Collocation, words which regularly occur in sentences with the unknown word, also provides additional contextual clues to meaning.

At A/AS level the learner needs to take responsibility for active learning him- or herself. Grauberg suggests a process consisting of four stages. Figure 3.7 represents this process and his examples of activities (see Grauberg 1997, pp. 5–33).

At A/AS level, vocabulary is learnt/absorbed in different ways for different purposes. There is no defined list and the range is far wider. Consequently, learners need to maintain an active approach and at the same time develop strategies to cope with unknown words. As a result the learning of vocabulary is inevitably linked and integrated with other skills.

Speaking and writing require active knowledge of key words relative to each topic. Learners' own needs in terms of vocabulary are obviously linked to the opinions and views they wish to express relative to a given topic. Unlike at GCSE, teachers cannot produce a comprehensive list; it is for the learner to develop his or her own. Lonsdale advocates (see 1996, p. 18) that the learner develops his or her own method of collecting and learning vocabulary and presents these methods to the rest of a group as an oral presentation. Thereafter the teacher needs to check that active vocabulary learning is taking place. The collection methods obviously vary from one learner to another. Some categorise according to topic, some according to grammatical function. Some prefer to colour code and others include

Stages	Activity types	Examples of activities
discrimination	pre-teaching	oral presentation of key words with visual aids
		explaining vocabulary in texts with synonyms
		providing a cultural contextualisation
		extensive reading
understanding meaning	relationships	grammatical analysis
		collocation
		teacher explanation/clarification
remembering and consolidation	recording and revising	lists
		semantic field mind mapping
		repeated use in context
		recital (e.g. poetry)
		colour coding
		preference ranking (e.g. food)
extension	production	answering focused comprehension questions
		puzzles
		writing short texts containing key vocabulary
		word association

Figure 3.7 Active vocabulary learning

key words within phrases and sentences to provide a meaningful context. More and more learners make use of computers to build databases containing relevant vocabulary.

REFLECTION

Activity 3.11 Shared development of vocabulary-learning strategies

Provide a group of learners with a difficult text containing a lot of unknown vocabulary. Inform the learners that you will test them on the vocabulary contained. Ask them to each use a different method to learn:

- categorise by topic
- categorise by grammatical function
- colour code, or
- place in context and learn phrases

Compare the results of the vocabulary test and carry out a discussion with the group in the TL where possible about the merits of the different learning strategies.

Clearly, at A/AS level it is crucial that learners develop a study schedule (see e.g. Lonsdale 1996, p. 23). This should not be separated from the content of the programme, but fully integrated. Lonsdale argues that the differences between GCSE and A/AS level should be openly discussed early in the course in order that learners can learn from each other. Such an open discussion avoids the risk of learners feeling threatened by the inadequacy of the study skills developed at an earlier stage. Learners need to feel in control of their learning. Learning strategies are more controllable by the learner whereas it is harder to face up to a lack of ability. Consequently, an awareness of a range of learning strategies is useful in that learners are able to experiment with alternatives if one particular technique is not effective (see Graham 1997, p. 119).

The collection of vocabulary, whether as separate words or parts of phrases, is only the first step. There is no escaping the need to learn actively for the purposes of producing personalised language. The idea of learner diaries is not new (see e.g. Dam 1990). In relation to vocabulary learning, the purpose of the diary is to note the learning outcomes and to point towards sources of evidence. Personal tutorials with the teacher should demand an oral presentation of recent learning achievements, based upon regularly written reports of the day's learning. This process requires the learner to revise topics and to make active use of vocabulary covered in context. The diary summarises, but draws the attention to all work covered. Targets can be set, which may involve the traditional GCSE-type vocabulary test on an individual basis.

Regular vocabulary testing can be tedious and takes up precious lesson time. Learners can and should test themselves and each other. Learners in Graham's study recommend (see 1997, p. 133) that vocabulary learning becomes more enjoyable if it forms part of a game. Drawing puzzles to assist each others' learning serves a dual purpose. Firstly, the design of such tasks requires careful attention and learning. Secondly, learners are able to challenge and test each other.

REFLECTION

Activity 3.12 Active vocabulary learning

Ask a group of learners in their second year of A/AS level study to devise some puzzles to assist learners in their first year to learn vocabulary related to a particular topic. Once the puzzles are completed test both groups of learners on the vocabulary contained and compare the results.

Receptive language skills require a commitment to different approaches. Firstly, dictionary skills are crucial. Looking up words in mono- and bi-lingual dictionaries demand particular competences (see Pachler and Field 1997, p. 68 and p. 112). To understand the content of a dictionary the learner requires a degree of grammatical knowledge. The use of reference material is, of course, a major difference between GCSE and A/AS level. At GCSE, textbooks and published vocabulary lists package words carefully within topics. At A/AS level, learners have to consider nuance and imagery when comprehending a text. Listening and reading are the principal sources of new vocabulary. However, gist understanding and 'reading for pleasure' can be frustrating if learners have to pause to use a dictionary every two or three lines. Other strategies include guessing meaning and glossing over unknown words.

Guessing meaning is a complex skill. Often clues are contained with words themselves (the stem, the root, homonyms, etc). The grammatical form/function (verb, tense, adjective, agreements) serves to assist in comprehension. Indeed, the context of the sentence can assist. Fluent reading does not mean translation and learners need to be encouraged to read and listen at pace. The provision of synonyms and notes in the margins of texts by the teacher is helpful to slow and ponderous readers. Speed-reading can be encouraged by the provision of easy comprehension questions. Pictures and diagrams to accompany both written and spoken texts can serve to guide comprehension and to support learning when learners encounter difficult words. The provision of summaries in advance can alleviate the need to reach for reference material.

In addition to being concerned with covering content, mfl teachers, as Graham points out (1997, p. 83), 'need to address the question of *how* their students are learning, rather than merely *what* they are learning' (see also Chapter 13).

The processes of learning have not yet been fully researched; teachers should, therefore, engage in research with their groups about how they learn. Vocabulary learning at A/AS level is the responsibility of the learner. At GCSE it can be seen to be the responsibility of the teacher through regular testing.

Summary

Underpinning the development of the four language skills at A/AS level are three running themes.

One such thread is the reliance on learners' general knowledge and cultural awareness. Learners are motivated by what they perceive as relevant and by what they are able to achieve. New A/AS levels include the study of novels, television and radio programmes, magazines and newspapers. Clearly, topicality stimulates interest. At the same time, it is important not to overstretch learners. Learners tend to be attracted by 'adult' and controversial issues, but teachers must be aware that learners of post-16 age are only in the process of developing ideas and opinions. And, they do not necessarily share their teacher's interest in political and socio-logical issues. Lonsdale (see 1996, p. 24) argues that most A/AS level learners draw on their own general knowledge rather than on the content of the course. Despite the inclusion of cultural awareness as part of the Programme of Study Part I in the 1995 National Curriculum mfl Orders, many schemes of work at Key Stage 4 provide little in terms of cultural awareness beyond the day-to-day habits of native speakers, perhaps because cultural knowledge and understanding is not assessed at the examination.

The second thread is the need for learners to develop independence and owner-ship of the learning process. It is, therefore, for teachers to select material which stimulates learners and to introduce achievable learning strategies. By opting to follow an A/AS level mfl course learners indicate an interest in the TL and culture. Learners must build on existing knowledge and skills and teachers must show respect for prior learning achievements. Learners need to develop independent learning skills and teachers must recognise traits and habits which lend themselves to active learning, such as analytical skills, a preparedness to experiment and make mistakes and finally a willingness and ability to monitor one's own performance.

Finally, the most obvious difference between GCSE and A/AS level study is the need to integrate the four language skills. Productive and receptive skills are interdependent. The overall approach which emerges is one where speaking and writing activities which resemble GCSE-type tasks are used to introduce topics. Higher-level linguistic competence is introduced through listening and reading. Speaking and writing are then redeveloped to enhance skills and exploit newly presented language forms.

References

Ausubel, D. (1968) *Educational Psychology: A Cognitive View.* New York: Holt, Rinehart and Winston.

Chambers, G. (1990) 'Wer die Wahl hat, hat die Qual: choosing an A level syllabus.' In *Language Learning Journal* 2. Rugby: Association of Language Learning, pp. 39–41.

Chambers, G. (1991) 'Suggested approaches to A level literature'. In *Language Learning Journal* 4. Rugby: Association of Language Learning, pp. 5–9.

Clark, A. (1993) 'Bridging the gap: GCSE to "A" level'. In *Language Learning Journal* 8. Rugby: Association for Language Learning, pp. 66–8.

Corless, F. and Gaskell, R. (1983) 'Foreign languages at the post O level stage'. In Richardson, G. (ed.) *Teaching Modern Languages*. Beckenham: Croom Helm, pp. 75–98.

Cummins, J. (1980) 'The cross-lingual dimensions of language proficiency: implications for bilingual education and the optimal age issue'. In *TESOL Quarterly*, 14, 2, pp. 175–87.

Dam, L. (1990) 'Learner autonomy in practice'. In Gathercole, I. (ed.) *Autonomy in Language Learning*. London: CILT, pp. 16 – 37.

DES (1981) *French 16–19: A New Perspective*. London: HMSO.

Eastman, J. (1987) 'Remedial training in listening comprehension'. In *System* 15, pp. 197–201.

Graham, S. (1997) *Effective Language Learning: Positive Strategies for Advanced Level Language Teaching*. Clevedon: Multilingual Matters.

Grauberg, W. (1997) *The Elements of Foreign Language Teaching*. Clevedon: Multilingual Matters.

Hatch, E (1974) *Second Language Learning Universals*. Working Papers on Bilingualism 3, pp. 11–18.

Johnstone, R. (1989) *Communicative Interaction: A Guide for Language Teachers*. London: CILT.

King, L. (1996) 'A matter of discourse – ways of developing learner competence.' In Shaw, G. (ed) *Aiming High: Approaches to Teaching A level*. London: CILT, pp. 40–56.

Lonsdale, T. (1996) 'Planning A level topics to achieve continuity and progression.' In Shaw, G. (ed) *Aiming High: Approaches to Teaching A Level*. London: CILT, pp. 17–30.

Pachler, N. and Field, K. (1997) *Learning to Teach Modern Foreign Languages in the Secondary School*. London: Routledge.

Pachler, N. and Allford, D. (forthcoming) 'Literature in the communicative classroom.' In Field, K. (ed.) *Issues in the Teaching of Modern Foreign Languages*. London: Routledge.

Peck, A. (1988) *Language Teachers at Work: A Description of Methods*. New York: Prentice Hall.

QCA, ACCAC and CCEA (1999) *Subject Criteria for Modern Foreign Languages: GCE Advanced Subsidiary and Advanced Level Specifications*. London.

Rees, P. (1995) 'Reading French from GCSE to A level: the student perspective.' In Grenfell, M. (ed) *Reflecting on Reading from GCSE to A Level*. London: CILT, pp. 27–58.

Searle, J. (1969) *Speech Acts: An Essay in the Philosophy of Language*. Cambridge: Cambridge University Press.

Shaw, G. and Anciaux, A. (1996) 'Bridging the Gap between GCSE and A level'. In Shaw, G. (ed) *Aiming High: Approaches to Teaching A Level*. London: CILT, pp. 8–16.

Skutnabb-Kangas, T. (1984) *Bilingualism or Not, the Education of Minorities*. Clevedon: Multilingual Matters.

Spack, N. (1985) 'Literature, reading, writing in ESL: bridging the gaps'. In *TESOL Quarterly* 19, 4, pp. 703–27.

Tebbut, S. (1996) 'Working with literary texts'. In Shaw, G. (ed) *Aiming High: Approaches to Teaching A level*. London: CILT, pp. 86–96.

Van Ek, J. (1976) *Threshold Level for Modern Language Learning in Schools*. Council of Europe.

Wringe, C. (1976) *Developments in Modern Language Teaching*. London: Open Books Publishing.

Chapter 4

Learner independence

Norbert Pachler and Kit Field

Introduction

An important thread running through many chapters·of this book on teaching modern foreign languages (mfl) at GCE Advanced (A) and Advanced Subsidiary (AS) level is the importance of learner independence.[1] An inherent feature of classroom-based mfl learning at advanced level is the limited time and opportunities available to reach the required level of linguistic proficiency and cover the wide range of topics to be studied. Mfl teachers at advanced level increasingly have to rely on learners practising, reinforcing and extending what is covered during contact time outside lessons. Indeed, the ability to increasingly dispense with the teacher and generate language of their own can be seen to be characteristic features of effective mfl learners (see Allford and Pachler 1998, p. 1). However, as mfl teachers, we must not assume that learners will necessarily bring with them the requisite skills to supplement what is on offer during contact time. There is, therefore, a real need to build into our teaching opportunities for learners to learn how to become effective independent learners.

With Ernesto Macaro we feel that learner independence should draw its rationale from the importance of addressing individual learners' needs (see 1997, p. 168). Elsewhere we draw attention to the fact that mfl learners have differing learning styles (see Pachler and Field 1997, ch. 2); catering for these differing learning styles is a considerable challenge for mfl teachers. Learners tend to display 'personal variables such as intentions, attributes, expectancies and beliefs about [their] own competence and learning abilities' (Little 1991, p. 13). From this follows not only that there should be variety in teaching material and activities but also opportunity for learners to contribute to the teaching and learning process. In addition, there should be scope for learners to use language individually and creatively (see also Kahl and Unruh 1993, p. 11).

As teachers we cannot learn for our learners, but we can provide an environment conducive to learning, both by appropriately and effectively structuring the teaching process as well as by ensuring an appropriate atmosphere enabling the learner to become cognitively and affectively involved and 'active'.

We need to gradually delegate responsibility for learning to learners. According to Leni Dam and Gerd Gabrielsen, learners need to be guided towards active use of the target language (TL), an awareness of the ability and necessity to learn and an understanding of the value and purpose of learning activities (see 1988). This implies the need for explicit coverage of learning strategies and learner training.

> Learner training aims to help learners consider the factors that affect their learning and discover the learning strategies that suit them best. It focuses their attention on the process of learning so that the emphasis is on *how* to learn rather than on *what* to learn. Learner training, therefore, aims to provide learners with the alternatives from which they can make informed choices about *what, how, why, when* and *where* they learn.
>
> (Ellis and Sinclair quoted in Dickinson 1992, p. 13)

Teaching learners how to learn is one aspect of learner independence which needs to build on an awareness, on the part of learners, of the key characteristics of effective (mfl) learning. These characteristics include first and foremost the development of the will and ability to work unsupervised (see Sheerin 1997, p. 58). Others are: being a good guesser of meaning and being driven by the wish to communicate which involves overcoming inhibition (see Rubin 1987, p. 38). Jack Rubin touches upon additional affective concerns, such as being keen to practise and being intrigued by the foreign culture(s). Evidently also, good learners focus their study, through choice, on form and language patterns and continually monitor their progress and achievement.

Awareness raising about characteristics of effective mfl learning is central. One of the key purposes of developing the ability in learners to learn independently is to produce more effective learners as well as better language users. Successful communication requires independence, self-reliance and self-confidence (see Little 1991, p. 8). Financial stringencies and staffing exigencies do not of themselves provide a rationale for learner independence at A/AS level (see Allford and Pachler 1998, p. 4).

REFLECTION
Activity 4.1 Raising awareness about learner strategies
Observe some A/AS level lessons and scan the schemes of work. Make a note of how teachers cover key learner strategies listed below (adapted from Wenden 1986, p. 41):
- having an insight into one's own preferred learner strategies
- adopting an active approach to learning
- being willing to take risks
- attending to form as well as content
- using the TL as a new referencing system
- being of an outgoing disposition

When promoting learner independence, teachers must have a clear perception of their own roles as well as of those of the learners. Independent learners must have ample opportunity to experiment, research, negotiate, explore and initiate (see Nunan and Lamb 1996, p. 141). Learner independence to some extent involves the ability of learners to detach themselves from the learning experience in a critical, reflective way.

This, in turn, has implications for the learning environment, i.e. the methodology and material employed. Eclecticism, i.e. methodological diversity and multi-resourcing, appears to be a way ahead (see also Chapters 7 and 8).

Peter Kahl and Thomas Unruh note the following quality indicators (for multi-resourcing) (loosely translated from German) (see 1993, p. 13):

- there needs to be sufficient material to allow learners to make choices
- resources need to be differentiated according to levels of difficulty and include spoken and written texts as well as practical activities
- instructions and guidance needs to be given in a way that they can be readily understood by the learner without the help of the teacher
- wherever possible material should include monitoring and self-assessment components, and
- material and activities should allow learners to pursue their needs, interests and abilities

Independent learners do need teachers, albeit ones with changing roles and responsibilities. An important role of teachers is to improve upon natural language learning processes (see Allford and Pachler 1998, p. 7). Teachers' pedagogic and didactic expertise in

- selecting appropriate learning objectives
- choosing relevant material
- designing, structuring and grading learning activities, and
- providing constructive feedback as learners progress

remains key to success at A/AS level mfl learning.

Another important role for the teacher, we feel, is to prepare learners for greater independence. Adopting an approach which fosters learner independence is not easy. Shifting roles of the teacher, from someone who provides information to someone who counsels and facilitates, invariably represents a not inconsiderable challenge. This change must not be seen as an abdication of responsibility. As teachers, we remain central to the learning process but we need to ensure that the classroom environment is conducive to learner independence. The atmosphere must be positive, caring, supportive, secure, trusting one where teachers value and learn from learners and tolerate error in the spirit of risk taking and in view of their importance in the learning process (see Chapter 6). The atmosphere should be active and interactive, requiring a sense of partnership between teacher and learner.

The actual content of the learning programme does, of course, remain central, too. It is for the teacher to ensure that language development and language learning development are integrated and that learners know why, when and where to employ independent modes of learning.

Objectives

The objectives of this chapter are to:

* illustrate the need for learner independence at A/AS level
* demonstrate the value of learner independence at A/AS level
* explain the process of becoming an independent learner
* identify aspects of language learning at A/AS level which are well suited to learner independence, and
* clarify the role of the teacher in an approach which fosters learner independence

What is learner independence?

The literature on learner independence is vast and the definitions are manifold. As the purpose of this chapter is not a review of relevant research literature, a brief outline of the term will suffice.

Learner independence[2] at A/AS level we view as a continuum stretching from guided learner independence from the teacher in the classroom characterised, for example, by simulations/role plays, pair- and groupwork, dictionary use or problem solving, to guided learner independence from the teacher outside the classroom, e.g. learners carrying out research activities or project work etc, accompanied by regular reflection on the learning process and the deliberate use of learning strategies. Mfl learning outside the context of a taught programme, e.g. through self-access study, or through distance modes is not considered here. At A/AS level, learner independence for our purposes can, therefore, be seen as the judicious use of learner-centred strategies and reflection on the learning process within a teacher-led learning programme.

Ute Rampillon puts forward a number of characteristics of independent learners (translated loosely from German) (see 1994, pp. 456–9). Independent learners:

* enjoy learning
* are aware of factors impeding their learning and try to overcome them
* are able to articulate factors impeding their learning
* combine known and new
* understand the importance of the subject matter for their own lives
* organise their own learning
* identify their own needs and act upon them
* use learning strategies and techniques

- monitor and review the learning strategies they use
- learn through communicating, and
- ask the teacher questions which improve their understanding of the subject matter as well as of the learning process

If we are seriously concerned with preparing A/AS level learners for lifelong mfl learning, we need to consider how we can move learners towards developing these characteristics.

Why learner independence?

REFLECTION

Activity 4.2 Why learner independence?

What are your personal and your departmental views and working definitions of learner independence? Do they compare with or differ from the views expressed in this chapter?

An 'A' level course involves approximately 300 hours of contact time which, when added to the number of hours of exposure to the TL up to GCSE, amounts to approximately 700 hours of mfl learning in total; this represents only 20 per cent of the time a child is exposed to the mother tongue from the first word to the point where she can be said to have recognisable language proficiency (see Macaro 1997, p. 99). Evidently the degree of language development possible as well as required in the 300 hours of study is vast. Teachers and learners cannot rely on lesson time alone.

Flexible and independent learning at A/AS level can be seen as a continuation of differentiation at GCSE (see also Lamb 1998, p. 33). Seen in this light, independent learning is a strategy of catering for learners' needs and it allows teachers to build on an assertion in Brian Page's book that 'the best sort of input arises from learner demand' (1992, p. 58). Underpinning this view of independent learning is a partnership model of the teacher and learners.

In the same way as the teacher cannot learn for his or her learners, teaching does not always lead to learning (see Page 1992, p. 70). How the learner assimilates input and converts it to intake is, therefore, one important question facing mfl teachers. As can be seen in Chapter 6, learner output and the negotiation of meaning play an important role. Research into how we learn suggests that the construction of meaning through social interaction and 'scaffolding' by significant others, e.g. through graded question-and-answer work, is crucial to successful learning (see Williams and Burden 1997, chs 1 and 2). From this we conclude that the learner needs to have ample opportunities to become an 'active' meaning maker and participant in the learning process. Learner independence seems key to this process.

Enjoyment of the learning process also offers support for a learner-centred and independent approach. Macaro reports that learners enjoy group work because they are able to work at their own pace and level and thus feel less threatened, and that the activity types involved require the teacher to adopt a 'nicer' role (see 1997, p. 135). But his research also highlights possible drawbacks, such as the over-use of English and the opportunity for some learners to avoid work (see also Allford and Pachler 1998, p. 6).

Manuel Jimenez Raya notes that successful learning is the outcome of the interrelationship between cognition (ability to learn) and affective and emotional factors (the will to learn) (see 1998, p. 21). Positive attitudes are, of course, reinforced by successful learning. By allowing learners to draw on their own curiosity, interests and active involvement through independent learning, successful outcomes can be seen to be more likely, leading in turn to yet more positive attitudes.

Another argument in support of independent learning is that learners who are over-dependent on the teacher will not give consideration to the range of learning opportunities available to them. Ian Tudor argues just this point (see 1996, p. 36). For him the key objective is to help learners develop their understanding of language simultaneously with the ability to make 'learner' decisions: independent learners need to select objectives for themselves, choose appropriate content and material as well as select methods to develop language and learning skills.

The size of the task should not be off-putting. Raya notes that the successful learning of learner strategies actually accelerates the process of subject learning (see 1998, p. 22). Learners become able to transfer successful strategies to new situations. This process ideally leads to a situation where learners can develop the skills to learn outside the classroom. After all, in order to become effective users of the TL, learners need to use the TL independently of the teacher. We cannot take this process for granted. Mfl teachers need to guide learners towards independence in learning and TL use (see Allford and Pachler 1998, p. 7).

At A/AS level, learners have by and large made a positive choice about the study of mfl. Only rarely will they enrol on an A/AS level course in mfl for reasons other than interest in the language. The reasons for their choice may coincide with Gardner and Lambert's (1972) types of motivational orientation: 'integrative' motivation represents an intrinsic interest in the TL culture; 'instrumental' motivation concerns a wish to achieve good examination results and/or use the language in functional situations. By allowing learners to select objectives, material and methods independently, teachers, in fact, allow learners to pursue their interests in the subject.

REFLECTION
Activity 4.3 Identifying learners' needs
Interview some learners studying A/AS level mfl in order to find out what their 'needs', 'wants' and 'lacks' are. Do their answers furnish you with a rationale for learner independence?

In our view learner independence is essential at A/AS level. Learners need an insight into language and its use in order to be able to apply the TL outside the classroom independently of the teacher, generating their own meaning; they need to process and proceduralise random input they are exposed to when using the TL in and outside the classroom, e.g. when listening to the TL, speaking with TL speakers or reading TL sources. All of these skills require learners to apply discourse strategies independently of the teacher. One set of learning objectives during an A/AS level mfl course must, therefore, relate to the development of respective skills.

Learner independence: when and how?

An important, if obvious, point to note in the context of when to introduce elements of learner independence is that learners need to be ready. Learner readiness cannot be taken for granted but can, in our view, be nurtured. Experience suggests that learners are often uncertain about attempts on the part of the teacher to withdraw as sole linguistic and cultural reference point in lessons. In many cases they have become socialised into certain expectations concerning the role of the teacher and have to learn, and be taught, to solve (linguistic) problems by drawing on a range of resources and not to rely solely on the teacher (see also Kahl and Unruh 1993, p. 13).

REFLECTION

Activity 4.4 Assessing your learners' readiness for independence

Carry out a brainstorming session with A/AS level mfl learners: what are their views about learner independence? what role do they think it should play in their mfl learning?

Whilst one reason for encouraging learners to develop learning strategies is that they eventually are used by learners outside the classroom in real-life TL application, the development of such techniques needs to begin in the classroom. Learner independence needs to be seen as a developmental process, with strategies and skills being introduced to the learner in a gradual way. Starting the process of learner independence in the classroom does not imply that the teacher hands over all responsibility to the learner, but that – as learners develop signs of responsibility – the teacher provides appropriate activities which encourage discussion and negotiation of the learning process. This should involve a debate about the effectiveness of the material and activities used and, subsequently, the design of, and participation in, exercises which learners feel best suit their own needs. The teacher develops the role of facilitator and tutor and learners become a resource for each other.

Some work on metacognitive strategies, i.e. strategies concerning the learning process, identifies three key phases: planning, monitoring and evaluating (see e.g. Tudor 1996, p. 57). Whilst at A/AS level the planning of a programme of study will be predominately teacher-led, it is very important that learners are involved in monitoring their progress and achievement against expected learning outcomes, i.e. that they carry out self-assessment. They also need to be involved in evaluating the effectiveness of the learning activities they undertake, ideally ones allowing active learner participation. Learners also need to reflect on how well these activities match their own learning styles. From there, learners can proceed to making suggestions and, eventually, to making decisions about the learning process itself. At A/AS level this also means that the teacher needs to select appropriate moments for the introduction of course work options and for the setting of open-ended tasks.

Involvement in planning, monitoring and evaluating can, therefore, be seen as an important step towards learner independence. This notion is reflected in Nunan's process-based approach (see 1997, p. 196). In this model, learners initially need to be made aware of the pedagogical goals and content of a unit of work. Secondly, they should be involved in analysing the goals and content of the unit and relate these to their own needs and 'wants', which can lead to learners selecting and adapting learning opportunities for themselves. In a third stage, learners create their own objectives, select their own material and complete tasks in their own time and in order to meet personal learning objectives. Finally, in a stage Nunan calls 'transcendence', learners aim to link what they have learnt to the outside world. It seems to us that such a model is very appropriate for A/AS level learners of mfl who wish to continue to pursue the study of mfl beyond 19. As mfl teachers, we need to provide learners with a core of knowledge and skills which enables them to research, practise and exploit the TL.

Independent learning opportunities present themselves whenever learners are confronted with input and 'texts' of various descriptions. By devising questions, wherever possible in the TL, which go beyond 'checking' content, such as

- how did you read the text?
- what are your reactions to . . .? or
- how could you be sure that . . .?

the teacher can generate active involvement and provoke responses to spoken as well as written texts which go beyond comprehension (see King 1996, p. 47).

Kahl and Unruh suggest that independent project work provides ample opportunity for learners to apply the knowledge, skills and understanding they have acquired, use their creativity and initiative and 'put the foreign language to the test', i.e. explore what they are able to do with what they have learnt. Independent project work will allow learners to experience success but, invariably, it will also highlight any shortcomings they still have and, hopefully, provide motivation to make up deficiencies (see 1993, p. 12).

Kahl and Unruh also point to the importance of the presentation and evaluation of independent or collaborative learning outcomes (see 1993, p. 15). In their own attempts to move towards teaching modes which foster learner independence they found that requiring learners to present their own work, for example in the form of role plays, tape-recordings, brochures, etc, and to evaluate work of peers proved to be of great educational value. Learners were asked to report on the outcomes of their work, how they went about completing the task, how good and focused their work had been and whether they were content with what they had produced. Learners were also asked to complete an evaluation/self-assessment checklist.

REFLECTION
Activity 4.5 Teaching and learning activity audit
On the basis of observation, list teaching and learning activities conducive to learner independence. Categorise them in the following way:
- planning
- practising
- interacting
- elaborating, and
- researching
How can learner responsibility be maximised in these activities whilst ensuring quality of learning?

Establishing ownership

Learners need to understand the foreign language learning process to some extent as well as some of the thinking that goes into course planning in order to be able to negotiate their own learning paths. In practical terms this can mean teachers engaging learners in discussions about the role and importance of learner independence. It also means that learning objectives not only have to be clearly defined but also that they are being made explicit to learners and are open to negotiation. Equally, expectations of examinations need to be clear as do pathways through the learning process.

One approach to establishing ownership is the drawing-up of a learning contract. Nunan and Lamb, for example, suggest the discussion with learners of the following issues when introducing a new unit of work or topic (see 1996, p. 158):

- what are the objectives?
- what activities help fulfil the objectives?
- what resources are needed?
- what evidence of success will be needed to be generated? or
- what is an appropriate time scale?

By being involved in this way learners become more aware of the process and content of their learning inside and outside the classroom and are better able to identify, supplement and extend those aspects which are in need of development and improvement as well as to make informed decisions about their learning.

REFLECTION
Activity 4.6 Establishing ownership
When introducing your next unit of work/topic, discuss the questions suggested by Nunan and Lamb with your learners. Then, reflect on the discussion: how did learners react? how willingly did they participate? what is your personal reaction?

Such a discussion, organised and recorded in a formal way, enables learners and teachers to make explicit their own expectations and for both parties to establish their roles and responsibilities.

Ownership of the learning process, therefore, develops as an outcome of teacher–learner dialogue, which must take place at all stages of the learning process. Learners need to engage in interaction and reflection on learning if real language learning is to take place (see also Macaro 1997, p. 143).

Ownership of the learning process also means an awareness, on the part of learners, of the place and value of material. Learners should be presented with choices about which material and activities to use, have access to a variety of them including spoken and written texts of different genres and in different media and be able to choose from a range of exercises and activities with which to exploit these material. A sense of ownership can evolve from an understanding of the value of types of material and activities in relation to personal learning styles. For planning multi-resourced topics, see Chapter 8.

REFLECTION
Activity 4.7 Exploiting material
Ask a group of A/AS level learners to analyse some material and devise some tasks in relation to the stated (and negotiated?) learning objectives.
Reflect on the characteristics of the tasks the learners have developed. What, if any, are the implications for your future planning?

Developing a bank of learner strategies

In order to be able to select appropriate learning strategies for themselves, learners need to understand the learning goal of a unit of work, see the value in terms of their own short-term learning objectives, appreciate the potential of material available and know how they personally learn best (see Macaro 1997, p. 171).

Learners also need the confidence to experiment with new learning strategies (see Raya 1998, pp. 22–3). This can be achieved by setting individual tasks which require learners to explain how the task was attempted, rather than simply to demonstrate outcomes. The completion by learners of a profile sheet, which allows them to tick strategies employed, is one possible way of learners reflecting on strategy use. If new strategies are introduced one at a time, learners are less likely to be confused. Another way of encouraging reflection on strategy use is to devote individual tutorial time to a discussion of the effectiveness of particular strategies.

One way of building a bank of learning strategies is to get peers to share and pool ideas on a 'graffiti' wall (see Johnson *et al.* 1990, p. 53). This way an agenda for discussion can be generated.

Speaking in the TL, for instance, is often impeded by lack of confidence. Independent practice and rehearsal in advance of a learner contribution to a discussion might help. Macaro (1997, p. 119) makes some useful suggestions in this context (see Activity 4.8).

REFLECTION
Activity 4.8 Strategies for developing oral competence
Survey a group of learners to find out which of the learning strategies listed below are popular, known but not used or not known. Can you add more to the list as an outcome of your study?
- practising out loud
- practising 'under one's breath'
- devising songs and rhymes
- acting out role plays
- predicting points of view
- using the teacher to correct, or
- learning from mistakes

Following Lamb (see 1998, p. 41) other learning opportunities, which are pertinent to rehearsal and practice, can be added:

- selecting appropriate material/worksheets to practise useful structures
- adapting ideas and opinions from text/course books and authentic material
- devising and planning games with a partner, or
- using new technologies to present arguments and to invite responses (see Chapter 14)

Implicit in many of these ideas is the notion of working collaboratively. Johnson *et al.* (1990) argue forcibly that the teacher has an important role to play in ensuring an atmosphere of cooperation in the classroom. They suggest an activity which allows learners to contribute, or to withdraw, as they see fit (see 1990, p. 53): the passing round of an artefact in a circle is a useful way of inviting comment as well as of establishing a sense of trust in the group. During such activities, the teacher can observe learners to see who contributes, who doesn't and why. Individual tutorials provide an opportunity to explore any anxieties learners might have that stop them from learning.

REFLECTION
Activity 4.9 Learner attitudes and levels of participation
Design an observation sheet which enables you to generate evidence of learners' attitudes and levels of participation. Use the sheet to conduct an observation and then use the observations as the basis of a discussion with learners.

Practising language in preparation for an 'event', such as a debate or 'public discussion', can involve independent exploration. This exploration needs to be focused. The teacher, through discussions with individuals, can direct learners to issues of particular concern such as arguments to be advanced but also, of course, lexis and language structures to be used.

The conversion of input into intake is an important aspect of mfl learning which requires learners to retain and store information in their long-term rather than short-term memories (see Chapter 6). Thompson 1987 (see pp. 45–6), for example, lists strategies for retaining information which are relevant to language learners (see Figure 4.1) and which relate to different learning styles. Teachers can help learners identify which techniques relate to their learning styles.

Verbal elaboration:	the organisation of components thematically (e.g. sound similarities, grammatical classifications, visual representations)
Physical response:	the re-enactment of what has been learnt in a problem-solving situation
Spatial mnemonics:	imagining information is placed in certain locations (e.g. rooms of a house, files of a filing cabinet)
Visual methods:	representing ideas through images which can be visualised mentally by the learner
Linguistic mnemonics:	the use of 'peg words' which, when remembered, trigger a stream of consciousness

Figure 4.1 Strategies for retaining information

There exists a growing number of books on learning strategies, many of which tend to confine themselves to the presentation of typologies. There appears to be a focus on metacognitive strategies concerned with the management of the learning process. However, some publications are emerging which apply typologies to mfl settings and offer useful suggestions for practical application (see e.g. Harris 1997).

Self-monitoring

The teacher has a major role to play in the monitoring of learning. Observations of learners' application, attitudes, questions, anxieties, difficulties, strengths, weaknesses and successes can generate useful information which may partly form the basis of individual tutorials (see McDonell 1992, p. 167). Such observations form vital input to an ongoing needs analysis.

> A learner centred approach to needs analysis rests on the belief that a full specification of learner's needs can only emerge over time, as learners gradually come to understand their needs and acquire the ability to express them in a pedagogically useful manner
>
> (Tudor 1996, p. 88)

Learners, too, have a crucial role to play in this but they need to be trained so that they can 'talk through the issues [with the teacher] and to give study and social skills an equal status to linguistic skills' (Carty and Harris in Page 1992, p. 54).

One way of enabling learners to monitor their progress is to break down learning tasks and to provide checklists which allow a step-by-step evaluation of the learning process by learners drawing on existing knowledge and making thematic links, thereby developing skill transfer.

REFLECTION
Activity 4.10 Analysing a task
Analyse a task on the current scheme of work and break it down into component parts. Use the components as a checklist and apply the checks to a particular learner working through this task. Where do his or her difficulties lie? Does he or she agree with your analysis? How do the outcomes match with his or her needs analysis?

A lot of the literature on independent learning involves mention of learner diaries. The learner diary can be seen as a tool for evaluating teaching and learning techniques on an individual basis. Raya notes (see 1998, p. 26) that it allows for the development of an awareness of cognitive abilities and provides both teacher and learner with an insight into the processes of language learning and also personal strategic behaviour. There is the risk that in completing a learner diary, the learner will make over-generalisations (see Page 1992, p. 75). The teacher must, therefore, check the diary regularly and provide some structure. Tudor recommends to advise learners in the early stages to record specific difficulties, which in turn enables the teacher to take remedial action if and when necessary (see 1996, p. 92). A later development is for the learner to record language use, particularly that which takes place outside the classroom. A detailed analysis of out-of-class language learning allows for the relationship between classroom learning and independent language use to become more transparent for the learner.

By definition, a learner diary provides a retrospective view of the learning process. Little warns against over-complication, recommending a simple record of 'what is done', 'how it is done' and 'what is learnt' (see 1991, p. 52). Raya is more specific, suggesting four key questions to be answered regularly (see 1998, p. 24):

1   What have you learnt today?
2   Who have you learnt it from?
3   How have you learnt it?
4   How did you feel?

Henry Holec makes the suggestion for learners to evaluate the use of material in terms of their contribution to the learning process (see 1987, p. 148).

Completing a learner diary demands that the learner reflects and through it learners can engage in what Macaro calls 'contrastive analysis' (see 1997, p. 99), a comparison of rules and patterns between mother tongue and TL. Such a process can be seen to aid the process of conceptualisation. Wherever possible details should be noted and recorded in the TL.

Monitoring during the learning process provides stimulus for discussion. Learner independence is not concerned with imposing learning methods, but with identifying strategies which best suit individual learners. Learners need, therefore, to be introduced to learning strategies and be aware of their potential, but also be left to reject/accept them on the basis of their own needs and wishes.

Self-assessment

Self-assessment can make a valuable contribution to the learning process. It can be concerned, amongst other things, with accuracy, improvement or fluency (see also Chapter 6). Self-assessment should cover the full range of language skills and should, therefore, include use of the video and audio tapes to assess oral and aural work. For a detailed discussion of self-assessment, see Chapter 13.

REFLECTION
Activity 4.11 Learner audit
Talk to some A/AS level mfl learners and explore in what ways they feel they:
- 'own' the learning process
- have developed a range of learning strategies
- monitor their own learning, and
- are able to self-assess

Summary

Learner independence is a complicated process which is developmental. It is negotiated between the teacher and learner and, therefore, must be planned. For Macaro the process is one where teachers must learn to predispose learners to language learning (see 1997, pp. 129–30). This involves presenting and sharing in the evaluation of known and new learning strategies and informing learners about pedagogy relevant to their own needs. Indeed, by explaining and negotiating objectives and by reviewing progress through a tutoring role, teacher and learners can develop an effective working relationship.

Notes

1 The use of 'learner independence' rather than 'independent learning' in this chapter is deliberate as, in our view, the term 'learner independence' reflects more clearly the implicit rationale: the emphasis is on the needs of the learner, not the 'prescriptions' of a 'method' or an 'approach'.
2 It should be noted that, apart from 'independence', the term 'autonomy' features frequently in background literature. For the purposes of our discussion we prefer to use the term 'independence' as, in our view, its connotations relate more closely to the relationship of learners and teachers we feel is most effective.

References

Allford, D. and Pachler, N. (1998) 'Learner autonomy, communication and discourse.' In *Proceedings of the Institution-Wide Language Programmes 7th National Conference*, Sheffield Hallam University, pp. 1–24.
Dam, L. with Gabrielsen, G. (1988) 'Developing learner autonomy in a school context.' In Holec, H. (ed) *Autonomie et Apprentissage Autodirigé: Applications dans le Contexte Européen*. Council of Europe: Strasbourg.
Dickinson, L. (1992) *Learner Training for Language Learning.* Dublin: Authentik.
Gardner, R. and Lambert, W. (1972) *Attitudes and Motivation in Second Language Learning.* Rowley, MA: Newbury House.
Harris, V. (1997) *Teaching Learners How to Learn: Strategy Training in the ML Classroom.* London: CILT.
Holec, H. (1987) 'The Learner as manager: managing learning or managing to learn?' In

Wenden, A. and Rubin, J. (eds) *Learner Strategies in Language Learning*. Hemel Hemstead: Prentice Hall, pp. 145–58.

Johnson, J. with Pardesi, H. and Paine, C. (1990) 'Autonomy in Primary school'. In Gathercole, I. (ed) *Autonomy in Language Learning*. London: CILT, pp. 46–54.

Kahl, P. and Unruh, T. (1993) 'Eigenverantwortliches Lernen im Englischunterricht eine Alternative zur lehrerorientierten Arbeit'. In *Der Fremdsprachliche Unterricht Englisch*. Heft 10. Erhard Friedrich Verlag/Klett, pp. 11–15.

King, L. (1996) 'A matter of discourse – ways of developing learner competence.' In Shaw (ed) *Aiming High: Approaches to Teaching A level*. London: CILT, pp. 40–56.

Lamb, T. (1998) 'Now you are on your own! Developing independent learning strategies'. In Gewehr, W. (ed) *Aspects of Modern Language Teaching in Europe*. London: Routledge, pp. 30–47.

Little, D. (1990) 'Autonomy in language learning'. In Gathercole, I. (ed) *Autonomy in Language Learning*. London: CILT, pp. 7–15.

Little, D. (1991) *Learner Autonomy: Definitions, Issues and Problems*. Dublin: Authentik.

Macaro, E. (1997) *Target Language: Collaborative Learning and Autonomy*. Clevedon: Multilingual Matters.

McDonell, W. (1992) 'The role of the teacher in the co-operative learning classroom'. In Kessler, C. (ed) *Co-operative Language Learning: A Teacher's Resource Book*. London: Prentice Hall, pp. 163–74.

Nunan, D. (1997) 'Developing and adapting materials to encourage learner autonomy'. In Benson, P. and Voller, P. (eds) *Autonomy and Independence in Language Learning*. London: Longman, pp. 192–203.

Nunan, D. and Lamb, T. (1996) *The Self-Directed Teacher: Managing the Learning Process*. Cambridge: Cambridge University Press.

Pachler, N. and Field, K. (1997) *Learning to Teach Modern Foreign Languages in the Secondary School*. Routledge: London.

Page, B. (1992) (ed) *Letting Go: Taking Hold!* London: CILT.

Rampillon, U. (1994) 'Autonomes Lernen im Fremdsprachenunterricht – ein Widerspruch in sich oder eine neue Perspektive?' In *Die Neueren Sprachen 93*, 5, pp. 455–466.

Raya, J. (1998) 'Training language learners to learn'. In Gewehr, W. (ed) *Aspects of Modern Language Teaching in Europe*. London: Routledge, pp. 13–29.

Rubin, J. (1987) 'Learner strategies: theoretical assumptions, research history and typology'. In Wenden, A. and Rubin, J. (eds) *Learner Strategies in Language Learning*. Hemel Hemstead: Prentice Hall, pp. 36–51.

Sheerin, S. (1997) 'An exploration of the relationship between self-access and independent learning'. In Benson, P. and Voller, P. (eds) *Autonomy and Independence in Language Learning*. London: Longman, pp. 54–65.

Thompson, I. (1987) 'Memory in language learning'. In Wenden, A. and Rubin, J. (eds) *Learner Strategies in Language Learning*. Hemel Hemstead: Prentice Hall, pp. 43–56.

Tudor, I. (1996) *Learner Centredness as Language Education*. Cambridge: Cambridge University Press.

Wenden, A. (1986) 'Incorporating learner training in the classroom'. In *System* 14/3, pp. 315–25.

Williams, M. and Burden, R. (1997) *Psychology for Language Teachers: A Social Constructivist Approach*. Cambridge: Cambridge University Press.

Chapter 5

Teaching and learning culture

Norbert Pachler

Introduction

Issues concerning the teaching and learning of culture have attracted considerable interest from researchers into and commentators on foreign language teaching and learning in recent years. This chapter examines what is currently known about the teaching and learning of (language and) culture and how this relates to A/AS level modern foreign languages (mfl) courses.

Objectives

By the end of this chapter you should have an awareness of:

- what constitutes culture
- why to teach culture
- some differences between target language and target culture learning, and
- some approaches to and strategies for teaching culture at A/AS level

What is culture?

Numerous researchers into and commentators on the cultural component of mfl teaching have been arguing for some time now the need to challenge traditional notions of what constitutes culture.

REFLECTION
Activity 5.1 What is culture?
What are your personal and your departmental working definitions of culture? Do they match with or differ from the definitions offered later in this chapter?

Also, carry out a brainstorming session with your A/AS level learners: what is their understanding of culture? What role do they think it should play in their mfl learning?

In an important contribution to the discussion of the cultural component of language teaching, Claire Kramsch distinguishes two definitions of culture, one coming from the humanities, the other from the social sciences. The one

> focuses on the way a social group represents itself and others through its material productions, be they works of art, literature, social institutions, or artefacts of everyday life, and the mechanisms for their reproduction and preservation through history.
>
> (Kramsch 1996, p. 2)

The other refers to 'the attitudes and beliefs, ways of thinking, behaving and remembering shared by members of that community.' (Kramsch 1996, p. 2).

Traditionally the notion of 'material culture' has prevailed which manifested itself in mfl teaching in the study of written sources, particularly literary texts, or that of 'time-honoured institutions' (Kramsch 1996, p. 2) such as the political or education systems of the target country, etc. With the inclusion of approaches from the social sciences such as ethnographic methods into mfl research, learning and teaching culture is increasingly seen as a social construct and as relative.

> [Culture] is arbitrary, which doesn't mean it is gratuitous, only that different events could have been recorded if other people had had the power to record them, different patterns could have been identified, these patterns in turn could have been differently enunciated; which is why culture, in order to be legitimate, has always had to justify itself and cloak its laws in the mantle of what is 'right and just' rather than appear in the naked power of its arbitrariness.
>
> (Kramsch 1996, p. 3)

In the wake of culture being viewed as a socially diverse phenomenon, observation and data collection, particularly through first hand experiences with target language speakers and the target cultures, have come to the fore in mfl teaching and learning. Indeed, the endeavour of imparting a modern foreign language is increasingly becoming mfl *education* rather than merely knowledge or skill acquisition.

In defining what culture is and what culture we can or should teach, the differentiation of culture constituting itself along three axes seems helpful (see Kramsch 1996, p. 3):

- the diachronic axis of time
- the synchronic axis of space, and
- the metaphoric axis of the imagination.

According to this taxonomy, then, culture includes historic traditions, social diversity and local specificity as well as the ephemerality of the status quo concerning the target culture.

Important questions for mfl teachers, however, remain, for instance: which aspects of culture are mfl teachers at A/AS level responsible for? A cursory look at language-and-culture teaching methodology suggests a move away from a cognitive approach with the aim 'to impart as many historical, geographical and institutional facts as possible while teaching language skills' via the communicative approach with the aim 'to behave "correctly" when communicating with members of that culture and to be able to cope in situations which they *(learners)* might encounter' to an intercultural communicative approach aiming at enabling learners 'to mediate attitudes, value-systems and viewpoints of their own culture and those of the target culture' (Wallner 1995, p. 8; see also Pachler and Field 1997, ch. 7).

An important question to be answered before we can address methodological issues is why culture deserves inclusion in an A/AS level mfl programme.

Why teach culture?

REFLECTION
Activity 5.2 What role does culture play in your A/AS level syllabus subject specifications and teaching?
Examine the A/AS level syllabus subject specifications you are currently using: what role does culture play in it?

Then examine your current A/AS level programme of study: what role, if any, does culture play there? what, if any, is your rationale for including culture in your mfl teaching?

Language is both part of culture as well as the medium by which culture is defined and described (see Pachler and Field 1997, p. 144). And, '[culture] in the final analysis is always *linguistically mediated membership into a discourse community, that is both real and imagined*' (Kramsch 1996, p. 3; italics in original). Language and culture are, thus, inextricably linked to one another. Michael Byram and Carol Morgan *et al.* succinctly express this interrelationship through hyphenation: language-and-culture (see Byram, Morgan *et al.* 1994). The main argument for teaching culture as part of the mfl curriculum at A/AS level, then, is a linguistic one: in order to understand language fully and use it fluently, learners need not only linguistic, pragmatic, discourse and strategic competence but also socio-cultural and world knowledge (see e.g. Willems 1996, p. 90). The notion that differences in languages predicate differences in how speakers of different languages view the world, i.e. the relativist hypothesis (see e.g. Whorf 1956), has stimulated eager debates amongst linguists. Byram notes that recent studies have provided evidence in support of this hypothesis in a moderate form, namely that some areas of language appear to reflect a culture (see Byram 1997a, p. 52). In order to become proficient target language speakers, therefore, learners need to be aware of the cultural dimension of language.

One level of language which reflects culture is the idiomatic: words need to be understood not only in terms of their mother tongue dictionary equivalent – insofar as this even exists – but together with their target culture connotations; mfl learners at A/AS level need to learn to attach target culture, rather than their own, connotations to new words (see Byram 1997a, p. 53). In his discussion of cultural awareness as vocabulary learning, Byram gives the example of the Austrian German word 'Schmäh' as a particularly rich carrier of cultural meaning which requires detailed cultural knowledge in order to be fully understood (see Byram 1997a, p. 54). Certain grammatical structures at the level of syntax or morphology can equally be seen to reflect culture providing mfl learners at A/AS level ample opportunities to deal with language-and-culture; examples include grammatical gender, certain verb conjugations and verb forms or aspects of word order, etc.

The cultural dimension in the use of language is equally important for mfl learners as correct target language expressions can easily be used inappropriately due to socio-pragmatic failure at a discourse level, for instance when and how to thank or apologise to a native speaker interlocutor, when to use formal or informal modes of address, what conventions exist for greeting people, how to start and conclude conversations, how to structure one's line of argument in a conversation, in turn-taking, turn-keeping and turn-giving, in topic nomination and topic change, the use of gambits or, particularly important in German, modal particles, etc. (see e.g. Rost-Roth 1996). In her contrastive discourse analysis of German and English, Juliane House (see House 1996, p. 8) identified five dimensions along which members of German and Anglo-American language-and-culture groups can be seen to have different communicative preferences:

directness   ↔ indirectness
focus on self   ↔ focus on other
focus on content   ↔ focus on addressee
explicitness   ↔ implicitness
ad hoc formulations ↔ linguistic routines

German native speakers, according to House, tend to prefer values towards the left of these five continua. Although House is careful to stress that these dimensions are, indeed, continua and not dichotomies and that her findings suggest tendencies not categorical differences, we might be well advised as mfl teachers to take note of such findings and include in our teaching programmes material which allows A/AS level mfl students to familiarise themselves with potential cultural differences at a pragmatic discourse level. Indeed, Gerard Willems suggests that, in order to help learners avoid failures in communication, as mfl educators we should give the context of language use a more prominent place in language teaching (see Willems 1996, p. 80).

It can be seen, therefore, that culture is closely linked to language and its use and that in order to communicate successfully and proficiently knowledge of culture is important. There are, however, also other reasons why to teach culture: these are of political, educational and pragmatic nature.

Despite the identification in 1988 of a European dimension as an educational aim with a view to facilitating the move to full economic and monetary union by Education Ministers of the then still European Community, for instance through strengthening a sense of European identity in young people, improving their knowledge of the Community and its member states or supporting pupils' strategic social, economic, political and aesthetic understanding (see Capel and Pachler 1997, pp. 263–4, and Morrell 1996, p. 15), a recent study suggests that the European dimension has been virtually excluded from the National Curriculum (NC) (see Morrell 1996, p. 5). The difficulties of justifying mfl, invariably an important part of a European dimension, on the curriculum are well documented. Whilst the original 1992 NC mfl Orders made provision for all pupils to learn one foreign language from 11 to 16, the revised version of 1995 reduced the statutory requirement at Key Stage 4 to that of a Short Course; at the time of writing it remains to be seen what the second revision of the NC in 2000 has in store. In addition, mfl departments experience increasing difficulties in offering more than one modern foreign language, at a time when the European Commission posits that

> it is becoming necessary for everyone, irrespective of training and education routes chosen, to be able to acquire and keep up their ability to communicate in at least two Community languages other than their mother tongue.
>
> (European Commission 1996, p. 45)

In political terms, then, foreign language and culture teaching appears not to enjoy a high priority at a policy level. At the interface of policy making with practice in classrooms, however, a stronger commitment to culture teaching is evident than has existed before the publication of the Harris Report which advised on the National Curriculum (see DES 1990). At 11 to 16, for example, the 1995 NC mfl Orders include as part of the Programme of Study Part 1 a section on cultural awareness:

Pupils should be given opportunities to:
(a) work with authentic materials, including newspapers, magazines, books, films, radio and television, from the countries or communities of the target language
(b) come into contact with native speakers in this country and, where possible, abroad
(c) consider their own culture and compare it with the cultures of the countries and communities where the target language is spoken
(d) identify with the experiences and perspectives of people in these countries and communities
(e) recognise cultural attitudes as expressed in language and learn the use of social conventions, *e.g. forms of address.*

(DfE 1995, p. 3)

For A/AS level teachers an awareness and knowledge of these requirements is important insofar as they represent the basis to be built on during A/AS level mfl study.

The Subject Criteria drawn up by the Qualifications and Curriculum Authority (QCA) and others as a basis for A/AS level syllabus development are also at the interface of policy making with classroom practice. The 1999 Subject Criteria for mfl list the following as one of the aims of mfl teaching at A/AS level: to 'develop students' insights into, and encourage contact with, the contemporary society, cultural background and heritage of countries or communities where the target language is spoken' (QCA *et al.* 1999, p. 1). There is a requirement for students at AS level to '*explore and develop* understanding of the contemporary society, cultural background and heritage of one or more of the countries or communities whose language is being studied' (QCA *et al.* 1999, p. 2; my emphasis) and at A level '*to understand and study in greater depth* aspects of the contemporary society, cultural background and heritage of one or more of the countries or communities whose language is being studied, *demonstrating a higher level of critical awareness*' (QCA *et al.* 1999, p. 3; my emphasis).

In summary, the political rationale for culture teaching seems less pronounced in the UK context than might have been expected.

Beside linguistic and political reasons, culture is important for its educational potential. 'To be cultured' has traditionally been, and continues to be, an integral part of our notion of an educated person. Whilst in the past this has been operationalised in mfl teaching and learning mainly in terms of the study of literature written in the target language and the knowledge of facts about the target culture, more recently affective, skill-based learning objectives such as 'to learn how other people live', 'to identify with the experiences and perspectives of people in target countries and communities', 'to be able to empathise with target language speakers' or 'to understand that there is a reality beyond the (negative) stereotypes we may have of others' have come to the fore which emphasise social and affective domains (see also Chapter 14). Claire Kramsch, identifies an additional, pertinent objective: to understand that 'we are irreducibly unique and different, and that I could have been you, you could have been me, given different circumstances – in other words, that the stranger . . . is in us' (Kramsch 1996, p. 3).

Lastly, for the purposes of this chapter, a pragmatic rationale for the teaching of culture can be discerned. Focusing on cultural aspects of foreign language, i.e. going beyond the transactional and functional, allows the mfl teacher to add intellectual challenge to lessons in ways which go beyond attempts to understand the rule system governing the target language. The higher level of linguistic proficiency allows the mfl teacher to present material which reflects the cognitive development and the level of maturity of learners more accurately as well as makes the work in the classroom more challenging for themselves. Focusing on culture in A/AS level mfl teaching allows the teacher to introduce intellectually stimulating activities into the mfl classroom which enable learners to widen their frontiers in relation, for instance, to their general knowledge of the world with regard to economic and social conditions, the environment, political processes, communications, consumerism, commercialism or professional life.

REFLECTION
Activity 5.3 Reasons for teaching culture
To what extent do your reasons for including culture in your mfl teaching relate to the four categories in this chapter? Can you add other reasons?

Differences between foreign language and culture learning

Before we can address the question of how to teach culture it seems also relevant to briefly examine what differences there are, if any, between foreign language and culture learning.

In an interesting paper, Gary Libben and Oda Lindner identify important differences between both the process as well as the product of successful second/foreign language and culture acquisition/learning. Libben and Lindner suggest that '[unlike] SLA *(second language acquisition)* . . . SCA *(second culture acquisition)* involves the expansion of an existing system rather than the development of a new one' (Libben and Lindner 1996, p. 1). The authors posit that whilst a person embarking on SLA believes

> 1. that there is a system to be acquired (that can have a label such as English or Spanish)
> 2. that he or she is already in possession of such a labeled system, [in] the case of SCA, the acquirer believes himself to be in possession of values, beliefs, and opinions that he shares in varying degrees with members of his social group but he does not conceive of the second culture as comprising a separate labeled system.
>
> (Libben and Lindner 1996, p. 3)

According to the authors, from this follows that culture learning becomes very difficult as for the learner it is not clear what he or she already knows or what he or she is supposed to learn (see p. 4). A further difference they point out is that language processing is something that one does, whereas culture is in many ways who one is (see p. 6). A fundamental property of cultural knowledge according to Libben and Lindner is that, whilst peripheral aspects can be easily modified and do not seem to get in the way of each other if they are different in the target culture to the native culture, more central cultural elements, 'the ones that are really associated with who you are' (p. 7), can cause stress and the need for the learner to reduce stress. The authors conclude that one cannot really maintain two cultural systems.

Rather, what happens is that biculturalism creates and integrates elements of two cultures in the same cognitive space. At the periphery these elements are typically situationalised, so there is little difficulty. However, at the more central levels of the cultural system, there is more potential for conflict, more stress, and a greater need to reduce that stress. So, whereas successful SLA is the result of the development of inoculated systems, successful SCA is the result of successful stress reduction.

(Libben and Lindner 1996, p. 9)

Target culture learning is, therefore, potentially threatening for learners and needs to be handled with care by mfl teachers.

Foreign culture learners have been found to deal with new cultural elements in four ways (see Libben and Lindner 1996, pp. 9–12):

1   there was no problem
2   the acquirer abandoned one element in favour of another
3   two incongruous cultural elements were amalgamated into a new 'third cul-
    ture' element, or
4   potentially incongruous cultural elements were situationalised

---

REFLECTION

Activity 5.4 Similarities and differences of native and target cultures
Brainstorm aspects of target culture with your A/AS level learners: what features of the target culture can learners think of? which do they consider to be important?

Then, ask learners to 'rate' the features they have identified according to the following scale:

    ++   very similar to native culture
    +   similar to native culture
    −   different to native culture
    −− very different to native culture

Finally, discuss with learners what implications in terms of 'learning diffi-culties' their perceptions of target culture features might have.

How to teach culture?

The Harris Report (see DES 1990) recognised the link between language and culture and introduced the notion of 'cultural awareness' into foreign language teaching and learning at 11 to 16. For Byram the implicit theory of culture learning is as follows:

- exposure to documents and interaction with people from another country leads learners to notice similarities and differences between themselves and others

- noticing differences leads to taking up the perspective of others and being able to understand how they experience the world
- experiencing the world from a different perspective leads to a new perspective on one's own experience of the world, and to a new understanding of one's own experience.

(Byram 1997b, p. 6)

Mfl teaching, seen from such a perspective, has to start from the learner's point of view and take his or her experiences as a starting point. '[It] is no longer adequate to merely present the target culture from within. One has also to provide for the perspective of the learner' (Wallner 1995, p. 9). Wallner goes on to suggest that the selection, presentation and treatment of material 'should take into consideration the learners' conception of the "other" as well as their indigenous culture' (Wallner 1995, p. 9).

REFLECTION
Activity 5.5 A comparative approach to culture teaching
Based on the topic you are currently covering with your A/AS level group, consider what materials, in your view, lend themselves to intercultural comparisons.

One fundamental methodological problem for the mfl teacher, as Kramsch rightly points out, is whether the emphasis should be on stressing commonalities or emphasising the differences between native and target culture (see Kramsch 1996, p. 5). Research by Hall and Ramirez (1993) suggests that

> language learners who are not actively guided to seek similarities between themselves and speakers of the target languages . . . come to objectify both target language speakers and English speakers as different and distant from themselves. Hall and Ramirez attribute this distancing to the fact that students do not perceive themselves as cultural beings, that is, as having culture.
>
> (Robinson-Stuart and Nocon 1996, p. 433)

Furthermore, findings from perception psychology indicate that

> individuals tend first to focus on differences between people(s) and then to magnify and generalize those differences as applicable to the local minority community as a whole. The salience and exaggeration of group differences form a general frame of perception that exists even in apparent contradiction to positive one-to-one experiences. So strong is the human tendency for

consistency that subsequent information from personal experiences is often distorted to avoid modification of the initial frame of perception.

(Robinson-Stuart and Nocon 1996, p. 435)

From this Robinson-Stuart and Nocon conclude that mfl teachers should first give attention to similarities; doing so can undermine the human tendency to exaggerate and generalise differences and they outline a productive-integrative approach to culture teaching following Crawford-Lange and Lange (1984, p. 171) involving the following:

1   identification of discussable themes
2   required classroom discussion
3   personalisation of the discussion by drawing on the learner's home culture, and
4   discussion of students' emotions, arguments and opinions

To this Robinson-Stuart and Nocon add an ethnographic approach, namely personal contact with target language speakers through interviews and active listening. This can be done by inviting target language speakers into the classroom or by taking learners on visits, trips, residentials or work experience abroad. In addition to interviews, techniques such as surveys, questionnaires or guided observations can be employed. Personal contact is, of course, also easily possible through e-mail and video-conferencing (see Chapter 14; Pachler and Field 1997, Chapters 11 and 12; and Leask and Pachler 1999, Chapter 6).

The move towards exploring culture through personal contact with native target language speakers can be seen as a necessary consequence of viewing culture as a dialogic process 'of decentering, of relativising self and other in an effort to understand both on their own terms and from their own perspective, as well as from the outsider's perspective' (Kramsch 1996, p. 6), as something between individuals and as something 'at the rupture or disjuncture between interlocutors' assumptions and expectations' (Kramsch 1996, p. 7).

REFLECTION

Activity 5.6 Identifying topics for culture-based discussion

How can the list of aspects of target language culture identified by your learners in Acitivity 5.4 be matched to the A/AS level syllabus you currently follow? Which topics for discussion could you include in your programme of study?

As a precursor to personal interaction with target language speakers, culture teaching through vocabulary learning is one possible strategy. Michael Byram (1997a, p. 52) posits that '[the] essence of understanding the cultural content of words is in their connotations.' He outlines three methods of vocabulary-based culture teaching (see Byram 1997a, pp. 53–6):

- the dictionary method
- the ethnographic method, and
- the historical and literary methods

The dictionary method focuses on analysing the meanings and connotations of key words, such as 'school-école-Schule' or 'teacher-professeur-Lehrern' in the mother tongue and the target language. For ideas about which words to choose, see e.g. Williams 1976. Learners are first asked to write down their associations with words, for instance in the form of a spider diagram, and then to compare them with those of peers. The next step is looking up the translation of the word in a bilingual dictionary, followed by looking up the meaning of the translation in a monolingual dictionary. As a follow-up, learners can be provided with examples of the key target language word in context as well as texts which deal with the topic associated with the key word.

REFLECTION
Activity 5.7 Identifying key words
What other words for the dictionary method with relevance to your current programme of study can you think of for your specialist subject?

The ethnographic method revolves around the collection of data through interaction with target language speakers for analysis of the connotations of words.

REFLECTION
Activity 5.8 Using ethnographic methods
Ask your A/AS level learners to carry out a mini-survey amongst target language speakers in and around the school, such as native speaker mfl teachers or Foreign Language Assistants in the school and the area, around one of the key words identified in Activity 5.7. How does the data compare with learners' expectations?

The historical and literary methods use literary texts to gain insights into the culture of the target country. One particular advantage of using literary texts, Byram notes, is that they open up the historical dimension of tracing changes in the use of words over time.

[Novels] in particular (and some short stories) have a vivacity and life which goes way beyond that which the conventional texts can offer. Literature conveys the atmosphere, ethos, life and even linguistic element of German (French, Spanish, Italian, Russian . . .) life in a quite unique fashion, and provides a subjective and aesthetic view of reality which may be extremely illuminating and stimulating.

(Bloch 1996, p. 2)

In addition to interpersonal methods, therefore, more traditional, 'documentary' methods (see e.g. Mughan 1998, p. 45) remain equally valuable. Indeed, Jürgen Kramer points out that literary texts appeal to learners' affective domains and thereby often produce strong motivational impetus (see Kramer 1990, p. 61).

REFLECTION
Activity 5.9 Using literacy texts for culture teaching
Can you identify passages from literary texts for your specialist language which could enhance the cultural component of some of the topics in your programme of study?

Juliane House draws the following conclusions from her research for the teaching of (intercultural) communicative competence (see House 1996, pp. 12–7):

- for teachers to raise learners' awareness of differences in interactive behaviours between mother and target language
- focus on linguistic-cultural phenomena, so called 'rich points', which are different in the mother and target culture, in which, for example, linguistic structures follow different conventions which can lead to misunderstandings in intercultural communication, for example by way of analysis of sample dialogues, signs, film titles, subtitles, video and sound recordings, etc.

House offers the following example of German daily culture (*Alltagskultur*):

Zur Vermeidung von Gesundheitsschäden und unzumutbaren Belästigungen ist in den Hallen, Fluren, Treppenhäusern und Veranstaltungsräumen dieses Gebäudes mit Ausnahme der Cafeteria und der Eingangshalle das Rauchen untersagt! Bitte nehmen Sie Rücksicht auf die Gesundheit Ihrer Mitmenschen.

(House 1996, p. 15)

Unsurprisingly, students asked why there wasn't simply the equivalence to a 'No Smoking' sign. House comments further that teachers:

- focus on the process of learning and personal awareness raising through learner diaries or field notes in which learners can note their observations or analysis of their own communicative behaviour as well as that of others, including, of course, target language speakers

- use role plays and simulations or even multiple-choice exercises in which so called 'critical incidents' can be practised and analysed by way of follow-up group discussions
- prepare learners systematically for the fact that breakdowns in communication are likely and teach strategies for continually monitoring their communicative acts by looking out for linguistic and non-linguistic signs of misunderstandings as well as to remain prepared to change one's interpretation of a communicative act

As far as topics for intercultural comparisons are concerned, Terry Mughan refers to a book by Brislin and Cherrie (1985) which provides and analyses critical incidents relating to aspects of a period of stay in the target country such as (see Mughan 1998, p. 42):

- host customs
- interacting with hosts
- settling in and making adjustments
- tourist experiences
- the workplace
- the family
- education and schooling, and
- returning home

REFLECTION
Activity 5.10 Identifying and responding to critical incidents
What critical incidents linked to topics in your A/AS level programme of study can you think of in relation to the aspects of a period of stay abroad identified by Brislin and Cherrie?

One way of collecting an inventory of critical incidents for classroom exploitation is to ask learners to record personal critical experiences in the form of field notes or learner diaries whilst on a period of stay in the target country. These incidents can later be used as a basis for role plays or simulations.

With reference to Peter Groenewold, Hans-Jürgen Krumm suggests as one possible activity of culture learning the task of learners 'inventing' a target language speaker and her biography. This, he notes, requires of learners background research into socio-political and geographical factors of real people and much more (see Krumm 1992).

Gerhard Neuner and Hans Hunfeld (1993) suggest the use of what they call 'universal experiences of life' as a basis for intercultural comparison including (see Pachler and Field, pp. 168–9):

- fundamental experiences, e.g. birth, death, living
- personal identity, e.g. personal characteristics
- social identity, e.g. private self, family, neighbourhood, local community, nation
- partnership, e.g. friendship, love
- environment, e.g. house and home, local area, nature, civilisation
- work, e.g. making a living
- education
- subsistence, e.g. food, clothing
- mobility, e.g. traffic
- leisure and art
- communication, e.g. media
- health care, e.g. health, illness, hygiene
- ethics, e.g. morals, values, religion
- events, e.g. past, present, future
- spirituality, creativity, imagination, emotions, memory, etc.

The first step for learners could be awareness raising about themselves, i.e. exploring their own private (interacting at home), semi-private (interacting with friends) and public (interacting with teachers, the adult world, at work, etc.) identities, in relation to these 'universal experiences of life' as '[identity] appears more as a kaleidoscope with which each individual plays' (Zarate 1995, p. 24). Subsequently learners can be tasked to find out how individuals in the target culture operate in relation to some of the above categories. Remember, though, that understanding of certain aspects of the target culture in depth rather than comprehensive coverage should be the objective at A/AS level. Again, data can be collected through interaction with native speakers in or outside the classroom as well as by way of the study of 'authentic' material. The library of the Goethe Institut, London,[1] for example, offers a wide range of topic-based material for A/AS level learners of German; equally, it offers a web-based service called *Kaleidoskop: Alltag in Deutschland* providing information 'about how people in Germany live, think and feel'[2] (see also Chapter 14).

REFLECTION
Activity 5.11 Universal experiences of life
Examine how universal experiences of life can be incorporated into your programme of study at A/AS level.

In a talk about the virtues of residency abroad at an AMGS[3]/Goethe Institut conference in June 1998 entitled *Textbook Germans: Images of Germany in Education and the Media*, Jim Coleman pointed to the importance of strategy training, i.e. of preparing learners who are about to embark on personal interaction with target language speakers in a target culture environment for what they will need in order to get 'into' the society. This includes the ability to avoid rush judgements, to avoid jumping to conclusions, to counterbalance individual critical experiences as not to view them as characteristic of the whole as well as practical suggestions of how to gain access to life in the target culture so as not to remain an onlooker or spectator. Walter Grauberg notes that learners need to understand that norms are place- and time-specific, that one can get used to different norms and that one's norms may appear strange to others (see Grauberg 1997, pp. 245–8).

Summary

I have attempted to demonstrate in this chapter how culture teaching has moved away in recent years from the teaching about culture towards teaching learners how to interact with culture in line with changes in perceptions of what constitutes culture. General methodological principles which have emerged in the course of the chapter relate to the need to integrate language and culture teaching, to build on the learners' experiences and to explore issues from differing perspectives includ-ing, importantly, data gathered through personal interaction with target language speakers (see also Anderson 1997, p. 61).

The approaches to culture teaching in this chapter are related to any specific A/AS level mfl syllabus and are compatible with a wide range of syllabuses.

Some problems of cultural awareness/competence, such as the questions of its assessment and the use of the target language, were addressed indirectly: by stressing the interrelatedness of language-and-culture it became clear that culture teaching must be about target language use and that, consequently, cultural aware-ness and knowledge can to some extent be assessed through how fluently, accu-rately and appropriately learners use the target language.

Notes

1 Goethe-Institut London, 50 Princess Gate, London SW7 2PH, Tel. 0171-411-3400, Fax: 0171-581-0974. http://www.goethe.de/gr/lon/
2 Available at: http://www.goethe.de/z/50/alltag/deindex.htm.
3 Association for Modern German Studies Membership Secretary, 27 Exeter Gardens, Ilford, Essex, IG1 3LA

References

Anderson, J. (1997) 'Communicating culture – approaches to teaching about German reuni-fication'. In Shaw G (ed) *Aiming High: Approaches to Teaching 'A' level*. London: CILT, pp. 58–69.
Bloch, B. (1996) 'Teaching business German and regional studies through novels'. In

Zeitschrift für interkulturellen Fremdsprachenunterricht 1, 1. Online available at: http://www.ualberta.ca/~german/ejournal/archive/bloch1.htm

Brislin, C. and Cherrie, Y. (1985) *Intercultural Interactions: a Practical Guide*. London: Sage.

Byram, M. (1997a) ' "Cultural awareness" as vocabulary learning'. In Chambers, G. (ed) *Language Learning Journal* 16. Rugby: Association for Language Learning, pp. 51–7.

Byram, M. (1997b) 'Introduction. Towards a pedagogical framework for visits and exchanges.' In Byram (ed) *Face to Face: Learning 'Language-and-Culture' through Visits and Exchanges*. London: CILT, pp. 3–16.

Byram, M., Morgan, C. et al. (1994) *Teaching-and-Learning Language-and-Culture*. Clevedon: Multilingual Matters.

Capel, S. and Pachler, N. (1997) 'Further professional development'. In Capel, S., Leask, M., Turner, T. (eds) *Starting to Teach in the Secondary School*. London: Routledge pp. 257–269.

Crawford-Lange, L. and Lange, D. (1984) 'Doing the unthinkable in the second-language classroom: a process for the integration of language and culture'. In Higgs, T. (ed) *Teaching for Proficiency, the Organizing Principle*. American Council of Teachers of Foreign Language, pp. 139–77.

DES (1990) *Modern Foreign Languages in the National Curriculum*. London: HMSO.

DfE (1995) *Modern Foreign Languages in the National Curriculum*. London: HMSO.

European Commission (1996) *Teaching and Learning: Towards a Learning Society*. Brussels.

Grauberg, W. (1997) *The Elements of Foreign Language Teaching*. Multilingual Matters: Clevedon.

Hall, J. and Ramirez, A. (1993) 'How a group of high school learners of Spanish perceives the cultural identities of Spanish speakers, English speakers and themselves'. In *Hispanica* 76, pp. 613–20.

House, J. (1996) 'Zum Erwerb interkultureller Kompetenz im Unterricht des Deutschen als Fremdsprache'. In *Zeitschrift für interkulturellen Fremdsprachenunterricht* 1, 3. Online available at: http://www.ualberta.ca/~german/ejournal/archive/house1.htm

Kramer, J. (1990) 'Teaching cultural, historical, and intercultural to advanced language-learners'. In Wringe, C. (ed) *Language Learning Journal* 2. Rugby: Association for Language Learning, pp. 58–61.

Kramsch, C. (1996) 'The cultural component of language teaching.' In *Zeitschrift für interkulturellen Fremdsprachenunterricht* 1, 2. Online available at: http://www.ualberta.ca/~german/ejournal/archive/kramsch2.htm

Krumm, H-J. (1992) 'Bilder im Kopf: interkulturelles Lernen und Landeskunde'. In *Fremdsprache Deutsch* 6. Edition Klett/Goethe-Institut.

Leask, M. and Pachler, N. (1999) (eds) *Learning to Teach Using ICT in Secondary Schools*. London: Routledge.

Libben, G. and Lindner, O. (1996) 'Second culture acquisition and second culture acquisition: faux amis?' In *Zeitschrift für interkulturellen Fremdsprachenunterricht* 1, 1. Online available at: http://www.ualberta.ca/~german/ejournal/archive/libben2.htm

Morrell, F. (1996) *Continent Isolated: A Study of the European Dimension in the National Curriculum in England*. London: Federal Trust.

Mughan, T. (1998) 'Integration of foreign culture awareness into business language teaching materials and methods'. In Chambers, G. (ed) *Language Learning Journal* 17. Rugby: Association for Language Learning, pp. 41–7.

Neuner, G. and Hunfeld, H. (1993) *Methoden des fremdsprachlichen Deutschunterrichts. Eine Einführung*. Berlin: Langenscheidt.

Pachler, N. and Field, K. (1997) *Learning to Teach Modern Foreign Languages in the Secondary School.* London: Routledge.

QCA, ACCAC and CCEA (1999) *Subject Criteria for Modern Foreign Languages: GCE Advanced Subsidiary and Advanced Level Specifications.* London.

Robinson-Stuart, G. and Nocon, H. (1996) 'Second culture acquisition: ethnography in the foreign language classroom'. In *The Modern Language Journal* 80, 4, pp. 431–49.

Rost-Roth, M. (1996) 'Deutsch als Fremdsprache und interkulturelle Kommunikation: Relevanzbereich für den Fremdsprachenunterricht und Untersuchungen zu ethnographischen Besonderheiten deutschsprachiger Interaktionen im Kulturvergleich.' In *Zeitschrift für interkulturellen Fremdsprachenunterricht* 1, 1. Online available at: http://www.ualberta.ca/~german/ejournal/archieve/rost11.htm

Wallner, M. (1995) 'The value of A-Level textbooks for teaching German culture'. In *German Teaching* 12. Rugby: Association for Language Learning, pp. 8–12.

Whorf, B. (1956) *Language, Thought, and Reality.* New York: Wiley.

Willems, G. (1996) 'Culture in language learning and teaching: requirements for the creation of a context of negotiation'. In Willems (ed) *Issues in Cross-Cultural Communication: The European Dimension in Language Teaching.* Nijmegen: Hogeschool Gelderland, pp. 69–106.

Williams, R. (1976) *Keywords.* London: Fontana.

Zarate, G. (1995) 'Cultural awareness and the classification of documents for the description of foreign culture.' In Wringe, C. (ed) *Language Learning Journal* 11. Rugby: Association for Language Learning, pp. 24–5.

Chapter 6

Teaching and learning grammar

Norbert Pachler with some examples by Jo Bond

Introduction

Issues concerning the notion of grammar, such as its nature and how to describe it or its relevance and role in foreign language (FL) teaching and learning, have traditionally occupied theoretical linguists as well as language teachers. They have given rise to heated debates and considerable fluctuations in the importance grammar has been afforded in FL classrooms. In recent years, after a period of two decades or so during which the role of grammar in school-based FL teaching and learning in the UK has been marginalised if not actively discouraged, voices in support of the need for explicit and coherent grammar teaching can increasingly be heard. In this chapter, the role of grammar in FL teaching and learning in general and in A/AS level modern foreign languages (mfl) teaching in particular will be discussed.

Objectives

By the end of this chapter you should have some awareness of:

- what grammar is
- why to teach grammar and how grammar is learnt, and
- how grammar can be taught at A/AS level

What is grammar?

> REFLECTION
> *Activity 6.1* What is grammar?
> What is your understanding of 'grammar' and what are your associations with the term? How do they compare with those discussed in this chapter?
>   Also, ask colleagues in your department: what views do they hold?

In an important paper on grammar, Henry Widdowson argues (1988, p. 151) that grammar 'frees us from a dependency on context and the limitations of a purely lexical categorization of reality'. In other words, grammar allows us to generate an unlimited number of utterances with a finite set of linguistic resources and to talk about the world beyond the here and now. Similarly, in his book on grammar, Rob Batstone points out (1994, p. 4) that it is through grammar that we can modify words systematically 'to enhance and sharpen the expression of meaning' and that, without grammar, language would be chaotic.

We use grammar when we modify words and when we relate them to one another to express widely applicable concepts, such as:[1]

- tense, e.g. present, future, past signalled by verb inflection
- aspect, e.g. temporality (such as progressive) signalled by verb inflection
- mood, e.g. declarative, interrogative, imperative or subjunctive expressed by verb inflection
- hypothetical distance, e.g. imagination communicated through 'if clauses'
- the relationship between sender and receiver, realised e.g. through word order, cases and prepositions
- social proximity or distance, e.g. directness versus indirectness expressed by choice of formal or informal modes of address
- psychological proximity or distance, expressed e.g. through use of direct or indirect speech, or
- point of view, expressed e.g. through lexical phrases such as *Meiner Meinung nach . . .* or *Ich glaube, dass . . .* etc. (see also Widdowson 1988 and Batstone 1994, pp. 16–24)

Thereby, the 'rules' of grammar facilitate communicative economy: 'grammar is a device for indicating the most common and recurrent aspects of meaning which it would be tedious and inefficient to incorporate into separate lexical items' (Widdowson 1988, p. 151); that is, grammar allows us to keep manageable the vocabulary we need to communicate effectively and accurately about both simple and complex matters.

Importantly, grammar also allows us to establish relationships of words within sentences or across sentences, for instance by referring back to the known by way of pronouns etc. (see also Batstone 1994, pp. 32–5). Grammar, therefore, also has 'discoursal and pragmatic dimensions' (Little 1994, p. 99), i.e. it allows us to structure longer spoken and written utterances, engage in linguistic exchanges with interlocutors and behave socio-culturally appropriately in a variety of different situations (e.g. formal versus informal registers), which may be known or may be new to us.

REFLECTION
Activity 6.2 What do learners think about grammar?
Ask your learners what associations they have with the term 'grammar':
- how do their views compare with yours and those of your colleagues?
- what implications do their views have for your teaching, e.g. how might you convince learners of the need for and importance of grammar?

Think of strategies to 'de-mystify' the concept for your learners.

An important distinction may be drawn between grammar as product and grammar as process.

Whilst grammar as product can be represented in numerous ways, e.g. as learning, teaching, reference or linguistic grammar, there is the underlying assumption of grammar as being static, i.e. as analysable and describable. By definition, grammar as product implies explicit knowledge and involves a degree of meta-language, i.e. grammatical terminology or language about language. Acknowledging grammar as product has considerable implications for the FL classroom such as whether and/or how to make linguistic structures and rules explicit to learners and whether or not, and if so to what extent, to use metalanguage.

Grammar as process, on the other hand, is concerned with how grammar is operationalised and proceduralised, i.e. applied with speed and in real time, without lengthy reflection and often unconsciously in communicative acts. The important question for FL teachers with regard to grammar as process is how to enable learners to use grammar as an 'on-line processing component of discourse' (Rutherford 1987, p. 104), i.e. effectively in simulated or face-to-face interactions with target language (TL) speakers.

Why teach grammar? How is grammar learnt?

The evidence relating high levels of grammatical and socio-linguistic competence to explicit grammar teaching, whilst not conclusive, would appear to be substantial (see Ellis 1997, p. 71). It may be the case that explicit grammar instruction has a particular role to play in the acquisition-poor environment of the mfl classroom. In this chapter some of the available evidence is examined.

Language learning is non-linear and not instantaneous

Batstone's assertion (1994, p. 38) that learners 'do not absorb grammar instantly, they internalize it gradually' seems an important starting point for the discussion of how grammar is learnt and should be taught in the context of the FL classroom (at A/AS level).

Lightbown and Spada make a similar observation:

[language] learning is not linear in its development. Learners may use a particular form accurately at stage X in their development (suggesting that they have learned that form), fail to produce that form correctly at stage Y, and produce it accurately again at stage Z. This usually happens when learners are incorporating new information about the language into their own internal system of rules.

(Lightbown and Spada 1993, p. 113)

These assertions have profound methodological implications for FL teachers: recycling of linguistic structures and rules that have already been covered and their transfer from one context/topic to another become central concepts in planning. Equally important is enabling learners to notice and renotice new language structures and to structure and restructure their existing linguistic repertoire in the process of FL learning. This allows them to convert input, language and structures they are exposed to, to intake, language and structures which are stored in their short term memory (see e.g. Batstone 1994, p. 42, and Ellis 1994b, p. 93).

REFLECTION

Activity 6.3 Recycling

Look at the grammatical progression in your current programme of study: which linguistic forms and structures do you revisit? which do you only cover once?

A number of language features are acquired simultaneously

Learners do not acquire linguistic features as a set of distinct entities, one after the other, but they work on a number of them simultaneously and they gradually move through stages of interlanguage, i.e. hypotheses about the TL and its grammar (see Ellis 1997, p. 61). Not enough research exists to allow us to formulate reliable guidelines concerning an optimal sequence of grammar acquisition for FL teachers to use as a planning tool. For FL teaching (at A/AS level) this suggests that, as teachers, we need to use our professional judgement as well as general pedagogic knowledge and common sense when planning grammatical progression into our programmes of study. Lightbown and Spada believe (1993, p. 114) that 'it is neither necessary nor desirable to restrict learners' exposure to certain linguistic structures which are perceived . . . as being "simple"'.

REFLECTION
Activity 6.4 Grammatical progression
Examine your current programme of study for the A/AS level course: what grammatical progression is implicit in your A/AS level teaching? What is the rationale for the progression in your planning?

The FL learning process

In an attempt to conceptualise the role of instruction in the process of FL learning, Rod Ellis (1994b, p. 84) differentiates between explicit and implicit FL knowledge, both of which he considers to be important in the FL learning process and both of which he feels need to be applied 'actively' by the learner, i.e. through language use and reflection about language use.

Current theories of second language acquisition, according to Ellis (1994b, p. 93), suggest that input becomes intake, i.e. part of the learner's short/medium-term memory, via noticing new language and linguistic features and comparing the TL ideal with their own language production. In order to effect a change in the learner's developing FL system, or interlanguage, the new knowledge has to be integrated into his or her long term memory, i.e. the learner needs to proceduralise and internalise linguistic features by being able to gain quick access to them in (real-time) language use.

It is thought by a number of researchers that it is the process of noticing-the-gap between TL ideal and the learner's current stage of linguistic development, i.e. his or her personal interlanguage, which is *the* important factor in FL learning. Noticing-the-gap might, for example, mean the learner realises he or she has problems with the pronunciation of a particular word and makes a specific effort to compare his or her utterances against a native speaker model.

The role of explicit knowledge

One way of leading learners towards noticing-the-gap is through explicit knowledge, i.e. knowledge which the learner is conscious of but which, nevertheless, can exist in the mind of the learner in an un-articulated way (see Ellis 1994b, p. 84). Ellis points out (1994b, pp. 97–8) that explicit knowledge, acquired through what has been called form-focused instruction or explicit grammar teaching – may help learners notice certain features in the input which may otherwise have been ignored.

Explicit grammar teaching can differ according to a number of variables:

- the amount of time taken to present the rule can be varied
- the source of explanation can be changed, e.g. the teacher, peers, the course book etc., or

• the manner of presentation can be modified, e.g. oral or written (see Ellis 1994b, p. 82–3).

Explicit grammar teaching seems to be one useful strategy to improve on the 'acquisition-poor' nature inherent in FL classrooms; it is important to remember, nevertheless, that whilst

> formal instruction results in faster and more successful language learning . . . it often fails to teach learners specific linguistic features . . . formal instruction contributes primarily to explicit knowledge which can facilitate later development of implicit knowledge . . . it will often have a delayed rather than an immediate effect.
>
> (Ellis 1994b, p. 107)

In other words, explicit grammar teaching is no panacea. As FL teachers we cannot expect grammar teaching to lead to instant success and we must view formal instruction as a medium- and long-term investment. Grammar teaching can, nevertheless, be considered to be instrumental in speeding up the acquisition process.

It is important that we find the right balance between explicit grammar teaching and use of the TL for expressing personal meaning in communicative contexts, because 'much of the language learning that takes place in the classroom takes place "naturally", as a result of learners processing input to which they are exposed' (Ellis 1994a, p. 657).

The importance of negotiation of meaning

The negotiation of meaning, i.e. learners trying out their own language, making their own choices and errors when using the TL in communicative contexts, plays a vital role in the learner's linguistic development. The teacher is central to enabling the learner to 'notice the gap'. This can be achieved, e.g. through choice, sequencing and structuring of input and the way it is provided. Other possibilities are to provide opportunities for learners to engage 'actively', i.e. mentally/cognitively, affectively and/or physically, with the TL through use and reflection.

Creating an environment which facilitates the negotiation of meaning, e.g. enabling learners to ask for clarification, confirmation, repetition etc., is an important strategy to address potentially inhibiting factors such as the large number of learners in many classes.

The role of metalanguage and the knowledge of rules

Explicit grammar teaching comes in many different guises but it tends to be characterised by various degrees of reference to the rules which govern the FL and the terminology used to describe linguistic phenomena, i.e. metalanguage. Whilst this explicit or declarative knowledge of grammar has to be learnt in addition to the language itself, it can offer learners real advantages in so far as it enables them to use reference material such as dictionaries and grammar books independently from the teacher.

Research seems to suggest that some rules seem to be easier to learn as explicit knowledge than others:

> The rules that were easy to learn were those that (1) referred to easily recognised categories, (2) could be applied mechanically and (3) were not dependent on large contexts . . . Difficult rules were those that did not permit 'simple exhaustive descriptions' or were not always governed by features of the immediate contexts . . .
>
> (Ellis 1994b, p. 91 referring to Green and Hecht 1992)

FL teachers (at A/AS level) might bear this in mind when deciding which rules to teach explicitly.

Pachler and Field note (1997, p. 154) that the amount of metalanguage, i.e. explicitness, best be left to the professional judgement of the teacher and that language about language be used according to the age and developmental stage of the learner. They point to an article by Alan Cornell who suggests that, by the end of their A/AS levels, FL learners should understand and use, i.e. have in their active repertoire, the following terms and concepts:

- 'the 'word classes' or 'parts of speech' (noun, verb, adjective, etc.)
- the main sentence constituents (subject, direct object, indirect object; clause)
- the concept of tense
- for German, the nomenclature of the case system
- miscellaneous terms which would include, for example, relative pronoun, reflexive pronoun/verb, subjunctive, imperative, modal verb, auxiliary verb, past participle, active/passive, but not that many more' (Cornell 1996, p. 28)

REFLECTION

Activity 6.5 Metalanguage

Make a list of the grammatical terms you use in your teaching. Which of them do you expect your learners to use actively and which passively?

Now choose three of them at random: reflect on how you go about introducing them to your class.

The role of implicit knowledge

Implicit knowledge, according to Ellis (1994b, p. 85), comprises formulaic knowledge and intuitive rule-based knowledge, with the learner unaware of having ever learnt and often unaware of possessing knowledge of certain linguistic features.

Whilst formulaic knowledge can be learnt explicitly, for instance by memorising patterns or fixed expressions such as idiomatic verbs and proverbs, implicit knowledge tends to be learnt incidentally from exposure to input in which certain linguistic features occur frequently (see Ellis 1994b, p. 92) and through practice in language use (see Batstone 1994, p. 44). An important role for the FL teacher, therefore, is that of providing rich input and creating opportunities for learners to use and manipulate the TL for themselves.

It seems important to emphasise at this stage that the learning process does not necessarily move from declarative, i.e. explicit, to proceduralised, i.e. automatic, knowledge and that FL learning can just as easily happen in an implicit form and, maybe, become explicit at a later stage; after all, common sense suggests that the myriad of language structures and rules that comprise the grammar of a language need not be known explicitly by learners in order for FL learning to take place (see Ellis 1994b, p. 87). From this follows that FL teachers must not only focus on developing the learner's explicit but also on facilitating the development of his or her implicit knowledge by creating an 'acquisition-rich' classroom environment.

The teacher's role in structuring input

The development of effective strategies to address the problem of the relatively 'acquisition-poor' nature of classroom-based FL learning imposed by the artificiality of the setting is an important concern for mfl teachers (at A/AS level). In the FL classroom, therefore, the teacher faces the challenge of enhancing opportunities for the learner to apply his or her natural FL learning processes in an 'unnatural' environment.

Broadly speaking, the following options are available to the teacher to structure exposure to the TL:

- presenting new language through (authentic) spoken and written texts
- making certain FL features artificially frequent and, thereby, potentially more learnable
- explicit or implicit grammar teaching, and
- the correction of errors, thereby making certain FL features more salient

With reference to Parker and Chaudron (1987), Ellis notes (1994, p. 83) that a number of modifications can take place in teacher-talk in order to make input comprehensible and, thereby, facilitate the natural development of the FL:

- simplification, e.g. shorter utterances and the use of less complex syntax and lexis
- elaboration involving redundancy, e.g. paraphrasing, use of synonyms, slower speech and rhetorical signalling and framing, and
- alterations to the thematic structure, e.g. emphasis of certain parts of speech/ utterances

Other modifications concern interaction:

- avoiding of mis- or non-understanding, e.g. by choosing simple topics, or
- repair of breakdown in communication, e.g. by requesting clarification or confirmation

There are, therefore, a number of options for the FL teacher to consider when using the TL for interacting with learners.

Socio-political reasons for grammar teaching

We also need to consider teaching grammar because of the social function it fulfils. Accuracy of language use and register 'tells the world something about what sort of person we are in the same way as our clothes, our lifestyle, and the newspapers we read' (Page 1990, pp. 103–4). As FL teachers at A/AS level, we can, of course, not ignore the requirement for the teaching of grammar set down by the GCE A/AS Level Subject Criteria for Modern Foreign Languages which include explicit reference to grammar and specify a range of grammatical structures for French, German, Spanish and Urdu for AS and A level respectively (see QCA et al. 1999).

The importance of learner differences

Whether or not grammar teaching works appears to depend on learner differences and their stage of linguistic development as much as the learning environment and FL teachers. Teachers, therefore, need to get to know their learners and their preferences as much as possible (see e.g. Pachler and Field 1997, ch. 2).

How to teach grammar?

REFLECTION
Activity 6.6 Your personal approach to grammar teaching
Ask yourself the following questions:
- what is your personal approach to grammar teaching?
- what works for you?
- what is your rationale for the strategies you currently use?
- do you use the same strategies with all groups? If not, why not?

The importance of building on good practice pre-16

Firstly, and most importantly, the teaching of grammar at A/AS level has to be seen in the context of what has gone before. Pachler and Field note (1997, pp. 332–4) that at GCSE learners are required to operate, through pair- and group-work, by and large at a transactional level within (quasi-)communicative contexts in relation to clearly defined topics, structures and vocabulary. At A/AS level, FL teachers need to build on the strengths and compensate for the limitations this entails. In practice this means not overwhelming learners at the beginning and gradually building-up knowledge of linguistic structures. A possible model for grammatical progression based on the A/AS level Subject Criteria for Modern Foreign Languages can be seen in Figure 6.1.

Some general suggestions for grammar teaching

According to Widdowson (1988, p. 154), grammar is subservient to lexis and, therefore, teaching should begin with words and should be concerned with what grammatical modifications make them communicatively effective. FL teaching, viewed in this way, should concentrate more on the power of the lexicon as generator of meaning (see also Little and Singleton 1991, pp. 128–9). Particular emphasis might be given to verbs as the 'engine of linguistic structure' (Little and Singleton 1991, p. 131).

Batstone suggests a three-pronged approach to grammar teaching:

- focusing attention on structures by encouraging learners to notice new structures in input and by helping them structure their own knowledge of the target grammar
- engaging learners in language use by formulating personal meaning, and
- engaging learners to reflect on the language learning process and how their own use of grammar can be improved (see Batstone 1994, section 2)

Methodological options in grammar teaching (Ellis's model)

According to Ellis, good grammar teaching currently is seen to consist of the systematic teaching of functional meanings of grammatical forms in materials designed to encourage communication (see Ellis 1997, p. 58). He describes a system of methodological options in grammar teaching, summarised in Figure 6.2, based on a combination of learner performance and feedback options. He describes along the 'learner performance options' branch the teacher's choices for eliciting from learners language which includes the use of a specific grammatical feature; along the 'feedback options' branch, he describes the teacher's choices for providing feedback to learners about their use of a specific grammatical feature.

Initially the teacher has the choice between isolating linguistic items and teaching and testing them one by one (feature-focused) or drawing the learner's attention to certain grammatical features by carrying out a meaning-based activity (focused communication). 'Feature-focused' instruction subdivides into a focus on explicit or implicit knowledge of the target grammar; explicit grammar teaching can either

	GCSE	AS level	A level
Nouns	gender, number and irregular forms contained within defined vocabulary list	nouns, unspecified but related to general issues	nouns, unspecified but related to general issues
Articles	all forms of direct, indirect and partitive articles	all forms including irregularities	all forms including irregularities
Adjectives	regular formation and position; irregular forms within a defined vocabulary list; possessive adjectives and recognition of comparatives and superlatives as lexical items	active knowledge of comparatives and superlatives, indefinite adjectives and position and formation of adverbs	position and agreement of all adjectives including interrogative adjectives; superlatives in concessive clauses
Pronouns	subject pronouns, recognition of object pronouns as lexical items; emphatic pronouns as lexical items and the recognition of interrogative and relative pronouns	active use of object pronouns, including correct positioning; use of disjunctive and relative pronouns	accurate use of direct and indirect object pronouns with correct past participle agreement; 'en' as a pronoun; use of demonstrative, indefinite and relative pronouns
Verbs and tenses	present indicative, perfect and immediate future; recognition of future, imperfect; past participle agreement with reflexive and 'être' verbs; active use of the imperative and the negative form of 'ne . . . pas'; recognition of the government of verbs and the present participle	active knowledge of imperfect, future, conditional pluperfect, present subjunctive after 'il faut que'; all past participle agreements, government of verbs and the use of modal verbs; all negative forms including negatives with infinitives; recognition of the present subjunctive with expressions of fear; wishing, possibility and doubt	active knowledge of all tenses; use of the subjunctive in all tenses; all verbal agreements and inflections; use of the present participle and gerund; accurate use of verbs governing the use of the infinitive and all negative forms
Quantity	cardinal and ordinal numbers, dates and the time; basic expressions of quantity	fractions and dimensions	
Other	use of 'depuis' and recognition of common structures	use of conjunctions and complicated structures	use of idiom and complicated structures; conjunctions requiring use of the subjunctive
	Much of the grammar at this level is taught as lexical items and is implicit. The focus is on recognition and there is scope for the learning of paradigms and set phrases.	*At AS level most knowledge should be active and explicit; additional items are added to the GCSE repertoire.*	*At A level all knowledge is assumed to be active to enable the generation and manipulation of language forms.*

Figure 6.1 Bridging the gap to post-16: grammar (French)
Source: Pachler and Field 1997, p. 341

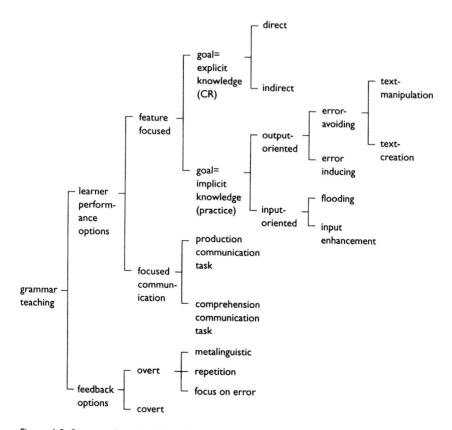

Figure 6.2 System of methodological options in grammar teaching
Source: Ellis 1997, p. 79, reprinted with permission, © Oxford University Press.

be deductive or inductive. 'Focused communication' divides into production and comprehension.

Ellis notes (1994b, p. 91) that empirical studies have failed to show a clear advantage for either the deductive approach, i.e. the provision of a grammatical rule followed by examples, or the inductive approach, i.e. the introduction of linguistic structures through examples from which to develop general rules (see e.g. Pachler and Field 1997, p. 148, or Grauberg 1997, pp. 103–6 for practical examples and further discussion). FL teachers might conclude from this that the application of a variety of methods in presenting new language is advisable.

Feedback can, according to Ellis, either be overt or covert with the former addressing the error by clarifying the learner's understanding of a rule or by the teacher providing a rule etc. (metalinguistic), by repeating the learner's mistake with a change in intonation to signal incorrectness or by directly signalling incorrect language production to the learner; when giving covert feedback the teacher provides information about incorrect utterances by reformulating what the learner has said (for a detailed discussion see Ellis 1997, ch. 3).

> Errors are a natural part of language learning . . . The errors reveal the patterns of learners' developing interlanguage systems – showing where they have overgeneralized a second language rule or where they have inappropriately transferred a first language rule to the second language.
>
> (Lightbown and Spada 1993, p. 114)

It can be noted, therefore, that it is important for mfl teachers to give ample opportunities to learners to try out their own language; there seems to be no substitute for giving learners the choice to use the language as often as possible.

REFLECTION

Activity 6.7 Ellis's system of methodological options in grammar teaching

- do you tend to focus on form or on meaning in your grammar teaching? do you prefer explicit or implicit approaches? what works well for you and what doesn't work so well?
- what is your personal approach to error correction? which of Ellis's three options do you favour and why?

The task-based approach

Following Peter Skehan (see 1994, pp. 194–7), Batstone suggests (1994, p. 97) a task-based approach with a gradation from pre-task via task to post-task, including the subtle tackling of factors affecting language production.

At the *pre-task stage* learners can be given planning time in order to be able to notice and re-structure (new) language (features); at the *task stage* the level of difficulty of real-time language use can be controlled by varying the familiarity of the topic, the extent to which the task requires the expression of shared or new knowledge or the amount of time available; at the *post-task stage*, learners can be given the opportunity to perform the task publicly or to reflect on grammatical aspects relating to the task-completion process. (For a more detailed discussion of learners reflecting on language production see Chapters 4 and 13.)

Making certain linguistic features in input more prominent

Ellis lists (1994b, p. 94) a number of factors of relevance to FL teachers which may help the learner in 'noticing' certain linguistic aspects in the input:

- task demands, i.e. making certain linguistic features pre-requisites for task completion

- frequency
- unusual features which surprise the learner for not conforming to expectations
- salience, e.g. phonological form or word position in sentence
- interactional modification during the negotiation of meaning, i.e. dealing with communication problems, and
- existing linguistic (mother tongue) knowledge

FL teachers might want to examine to what extent the input they provide to their learners takes account of these criteria.

REFLECTION

Activity 6.8 The role of the course material
- to what extent does the course book determine grammatical progression in your teaching?
- to what extent are your approaches to grammar teaching dependent on the course material?

What mfl teachers should consider in relation to explicit grammar teaching

By way of a summary, then, of what mfl teachers should consider in relation to explicit grammar teaching, the following can be said.

- New language structures are not acquired instantaneously and not in a linear manner. Expectations of what explicit grammar teaching can achieve in the short and medium term, therefore, need to be realistic. Recycling and transfer of linguistic features across topics, etc. are essential.
- Both explicit and implicit knowledge are important in the FL learning process and both need to be used 'actively' by learners. Explicit grammar teaching by itself is insufficient. There needs to be ample opportunity in the FL classroom for learners to use the TL and produce TL utterances. Also, exposure to the TL is essential for learners to gain implicit knowledge.
- It is essential for mfl teachers to create ample opportunity for learners to 'notice the gap' between TL features and their own language production. Explicit grammar teaching can help in this process but is not the only option. Reflection on the TL can also be seen to be important as can the negotiation of meaning during actual language use.
- Explicit grammar teaching can improve on the inherently 'acquisition-poor' nature of FL classrooms and speed up the natural acquisition process but needs to go hand in hand with TL use to express personal meaning.
- Knowledge of metalanguage and rules can be beneficial but need to be learnt in

addition to the language itself. The ability to *use* grammar 'on-line' (in real time) is important.

- Whether or not and what kind of explicit grammar teaching works depends also on learner differences and preferences.
- In order to make TL input more accessible, the role of the teacher in selecting, structuring and sequencing is crucial in making certain language features more salient, i.e. potentially more learnable.
- FL learners should not be overwhelmed, but instead knowledge of language structures should be built up gradually.
- Explicit grammar teaching can be inductive or deductive. The use of a variety of methods seems advisable.

Whilst the chapter has thus far been concerned with outlining general principles concerning the learning of grammar in order to establish a theoretical and conceptual framework against which to plan a coherent approach to grammar teaching, the following section offers a number of practical suggestions as to how form-focused instruction can be combined with the expression of meaning in A/AS level mfl classes.

Grammar teaching at A/AS level – some examples by Jo Bond

If during their pre-A/AS level years of FL learning pupils are taught only the vocabulary and structures needed to pass the GCSE, they will approach the more rigorous demands of A/AS level with a considerable disadvantage. It is, therefore, necessary to reach a compromise and put grammar back in the toolbox from Key Stage 3 onwards.

As with vocabulary, practice is the key to confidence and familiarity by building a programme of basic grammar into the Key Stage 3 curriculum. This is of particular relevance given the often prevailing lack of knowledge of grammatical terms in English of pupils entering Year 7. This programme may then be revised and extended in Key Stage 4 so that those who wish to continue their language studies will be in a much better position to do so. It is important to view the teaching and learning of grammar as a seven-year experience, rather than a mad panic in the first year of A/AS level study.

It would certainly be unwise to plan grammar teaching without an awareness of the target group: what do they understand already (English or FL)? what is the ability of the group? how do I cater for a small number of potential A/AS level learners in a large top set?

When learners enter the A/AS level classroom, certain basic grammatical notions should already be in place. Alas, this is not always the case. If you are new to the school or have not taught the learners before, the following suggestions may be helpful:

- check out the group's history of language learning by liaising with their previous teachers and looking through the schemes of work
- read the A/AS level Subject Criteria and exam specifications as well as past papers. This is particularly important if you have weaker candidates in your group. Find out about the board's marking criteria so that you can prioritise in what you teach them
- in order to avoid overwhelming learners in the first few weeks, spread your grammar programme over the course of the programme. Make yourself a checklist so that you know you will have covered everything you need to cover. With a group of able learners, it will simply be a case of revision and going into greater depth, and
- if the learners are doing the course work option they will need a format for checking the accuracy of their work (see Figure 6.3; see also Chapter 13)

Frequent practice is essential if learners are not only to learn grammar points, but also remember them. Variety is important as is adding an element of enjoyment to what, for some learners, can be a difficult area. Below are some ideas which may be used with most topics: although the focus is on German, the examples are equally applicable to other mfl with (minor) modifications.

Using texts

Whatever its subject or difficulty, be it topic-based or a work of literature, all or part of a text can be exploited for grammar work. Some of the ideas below may take time to set up, but if the text is chosen carefully, it can be used over many years. Working with wordprocessed texts makes preparation relatively easy:

- delete only the articles/possessives/pronouns (depending upon what your focus is or what the text has to offer)
- play 'spot the noun/dative plural, etc'. A packet of pencil crayons makes this exercise even more appealing for some reason, although it can be done orally. This exercise can take very little time and is a good source of revision. It may be played individually or in pairs. You may wish to focus on a single grammar point or practise several at once. Have your answers prepared by highlighting them on an OHT
- change most of the verbs back into the infinitive – let the learners sort out the tenses and justify their answers
- remove all the punctuation
- jigsaw puzzle: cut the text up with a pair of scissors and ask learners to reassemble it
- pupils change all the verbs to a given tense
- alter the verbs/articles etc. so that some are incorrect – learners have to pick them out, or
- take out individual sentences and jumble them up, starting with short

When each box is ticked, you are ready to hand in your essay!

	Tick here
Style	
The essay has **paragraphs**	
The essay is very **neat** and **easy to read**	
The essay is illustrated (if appropriate)	
The essay looks stylish!	
The **punctuation** is correct	
Nouns	
All have CAPITAL LETTERS	
I have checked all the **spellings**	
I have checked **case** and **gender**	
I have checked the **plurals**	
Adjectives	
before a noun – **ending**	
I have checked the **adjectival endings** carefully	
Adjectival nouns have endings	
Comparatives are correct	
Verbs	
Each verb **agrees with its subject**	
Tenses are formed correctly	
I have not changed tense unnecessarily	
I have checked **irregular verbs**	
I have not forgotten the **separable prefix**	
Nor have I forgotten the **reflexive**	
I have checked for verbs which take the dative or genitive	
Word order	
The verb is **second idea** in each **main clause**	
Subordinating clause: the verb is at the **end**	
Relative clause: the **verb** is also at the **end**	
I have followed the rules of **time, manner, place**	
Prepositions	
I have checked the **meaning** of each preposition	
Each preposition is followed by the **correct case**	
Verbs are followed by the correct preposition	

Figure 6.3 Essay-writing checklist

sentences, working up towards longer ones. Synonyms can also be useful in this exercise.

Books and films can be used effectively for the practice of tenses: the imperfect tense can, for instance, be practised by asking students to describe briefly the plot of a book they have recently read or a film they have just seen using only certain verbs: e.g. *gehen, fahren, sagen, schlafen, töten, lieben, sein, haben, müssen, wollen, können, mögen, finden* or *laufen*.

Using the dictionary

A dictionary is another important linguistic tool which requires practice if it is to be used quickly and efficiently. It is wise to encourage pupils to develop their skills from Year 7. Publishers have realised this and are now producing a variety of colourful, pupil-friendly versions of their bi-lingual dictionaries, some of which are appropriate for use at Key Stage 3. It can, therefore, be expected that learners already know their way round a dictionary by the time they reach the A/AS level classroom. A more thorough knowledge is required, however, if pupils are to make full use of a larger or monolingual dictionary and at the start of their A/AS level study learners would benefit from guidance and a list of terminology and common abbreviations, both in English and the TL. Figure 6.4 provides a possible, although incomplete, example.

Use of pictures and flashcards

Pictures are certainly not inappropriate at this level and can add variety and fun. Learners have the freedom to choose their own language while practising a specific

Terminology		Abbreviation	Example	
bestimmter Artikel	definite article	**def**	der, die, das	the
unbestimmter Artikel	indefinite article	**indef**	ein, eine, ein	a
Maskulinum	masculine	**m**	der, ein	the, a
Femininum	feminine	**f**	die, eine	the, a
Neutrum	neuter	**nt**	das, ein	he, a
Substantiv	noun	**n**	Hund	dog
Pronomen	pronoun	**pron**	er, sie, es	he, she, it
Präposition	preposition	**prep**	auf, unter	on, under
Präsens	present	**pres**	ich spiele	I play, am playing
Partizip Perfekt	past participle	**ptp**	gespielt	played

Figure 6.4 Dictionary work

grammar point. Learners are simply told to write sentences using the information given.

Flashcards can be used to practise tenses: this may seem childish, but can prove an effective and quick way of revising GCSE work and increasing the confidence of your learners by the familiar context.

Similar techniques can be used with comparatives and superlatives, possessives and demonstratives, practising cases. Once prepared, such exercises may be used repeatedly to add pace and colour to your lessons. An obvious choice for the classroom is the OHP, but if learners have access to computers, grammar practice software can provide an excellent source of self-study, especially if some learners feel they need extra practice in a certain area.

Games

Variety, pace and concentration can result from the careful incorporation of games into your lesson.

Card games

Jumble up sentences by writing each word on a square in a grid and then cut the grid up to make a number of cards. Try not to make the cards too small or they will be hard to handle (a good size is 6cm × 4cm as you can fit twenty-four cards on a piece of A4). This way you can practise tenses, general word order, subordinating conjunctions, prepositions, separable and reflexive verbs and adjectival endings. It is a particularly good way of practising compound nouns as it enables you to demonstrate exactly how they function.

Matching

Match each ending to the correct word and give the meaning – this looks quite straightforward . . . until you cut up the grid in Figure 6.5!

Learners make as many compound nouns as possible from the words in Figure 6.6. This can be done in two consecutive lessons, in the second as a timed exercise. As an additional variable, articles could be introduced.

 A similar technique can be used with important quotations from literary texts, significant topic phrases or verbs and prepositions.

Wordsearches

Even these have their place at A/AS level as they demand concentration, perseverance and a knowledge of spelling as well as providing a relaxing way to reinforce vocabulary such as prepositions, subordinating conjunctions, relative pronouns. 'Find fifteen irregular verbs in the imperfect tense in this wordsearch

Umgeb	ung	Notwendig	keit	Sicher	heit
Einzel	heit	Entscheid	ung	Feind	schaft
Vollend	ung	Fähig	keit	Gesell	schaft
Wissen	schaft	Erklär	ung	Möglich	keit

Figure 6.5 Matching exercise-word endings

Werk	Flug	Spiel	Zeug	Platz	Hafen
Sache	Haupt	Stadt	Mitte	Brief	Träger
Marke	Kasten	Tasche	Tuch	Hand	Platz
Kinder	Buch	Wörter	Fußball	Koffer	Schuh

Figure 6.6 Matching exercise-compound nouns

Taking the biscuit

Translating only the pronouns, rewrite in German word order:

1   Give me the biscuit, please!
2   Give it to me immediately!
3   It's my biscuit.
4   Those are not his biscuits.
5   He can't have them. They are all mine.
6   You've eaten all the biscuits!
7   I hate you and her and him and it (the dog).
8   Oh good, there's still one left.
9   Pass it to me, please.
10   Thank you. You can have it back now.
11   I don't really like them anyway.
12   Give it to him then. I don't want it.

Figure 6.7 Translation as grammar practice

and then learn them' tends to be more effective than just referring students to a column of their irregular verb table.

Quizzes

An end-of-term quiz (in teams of two if you have a small group) can be an efficient way of informally practising the grammar points you have covered.

Translation

This is a straightforward way to practise specific grammar points and show in depth understanding by the learner. A little humour can make the exercise more appealing (see Figure 6.7).

Most learners tend to be addicted to one or another of the television soaps so why not ask them to translate the latest emotional upheaval into the TL, either as a piece of dialogue, indirect speech (subjunctive) or a summary of events in the style of a newspaper report (imperfect tense). This is also a useful way of practising relative clauses, as all the characters are either related or have a relationship with each other. A simple question, such as 'Wer ist Deirdre?' could keep the class going for a couple of weeks! (For translation see also Chapter 12.)

Summary

Throughout the debate about whether or not grammar should be taught and, if so, whether explicitly or implicitly, we need to remember that learners don't learn everything they are taught; neither will they eventually only know what they were taught:

> [They] are able to use their own internal learning mechanism to discover many of the complex rules and relationships which underlie the language they wish to learn.
>
> (Lightbown and Spada 1993, p. 116).

Exposure to new and known language, opportunities allowing learners to notice and restructure the FL and compare it to their own tentative understanding of the TL through the expression of meaning, seems particularly important. The teaching of grammar should support and not hinder the learner's natural rule-discovery procedure (see also Mohammed 1997, p. 50).

> Grammar develops in the long term as a function of extensive exposure to, imitation and adaptation of the richest possible variety of language forms. The process can certainly be supported and indeed accelerated through conscious focusing on isolated grammatical forms allied to regular, targeted practice and reinforcement, but it is only through freer, more creative and more contextualised activity that knowledge of grammatical forms can be transformed into habitual productive skills.
>
> (Klapper 1997, p. 24)

Importantly, this chapter has intended to show that methodological diversity, i.e. the use of a variety of approaches to the teaching of grammar, appears to be most effective.

Note

1 Different languages use different ways to express these concepts; the examples given here, broadly speaking, relate to European languages.

References

Batstone, R. (1994) *Grammar.* Oxford: Oxford University Press.

Cornell, A. (1996) 'Grammar – grinding or grounding?' In Brien, A. (ed) *German Teaching* 13. Rugby: Association for Language Learning, pp. 26–9.

Ellis, R. (1994a) *The Study of Second Language Acquisition.* Oxford: Oxford University Press.

Ellis, R. (1994b) 'A theory of instructed second language acquisition'. In Ellis, N. (ed) *Implicit and Explicit Learning of Languages.* London: Academic Press, pp. 79–114.

Ellis, R. (1997) *SLA Research and Language Teaching.* Oxford: Oxford University Press.

Grauberg, W. (1997) *The Elements of Foreign Language Teaching.* Clevedon: Multilingual Matters.

Green, P. and Hecht, K. (1992) 'Implicit and explicit grammar: an empirical study.' In *Applied Linguistics* 13, pp. 168–84.

Klapper, J. (1997) 'Language learning at school and university: the great grammar debate continues (I)'. In Chambers, G. (ed) *Language Learning Journal* 16. Rugby: Association for Language Learning, pp. 22–27.

Lightbown, P. and Spada, N. (1993) *How Languages Are Learned.* Oxford: Oxford University Press.

Little, D. (1994) 'Words and their properties: arguments for a lexical approach to pedagogical grammar'. In Odlin, T. (ed) *Perspectives on Pedagogical Grammar.* Cambridge: Cambridge University Press, pp. 99–122.

Little, D. and Singleton, D. (1991) 'Authentic texts, pedagogical grammar and Language Awareness in foreign language learning'. In James, C. and Garrett, P. (eds) *Language Awareness in the classroom.* London: Longman, pp. 123–32.

Long, M. (1983) 'Does second language instruction make a difference? A review of the research'. In *TESOL Quarterly* 17, pp. 359–82.

Mohammed, A. (1997) 'Learner-centered grammar instruction.' In *English Teaching Forum* 35, 1, pp. 50–1.

Pachler, N. and Field, K. (1997) *Learning to Teach Modern Foreign Languages in the Secondary School.* London: Routledge.

Page, B. (1990) 'Why do I have to get it right anyway?' In Page, B. (ed) *What Do You Mean It's Wrong?* London: CILT, pp. 102–6

Parker, K. and Chaudron, C. (1987) 'The effects of linguistic simplification and elaborative modifications on L2 comprehension'. *University of Hawaii Working Papers in ESL* 6, pp. 107–33.

Rutherford, W. (1987) *Second Language Grammar: Learning and Teaching.* London: Longman.

QCA, ACCAC and CCEA (1999) *GCE AS and A Level Specifications Subject Criteria for Modern Foreign Languages.* London.

Skehan, P. (1994) 'Second language acquisition strategies and task-based learning'. In Bygate, M., Tonkyn, A. and Williams, E. (eds) *Grammar and the Language Teacher.* New York: Prentice Hall.

Spada, N. (1997) 'Form-focussed instruction and second language acquisition: a review of classroom and laboratory research'. In *Language Teaching* 30, pp. 73–87.

Widdowson, H. (1988) 'Grammar, and nonsense, and learning'. In Rutherford, W. and Sharwood-Smith, M. (eds) *Grammar and Second Language Teaching: A Book of Readings.* New York: Newbury House, pp. 146–55.

Part III

Planning, teaching and assessment at A/AS level

Chapter 7

Planning a programme of work

Lynne Meiring and Nigel Norman

Introduction

The planning of a programme of work is fundamental to modern foreign languages (mfl) teaching. This chapter aims to establish principles of macro-level planning affecting both teacher and learner at GCE Advanced (A)/Advanced Subsidiary (AS) level. It draws upon existing practice, whilst at the same time proposing new ways of working that reflect recent research.

Objectives

By the end of this chapter you should have an awareness of three interrelating elements that inform the planning of a programme of work at A/AS level:

- the need to develop structure, autonomy and reflection
- the need to monitor development through moving the learner from transition via progress to mastery, and
- the need to focus on lesson content, directed time programmes and learners' organisation of their own work

Getting started

In order to address the issue of macro-planning we must first consider A/AS level subject specifications, formerly syllabuses. It is not possible in this context to analyse all existing A/AS level syllabuses/specifications, so we have taken as an example the 2000 WJEC (Welsh Joint Examinations Council) syllabuses for French, German and Spanish. Some reference has been possible to the A/AS Level Subject Criteria for Modern Foreign Languages (see QCA et al. 1999).

We would suggest that the general philosophy emerging is not one concerned with producing technical experts in topic fields, with an encyclopaedic grasp of facts and information. Derek McCulloch (1995, p. 18) sees the danger that

> teachers appear to be working round the clock, finding materials, videoing TV programmes etc. etc., to be able to cover the 22 or however many topics. But

the result is students who have discussed urban pollution, but do not know the plural of *Stadt*; students who can list the political parties, but do not know the gender of *Partei* . . . If changes are to be made . . . then it is at the post-GCSE stage that the most radical revisions must be undertaken.

The focus must be on practical communication, insights into culture, ability to discuss, analyse and reflect upon contemporary social and political issues. The topics must, therefore, clearly be seen within the context of the aims of the syllabus. This is apparent in the WJEC French syllabus in which the content is defined by a list of 'general' topic areas and issues; candidates 'should acquire *basic* information about France within each topic area' (our emphasis). In addition there is wider focus, which clearly emerges from the stated aims.

> To introduce new material and skill areas, therefore promoting greater knowledge and enjoyment of France, encouraging an interest in contemporary issues and extending an awareness of the French language and its uses.
> i   To provide for courses which will cater for the wide range of interests and abilities to be found in current sixth-formers, while ensuring there is a common basis of language learning and comparability between the different options.
> ii   To meet the needs of candidates who wish to pursue their study of French in higher education and, at the same time, to provide courses which are valid in their own right for those whose studies will end in the sixth-form.
> iii To provide an introduction to the study and appreciation of French literature, while fostering the ability to analyse, evaluate and express opinions clearly and cogently.
> iv   To provide an extended language option for candidates who do not wish to pursue a study of literature, while fostering the ability to analyse, and express themselves clearly and cogently.
> v   To provide for elements of teacher-assessed course work which may be based on study of either language or literature.
> vi   To provide for school-based project work for candidates who wish to pursue particular interest relating to France through the medium of French.
>
> (WJEC 1998 French, p. 2)

As curriculum planners, we welcome the flexibility offered for interpretation of topics and issues. This philosophy should inform macro-planning at all levels. At the same time we recognise teachers' needs for guiding principles in their interpretation (especially PGCE student teachers and newly qualified teachers).

REFLECTION
Activity 7.1 Matching schemes of work with subject specifications
Consider the extent to which your scheme of work for the A/AS level course
addresses each of the aims in the examination specifications that you follow.
What changes would be necessary in order to incorporate all the aims?

Priorities

Discussions with teachers, learners and student teachers would suggest that practical communication emerges as a strength at the post-16 stage. The time-gap
between GCSE and the start of the A/AS level can, however, be an impeding
factor. Learners often embark on A/AS level courses having taken a step back from
GCSE, in terms of knowledge and confidence. This time can be used constructively
to lay foundations for new ways of working which we shall discuss below.

Taster courses have been successfully run in some institutions, providing a
flavour of advanced level work and thus minimising the nature of the gap. It would
seem more feasible logistically to develop directed time packs, which would
encourage self-study skills, but also reinforce GCSE language (e.g. cassette tapes,
videotapes, advanced dictionary work, games with words and phrases). The most
important point is that language skills are being maintained and that the more
sophisticated skill of independent learning is gradually being introduced.

REFLECTION
Activity 7.2 Planning a post-GCSE 'taster' pack
In planning pre-A/AS level material what knowledge, understanding and
skills would you seek to reinforce and develop?

Planning priorities to address transition, consolidation and logical continuation at
A/AS level needs to take account of the perceived gap in grammatical competence,
independent study skills and the ability to analyse and marshal argument. These
key issues may be summarised as:

1 STructure;
2 Autonomy; and
3 Reflection (analysis and inference).

We therefore propose that the focus at A/AS level be the STAR model (see Figure
7.1).

In addressing structure, the A/AS level learner will need to be conversant with
appropriate technical terminology, whether this be in English or the target language

Key areas	Issues	Recommendations
Structure	(a) knowledge of terminology	establishment of self-discovery strategies
	(b) understanding of concepts	development of reference skills
Autonomy	(a) choice	multi-resourcing
	(b) responsibility	division of time:
		teacher-controlled
		teacher-directed
	(c) independence	learner-controlled
Reflection	(a) analysis	collection of variety of ideas, opinions
	(b) inference	synthesis and consolidation of ideas
	(c) reasoning	presentation of arguments

Figure 7.1 **The STAR model**

(TL), e.g. the perfect tense or *le passé composé*. More fundamentally, he or she will need to be able to grasp whole concepts, such as verbs and tenses, nouns and pronouns – in short develop an understanding of the workings of language. Learners should be encouraged to take responsibility for 'discovering' this for themselves, by developing individual learning strategies, dictionary and referencing skills. In directing and supporting learners, teachers can provide a choice of tasks, resources, reference materials etc. within the framework of the given topic, thus moving the focus from teacher control to learner control. Fostering reflection in the advanced learner is perhaps the most challenging of all. Learners need to be given the opportunity to be exposed to a wide variety of stimuli, of ideas and language, in the TL and English, in order to promote the skills of analysis and inference. This will enable them to formulate, argue and present their ideas in oral and written form (see also Chapter 6).

REFLECTION
Activity 7.3 Developing awareness of terminology
What planning strategies do you use to enable A/AS learners to access appropriate technical terminology? Is this terminology identified in the TL or the mother tongue?
How can learning strategies be developed to promote an understanding of linguistic concepts?

It is recognised that genuine autonomy is an unrealistic ideal for the majority of learners, but that significant steps can be made towards it. Stella Hurd (1998, p. 70) states: '[it] is not simply a matter of teachers setting up tasks and from then on ignoring their students until assessment time'. Both the teacher and the learner have complementary but distinctive roles in the process:

> It is what the learner brings to the learning process and the learning materials, which not only determines his or her degree of autonomy, but is also often a measure of learning success. The 'capacity' to learn autonomously develops from a state of self-awareness and willingness to take an active part. In order for learners to achieve this state teachers must also play their part. It is no easy option for either side.
>
> (Hurd 1998, p. 70)

There is almost a reversal of roles that comes about in developing autonomy: '[it] is the teacher's responsibility to help learners achieve that state of independence, to act as counsellor, helper, and facilitator, while recognising that as learner expertise increases teacher involvement inevitably decreases' (Hurd 1998, p. 70).

Henri Holec places the learner at the centre of the process in viewing autonomy as 'the ability to take charge of one's learning . . . to be acquired by "natural" means or in a systematic, deliberate way' (quoted in Hurd 1998, p. 70).

Along with other researchers, David Little (1991) highlights other important aspects of autonomy: 'a capacity for detachment, critical reflection, decision-making and independent action' (quoted in Hurd 1998, p. 70), whilst T. Lonsdale (1996, p. 18) writes of the 'need to define and structure a route through from defined-topic-vocabulary-dependency-with-limited-operational-effectiveness   to autonomous-independent-language-acquisition-for-transferable-linguistic-skills'.

Careful training in autonomous modes of learning is, however, fundamental to success: '[if] learners are not trained for autonomy, no amount of surrounding them with resources will foster in them that capacity for active involvement and conscious choice, although it might appear to do so' (Hurd 1998, p. 72). This is confirmed by Pachler and Field (1997, p. 342) who state: 'The students need to assume responsibility for their learning from the very start of the course, but mfl teachers should not take this ability for granted.' Suzanne Graham (1997, p. 171) emphasises the pro-active role of the teacher in this process, quoting D. Norman (1980): 'It is strange that we expect students to learn, yet seldom teach them anything about learning.' In other words, as L. Barnett suggests, learners must neither be 'too carefully led nor too carelessly left alone' (cited in Hurd 1998, p. 73) (see also Chapters 4 and 13).

REFLECTION
Activity 7.4 Initial steps in developing learner autonomy
What steps can you take in the initial stages of the A/AS level course to move the learner from dependence on the teacher to increased choice and responsibility for his or her own learning?
What are the implications of this move for the provision and accessibility of resources within your department?

Planning targets

Preliminary consultation amongst practising A/AS level teachers and learners suggests that there is a need in macro-planning to look at:

- content of lessons
- directed time programmes, and
- learners' organisation of their own work

John Thorogood and Lid King (1991, p. 5) acknowledge the latter as a by-product of GCSE ways of working, referring to a 'willingness to tackle the unfamiliar. GCSE authentic reading and listening texts encourage the future "A" level aspirant to be bolder in adopting comprehension strategies than their predecessors reared on "doctored" "O" level texts'.

The transactional competence developed at GCSE should be maximised and enhanced through a transition to more self-sufficient, linguistically aware modes of operation.

This must be addressed through a dual focus on:

- *structure/language*: a grammar deficit manifests itself in the inability to transfer and manipulate language outside a narrow range of contexts and acquired phrases, and
- *reflection/thought*: under-developed cognitive skills need careful cultivation in order to move learners forward from concrete-physical (transactional) language to abstract-conceptual (cognitive).

Whilst the grammar deficit can, to some extent, be addressed systematically through an instructional framework and autonomy by means of clearly delineated support guidelines, the issue of reflection is more problematic. The development of opinions and ability to analyse and structure arguments has been fostered in other curriculum areas such as Geography (DfE, 1995): 'pupils should be given opportunities to: analyse and evaluate the evidence, draw conclusions and communicate findings', but has been conspicuously neglected in the more heavily transactional GCSE mfl courses. Therefore, learners embarking on A/AS level courses should initially be helped to transfer the reflective skills acquired in these other subject areas to their modern foreign language(s) course(s), particularly as the 1999 Subject Criteria for A/AS level require candidates to 'use the target language to analyse, hypothesise, evaluate, argue a case, justify, persuade, rebut, develop arguments, and present viewpoints in speech and in writing' (QCA *et al.* 1999, p. 7).

More significantly, however, the language required to formulate and articulate opinions and arguments needs to be established at an early stage of the course. Learners need to be taken to a further stage of sophistication by developing and practising additional strategies, such as analysis, inference and reasoning, summarising and synthesis. Thus, for example, several short stimuli representing contrasting viewpoints, designed to elicit strongly held views, will stimulate these cognitive processes. Two such tendentious articles can be found in Carter *et al.* (1998, pp. 32–3): *L'écologie en terrain conquis* and *La pollution a tous les droits*.

REFLECTION
Activity 7.5 Developing analysis, inference and reasoning
When planning your A/AS level course what techniques do you use to transfer and develop the reflective skills of analysis, inference and reasoning? How can the necessary language be effectively established?

The A/AS level mfl course should thus move naturally from dependence to self-sufficiency, from transition to progress to mastery (see Figure 7.2).

In the transition stage from GCSE to A/AS level the content of lessons will be based initially upon what learners already know. Ann Barnes (1996, p. 28) expresses it thus: '[they] should not . . . be confronted by a lot of "unknowns"'. There will be a gradual move from the known to the unknown and a continuation of effective communicative methodology, i.e. sequenced application of the four skills: listening, speaking, reading and writing. An emphasis will be placed on enjoyment through participation and interaction. Barnes (1996, p. 28) describes the gradual increase in 'more sophisticated phrases [which] "infiltrate" into the students' utterances involving the giving of opinions, for example' and goes on to characterise this process as a 'move from the more transactional [pre-16] language to more creative, personal language'.

As learners progress there is likely to be a shift in the nature of tasks undertaken, from individual prescribed homework tasks to more diverse, tightly teacher-structured (i.e. directed time) learning outcomes. Accompanying this there is likely to be a change in perception of the teacher's role: from that of teacher-instructor to 'learning manager'. Outcomes from directed time tasks constitute diversification in learning, exemplified through learner presentations and peer teaching. Additional media and resources can make for multi-media work, using, for example, CD-ROM, the internet, language-learning software or video. Pachler and Field

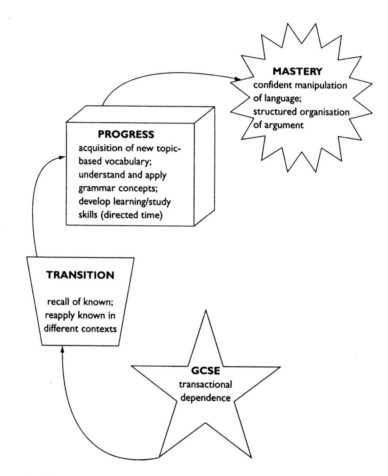

Figure 7.2 Monitoring progression

(1997, p. 342) note that '[students] have to develop new study skills such as time management, learning strategies, personal organisation, use of reference material or research skills'. In this way also learners are improving their own learning and performance, a key skill in the proposals for the new A/AS level (see QCA *et al.* 1999, p. 3).

REFLECTION
Activity 7.6 Identifying directed-time activities
Select a topic from your scheme of work for the first year of the A/AS level course. Consider which activities might be undertaken in directed time. What steps would you need to take to support learners in this?

In the later stages a degree of mastery will be achieved. This will manifest itself in independent recall and application of the 'known' (vocabulary and structures). Language items such as vocabulary, structures, ideas, essay phrases, idioms will be identified by the learners themselves and they will have a measure of responsibility for recording their own progress within a topic. This will ultimately lead to the collation of a range of work in different formats, in a dossier, to demonstrate mastery within a topic and as an aid to revision. Work could include written reports, recorded oral presentations, interpretation and evaluation and précis of written data, e.g. graphs or statistics.

REFLECTION
Activity 7.7 Allowing for progression
In planning your A/AS level course, evaluate the importance of the stages of transition, progress and mastery.
How do they apply (a) over a one-/two-year period, (b) within each topic?

Transition stage

> The real villain of the piece . . . has to be seen to be 'A' level. Little or nothing appears to be done during those two critical years to divert the alleged enthusiasm for the subject up to GCSE (though often it appears that enthusiasm is wrongly confused with the high grade achieved, towards a more rigorous and critical look at the way in which the language functions.)
> (McCulloch 1995, p. 18)

Whether or not one agrees with McCulloch's contentious claim, one must agree that learners embarking upon A/AS level courses bring with them a host of positive qualities and skills. These include confidence in listening and speaking in transactional situations, enthusiasm for the TL and target culture, a desire to improve and develop communication skills and increase their understanding of language structure. It is essential that these qualities are acknowledged and positively channelled, particularly in the initial stages of the A/AS level course. This transition stage, therefore, enables learners to recycle language previously acquired at GCSE. Techniques such as brainstorming and oral warm-up activities can be useful strategies to stimulate vocabulary and structure recall. Established good practice at pre-GCSE stage, i.e. presentation – practice – production, should not be overlooked, but capitalised upon and refined. Thus visuals, realia, gesture all still have a part to play in 'fixing' language in the learner. Over-insistence on language form (*excès de rigueur*) can de-motivate and create barriers to learning.

This transition stage goes beyond GCSE and should be channelled into more sophisticated, age-related activities. Learners need to move on from single items of vocabulary and prelearnt phrases to larger, independently generated 'chunks' of

language. This will involve transfer of previously acquired material, both individual and from peers, to different contexts. (See Pachler and Field 1997, p. 336 for
progression in skill development.) Outcome activities will often be collaborative
and may, for example, take the form of a sketch, exposé, presentation, simulation,
interviews, surveys, 'Question Time' or information gap.

Suggested activities might include simulations, which allow learners to draw on
skills from several areas. The principle of generalisable game activities suggested by
G. Rumley and K. Sharpe (1993, p. 8), which 'foster interest and motivation,
provide opportunities for real communication in a meaningful setting . . . and
facilitate plenty of repetition without seeming tedious', is equally applicable at
A/AS level, simulation-type activities replacing games. Asking learners to imagine
that they are in an area of France, for example, providing them with an identity, a
job, a specific day and time on which an event occurred (an accident, a tourist
reported missing, etc.) sets the scene for a rich source of language interaction,
involving interviews, written statements and the like.

REFLECTION
Activity 7.8 Designing advanced imaginative activities
Design an activity (sketch, exposé, presentation, simulation, interview, survey) that allows learners to develop more sophisticated and imaginative
language and transfer previously acquired material to a different context.

It is worth emphasising that this transition stage is not merely a desirable option,
but is crucial in developing advanced language-learning skills. Learners will not
have magically acquired new skills in the post-GCSE summer holidays. It is up to
teachers to revive and extend existing habits and modes of learning. GCSE topics
lend themselves to recycling and extending. Thus for example the topic of personal
identification and the family provides an accessible point of departure for issues
concerning young people such as generation gap, etc. (For other examples see
Pachler and Field 1997, p. 337.)

A template for organising the three stages we have been discussing will provide a
useful graphic framework for both teacher and learner. We have chosen to represent this as a topic organiser (see Figure 7.3), which summarises work done and
vocabulary and grammar acquired or revisited at this stage.

Progress stage

At the progress stage learners take a significant step forward in terms of their
methods of learning and working. It is essential that a variety of learning techniques
is used. Thus there will be teacher input, directed time tasks, pair and group work,
research, access to Information and Communications Technology (ICT), peer
teaching, learner presentations or spontaneous management (coping strategies).

TOPIC: ....

Transition stage: Recycled language

Vocabulary	Useful structures

Outcome activities

Figure 7.3 Topic organiser – transition stage

Current assessment criteria for A/AS level oral include linguistic accuracy, as well as defending your viewpoint and responding to the unpredictable.

Underpinning all of this is the fundamental principle of access to text by the learner, whether this is written, oral or aural. Dense text can be very demoralising, even counter-productive; Suzanne Graham (1997, p. 141) quotes a teacher who calls it 'the cold shower approach'. Therefore, it is crucial that 'text-bites', i.e. short and manageable chunks of language, are used which are accessible to the learner as well as the teacher. Graham (1997, p. 142), referring to Langer *et al.* (1974) summarised by Schulz (1981), suggests some realistic criteria for the selection of texts:

1   Text simplicity – simple sentences employing common words
2   Text structure – clear and logical structure and sequence to the text
3   Length and conciseness of essential information
4   The inclusion of special 'interest-stimulators', such as direct speech or exclamations

If denser texts are chosen for reasons of simple availability or suitability, these must be sympathetically exploited, for example small groups of learners working on individual paragraphs (see also Chapter 12).

At the same time as language is being generated in this user-friendly way, there is a need to trigger relevant thought processes, perhaps through an appeal to familiar aspects of learners' daily lives. In discussing vegetarianism, for example, such appeal could be made through an initial visual stimulus of the late Linda McCartney, asking who she was, why she was in the news, what she represented. Both linguistically and cognitively this acts as a catalyst for the generation of content and language. The technique of brainstorming also enables learners to bring what they already know to a topic. We are getting a foot in the door of language and understanding of subject matter and are allowing learners to learn: 'Give a man a fish and you feed him for a day. Teach a man to fish and you feed him for a lifetime' (Confucius).

From such beginnings learners will progress to a variety of 'texts' through a variety of approaches. The teacher's role at this stage is to organise the selection and exploitation of appropriate texts. However, there must be the potential for the teacher to 'let go' of controlling the learning situation (see e.g. Page 1992) and hand over to the learner this selection and exploitation, thus developing genuine autonomous learning skills. Hurd states (1998, p. 72):

> asking students to watch the news in the target language and prepare a résumé of a news item of their choice, involves some autonomy; stating which news item and exactly what to do with it does not. In the same way directing students to a particular self-correcting language-learning package is not asking them to exercise, merely to follow instructions.

REFLECTION

Activity 7.9 Selection of texts

Consider the appropriacy of texts that you use for A/AS learners in terms of:
(a) simplicity
(b) text structure
(c) length, and
(d) interest of content and presentation

How can longer, denser texts be made more accessible to A/AS learners?

Vocabulary and structures

During the progress stage, significant strides will be made in the acquisition of vocabulary and in bridging the grammar gap. The topic organiser (see Figure 7.3) shows how learners can document their progress. Core vocabulary will already have been identified in planning. This could be defined as vocabulary which is essential to an understanding of the topic, referred to by J. Ollerenshaw (1998, p. 8) as *mots-clés*. These are identified as starting points for comprehension of the text. She uses a variety of exploitation techniques to ensure comprehension, for example, reordering definitions. The core vocabulary is reused in exercises as a catalyst for lexical understanding, which is described as '*élargissement du vocabulaire*'. One strategy is encouraging learners to create their own vocabulary fields (see Figure 7.4).

Extended vocabulary will consist of unpredicted, unplanned items that the learner will have discovered autonomously and which will bring with it a further level of sophistication, precision and linguistic insight.

It is vital that teachers provide opportunities for learners to develop their own vocabulary learning strategies (see also ch. 3).

> The central issue is the need to invite students to try out and evaluate methods of vocabulary learning that go beyond the mainly rote-based techniques so many of them appear to employ – such as composing sentences that include the item to be learnt and mnemonic devices.
>
> (Graham 1997, p. 89–90)

Many suggestions for such techniques are proposed by Oxford (1989) and Rubin and Thompson (1982) (quoted in Graham 1997, p. 90). These can be effectively carried out in small groups during directed time.

REFLECTION
Activity 7.10 Developing vocabulary building
What techniques can be used to produce an *élargissement du vocabulaire*?
How can this process be monitored effectively?

Learners will research specific grammar points during directed time and under the guidance of the teacher. Once identified, these points can be practised using grammar reference materials according to individual need. The teacher's role then changes into one of coordinating the outcome and ensuring understanding,

verbes	noms	adjectifs/participes	adverbes
soigner se soigner	le soin/les soins	soignant soigné soigneux	soigneusement

Figure 7.4 Creating vocabulary fields
Source: Ollerenshaw 1998, p. 17.

acting as an additional resource, in effect a 'learning manager'. This represents a reversal of the common practice of teacher input, followed by learner practice, which can be de-motivating and confusing, relying, as it does, on unfamiliar terminology and methodology. Learners will instead deduce principles of grammar themselves, with varying degrees of accuracy, which will then be clarified in contact time, with a focus on shorter, less didactic, more accessible key points. This mode of working reflects the requirements of the 1999 A/AS level Subject Criteria.

At the brainstorm/warm-up stage, learners will have acquired/recycled vocabulary that will have generated all-important thought and language. The text must now be exploited for more extended, sophisticated, idiomatic vocabulary and structures, ideas and opinions and useful essay phrases. A common grammar reference book or ICT package is useful here, to establish a consistent working core. Learners can then exploit strategies such as peer teaching to consolidate their own knowledge, instruct others, thus developing communication skills and highlight problem areas, where the teacher can intervene.

If, for example, a learner has problems with the perfect tense, he or she should refer initially to what is already known. The average GCSE learner will be familiar with a range of first-person singular verb forms, for example, *j'ai mangé, je suis allé, je me suis levé, j'ai fini, je suis descendu, j'ai vu*. This immediately raises several aspects of the same grammatical point, which can be dealt with by separate groups of learners. The teacher could assign the following to each distinct group:

1   regular -er, -ir and -re verbs, which take *avoir*
2   all verbs which take *être*, including agreements (this could be a differentiated task for the more able learners)
3   all reflexive verbs, or
4   all verbs with irregular past participles, including *avoir* and *être*. (Again this would be differentiated for more able learners.)

There would be a three-part research and presentation exercise:

1   learners collect other examples of verbs in their allocated category in groups
2   in groups, using the common grammar reference book, they extrapolate simple rules
3   learners prepare simple presentations and devise tasks for their peers to ensure appropriate application of principle. In the initial stages of the A/AS level course peer teaching may be perceived as demanding and unrealistic. It can be developed more gradually through 'reciprocal teaching' (see Palinscar and Brown 1984 referred to in Graham 1997, p. 144). The teacher will initially model the strategy to be used and the learners will assume the same role in small groups.

For teaching grammar at A/AS level, see also Chapter 6.

Recent course materials, at the time of writing, appear to reflect this shift in pedagogy and provide appropriate support and practice for the learner and make the move towards independent learning less daunting for the teacher (see e.g. Ollerenshaw 1998).

This provides a framework for the approach to any point or structure, a *point de repère*, arrived at primarily by learners, which enables teachers to progress to more sophisticated, idiomatic usage in other contexts. The perfect tense in French, for example, is used extensively in standard form in such texts as *Le petit Nicolas* by Sempé-Goscinny (1960). Each chapter is short, self-contained and humorous with relevant, accessible content and provides numerous opportunities for this three-fold process. For example: '[il] a été tellement étonné qu'il n'a même pas pleuré' (Sempé-Goscinny 1960, p. 13). The following example illustrates more complex verbal use, which would significantly enhance learners' speaking and writing skills: '[nous], on a ramassé la balle et on est retournés à nos places' (Sempé-Goscinny 1960, p. 27).

However, it is important that the teacher retains the control and direction of this more advanced material to ensure continuing motivation. Such texts provide a wealth of potential essay formulae which can be collated on the topic organiser. Although the focus has been linguistic, learners will also benefit from the ideas and opinions contained in the texts.

The variety of texts will provide learners with a range of opinions relative to the new topic, which will in turn furnish them with the required language and ideas to formulate their own opinions. Useful essay set phrases can also be identified and will improve the quality of learners' expression. Figure 7.5 again shows how learners can record this and it is anticipated that for each topic several of these topic organiser proformas would be used.

REFLECTION

Activity 7.11 Using common grammar reference material

How necessary is the availability of a common grammar reference book for learners to work autonomously and to peer teach?

What are the relative merits of grammatical terminology presented in English and the TL? (See also Chapter 6.)

Mastery stage

For each topic learners need to be able to reach a stage of mastery, in which independent confident knowledge of subject matter and language [is demonstrated] and a greater sophistication of ideas, teacher support will need to be given in helping learners to organise their language and ideas appropriately, for example the introduction of ideas, presentation of arguments or drawing of conclusions.

Vocabulary	Core	
	Extended	
Structures	Identification of term	Grammar book reference
TL phrase ideas, opinions	Key issues (in English)	
Essay set phrases		

Figure 7.5 Topic organiser – progress stage

There is the suggestion that this represents a move from Basic Interpersonal and Communicative Skills (BICS) to Cognitive Academic Proficiency (CALP) (see Graham 1997, p. 18). BICS is defined as 'proficiency in everyday communicative contexts' and CALP as 'the manipulation of language in de-contextualized academic situations'. It is unrealistic to expect learners to achieve CALP before the mastery stage. It develops over time and with maturation.

At the later stage of the A/AS level course this can be achieved during the study of the topic, but earlier in the course, this should not necessarily be expected. Learners have the opportunity, throughout the course, to revisit topics and demonstrate their mastery. In this context Graham suggests (see 1997, p. 143) that drafting, monitoring, evaluation and cooperation, which can be developed in small groups, have a significant role to play. Schulz (1991) (referred to in Graham 1997, p. 143) goes further in advocating that learners review each other's draft work.

The establishment of a dossier allows for progressive improvement of work, in the manner of a portfolio of best pieces. These could include tapes, videos, written work, songs or poems. Although the dossier would not have formal assessment status, it gives value to learners' work, it provides teachers with formative information and it is a very valuable revision aid. Figure 7.6 enables learners to assemble a selection of representative pieces of work.

REFLECTION
Activity 7.12 Selecting work for the dossier
For each of the A/AS level topics identify items of work which could be included in the dossier to demonstrate mastery.

Topic organisers are, therefore, of primary importance to the learner as a useful aid to effective organisation.

Directed time

The notion of directed time challenges traditional concepts of teaching and learning, but is a fundamental component of autonomous learning. Once a degree of autonomy is established, independent learning beyond teacher control is more likely to take place. 'Those learners who are responsible for their own learning can carry on learning outside the classroom.' (Ellis and Sinclair 1989 quoted in Graham 1997, p. 170). Directed time is thus a waystage on the path to autonomy – the crucial factor being the interdependence of teacher and learner.

Time spent on advanced study can be divided into contact time and non-contact time/private study. The status quo (approximately six hours each) and quality of the non-contact time is in need of review. There must be an acceptance on the part

---

Items to include in dossier

1.

2.

3.

Figure 7.6 Topic organiser – mastery stage

of learners that a significant time commitment is needed; we would suggest a minimum requirement of twelve hours for non-contact time.

The organisation of non-contact time is challenging because a variety of learning skills are acquired, which will not only inform and enhance contact time, but develop new working habits. This will include working collaboratively, in pairs or groups, as well as undertaking individual tasks. Thus, a teacher may set a project for completion within a given time, that could be investigated using a range of resources and media and involving various outcomes: newspaper report, television or radio broadcast, dramatic sketch, debate or discussion. The choice would be left to the learners themselves, who would in the process be developing task management skills such as decision-making, leadership roles, delegation or team work.

The significance of this is highlighted by Mike Grenfell and Vee Harris (1998, p. 23) who synthesise recent research on learner strategies and conclude with evidence from OFSTED (1995) that 'pupils appear to lack the strategies they need to be able to work independently'.

O'Malley and Chamot (1990, p. 46) provide a useful categorisation and explanation of these strategies as metacognitive, cognitive and social/affective. These are interpreted by Vee Harris (1997, p. 5) as follows.

> Metacognitive: relating to more global strategies, involved in planning, monitoring and then evaluating learning; deciding, for example, how to tackle a particular task and then evaluating how successfully we have done it.
> Cognitive: this refers to strategies used for specific language tasks involving direct manipulation of language, whether it is basic 'study skills', like memorisation strategies, or more complex ones, like applying grammar rules.
> Social/affective: strategies through which the learner may seek help from others or control emotional responses, such as level of anxiety.

Other benefits of this way of working would include the development of imagination and creativity. These are evident in the 1995 National Curriculum mfl Orders and are often apparent at Key Stage 3, but diluted at Key Stage 4 under the requirements of GCSE syllabuses and sidelined at A/AS level because of the grammar gap which can be very well addressed during directed time (see above).

What then are the implications of all this for the teacher? Clearly we are developing process skills at A/AS level and we should not confuse outcomes with processes. Whereas outcomes must be, and are, carefully monitored by the teacher, processes have their own intrinsic value and do not require the same close scrutiny. Thus all tasks are not automatically items for assessment, but rather a record of research completed. Formal assessment at the progress and mastery stages and linguistic performance in the classroom will reflect formative grasp of the grammar acquired and the development of ideas, opinions and reflection.

Summary

Planning an A/AS level mfl course has to take account of examination require-ments which demand skills from the learner that are either new, deficient or lacking. These, we have proposed, can be addressed by adopting the STAR model. The topic organiser provides a systematic framework that can arrange the teaching and learning effectively and document progress throughout the course.

Learner progress will be evident in linguistic skills with the accumulation of vocabulary and structure in both taught lessons and directed time and in new learning skills with the development of learning strategies and autonomous modes of working.

References

Barnes, A. (1996) 'Getting them off to a good start: the lead-up to that first 'A' Level class.' In *German Teaching* 14. Rugby: Association for Language Learning, pp. 23–8.

Carter, J., Jannetta, J., Langlais, J. and Moreton, M. (1998) *Nouvelles perspectives. Découvertes.* Hodder and Stoughton.

Department for Education (1995) *Geography in the National Curriculum.* London: HMSO.

Graham, S. (1997) *Effective Language Learning: Positive Strategies for Advanced Language Learners.* Clevedon: Multilingual Matters.

Graham, S. and Powell, B. (1992) 'From GCSE to A Level: a natural progression?' In *Language Learning Journal* 6. Rugby: Association for Language Learning, pp. 62–5.

Grenfell, M. (1996) 'Theory and practice in Modern Language teacher training'. In *Links* 14. London: CILT, pp. 13–5.

Grenfell, M. and Harris, V. (1993) 'How do pupils learn? Part 1' In *Language Learning Journal* 8. Rugby: Association for Language Learning, pp. 22–5

Grenfell, M. and Harris, V. (1998) 'Learner strategies and the advanced language learner: problems and causes'. In *Language Learning Journal* 17. Rugby: Association for Language Learning, pp. 23–8.

Harris, V. (1997) *Teaching Learners How to Learn: Strategy Training in the ML Classroom.* London: CILT.

Hurd, S. (1998) 'Too carefully led or too carelessly left alone?' In *Language Learning Journal* 17. Rugby: Association for Language Learning, pp. 70–4.

Lonsdale, T. (1996) 'Planning 'A' level topics to achieve continuity and progression'. In Shaw, G. (ed) *Aiming High: Approaches to Teaching 'A' Level.* London: CILT, pp. 17–29.

McCulloch, D. (1995) 'Where has all the grammar gone? An "accusative" search'. In *German Teaching* 12. Rugby: Association for Language Learning, pp. 13–8.

Naiman, N., Fröhlich, M., Stern, H.H. and Tedesco, A. (1996) *The Good Language Learner.* Clevedon: Multilingual Matters.

Ollerenshaw, J. (1998) *Facettes de la France Contemporaine.* Sandy: Bedfordshire.

O'Malley, J. and Chamot, A. (1990) *Learning Strategies in Second Language Acquisition.* Cambridge: Cambridge University Press.

Oxford, R. (1989) *Language Learning Strategies: What Every Teacher Should Know.* Boston: Heinle and Heinle.

Oxford, R. (1993) 'Research on second language learning strategies'. In *Annual Review of Applied Linguistics* 13, pp. 175–87

Pachler, N. and Field, K. (1997) *Learning to Teach Modern Foreign Languages in the Secondary School*. London: Routledge.

Page, B. (1992) (ed) *Letting Go, Taking Hold*. London: CILT.

Pickering, R. (1992) *Planning and Resourcing 'A' Level French: A Handbook for Teachers*. London: CILT

QCA, ACCAC and CCEA (1999) *A/AS Level Subject Criteria for Modern Foreign Languages 1999*. London.

Rumley, G. and Sharpe K. (1993) 'Generalisable game activities in modern language learning'. In *Language Learning Journal* 8. Rugby: Association for Language Learning, pp. 35–8.

Sempé-Goscinny (1960) *Le Petit Nicolas*. Folio: Editions Denoël.

Thorogood, J. and King, L. (1991) *Bridging the Gap: from GCSE to 'A' Level*. London: CILT.

Tumber, M. (1991) 'Developing pupil autonomy'. In *Language Learning Journal* 4. Rugby: Association for Language Learning, pp. 24–6.

WJEC (1998) *Syllabus for GCE Advanced Level French, German, Spanish 2000*. Cardiff.

Chapter 8

Planning an integrated topic

Lynne Meiring and Nigel Norman

Introduction

The planning of an integrated topic is dependent upon the framework established in macro-level planning and is concerned with the application of principles in practice. The main emphasis is on examples of practical teaching and learning that reflect current methodology and material in addition to innovative modes implicit in the development of new technologies and new styles of learning.

Objectives

By the end of this chapter you should have an awareness of:

- appropriate selection of subject matter and material
- integration of the four skills
- the development of knowledge and understanding, and
- integration of language, literature and other material

Appropriate selection of subject matter and material

Sequencing topics

The initial challenge facing the teacher of A/AS level language courses is determining the selection and sequencing of topics to reflect the cyclical nature of maturation in the learner. In the post-GCSE transition stage certain topics are more appropriate, although their mastery is an unrealistic goal. Pachler and Field (see 1997, p. 337) show how GCSE topics provide a point of departure for A/AS level topics and issues. As learners' knowledge and understanding increase, there must be the potential to revisit some of the earlier topics and bring to them added depth acquired through the learning process (see Chapter 7, Figure 7.2 transition > progress > mastery). In the 1998 Welsh Joint Examinations Council (WJEC)

No.	French	German
1	*La France et sa société*	*Die Gesellschaft in der BRD*
2	*La Vie de famille et les rapports entre individus*	*Das politische Leben*
3	*L'Environnement*	*Das wirtschaftliche Leben*
4	*L'Enseignement*	*Die Umwelt*
5	*La Vie active*	*Bildung und Erziehung*
6	*La Vie politique et économique*	*Die Welt der Jugend*
7	*Les Médias*	*Freizeit und Urlaub*
8	*Les Loisirs*	*Die Medien*

Figure 8.1 Topics in the 1998 WJEC syllabus

syllabus for French and German – now called subject specifications – for example, the topics are sequenced as in Figure 8.1.

There is no explicit rationale for this sequence and neither is the order parallel in both French and German. However, it would clearly be more appropriate for A/AS learners to begin their course with topic 2 in French and 6 in German than with the first in the sequence. Some of the topics do lend themselves to revisiting in that for each topic there are suggested issues (*thèmes*) that reflect a development in the treatment of the topic. For example, in *La Vie de famille et les rapports entre individus* the suggested *thèmes* illustrate a marked progression from 1. *Problèmes de l'adolescence*, more appropriately dealt with in the early stage of the course, to 2. *Égalité des sexes*, requiring greater sophistication in language and level of understanding. Similarly, in German a suitable start to the course could be made with topic 6, *Die Welt der Jugend*, rather than that of topic 1, *Die Gesellschaft in der BRD*, with its heavy factual load and more demanding level of language. In topic 6 a progression is evident from individual attitudes (*Einstellungen zum Leben als Jugendliche*) to the more discursive arguments required for dealing with problems (*Probleme für Jugendliche in der BRD*) and military service and conscientious objection (*Wehrdienst und Zivildienst*), which presuppose a greater cultural awareness and maturity of argument.

Although in general such principles will apply, there will be other factors affecting selection of topics. These will include the accessibility of the vocabulary, structure and ideas in the resources available to the learners. Since these are highly variable factors, individual to the learning context, we have suggested the following planning models for French and German (see Figures 8.2 and 8.3).

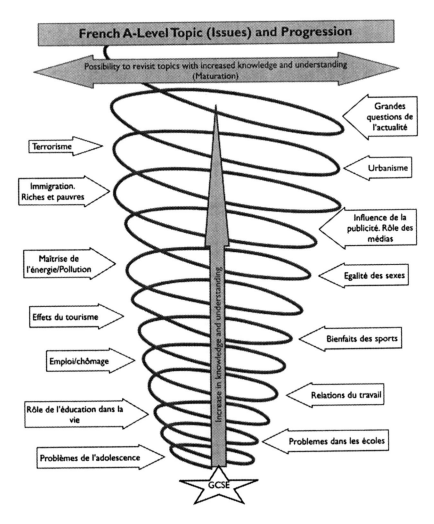

Figure 8.2 French spiral

REFLECTION
Activity 8.1 Sequencing topics
Using the examination subject specifications (formerly syllabuses) followed in your institution and material available, how would you sequence the topics within the model suggested? What was the most decisive factor in determining your choice?

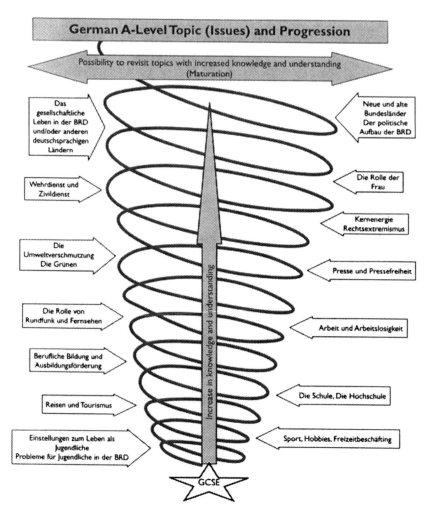

Figure 8.3 German spiral

Selecting material

The second planning priority concerns the selection of material, the underlying principle of which must be one of multi-resourcing, a particularly significant factor in the development of autonomy (see Chapter 7). Traditional paper-based and audio resources such as those represented by the major commercial coursebooks will play their part. One must be alert, however, to the danger that coursebooks can act as vehicles for the artificial introduction of certain vocabulary and structure items. Valid as they are as a *cours de base*, they are, nevertheless, to be seen as one of a whole battery of supplementary material, including 'live' authentic magazine and newspaper articles, TV and video, songs, Information and Communications Technology (ICT) (including CD-ROMs and the internet) and literature. A classroom case study referred to by David Little, in which a text selected by the teacher is used with disappointing response from the learners, underlines the demotivating effect of jumping through instructional hoops: 'every utterance that the learners produce is generated out of the text they have in front of them, which acts as a prompt' (1991, p. 29). What does not emerge is the interest and motivation to be generated from the element of choice of resources on the part of the learner. Little continues:

> perhaps most important of all, the learners clearly do not feel that they have any particular stake in what is going on. The text they are working on was certainly not their choice, and most of them seemed to find difficulty in showing even a polite interest in it.
>
> (1991, p. 30)

If the learner is to have more than merely a 'polite interest', it is essential to draw on as wide a menu of resources as possible. A resource planning checklist provides a valuable instrument for teachers to verify the effectiveness of the material in covering a variety of skills and activities. Thus, each resource is identified and cross-checked for its appropriacy to prescribed language functions and skills (see Figure 8.4).

TOPIC: ....

Resource	Grammar focus	Listening	Speaking	Reading	Writing	Study skills
Course book						
Audio cassette						
TV/video						
Songs						
ICT						
Authentic material						

Figure 8.4 Resource planning checklist

It is also useful to take account of a number of criteria when selecting material, some of which will assume more significance than others: for example, length of text, level and type of support or layout.

REFLECTION
Activity 8.2 Criteria for the selection of material
Which of the following would govern your choice of material: length, density, level of difficulty, relevance to topic, interest, variety and/or coverage of structures? What other considerations might affect your choice?

There is a caveat, however: the risk in multi-resourcing lies in compartmentalising discrete language activities, leading to a lack of continuity and cohesion. Glenis Shaw (1996, p. 3) refers to the difficulties of

> reading an article, then watching some TV, discussion, grammar . . . Experience suggested that students became better learners if the teaching processes were made explicit, for example, by the distribution of a half-termly programme of objectives, including materials and tasks.

Clearly, the overriding concern in planning has to be one of maximum exploitation of single resource items, such that an integration of skills takes place, rather than discrete practice of individual skills.

Integrating skills

Despite the tendency in assessment towards discrete skill testing, in order not to prejudice ability by poor performance in other skills, such artificial compartmentalisation lacks authenticity and is not desirable in teaching and learning. Colin Wringe (1989, pp. 7–8) supports this:

> [separating] the four skills for theoretical or assessment purposes does not mean that we necessarily have to *teach* them separately or avoid the use of multi-skill activities such as carrying on a conversation or responding in the foreign language to spoken or printed material, which are characteristic of everyday communication.

Smalley and Morris (1992, p. 24), referring to reading and speaking, demonstrate the lack of authenticity in teaching skills separately: 'there are few cases in real life where people do not talk or write about what they have read or act upon the information gleaned' and: 'most of the speaking people engage in is in the form of a dialogue and less often in the form of a monologue of rehearsed speech' (1992, p. 27). Pachler and Field (see 1997, p. 119) stress the importance of a multi-skill approach, supporting their point by referring to the terminology of the statutory frameworks, which include such terms as 'respond', 'react' and 'summarise', all of which presuppose a mixture of skills. This has been acknowledged in the revised National Curriculum for mfl Attainment Targets: AT 1 Listening *and Responding* and AT 3 Reading *and Responding* (see DfE/Welsh Office 1995). The assessment objectives AO1 and AO2 of the new Subject Criteria for A/AS level (QCA *et al.* 1999, p. 7) similarly reflect this move:

> understand and respond, in speech and writing, to spoken language.
>
> (AO1)

> understand and respond, in speech and writing, to written language.
>
> (AO2)

Hence, the example assessment task in the new Subject Criteria (QCA *et al.* 1999, p. 8) suggests 'an examination of internal assessment module in which candidates study a topic through both written and recorded documents and respond to these in both speech and writing'.

Terry Atkinson and Elizabeth Lazarus give an example of a multi-skill activity based on authentic tasks:

> [provide] students with a *tape from an answering-machine* containing phoned-in orders, requests, complaints etc. and for which they must take appropriate action. In the context of a tourist-information office these messages will request hotel bookings and details of excursions or restaurants. Students *use brochures*, photos or *computerised databases* to find the appropriate information. They then pass on the information to clients *by letter*, or *face-to-face*, or by *ringing back* on the number left on the answering-machine. A nice twist is to have them faced with an *answering-machine* when they ring to *provide the requested information*.
>
> (1998, p. 24; our emphasis)

Similarly, a suggested activity in the video accompanying the computer program Granville (Jones 1986, sequence 2) demonstrates the interrelationship of all four skills in the accomplishment of a task, like the one above. A written request for information is transferred to a telephone message, which is relayed to an employee of a tourist information centre, who requires further details from a hotel and other services in the French town of Granville using a database. When all the information has been collated it is telephoned back to the original enquirer, who notes the contents down and passes it on. Such activities would be particularly appropriate for the 'transition' stage (see Chapter 7), enabling the learner to draw upon previous knowledge and extend and reapply it in a multi-skill context. In this way, the GCSE topics of town and free time and requesting information are being built on.

At the later 'progress' stage more sophisticated material and tasks can be exploited in a multi-skill way. The issue of *Die Rolle der Frau* within the topic

Die Gesellschaft in der BRD (see WJEC 1998, p. 3) could be researched using a variety of media (including, for example, the CD-ROM *Stop Press* by the Foreign and Commonwealth Office/Auswärtiges Amt/British Council/Goethe-Institut [see also Chapter 14], texts from the internet or course material). This could lead on to a class debate (listening and speaking) and the production of an article for an electronic newspaper. This style of collaborative research and production is well-suited to directed time (see Chapter 7) and clearly develops additional skills to the familiar four language skills.

REFLECTION

Activity 8.3 Devising an integrated skill activity
Devise an activity from any given topic that practises a combination of at least three of the skills.

How did learners benefit from the integrated, as distinct from the discrete skill approach?

The development of knowledge and understanding

Knowledge and understanding will develop gradually over the course as learners move from transition to progress to mastery within topics. Because of this gradual development it is essential that the A/AS level subject specifications are viewed in terms of a spiral (see Figures 8.2 and 8.3) with the possibility of revisiting topics to achieve the mastery level, when there is sufficient maturation in knowledge and understanding. Graham (1992, p. 65) re-emphasises the significance of the 'gap' between ideas and language:

> [the] essence of the gap so often mentioned when referring to the transition from GCSEs to A Level seems to lie in the mismatch between the sophisticated concepts students need and want to discuss and the rather less sophisticated means they have at their disposal.

This maturation will involve developing the skills of autonomous learning, collaborative research and peer teaching (see the 'STAR' model in Chapter 7).

The topics at A/AS level lend themselves to acquisition of specific knowledge/facts/information, but if the learner remains at this stage he or she is ultimately unable to operate independently, beyond the structured environment of the classroom and the control of the teacher. Traditionally, many foreign language activities are artificially designed around the practice of discrete skills with predictable outcomes (e.g. correct answers to questions, accurate manipulation of certain structures). However, if the activity is authentic and mixed-skill, requiring transfer/application of knowledge, understanding tends to be developed. Chris Kyriacou (1986, p. 49) supports this: '"transfer of learning" refers to the pupil's ability to make use of previous learning in dealing with new tasks and in new situations. To facilitate such transfer is perhaps one of the most important tasks of effective teaching.' Enriching knowledge and understanding at A/AS level requires development of cognitive (e.g. analysis, criticism, reflection) and discursive skills (e.g. opinions, argument, debate), in addition to the affective dimension (i.e. personal, social, emotional). Pachler and Field (1997, Figure E1, p. 336) show how some of these skills can be developed. As learners develop they will move from a more passive, structured mode to a more active, open-ended one.

Pachler and Field (1997, p. 341), in discussing post-16 development of grammar, stress the importance of moving from recognition and learning of paradigms and set phrases (passive) to the manipulation of language forms (active). This will be a feature of the 'progress' stage, which will include a wide variety of stimuli and multi-skill tasks, and there will be a consequent shift from dependence to autonomy (see the 'STAR' model in Chapter 7).

Activities such as those mentioned above (see Atkinson and Lazarus 1998, p. 24, and Jones 1986, Sequence 2) will develop spontaneous personal responses, involving mood and emotion. When trying to book a hotel room, for example, the enquirer is told that everything is full, or when processing an answerphone enquiry, one is informed that weather conditions have caused cancellation of certain services (e.g. coach trips, ferry crossings, excursions). Whereas the affective dimension simply requires an outlet and practice, the cognitive and discursive dimensions need to be systematically developed and will certainly not happen spontaneously.

Presenting learners with a wide variety of often neutral stimuli and communicative functions will not guarantee the development of cognitive and discursive skills. Instead, a selection of contentious opinions from audio, songs, video, text, CD-ROM, etc. sources will generate ideas and provoke personal reaction as well as providing all-important factual information. An example of a resource that consciously develops thinking skills through structured debate is Beile and Beile (1995). An authentic text is presented, but more importantly issues that emerge from it are debated by young people, their parents, and others, which provides a waystage between passive acquisition of factual detail and their active manipulation and interpretation. This represents a significant progression from the lower-order comprehension questioning which characterises many authentic materials at present. Thus a short extract on the law concerning young peoples' rights stimulates strong viewpoints from school-pupils, students and parents (see Beile and Beile 1995, pp. 51–3)

Following this a role play (see Beile and Beile 1995, p. 55) enables all contrasting opinions to be given active expression in a motivating context, ensuring development of discursive skills. At this stage the learner will be in a position to record a series of contrasting opinions in note form (bullet points) and from these eventually to formulate his or her own ideas. This methodology is exemplified in Carter et al. (1998), where the learner is invited to process texts, extract ideas, reasons, viewpoints and to move on to active reworking in the form of presentations, letters, articles, surveys. For example in the unit *Poitou-Charentes* (see Carter *et al.* 1998, p. 34) learners read an article and are asked to complete a table giving evidence of attitudes, reasons and suggestions for improvement on the topic of environmental pollution. Following this a survey is conducted in which learners can choose aspects of the topic to investigate and formulate their own questions. In doing this they will obtain an original and personalised angle on the topic that involves their peers and teachers and will simultaneously create a unique and highly motivating resource for presentation. At this stage a short, written consolidation of ideas is a useful precursor to the more formal convention of an essay. In this instance the learner writes two letters based on the texts:

> la première destinée au rédacteur de *Sud-Ouest (Charente-Maritime)* et la deuxième au rédacteur en chef d'*Al-Ahram Hebdo*. Vous devrez exprimer vos réactions aux articles des journaux respectifs. Proposez vos idées d'une façon encourageante sur les moyens possibles d'empêcher la pollution et de sensibiliser la population.

Before a final formal written outcome in the form of an essay is possible ('mastery' stage) a draft stage is required in which the notes, letters, tabulated evidence are marshalled into coherent sentences, points are organised into structured paragraphs and a reflective conclusion is reached. For example, in his book Ross Steele (1998) includes two useful sections in each 'dossier' entitled *Points de vue* and *A votre tour,* which are skilfully structured to stimulate and organise ideas and provide a useful bank of short items, which could eventually be drawn together into an essay.

REFLECTION
Activity 8.4 Developing ideas and arguments
Select a number of authentic resources on a topic and evaluate their effectiveness in expressing strongly contrasting viewpoints. What supplementary measures would be required to enable such viewpoints to be developed?

Integrating language, literature and other material

Literature

In past A level modern foreign languages syllabuses there tended to be an artificial divide between language and literature, with considerable emphasis placed upon close textual analysis and techniques of literary appreciation, culminating in essays in English on a number of prescribed texts. In language work there were precise translations to and from the foreign language and tightly structured essays in the target language. This gave way to a 'texts and topics' approach, which set in train a gradual process of marginalisation of literature. This increased when a greater emphasis was placed on topics, and literature was relegated to the status of an option. Susan Tebbutt (1996, p. 95) refers to 'an unfortunate fact in the 1990s that many university students may complete a degree without ever having read a whole book, be it fiction or non-fiction.' Increasing emphasis on socio-cultural aspects has led to the requirement of the new Subject Criteria to 'develop students' insight into, and encourage contact with, the contemporary society, cultural background and heritage of countries or communities where the foreign language is spoken' (QCA *et al.* 1999, p. 5). Literature is not actually mentioned here, but, of course, represents a significant part of the cultural heritage of a country and leads to an understanding of the culture and society in question. (See also Chapter 11.)

Literature needs to be re-established as a source of text and assume its valid place alongside the vast wealth of other source material made available through new technologies. Emma Haughton (1998, p. 14) highlights the resources available in the information society:

ICT makes a real difference by literally opening up new worlds for teachers and pupils. E-mail and video-conferencing can put you in touch with native speakers across the globe, the Internet allows virtual visits to almost any country; multi-media and CD-ROMs bring languages and cultures to life.

Terry Atkinson (quoted in Haughton 1998) affirms this: 'you're aiming for a rounded learning experience, with books, videos, language assistants and other things, as well as computers.' Daniel Tierney (quoted in Haughton 1998) says: 'while books are still very important and popular, ICT can bring more variety.' (see also Chapter 14).

In planning a unit of work it is tempting to draw upon this wide range of resources, but a note of caution must be sounded, to avoid the pitfalls of resource overload, signalled by Kyriacou (see 1991, p. 45).

In his detailed description on 'Producing an integrated unit' on the topic of *L'impressionisme* Robin Pickering (1992, p. 124) advises restraint:

[since] it is important not to overload the students with material, only three texts have been selected, presenting a contrast in format and register. The first is of the kind one might find in an art history, the second comes from an exhibition catalogue and the third is a newspaper article about recent thefts in the art world. It is very easy to keep presenting written material of the same kind. It is quite difficult to vary and balance the register, but essential if the students are not to become narrow in linguistic experience or bored by the monotony of the presentation.

The challenge to the teacher is to develop an appropriate methodology which embraces literature as a constituent part of this plethora of information. Gary Chambers (1991a, p. 35) stresses the immediate authenticity and cultural significance of literature: 'literature . . . represents surely the most authentic material we can provide, and for which the authentic task of reading for enjoyment can be encouraged'. He also refers to the beneficial effect of literature on personal, social and affective development, offering vicarious experience to maturing individuals, which help 'a development of their facility to take an objective, critical stance and by association the establishment of personal principles and values' (1991a, p. 35). Finally, the facility of literature to provide coherence and integration to the otherwise potentially discrete components of language, literature and other material is signalled by Chambers (see 1991a, p. 35).

Out of a concern for the lack of enthusiasm amongst teachers to include literature, Mike Grenfell (1995, p. 88) carried out three case studies on the integration of literary texts into foreign language. From these he concluded that '[it] is possible for 16–19 year olds to enjoy literary texts in a foreign language and to learn from them.' He also points to the important contribution literature makes to language development.

Bernard Lien and Maureen Raud (in press) go some way towards incorporating literature into language work by providing lists of supplementary material within each 'dossier', e.g. in *La vie urbaine et la vie rurale* they refer to *Thérèse Desqueyroux*, *La Place*, *Germinal*, *La Gloire de mon père* and *Manon des sources*. Photocopiable dossiers are included in the tutor's book.

This integration of literary text into language work is also evident in Stuart Stockdale's unit (1993) in which a text involving personal description by Gabriele Wohmann is used to elicit learners' impressions and responses and, thereby, develop the language of opinion. Literature here is being used as a springboard from which other text types can be used, which lead to creative writing by the learners. This approach lends itself more to poems and short stories than novels and drama, which would become disjointed and lose their coherence if presented in short extracts. For working with literature see also Chapter 11.

Websites such as those of the Goethe-Institut (see e.g. *Literatur und Fremdsprachenlernen* available at: http://www.goethe.de/ne/hel/deslit.htm) and *France à la carte* (available at: http://www.francealacarte.org.uk) provide learners with useful ways of accessing literary texts, enabling them to work autonomously. A typical *Etude de texte* on Marcel Pagnol's *La Gloire de mon père* provides an *aide linguistique* on adjectives and difficult expressions, as they occur in the text, serving as a monolingual glossary and helping the establishment and development of style and range of linguistic expression. Further support is given in the form of target language character studies (*Les personnages*) including close cross-references to the text. Other *Etudes de texte* provide chapter by chapter *résumés* and hyperlinks to other useful support. Thus more time is made available for the teacher to integrate literature into language study, involving a variety of media. Ann Barnes and Bob Powell (1996, p. 24) suggest, for example: 'drama, formal debate of issues, press conference, radio or television programme design and presentation, newspaper front page creation via desktop publishing and e-mail correspondence'.

Gary Chambers (1991b, p. 6) similarly suggests activities that cover all four skills and are suitable for individual, pair and group work, for example: 'dramatisation of an excerpt on video, letter writing from one character to another, balloon debate'. Ann Barnes and Bob Powell (see 1996, p. 29) discuss ways of 'making reading more interactive', for example what they call 'the tabloid ploy', in which mini-headlines are extracted from the text and used to stimulate interest and prediction of possible content. This and other activities are shifting the focus from laborious, word-by-word textual analysis and interpretation towards a more creative and interactive engagement with text.

REFLECTION
Activity 8.5 Using a literary text as a basis for language work
Select a literary text and devise activities that will maximise its potential for classroom language work.

The internet

It must be emphasised at this point that any approach that uses new technologies must be structured carefully by the teacher. Assistance in processing text is available. For example, the Goethe-Institut page available at http://www.goethe.de/z/50/uebungen/deindex.htm enables teachers to enter text that will be transformed into manipulation exercises, such as gapped text, assigning headings to sections and sequencing sections, creating effectively a customised worksheet builder.

Aimless 'surfing' of the internet should not be transferred to the classroom. The Internet as a resource must be evaluated for benefits and pitfalls (see also Chapter 14 and Pachler 1999a and 1999b).

Pachler and Field (1997, p. 268), quoting Horsfall and Whitehead (1996), stress the need for new skills to be developed in school use of the internet: 'pupils need to be taught early how to sift, reject and reuse for their own purposes from the mass of material'. This presupposes an understanding of the materials on the part of the learner. As Pachler and Field note, the teacher needs

> to ensure that pupils using information obtained particularly via CD-ROM and/or the Internet, have actually understood the material and developed and/or consolidated linguistic skills, knowledge and understanding in the process of using this technology.
>
> (1997, p. 268)

The obvious advantage of CD-ROM is that it is a fixed database, a controlled resource, unlike the internet. Consequently it lends itself to activities that are similar but that are within a controlled environment. *Stop Press*, for example, is a multi-media resource which develops reporting and editing skills (*journalistische Fertigkeiten*) through reading and writing and learners will produce articles for a virtual newspaper. Ruth Bourne (quoted in Pachler and Field 1997, p. 274) gives a useful checklist for evaluating CD-ROMs. She stresses amongst other criteria the importance of asking how they link with/complement other material. For evaluation criteria see also Pachler 1999a and Bruntlett 1999.

The opportunity to pursue autonomous learning tasks in the relatively uncontrolled environment of the internet must be encouraged, but there must be clearly defined objectives. In circumstances where text is perceived to be too difficult to understand, and given the vast quantity of possible material, outcomes are nevertheless crucial, and learners must not leave the task empty-handed or frustrated. In her *Guiding principles for creating teaching units with the WWW* (which is available at: http://faraday.clas.virginia.edu/~iad4c/www.html), Inge DiBella puts it thus: '[a] text is never too difficult: it depends what you want the students to do with it and how you structure this activity'.

This could range from picking out headlines, composing lists and sorting information under headings to comparisons, analysis and hypothesis. Teachers can set tasks that require minimal gist understanding ('What is this text about?'). The template in Figure 8.5 can serve as a general guide for initial access by the

---

Location (URL): . . . .

Titre: . . . .

Thème: . . . .

Questions à résoudre:
  Vocabulaire (Mots inconnus)

  Idées (Points-clés)

  Grammaire (Structures à identifier)

Questions à poser au professeur/à l'assistant(e)

1.

2.

3.

4.

5.

etc

Figure 8.5 Access sheet for web-texts (French):

learner to more demanding, unfamiliar web-texts. This will release the teacher from the laborious and time-consuming obligation to process every text in advance. Initially the learner identifies the location (URL), the title, topic (and connection with the syllabus). Learners then formulate a series of questions on the web-text, which could provide the basis for fruitful discussion with a Foreign Language Assistant or the teacher and class. The focus is on unfamiliar vocabulary, key ideas and structures. At the same time, and crucially, however, learners are being given the support necessary to develop genuinely autonomous learning skills, using the internet in an individualised and self-selecting way. In a section entitled *Wie liest und versteht man fremde Texte? Tips zum Entschlüßeln deutscher Texte* (available at http://www.goethe.de/z/jetzt/dejlesev.htm on the Goethe-Institut website) reading strategies are provided that range from global understanding and previous knowledge, through key words and pictures to structure and associations.

Some of the practical considerations in using the internet as a language-learning resource can be exemplified in a case study of a PGCE student teacher, who set about using the internet to allow learners in their first year of advanced level mfl study to investigate the topic *L'immigration*. She searched the web to find suitable texts and devised a series of questions which the learners would address by accessing the technology themselves. Preparation included providing background vocabulary on a worksheet, which involved dictionary-skill activity. The student teacher's evaluation of the whole undertaking can be summarised in Figure 8.6.

The major concern for teachers will no doubt be the time required to research and prepare the material. A solution is the use of a template to cover a range of possible texts (as described in Figure 8.5) and in addition a shift of responsibility to the learner to discover meaning through, for example, drawing up a list of questions, instead of the traditional teacher-directed set of tasks. This would make the

	Benefits	Pitfalls
Student teacher	• innovative pedagogy, resulting in enthusiastic approach • personal development of ICT competence	• availability of resource • time-consuming preparation • technical problems
Learner	• enjoyment, fun • different learning experience • more active involvement • more interesting than searching through piles of books	• time-consuming • unfamiliarity of process • need for technical support

Figure 8.6 Case study evaluation of the use of the internet

resource more attractive to teachers, as well as developing significant learner strategies. Teachers would find it useful to collate information on appropriate websites and their potential application to topics in the form of a website planner (see Figure 8.7).

REFLECTION

Activity 8.6 Resourcing from websites

Using Figure 8.7, select a topic from your A/AS level syllabus and find a selection of useful websites. Show how the resources you find could be exploited.

Video and song

There are three ways video can be used in the language classroom:

- off-air authentic recordings
- commercially-produced series (e.g. BBC French Collection, German Collection, *Café des rêves*), and
- complementary component of coursebook

It has manifest advantages over other material. As Pachler and Field note (1997, p. 257): 'one of the reasons for using television in mfl teaching is that it is often

Topic (e.g. Environment):		
URL	Focus/Title	Exploitation
e.g. http://www.francealacarte.org.uk	e.g. nuclear energy, recycling	e.g. vocabulary synonyms, grammar exercise

Figure 8.7 Website planner

intrinsically motivating to pupils. It offers a degree of familiarity and with it security.' In addition Brain Hill (quoted in Pachler and Field 1997, p. 258) speaks of 'off-air recordings [providing] examples of real life which are potentially up-to-date and offer an intercultural perspective on life'. The impact of paralinguistic functions to support understanding is another palpably powerful benefit. Whichever of these three applications is used, it is vital that exploitation is carefully structured. The coursebook *Essor* (Bourdais *et al.* 1997) demonstrates how viewing skills can gradually be developed in the learner. In the introductory unit *Les vedettes* (Bourdais *et al.* 1997, p. 12) a clip from *Le juste prix* is shown and learners are asked to:

1   predict questions that will be asked
2   watch with the sound turned down
3   guess the occupation of the participants, and
4   verify their responses to (1) and (3)

At a more demanding level, learners are asked to elicit the character and personality of the host and the participants using paralinguistic clues and speech. Finally learners extract from the clip key expressions relating, for example, to reactions and emotions, and carry out role play which reworks these.

Songs, too, have a significant motivational role for learners, as well as providing enjoyment and stimulation. At post-16, authentic songs are far more appropriate than the 'custom-made' ones, such as those produced for Key Stage 3 (e.g. *Un kilo de chansons*). Songs are effectively another form of literature and can be integrated into topics. The song *Répondez-moi* by Francis Cabrel, for example, deals with city life, environment and pollution. The poetic style of the lyrics make it a rich resource for developing style, imagery and ideas. An approach to the text through synonym and definition exercises will enable easier access to the poetic images, for example:

> Mon coeur a peur d'être emmuré entre vos tours de glaces
> Condamné au bruit des camions qui passent

The following question could be asked: *Quelle est l'expression dans le texte qui correspond à 'enfermer dans un mur'?*

A mixed-media approach is adopted in *Rock und Deutsch* (1995), which incorporates songs on cassette with the magazine *Juma*[1] and a *Textheft mit Didaktisierungsangeboten*, including full transcripts of the lyrics. Fully worked exercises that include biographical background on the singers and largely linguistic exploitation of the songs can be found in *Mein Gespräch, meine Lieder* (1986). The disadvantage of such material, of course, is that the songs themselves date, in a way that news dates, but this does not invalidate the pedagogy. All of the songs mentioned would be particularly appropriate at the 'transition' stage, providing accessible text-bites based upon largely familiar vocabulary and structures.

Perhaps the final word on the use of such an abundance of potential resources for foreign language learning should be one of caution, as Pachler and Field note

(1997, p. 243): '[each] resource serves a particular purpose in the mfl teaching and learning process and it is important to devise appropriate activities to maximise the effectiveness of individual resources'.

REFLECTION

Activity 8.7 Using video and song as a teaching resource
Select a TV clip/extract of video or a song related to one of the topics. How suitable is it for developing linguistic skills and ideas and opinions?

Planning an A/AS level topic-based unit

In our discussions of A/AS level planning many recommendations have been made, which it is crucial to address in designing a unit of work. Figure 8.8 is a photocopiable pro-forma for applying these recommendations to planning. For reasons of space and practicality it is advisable to enlarge the form.

It is envisaged for one pro-forma to be used for each topic (i.e. approximately eight in all).

QCA *et al.* (1999) highlight six key skills, which 'will be written into AS/A Level specifications, where these can be integrated without distorting the integrity of the subject'. Figure 8.8 shows all the key skills, as, at the time of writing, it is not yet clear which ones will apply to mfl.

In planning, the teacher needs to consider teaching and learning activities (these could be distinguished as 'T' and 'L' in the narrow column alongside). 'Teaching and learning activities' refers primarily to classroom-based work, whereas 'Directed Time' indicates work carried out in non-contact time.

Other information to be documented will include the selection of texts, key vocabulary, grammar and opportunities for assessment and outcome tasks.

A key is included to indicate the level of the work (transition, progress and mastery). As the mastery level will not be achievable within every topic it is essential that time is built into planning to revisit certain aspects of topics.

Although a mixed-skill approach has been strongly recommended in this chapter, it might be reassuring for the teacher to indicate on the planning document the skills that are being practised through any given task/activity. This can be done by simply showing in brackets the appropriate skill.

Finally a list of the resources used should be itemised.

Key skills

Communication	IT	Application of number	Improving own learning and performance	Working with others	Problem-solving

A/AS Level Topic:

Activities (Teaching/Learning)	Directed Time	Texts	Key Vocabulary	Grammar	Assessment	Outcome Tasks

Time available for unit	Aspects to revisit and date	Key to levels	Resources
		Transition Progress Mastery	

Figure 8.8 A/AS level topic planner

REFLECTION
Activity 8.8 Planning an individual topic
Using the A/AS level topic planner in Figure 8.8, plan a topic from your scheme of work, to incorporate features introduced:
- transition, progress, mastery
- directed time, including autonomy
- ICT, including internet
- key skills, and
- multi-resourcing

Summary

Detailed planning of a topic needs to take account of subject content as defined in the examination specifications. From this, decisions can be made concerning material and modes of teaching and learning.

An inevitable implication is an approach based on multi-resourcing. This will enable alternative access to subject matter and simultaneously develop flexibility of learning styles. The transition, progress and mastery stages, which form the framework of each topic, will chart the maturation process. This process, we propose, can be represented as a spiral, which demonstrates the accompanying increase in knowledge and understanding over the duration of the course. We also propose greater authenticity of activities through an integration of skills and media, culminating in a range of outcome tasks at all three stages: transition, progress and mastery.

Notes

1 *Juma* is also available online at: http://www.juma.de.

References

Atkinson, T. and Lazarus, E. (1998) *A Guide to Teaching Languages.* Cheltenham: MGP/ALL.
Barnes, A. and Powell, B. (1996) *Developing Advanced Reading Skills in Modern Foreign Languages.* Cheltenham: Mary Glasgow/ALL.
Beile, W. and Beile, A. (1995) *Themen und Meinungen im Für und Wider.* Bonn: Inter Nationes.
Bourdais, D., Hope, M., Huntley, T. and Thorpe, C. (1997) *Essor.* Oxford: Oxford University Press.
Bruntlett, S. (1999) 'Selecting, using and producing classroom-based multimedia'. In Leask, M. and Pachler, N. (eds) *Learning to Teach Using ICT in the Secondary School.* London: Routledge.
Carter, J., Jannetta, J., Langlais, J. and Moreton, M. (1998) *Découvertes: Nouvelles perspectives.* London: Hodder and Stoughton.

Chambers, G. (1991a) 'A Level literature in the 90s: a fresh start'. In *Language Learning Journal*, 3. Rugby: Association for Language Learning, pp. 34–40.

Chambers, G. (1991b) 'Suggested approaches to A Level literature'. In *Language Learning Journal*, 4. Rugby: Association for Language Learning, pp. 5–9.

DfE/Welsh Office (1995) *Modern Foreign Languages in the National Curriculum*. London: HMSO.

Graham, S. (1992) 'GCSE to A level: a natural progression'. In *Language Learning Journal*, 6. Rugby: Association for Language Learning, pp. 62–5.

Grenfell, M. (ed) (1995) *Reflections on Reading: From GCSE to A Level*. London: CILT.

Haughton, E. (1998) 'Speaking in the same language.' In *Education Guardian*, 13 October.

Jones, B. (1986) *Granville*. Cambridge: Cambridge University Press/Cambridge Micro Software.

Juma Extra 1/96 Rock und Deutsch: Deutsche Rock- und Popmusik seit 1989. (1996) Cologne.

Kay, J. (1978) *Un kilo de chansons*. London: Mary Glasgow.

Kyriacou, C. (1986) *Effective Teaching in Schools*. Hemel Hempstead: Simon & Schuster Education.

Kyriacou, C. (1991) *Essential Teaching Skills*. Oxford: Blackwell.

Lien, B. and Raud, M. (in press) *Thèmes et Textes*. London: John Murray.

Little, D. (1991) *Learner Autonomy: Definitions, Issues and Problems*. Dublin: Authentik.

Mein Gespräch, meine Lieder: Liedermacher im Deutschunterricht. (1986) Munich: Langenscheidt.

Pachler, N. (1999a) 'Theories of learning and Information and Communications Technology'. In Leask, M. and Pachler, N. (eds) *Learning to Teach Using ICT in the Secondary School*. London: Routledge.

Pachler, N. (1999b) 'Using the Internet as a teaching and learning tool'. In Leask, M. and Pachler, N. (eds) *Learning to Teach Using ICT in the Secondary School*. London: Routledge.

Pachler, N. and Field, K. (1997) *Learning to Teach Modern Foreign Languages in the Secondary School*. London: Routledge.

Pickering, R. (1992) *Planning and Resourcing 'A' Level French: A Handbook for Teachers*. London: CILT.

QCA, ACCAC and CCEA (1999) *Subject Criteria for Modern Foreign Languages: GCE Advanced Subsidiary and Advanced Level Specifications*. London.

Shaw, G. (1996) 'Introduction: the "A" level examination a decade of change.' In Shaw (ed) *Aiming High: Approaches to Teaching A Level*. London: CILT, pp. 1–5.

Smalley, A. and Morris, D. (1992) *The Modern Language Teacher's Handbook*. Cheltenham: Stanley Thornes.

Steele, R. (1998) *L' Express: Perspectives Françaises*. Oxford: Oxford University Press.

Stockdale, S. (1993) 'Chapter 2.' In Bond, J. et al. *Aus eigener Erfahrung: Von GCSE bis 'A' Level*. London: CILT, pp. 25–41.

Tebbutt, S. (1996) 'Working with German literary texts'. In Shaw, G. (ed) *Aiming High: Approaches to Teaching 'A' Level*. London: CILT, pp. 9–24.

WJEC (1998) *GCE Advanced Level French and German*. Cardiff.

Wringe, C. (1989) *The Effective Teaching of Modern Languages*. Harlow: Longman.

Chapter 9

Developing 'receptive' language skills – listening and reading

Bob Powell

Introduction

The term 'receptive language skills' is one that is commonly used in the literature on language-teaching methods but it is open to various interpretations. The adjective 'receptive' is associated with receiving, with being in a position of one who accepts what is given, not therefore automatically an active participant in the proceedings. Indeed, there have been times when listening and reading have been labelled as 'passive skills' in stark contrast to the 'active skills' of speaking and writing. This unfortunate categorisation has brought with it the risk of assuming that by looking after the active skills, the passive skills will somehow develop by themselves. However, a quick glance at an English dictionary will remind us – if we needed to be reminded – that the word 'receptive' conveys also the notions of attentiveness, concentration and the ability or speed with which one can receive impressions or ideas and develop them. In the context of foreign language teaching and learning, it is this second set of meanings with which this chapter is concerned.

At the time of the introduction of the National Curriculum in England and Wales in the early nineties, most teachers welcomed the presentation of the so-called 'passive' skills as Attainment Targets defined as: Listening *and Responding* and Reading *and Responding* (DfE/Welsh Office 1995; my italics). The inclusion of the word 'responding' was in recognition that, as far as foreign language learning is concerned, most listening and reading activities, in keeping with the tenets of communicative language teaching, are best designed to lead to relevant and purposeful activity on the part of the learners. One should, of course, encourage listening and reading for their own sake. These activities have perhaps erroneously become known as listening and reading 'for pleasure' – as if all other forms of listening and reading are devoid of enjoyment! Teachers should be making sure that their learners engage with, react to, and produce something from the language to which they are exposed – and enjoy the experience at the same time. This is as true for A/AS level studies as it is for lower level work.

Objectives

By the end of this chapter, you should have:

- understood the importance of listening and reading in the whole of the foreign language learning experience 16–19
- become familiar with the requirements of A/AS examinations as regards listening and reading, and the relevant assessment criteria
- understood the value of thorough preparation on your part before introducing learners to listening and reading material
- familiarised yourself with a range of listening and reading strategies, and
- developed a scheme for integrating the teaching of these strategies into your scheme of work for A/AS level

Changing attitudes to listening and reading

The aims of foreign language education have developed and evolved considerably over the course of the last few decades. It is worth recalling that, when modern languages were introduced into the curriculum of secondary schools at the end of the nineteenth century, the model for instruction was based more or less entirely on the practice of teaching classical languages. The main priority was for many years the development of the ability to read the foreign language. Reading, however, actually meant translation into English and it was taken for granted that this implied a thorough grounding in grammar and syntax. Other skills were conspicuously absent apart, perhaps, from the need for learners to write sentences, based generally on models found in their reading passages, in order to prove that they could handle complex grammatical structures. The following extract from the statement of aims presented by a teachers' professional association in 1929, as well as inviting some interesting social comment in terms of its sexist use of language, may bring a wry smile to today's reader.

> One can reasonably expect of the average non-intellectual boy:
> 1   that he should read and understand straightforward narrative and description in the foreign language, in prose and in verse
> 2   that he should be able to give proof of his understanding by expressing in English what he has read in the foreign language – for which purpose some practice will be necessary
> 3   that he should be able to read aloud in a clear voice, with a reasonably accurate intonation, and with expression . . .
> (Association of Assistant Masters 1929, pp. 22–3)

In the complete list of aims there was no place for any mention of listening skills and, incidentally, speaking was limited to 'asking and answering simple questions on subjects familiar . . .'.

Gradual changes in approaches to teaching foreign languages – and most notably the development and adoption of the direct method – caused a shift in the focus of foreign language lessons. Not only was the supremacy of translation and writing challenged, but a recognisable order was established which influenced the sequencing of teaching activities and, eventually, the format and presentation of text books. Listen – speak – read – write became established as the advised method of presenting and exploiting language and this sequence is still accepted by many as a conventional and sensible guideline for lesson planning.

The efforts of language teachers in the sixties and seventies seem to have been concentrated, at least in the lower end of the secondary school, on the practical difficulties of managing the technology (tape recorder, film-strip projector, language laboratory) which was an essential feature of the new audio-visual and audio-lingual courses. Suddenly, listening and speaking were all-important. Reading was positively discouraged in the early stages of language learning since it was considered that seeing the written word would confuse learners and detrimentally affect the acquisition of a good foreign accent. Later, attention to reading tended to be limited to the problems of selecting suitable material and fitting reading time into an otherwise busy teaching schedule. One exhortation from an influential writer of the time abounds in metaphor but lacks practical detail with regard to implementation:

> [it] is important to show the student that what he [sic] is gaining is applicable knowledge – to let him see from the earliest possible moment that the language he is learning is a key to places worth visiting. Reading – released from the labour of the course book – can be a most fertile source of pleasure for him, as well as a means of turning over old ground and breaking sods in new.
>
> (Hilton 1974, p. 53)

With developments in A level examination syllabuses in the eighties, there was consistently more pressure on teachers to help learners listen to and make sense of the foreign language spoken at native speed. However, reading was still primarily a teacher-directed affair with literary texts often being painstakingly translated page by page with the content dissected and analysed – generally in English – in preparation for essay writing, also in English.

It is easy to criticise teaching methods of the past but it is now clear that failure to recognise the importance of a systematic approach to developing listening and reading skills in the early stages of foreign language learning had major consequences for later, more advanced work. Similarly, spending so much time during advanced level lessons discussing literary form and style, while providing learners with a reasonable grounding for traditional undergraduate courses, did not support the acquisition of a broad base of knowledge about contemporary foreign societies, nor did it encourage extensive reading habits.

As long ago as 1981, Eric Hawkins urged for a reappraisal of the forms of reading which were prevalent at that time, determined largely by the requirements of A level examinations. He concluded:

> both intensive and extensive reading . . . are essential but literary appreciation of works in a foreign language has no place in our conception of education at school level . . . We can move to motivated reading in sixth-forms by scrapping the set-books paper at A level and substituting for it a rigorous, varied programme which is tested in individual oral discussion with the examiner.
>
> (Hawkins 1981, p. 272)

Not everyone shared Hawkins's radical view, for 'scrapping the set-books paper' was tantamount to abandoning literature classes much loved by many teachers and there was still a majority of learners aspiring to study foreign languages in higher education where literary appreciation was the norm.

Changing approaches to listening and reading

The publication of Hawkins's framework for foreign language learning in school coincided with a practical demonstration of creative curriculum development by a working party comprising secondary and higher education teachers of foreign languages. This group produced a report which has strongly influenced A/AS level teaching and examination syllabuses. These teachers did not favour ditching literature altogether but rather wished the study of literary texts to be better integrated into the whole of the reading programme and exploited for its special worth with more varied and practical activities. The four principal characteristics of this 'new perspective' for teaching languages in the 16–19 age range were:

1   'The course is based on the study of authentic texts, oral and written, which embody a range of characteristic language uses and reflect real communicative needs.
2   These texts are exploited through a carefully controlled sequence of teaching procedures which enable the learner firstly to discover new language, ideas and information, then sort and practise the language and evaluate the content, and finally to make use of both language and content in sustained speech or writing.
3   These procedures require the learner to make use of language-handling skills, study skills which are common to the learning of all subjects.
4   The forms of assessment proposed reflect as closely as possible this teaching-learning process. Their purpose is to test language and study skills rather than an acquired body of language' (French 16–19 Study Group 1981, p. 2).

It is more or less taken for granted nowadays that learners will be using a range of foreign language skills in any single lesson. But the emphasis on linking general study skills to language-learning activities, on integrating so clearly receptive processes to active tasks, was a breath of fresh air at the time of the publication of the Study Group's report and their ideas had a significant impact on the organisation of teaching in the 16–19 curriculum and, eventually, examination reform. At the time, lessons tended to focus primarily on examination tasks: translation to and from the target language (TL); the essay, set-books, etc., with responsibility for preparing learners for the separate A level papers being given to different teachers. While this was very neat from an organisational point of view, it did not exactly encourage integration, cross-referencing or overlapping work.

What was also of great importance to the 1981 Study Group was the insistence that the same careful attention should be paid to helping learners understand and use the TL irrespective of whether the stimulus material was based on listening 'texts' or reading texts. It is worth delving a little further into what these teachers

Degree of support/independence	Examples of receptive processes	Examples of active tasks
1 WORKING WITHIN THE TEXT		
Discovering the text	decoding	transcribing
Collecting language/ideas	recognising	completing
	identifying	note taking
	selecting	making lists of
	classifying	language or facts
	sequencing	asking/answering
		questions
2 WORKING AROUND THE TEXT		
Sorting, practising language/ideas	matching	summarising
	reorganising	renarrating
	inferring	expanding condensed
		material
	interpreting	elucidating
	selecting/rejecting	interpreting
3 WORKING AWAY FROM THE TEXT		
Independent, integrated use of newly		role-playing
and previously acquired language/ideas/		dramatising
knowledge		adapting
		counter-argument
		personal/imaginative
		writing

Figure 9.1 The three-stage approach to listening and reading
Source: French 16–19 Study Group 1981, p. 12

called a 'three-stage approach' to handling listening and reading activities. Figure 9.1 is their schematic summary of the different stages and exemplifies, in general terms, some of the core activities.

The proposals of the 16–19 Study Group still have much to commend them. Their insistence on firstly *Discovery of the text* leading to *Sorting and practising* activities and then to *Spoken or written production* provides a helpful framework for lesson preparation for teachers today. Similarly their recommendations regarding the acquisition of grammatical knowledge through the identification and practice of examples *in context* before the reapplication of that knowledge in different contexts have become accepted as the common-sense way of dealing with grammar learning.

There are, however, a number of drawbacks to this approach, or at least in the way that the scheme tended to be adopted in classrooms. Firstly, we recognise now the importance of giving learners more control as early as possible in the language-learning cycle. The teacher should not dominate proceedings by asking all the questions and appearing to the learners as the single source of all the 'correct' interpretations. Also, we encourage nowadays much more collaborative work in class; pair-work practice and production have become standard activities in the early stages of language learning and there is no reason why advanced learners should not share the experience of making sense of a text through combination of practical exercises which involve working together without the teacher's constant interference. Communication, after all, requires active participation and shared meanings. Thirdly, the list of receptive processes suggested and the active tasks which were exemplified in the report (and which now form the main diet of many A/AS level coursebooks) are dependent primarily on what have become known as 'bottom-up' or 'text-driven' processes (see Eskey 1988; McDonough 1995). That is, they concentrate on recognition and 'de-coding' of features in the text rather than encouraging the use of personal, previously acquired knowledge. The application of this latter subset of skills has come to be known as 'top-down' or 'concept-driven' processes. The good A/AS reader, and listener for that matter, will have been introduced to and have gained experience of using *both* top-down and bottom-up processes through the course. It is certain that the examination questions will call for use, under pressure, of *both* sets of processes.

What is really needed to complete the picture is a *fourth stage* to the planning of lessons based on exploiting listening or reading texts. We can call this stage *Orientation* or *Arousal*. General theories about education reinforce the idea that learner readiness is one of the keys to creating optimum conditions for learning. In language-learning contexts, some have called this 'Sensing' as part of a four-stage model for developing better listening skills (see Steil *et al.* 1983). Gary Chambers stresses the value of pre-listening activities for learners and warns against going 'straight into the main course without having their taste buds awakened with an appropriate hors-d'oeuvre' (1996, p. 24). More recently, D. Clark (1998) reminds us that the starting-point for any 'instruction' should be the idea that the would-be learner is actually unaware that there is something worthwhile to be learned. This is probably true of many A/AS level foreign language learners!

The first task of any teacher, then, is to awaken in the learner the realisation that there is actually something of interest to be gained not just in terms of linguistic knowledge but personal enjoyment and fulfilment through the process of discovery, practice and productive use. This phase has been called 'a provocation or incentive to read [or listen] which depends on raising the curiosity factor of the chosen text' (Barnes and Powell 1996, p. 28). It can be done in a variety of ways. For example, the teacher shows a picture, photograph, diagram, graph, object, headline, etc. which may touch on some aspect of the text to be listened to or read, and then invites speculation among the class as to how it might relate to the text about to be studied.

Learners should also be encouraged to tell of their own experiences on the subject of the 'yet to be discovered' text, e.g. before studying a news item on urban traffic problems the teacher might ask learners to describe an occasion when they have been delayed while travelling. Questions, in the TL, should at first be at a purely factual level along the lines:

- when did this happen?
- where did it happen?
- how long was the delay?
- how many people were involved?
- what was the cause of the problem?

But, ideally, there should also be some questions at a more emotional or speculative level, such as:

- how did you feel at the time?
- could it happen again?
- how might the situation be avoided in the future?

This kind of conversation will provide ample opportunity for remembering or introducing some key vocabulary relating to transport but, equally important, it will inject an element of human interest right from the start into what can so often be a rather dull topic.

REFLECTION

Activity 9.1 Observation and/or self-analysis
Consider during your observations of teachers in action, or through analysis of your own practice, the following questions:
- how much preparation is given to A/AS level foreign language learners *before* embarking on a listening or reading activity?
- what kinds of activities are they asked to do *during* the listening/reading activity
- at what stage are they expected to *use* the language encountered during the listening/reading activity?

I have spent some time considering how foreign language teaching has evolved over the years and how, specifically, the skills of listening and reading have gained in status as more attention has been paid to their development. It is testimony to the innovatory work of the 1981 Study Group that language teachers in the 16–19 age range have been regularly referred to the 'New Perspectives' report ever since its publication, e.g. Pickering 1992. We need now, however, to:

1   examine more closely the requirements of current A/AS examinations
2   take account of some recent school-based research into the problems of advanced readers, and
3   develop some guidelines for supporting A/AS learners as they develop their receptive skills.

Aims and assessment criteria for listening and reading at A/AS level

Learners enter A/AS level courses with very varied experiences of listening and reading. One thing is certain: very few will have acquired the standard expected in the highest levels of the statutory orders of the 1995 National Curriculum. It is worth reminding ourselves of the definitions of 'exceptional performance' in the modern foreign languages attainment targets (see Figure 9.2).

The definition of exceptional performance in *Attainment Target 3: Reading and Responding* differs from the above only by the addition of the choice of material which may be 'official and formal material' and the inclusion of 'stories, articles and plays'. In reality, very few learners will have read anything much longer than the standard comprehension passages comprising a few short paragraphs which they are obliged to read in preparation for the GCSE examinations.

Attainment Target 1: Listening and Responding

Exceptional Performance:

Pupils show understanding of a wide range of factual and imaginative speech, some of which expresses different points of view, issues and concerns. They summarise in detail, report, and explain extracts, orally and in writing. They develop their independent listening by selecting from and responding to recorded sources according to their interests.

Figure 9.2 National Curriculum standards
Source: DfE/Welsh Office 1995, p. 6

REFLECTION

Activity 9.2 Reviewing expectations and resources

1   Examine a modern foreign languages department scheme of work for Key Stage 4 (14–16 year olds), concentrating especially on the aims and objectives for the more able pupils.
    What evidence can you find that suggests that the teachers in the department are:
    • providing a wide range of factual and imaginative texts? and
    • actively encouraging the development of independent listening and reading skills?

2   Familiarise yourself with the resources available for developing learners' independent reading and listening skills before and/or at the beginning of an A/AS level course by:
    • studying publishers' catalogues and the review sections of language-teaching journals, and
    • looking at the materials available in a department's resource centre/ staffroom

In recent years, much has been written about the gap between GCSE and A/AS level study. Patricia Rees, in an informative account of action research examining the transition from GCSE to A/AS level, examined in detail the reading habits of thirty-five learners. The main findings could be summarised as follows (see Rees 1995, p. 31):

• the main source of reading material had come from coursebooks
• past papers had been used by most learners to practise reading but specifically for 'examination task' purposes
• many had read photocopied texts or passages
• very few had read authentic magazines or newspapers
• only a quarter of the sample had been offered 'readers' – texts specially prepared for their level of language competence
• the readership of 'complete books' or poetry was minimal, and
• the majority had read 'nothing longer than, at best, four or five paragraphs of continuous text. Two to three paragraphs had been more usual'.

Suzanne Graham (1997) also concentrated on the learner perspective in her research. Part of her project involved investigation of the experiences of learners of French and learners of German at the beginning of their A level courses. For the French learners, listening emerged very high in the rank order of 'Things I have found difficult so far in my A level course' – second, in fact, only to 'tenses'. For the German learners, listening was less frequently cited as a difficulty but still a major source of anxiety and insecurity, along with 'cases', 'tenses' and 'vocabulary'. In general, Graham found that the learners were, as she understates it, 'very ready to express their feelings about *listening comprehension*' (p. 25). And when listening was cited as a difficulty, 'many respondents highlighted their comments with exclamation marks or underlinings, suggesting that the task was more than just a challenge' (Graham 1997, p. 25).

The problems seemed to arise when teachers had too high expectations of learners' ability to cope with authentic discourse. Mostly this was in the form of pre-recorded or off-air material but the language used by the teachers themselves also came in for criticism with one learner lamenting the fact his teacher addressed the class 'as if [we] were fluent A-levellers'. Clearly there is a huge difference in grammatical, lexical and syntactical complexity between the natural speech of a native or near-native speaker and the pseudo-reality language of GCSE listening tasks. Teachers should never forget how little prepared A/AS level learners are for 'real-life' language use.

Rees' and Graham's enquiries have provided very sensible advice for the teacher who is new to the job of preparing learners for the A/AS examinations. Their studies concentrated on the early stages of the course. The aims and assessment criteria for the examinations need to be studied, of course, and understood by teachers and learners alike but they must be seen as targets rather than 'ways of working' from the outset. So what are the current demands and expectations of the examinations for the receptive skills?

This year, new Subject Criteria for GCE A and AS level modern foreign languages were published (see QCA *et al.* 1999). These provide foreign language teachers and Examinations Boards with a list of aims and skills to be taught during the courses. The assessment objectives and grade descriptions provide the basis for subject specifications, formerly called examination syllabuses (see also Chapter 2). In addition, grade descriptions indicate the characteristic levels of attainment and a general indication of the required learning outcomes (see Figure 9.3 for grade distinctions for reading and listening).

Let us move now from general criteria to a specific example. All A/AS level teachers need to become totally familiar with the schemes of assessment and the range of tasks their learners will have to face at the end of the course. Of course it would be very short-sighted to restrict classroom activities throughout the course to those tasks. There is usually considerable difference between activities for learning and tasks for assessment. However, an awareness, from the beginning of the A/AS level course, of what learners will be required to do in the examination will enable the teacher to signal to learners how some activities they are presented with are especially relevant to the formal assessment requirements (see also Chapter 13).

The London Examination pilot syllabus for AS French, developed by the Edexcel Foundation for first examination 1999 and for A level French first examination 2000, sets out the typical range of tasks and the kinds of material from which examination questions will be formulated (and therefore the kinds of material to which they should be exposed during their course). Figure 9.4 gives details of the AS examination specifications.

GRADE A

Candidates show clear understanding of a wide range of complex spoken and written texts in a variety of registers. They have a very good understanding of grammatical markers, e.g. tense, mood and aspects, and a high level of awareness of structure, style and register. They not only understand the detail of the text but also show an ability to infer and appreciate. Where circumstances allow, they respond with insight and imagination. They appreciate the register and syntax of the original and when transferring meaning into English, Welsh or Irish they adapt their style appropriately.

GRADE C

Candidates understand a range of spoken and written texts in a variety of registers. They show understanding of grammatical markers, e.g. tense, mood and aspects, and show some awareness of structure and register. They grasp the significant details of the text and are able to identify points of view, attitudes and emotions. They show some appreciation of the register and syntax of the original and when transferring meaning into English, Welsh or Irish their style is sufficiently clear to convey meaning unambiguously.

GRADE E

Candidates respond to straightforward questions competently. They may experience difficulties with abstract or complex language. In the case of answers in the target language they may resort to copying parts of the text because of their lack of comprehension. In the case of questions in English, Welsh or Irish they may attempt to translate. They understand the gist and identify main points but their grasp of detail may be random and they have a limited ability to draw inferences, recognise points of view and emotions and draw conclusions. When transferring meaning into English, Welsh or Irish they manage to transmit some of the basic message, but often fail to appreciate grammatical markers, e.g. changes of tense. Their style is frequently clumsy.

Figure 9.3 A/AS grade descriptions – reading and listening
Source: QCA *et al.* 1999, pp. 5–7

In listening and writing at Advanced level (A2 Module 6a), as well as answering TL questions in the TL, there is a summary in English (90–120 words). In all, the material totals 300–400 words and lasts about 4–5 minutes. Responses to reading matter, drawn from such sources as magazines, newspapers, reports, books and other forms of extended writing, are also in the TL. The material totals 300–400 words and this part of the paper (A2 Module 6b) lasts half an hour. All timings and word limits are subject to QCA approval towards the end of 1999.

AS Module 1: Listening and writing

Candidates will be required to listen to authentic recorded target-language material and to retrieve and convey information given in the recorded material by responding to a range of mainly target-language questions. Candidates will need to show understanding for both general sense and specific detail; they will need to show knowledge and awareness of contemporary society and culture in the target country. The questions will elicit non-verbal responses, target-language answers and English answers requiring transfer of meaning from the target language.

Candidates will have individual control of the recording: they may stop, re-wind, and re-play the recording at will, and they may make notes and write answers at any point. The recorded target-language material will be drawn from contemporary sources such as news items, telephone messages, announcements, advertisements, interviews, radio talks, reviews, conversation, discussions, and current affairs broadcasts. The material will total 500–700 words and about 5–6 minutes' recording time.

AS Module 2: Reading and writing

(First paragraph virtually identical to the above, plus:)
Candidates will also be required to write about 200 words in the target language based on a short printed target-language stimulus and involving transfer of meaning from English instructions; the writing will be in the form of a letter, a report or an article.

Figure 9.4 AS examination specifications
Source: EDEXCEL 1998

REFLECTION
Activity 9.3 Comparing personal exam experience with those of your learners
Study the schemes of assessment and the range of tasks for listening and reading in the various models for AS and A level of the examination for which you are preparing/will prepare learners.
- How do they differ from the A/AS level or equivalent foreign language examination which you took at school or college?
- What do you consider to be the main implications for your own teaching?

A/AS level examinations present many new challenges. Not only is the modular framework a radical shift from past examinations, the emphasis on exposure to and use of the TL in the assessment schemes and the wide spectrum of text sources, styles and registers place extra responsibilities on coursebook writers and teachers. The learners themselves need to become aware of their responsibility to listen and read widely outside lesson time. Furthermore, the precise nature of the examination tasks, especially in the listening and reading sections, may vary from year to year. This may not be such a problem, however, since many of the day-to-day activities of foreign language learning find themselves in the list of examination question types now used by examination setters. Some of these will have become familiar also through pre-A/AS level learning. A survey of a few specimen papers in 1998 produced the list in Figure 9.5. There are probably many other types across the various examinations in the different languages.

Teachers must ensure adequate coverage of the test types likely to be encountered in the final examination without becoming slave to the subject specifications. They must also recognise the ranges of difficulty not only of the texts to be used during lessons but of the activities which they get their learners to do. Then there is the question of differentiation – since not all learners experience similar difficulties or have identical learning styles. There must be a sense of progression through the course so consideration must be given to text length, conceptual difficulty, etc., and, consequently, to the timing of topics during the programme. There are many other practical issues to be taken into account such as access to resources and

(NB text may be read or heard)
- answering TL questions on the text in the TL;
- answering English questions on the text in English
- ticking true/false boxes next to sentences based on text
- choosing and numbering words to fill gaps in a TL summary of a text (more words provided than gaps):
    (a) same parts of speech, tense, etc
    (b) random words
- writing brief factual TL notes in a table next to a short TL stimulus
- matching two parts of TL sentences to produce summary (more second parts provided than needed);
- choosing the correct answer among TL multiple choice questions (1 correct item, 2 distracters)
- finding TL equivalents to TL words and phrases
- explaining in the TL the meaning of phrases taken from the text
- responding to a TL stimulus (e.g. letter, announcement)
- summarising in English a TL text supported by notes in English
- writing a memo in English having read a business letter, and
- continuing a short TL text (dialogue) by imaginative writing.

Figure 9.5 Activity/question types used in testing listening and reading

equipment, the assessment and recording of progress. All these factors argue for the drawing up of a coherent programme of preparation and training of listening and reading skills.

Learners' difficulties and ways to overcome them

The first stage in developing the receptive skills is to understand the difficulties learners face when confronted with authentic listening and reading material at A/AS level.

REFLECTION
Activity 9.4 Identifying problems with listening and reading
- In your observation or teaching of A/AS level learners, have you noticed particular difficulties manifested during lessons based on listening or reading comprehension activities?
- Consider the physical arrangements as well as the teaching/learning activities.
- How might you set about remedying the situations or problems you have identified?

At the beginning of the A/AS course there can be a sudden leap from what were primarily basic interpersonal and communicative skills (BICS) to cognitive/academic language proficiency (CALP) (see Graham 1997, pp. 18–19; see also Chapters 3 and 7). Moreover, while the language being learned earlier in secondary school was contained, to a large extent, within a limited range of topics and settings, there seem suddenly to be no such restrictions and the whole of the TL is the source of enquiry and exploitation, and the medium for study. It is the teacher's task both to ease this transition and ensure rapid progress so as to increase the confidence of learners to be able to work more independently.

A/AS learners, especially at the beginning of their course, need a lot of support before they embark on what will be essentially an extended series of authentic listening or reading exercises. Of course, there may be specific problems arising out of the quality of the teaching material or the equipment used during lessons. Poor photocopying or poor quality recordings can present unnecessary frustrations. As regards the latter, recordings can easily deteriorate over time, and while teachers may still be able to understand easily what for them have become very familiar texts, learners can find listening to muffled sounds very off-putting, not to say impossibly difficult. Usually, these problems can easily be put right. However, much more demanding are the mental challenges A/AS level learners face when processing audio or reading material.

In the section below, drawn from the research literature, discussions with teachers and personal experience, the identification of the learner deficits, sometimes grouped together by similar problems, is followed rapidly by suggestions for improvement (R = reading; L = listening).

A/AS learners may be:
- daunted by longer texts (R/L), and/or
- prone to losing concentration because of the initial difficulty/speed of delivery of a text (L)

Keep texts short and listening extracts brief in the early stages. It is far better to tackle shorter items, repeating reading or listening several times, for different purposes, rather than presenting longer pieces with constant interruptions. Remember that 'global' understanding can assist comprehension of the details. Don't feel obliged to use the whole of an article. It is better to select a part of it or produce an edited version. One seemingly banal idea can have a positive effect on motivation: enlarging the print size when using photocopied material. This can also provide more space for making notes or giving meanings. In listening activities, give learners a few phrases from the transcript on the board or OHP, in the order in which they occur, as a framework for listening. Use more recordings of songs or poetry in which the pace is slower and there may be repetition.

A/AS learners may be:
- lacking in passive and active vocabulary knowledge (R/L)
- over-concerned with individual words or phrases (R/L), and/or
- weak at identifying 'key words' or 'key phrases' (R/L)

Lack of vocabulary can certainly be a major stumbling-block to fluent reading and listening. What may appear to the teacher as obvious 'key expressions' may be lost to the learner whose limited vocabulary causes stumbling-blocks on every line of text or every few seconds of a listening exercise. Learners have almost to make a leap of faith: from the stage of needing to know the meaning of *everything* before understanding *anything*, to accepting that they do not need to know *everything* before understanding *something*. Providing some of the more unusual vocabulary before seeing or hearing the text can ease the fear of confusion. It is helpful to let learners know that some examinations include occasional vocabulary notes, too. Learners need to come to the realisation, as John Klapper put it neatly (1992, p. 28): '[Meaning] does not depend on particular words; what we remember of what we have read is the meaning attributed to the words, not the actual words themselves.'

A/AS learners may have difficulty:
- identifying redundant ideas or language (R/L), and/or
- distinguishing or recognising individual words or phrases in the stream of speech (L)

Some learners genuinely have difficulty in distinguishing separate parts of sentences in the flow of spoken or written language. It always appears that a speaker of a foreign language pours out language far more quickly than speakers of one's mother tongue. That is why, for example, it is essential to ease learners gently into viewing or listening to broadcast news items since these really are delivered at a far more rapid pace than natural conversation. This is one occasion when judicious use of the pause button can help. Short bursts of speech can be played (4–5 seconds each time) immediately followed by questions in the TL, of course, such as:

- can you pick out any words or phrases?
- what was the last word you heard?
- what connection does it have to what was heard before?

This kind of 'listening training' may seem artificial but it can really help attune the ear to pick out relevant detail and also to pay less attention to superfluous language. In reading texts, there is no substitute for the recognition of essential grammatical markers such as subject, object and verb in order to make sense of compound sentences containing complex ideas.

One exercise that illustrates how much redundancy is contained in normal discourse is to let learners work together on a text or transcription, crossing out what they think is not absolutely necessary to the main ideas the person wishes to express. Learners then compare what is left in their version with that of the teacher's. Figure 9.6 contains an extract from an interview with a French policeman recorded some years ago. It contains little of substance but has a wealth of repetition and redundant language and is, therefore, very suitable for this kind of exercise.

'Pardon Monsieur, est-ce que vous pourriez me décrire un peu votre fonction? C'est une question vaste, je le sais.'

'La fonction, effectivement, la fonction de policier est très, très vaste. Effectivement, nous garantissons, bien sûr, en premier lieu, la sécurité du citoyen. Mais vous savez, chez nous, il existe énormément de spécialités. Pour moi, celle que je connais le mieux, c'est celle que j'ai à l'heure actuelle, c'est la circulation. Bien entendu, dans la circulation aussi il y a des spécialités. Mais enfin, c'est une question très, très vaste qu'on peut développer dans tous les sens. N'importe quoi dans notre métier est plein d'imprévu. On ne sait jamais ce qui va arriver.'

'Parlons d'abord de la circulation.'

'La circulation, alors là, pour Bordeaux, voyez, on tombe très bien là justement. Vous avez énormément de circulation, et il faut, dans la majorité des cas, réguler cette circulation . . .'

Figure 9.6 Redundancy in speech
Source: recorded by Ian Gathercole

When this exercise has been done during teachers' workshops, very little of the text remains! Most of the redundancy in this interview is the result of the speaker's hesitation, repetition and overall inability to express himself adequately. However, some of the phrases he uses can easily be employed by A/AS learners as fillers while they think of answers to difficult questions in speaking tests or, in writing, as link phrases in essays.

REFLECTION
Activity 9.5 Collecting redundant language
Listen again to native speakers of the language you teach and draw up a list of their hesitation or 'thinking-time' strategies. Record them if you can.
Consider also the use of 'filler phrases' in written texts. How might you ensure that your learners:
1   identify 'filler phrases' for what they are: non-essential elements of normal language use, and
2   use them appropriately in their own productive language?

A/AS learners may be:
- too slow in decoding the meaning of a text (R/L)

It is generally recognised that 'the slow 'de-coder' devotes the conscious mind to wrestling with unfamiliar language forms, often leaving little time for higher order skills' (Klapper 1992, p. 27). So the teacher has to present lots of opportunities for identification and familiarisation with grammatical and syntactical markers during the 'Discovery of the Text' phase of exploitation. It is best if this is done inter-actively, i.e. with learners actually 'marking up' a text by underlining or using a highlighter pen. One example in French is to get learners to pick out all the 'temporal markers', generally adverbial expressions or subordinate clauses, in an article, chapter, anecdote or witness account: e.g. *auparavant, à l'heure actuelle, entretemps, plus tard, finalement*. This sort of activity may not be 'communicative' in the strictest sense of the word but it will help learners, in this case, to gain a sense of the chronology of events.

Do not restrict this kind of activity to phrases which signal the sequence of ideas. Help learners identify other categories, for example, words and phrases which:

- introduce examples, clarifications or definitions, e.g. *c'est-à-dire, concrètement, tel que*
- introduce contrasting ideas or comparisons, e.g. *en revanche, par contre, d'autre part*
- introduce emphasis or reinforcement of ideas, e.g. *j'insiste sur le fait que . . . , certes, souligne-t-on*

- introduce recapitulation or summing-up, e.g. *après tout, en fin de compte, une dernière question*

A/AS learners may have problems:
- picking up 'signals' from the context (R/L)

Learners need to be taught what the context clues might be. The following passage was used in 1981 by Branson and Johnson (referred to in Cook 1991, p. 54) to demonstrate the importance of context in reading.

> The procedure is actually quite simple. First you arrange things into different groups depending on their makeup. Of course, one pile may be sufficient depending on how much there is to do. If you have to go somewhere else due to lack of facilities, that is the next step, otherwise you are pretty well set. It is important not to overdo any particular endeavour. That is, it is better to do too few things at once than too many . . .

Without one essential piece of background knowledge – the text is about doing the washing – the whole passage is pretty meaningless, even though the individual words and phrases are not necessarily complicated in themselves. Translate the passage into the language you teach. Prepare three versions: one with just the text, one with the text and a title, e.g. *La lessive* ('The washing'), and one with a small picture of a washing-machine. Then ask the question: *De quoi s'agit-il?* ('What is this text about?') making sure that you ask those first who have *only* the text. Watch their bewildered reactions and those of the others in the class when they observe their surprising confusion. This exercise should lead to interesting discussion of the importance of context.

Context can come from the background knowledge or 'schema' into which the text fits (see Carrell 1984). That is why it is so important to stress the value of checking for clues in titles and subtitles, illustrations, captions, diagrams, data in the form of statistics and other figures. Even the typeface used and lay-out of the text, the background noises or the tone of voice in recordings can provide valuable information. But, mostly, context comes from within the language of the text itself. The trouble is that those clues to meaning which teachers may find self-evident are not always obvious to learners. Text de-construction exercises can be usefully part of the joint discovery of the text. In these exercises, both the overall framework used to convey the ideas (see Barnes and Powell 1996, p. 38–9) *and* the individual parts which make up the paragraphs, the sentences and, in some cases, the separate words are examined, labelled and studied for both their function and meaning.

REFLECTION

Activity 9.6 Text de-construction

1   Select a number of short texts that present coherent, logically-sequenced arguments.

2   Enlarge one of them on the photocopier and make an overhead transparency.

3   Mark up the text with coloured pens to highlight words and phrases which

(a) *in the framework*:
* introduce new ideas
* show the writer's personal opinion
* provide counter-arguments
* give examples or further illustrations
* sum up ideas

(b) *in the detail*:
* link subject and verbs in compound sentences
* link adjectives to nouns
* contain the main ideas
* could be erased without detracting from the overall message

---

A/AS learners may be:
* using a limited range of reading subjects

The past few years have seen an explosion of interest in language-learning strategies. Most research has been concentrated on reading in the context of English as a foreign language. Several lists or taxonomies of language learning skills or strategies have been drawn up (see Graham 1997; O'Malley 1990; Oxford 1989). Steven McDonough lists some of the general categories of skills involved. I have already delved a little deeper into some of the skills listed in Figure 9.7.

Obviously most of these can apply to listening as well. Reading the literature on language learning skills and strategies can help teachers categorise their learners' approaches to using their receptive skills. However, more important is the task of getting learners, themselves, to employ a wider range of strategies and techniques while listening and reading. Firstly they have to know what strategies they *are* using and those which they could use to better effect.

Some of the techniques learners use when reading and listening are intuitive and difficult to define. But by using a 'thinkaloud technique' or by encouraging the use of learner diaries, teachers can share perceptions and insights into what goes on during learners' independent work and therefore extend their awareness of what needs to happen *during* listening and reading activities. Both these research tools

- identification of word meaning
- recognition of grammatical cues
- recognition of print and orthographic cues
- use of contextual information
- use of background knowledge
- discrimination of author's intention
- discrimination of main and supporting arguments
- reconstruction of the argument
- recognition of the type of text

Figure 9.7 Reading skills
Source: McDonough 1995, p. 36

have their merits if applied sparingly early in the course and at intervals later on. They can also be useful methods of annotating and being accountable for revision for specific examination techniques.

REFLECTION
Activity 9.7 Thinkaloud techniques
This activity is best done using a language with which you are less familiar.
1 Select an article from a TL newspaper.
2 As you read the text, talk to yourself about the ways in which you are reading, noting when and why you hesitate, how your eyes travel across the page, what ideas come to you as you read. Record yourself as you do this; playback and analyse what you said. What strategies were you using?
3 Try a similar activity listening to short recorded speech. But make notes this time.
4 Get an A/AS level learner to work as above, prompting where necessary but not intruding. You, the teacher, record and analyse what the learner says. Discuss the results of the exercise together. What other strategies might you recommend?

After discussing the range of strategies learners employ, the class should engage in activities which give opportunities for practice. It will rapidly become apparent how conscious use of more strategies can make the difference between confusion and comprehension. One recent study on strategy use suggests that regrettably, even reasonably competent language learners frequently resort to 'basic strategies of approximation, pre-packaged forms and "wild card" guessing' (Grenfell and Harris 1998, p. 27).

A/AS learners may be:

- worrying too much over the correctness of responses to text and failing, therefore, to check the logic and accuracy of their answers (R/L)

Gary Chambers (1996), writing primarily about listening at pre-GCSE level, reminds us about the importance of removing the notion of 'listening as testing' from the initial encounters with the text. He asks pertinent questions:

> 'Let's find out what you don't understand!' seems to be the general aim. Some teachers, in an effort to be supportive, even pose that very question: 'Tell me what you don't understand.' Why this focus on the negative? Why not focus on what *is* understood and then fill the gaps?
>
> (Chambers 1996, p. 24)

The message here is as applicable in A/AS level teaching as it is in earlier stages of foreign language learning. By first encouraging individual learners to identify parts of the text which look or sound familiar and pooling this knowledge, e.g. by the teacher 'collecting' the words and phrases on the OHP and placing them in the sequence of the original, very soon a skeletal framework of the text can be created. A second reading or listening through can add flesh to the bones and the overall meaning and quite a lot of the detail of the original will have been gathered.

Developing a sense of one's own 'fallibility' and the need to check answers thoroughly is a prerequisite for avoiding unnecessary errors in test situations. Teachers can encourage a collaborative approach to the problem by making learners examine each others' work occasionally. This must obviously be handled sensitively by taking into account the different levels of competence in the class and friendship groupings. Reading one's work aloud or whispering answers to oneself can also sometimes help error recognition, even in English answers!

A/AS learners may be:

- giving the impression of having understood a text but not really understand much at all (R/L), and/or
- misunderstanding the whole because of one or two misinterpretations (R/L)

It is difficult for a learner to feign understanding in *oral* exploitation or testing of a spoken or written text. However, one difficulty for teachers *and* examiners in testing comprehension by means of written TL questions is knowing exactly how much understanding the TL response really conveys. We know from the A/AS grade descriptions that 'copying from the text' is not likely to gain high marks. It is vital, therefore, that questions are asked:

1 requiring both global and detailed or selective understanding
2 in an appropriate order of difficulty, and
3 in such a way as to aid rather than hinder comprehension

Learners may also have problems with the degree of conceptual difficulty or 'world knowledge' required to comprehend and discuss certain topics. Current A/AS level courses place a lot of emphasis on assessing learners' insights into the contemporary society, culture and heritage of the TL countries. British learners, it has to be admitted, are not renown for their political, socio-economic, historical or general cultural awareness!

To gain the highest grades in the A/AS examinations, learners will have to demonstrate sophisticated levels of comprehension and response to text. However, teachers should avoid asking 'higher-order' questions at the beginning of a teaching/learning sequence. The 'easy to ask' question: 'Well, what do you think about that?' comes at the end of the 'difficult to answer' question spectrum. There have been many attempts to define a hierarchy or taxonomy of comprehension levels. Such a framework can assist the teacher or examiner in sequencing questions from simple to complex, from concrete to abstract. Figure 9.8 gives one attempt at distinguishing between the functions of questioning at various levels.

more simple	recognising facts and figures, dealing with literal meaning
↓	recalling, after initial reading/listening, elements/details of the argument, plot or account
↓	identifying, classifying and organising thoughts and using newly acquired language
↓	showing understanding of relationships between parts of the text and inferring meaning
↓	analysing the detail, interpreting figurative language or points of view
↓	evaluating the validity of the arguments and the language used to present them
more complex	demonstrating one's personal sensitivity to and appreciation of an argument, critically evaluating style, register and form

Figure 9.8 Levels of questioning

REFLECTION
Activity 9.8 Formulating questions
Choose a text – spoken or written – and try to produce at least one question
which corresponds to each of the categories in Figure 9.8.
How useful is a taxonomy of question functions when composing compre-
hension questions?

In this review of learner difficulties, I have concentrated deliberately on the early
stages of the A/AS level course. If the learners become aware of the processes
involved in comprehending audio and written text and if they are taught overtly
during this stage the strategies they need for developing their receptive skills, they
will gain confidence and move more easily into successful independent reading and
listening.

Summary

Learning a foreign language has sometimes been compared to learning to drive a
car: one learns a set of rules, one acquires a set of skills and then, after much
practice, the reactions become automatic and fluent. That is obviously far too
simplistic an analogy to describe the complex cognitive processes that are applied,
for example, in reading and listening to a foreign language. While one can drive a
car without necessarily understanding how the engine works, the advanced motor-
ist – and certainly the grand-prix driver – needs to know quite a lot about the
mechanical and technical aspects of the internal combustion engine. Similarly, the
advanced language learner needs to gain information both about the inside workings of text and the cognitive skills required to process meaning.

In this chapter I have shown how the receptive skills have gained in status over
the years, both in classroom practice and in examinations. A/AS level learners will
have most of their exposure to the TL through reading authentic texts and through
listening to pre-recorded material. They will be expected both to react to these
texts and to engage with the new language which, inevitably, they will come across. I
have examined the requirements of the A/AS examinations and have also stressed
the importance of easing the transition into more advanced language study by
carefully sequencing activities and by moving from simple to complex, from
concrete to abstract, in one's questioning. In the words of one researcher: '[listen-
ers] and readers must be good interpreters and good decoders of texts' (Graham
1997, p. 52).

Hence the need to inform learners about the wide range of strategies that can be
employed in developing one's receptive skills. Equally important is the need to
teach such strategies overtly in the context of a coherent programme of class-based
reading and listening. As learners become more secure in their comprehension
skills, they will be able to enjoy more readily, and be more successful in carrying

out, independent reading and listening tasks. This must be the main goal because, after all, they will be alone in their examination and, hopefully, they will continue to read and listen independently to the TL long after the examination course has finished.

References

Association of Assistant Masters in Secondary Schools (1929) *Memorandum on the Teaching of Modern Languages*. London: University of London Press.

Barnes, A. and Powell, B. (1996) *Developing Advanced Reading Skills*. Cheltenham: Mary Glasgow Publications.

Carrell, P. (1984) 'Schema theory and ESL reading: classroom implications and applications.' In *Modern Language Journal* 68, 4, pp. 332–43.

Chambers, G. (1996) 'Listening. How? Why?' In *Language Learning Journal* 14. Rugby: Association for Language Learning, pp. 23–7.

Clark, D. (1998) 'Right steps on the ladder to learning'. In *Times Higher Educational Supplement*, 5 May.

Cook, V. (1991) *Second Language Learning and Teaching*. London: Edward Arnold.

DfE/Welsh Office (1995) *Modern Foreign Languages in the National Curriculum*. London.

EDEXCEL (1998) *London Examinations GCE French AS/A Level Pilot Syllabus*. London.

Eskey, D. (1988) 'Holding in the bottom: an interactive approach to the language problems of second language readers'. In Carrell, P., Devine, J. and Eskey, D. (eds) *Interactive Approaches to Second Language Reading*. Cambridge: Cambridge University Press, pp. 93–100.

French 16–19 Study Group (1981) *French 16–19: A New Perspective*. London: Hodder and Stoughton.

Graham, S. (1997) *Effective Language Learning*. Clevedon: Multilingual Matters.

Grenfell, M. and Harris, V. (1998) 'Learner strategies and the advanced learner: problems and processes'. In *Language Learning Journal* 17. Rugby: Association for Language Learning, pp. 23–8.

Hawkins, E. (1981) *Modern Languages in the Curriculum*. Cambridge: Cambridge University Press.

Hilton, J. (1974) *Language Teaching: A Systems Approach*. London: Methuen.

Klapper, J. (1992) 'Reading in a foreign language: theoretical issues'. In *Language Learning Journal* 5. Rugby: Association for Language Learning, pp. 27–30.

McDonough, S. (1995) *Strategy and Skill in Learning a Foreign Language*. London: Edward Arnold.

O'Malley, J. (1990) *Learning Strategies in Second Language Acquisition*. Cambridge: Cambridge University Press.

Oxford, R. (1989) *Language Learning Strategies: What Every Teacher Should Know*. New York: Newbury House/Harper and Row.

Pickering, R. (1992) *Planning and Resourcing A level French*. London: CILT.

QCA, ACCAC and CCEA (1999) *Subject Criteria for Modern Foreign Languages: Advanced Subsidiary and Advanced Level Specifications*. London.

Rees, P. (1995) 'Reading in French from GCSE to A level: the learner perspective'. In Grenfell, M. (ed) *Reflections on Reading*, London: CILT, pp. 27–58.

Steil, L., Banker, L. and Watson, K. (1983) *Effective Listening: Key to Your Success*. London: Addison-Wesley.

Chapter 10

Developing productive language skills – speaking and writing

Kit Field

Introduction

A discussion of the development of speaking and writing at Advanced (A)/ Advanced Subsidiary (AS) level invariably needs to be multi-dimensional. Firstly, speaking and writing can be treated as discrete skills, assessed in their own right. However, productive language skills are also integrated with so called 'receptive' skills (listening and reading). It is normally through the *use* of the target language (TL), i.e. through speaking and writing, that listening and reading comprehension is demonstrated. Also, language skills are integrated at the assessment stage. Secondly, the new Subject Criteria for A/AS Level Modern Foreign Languages (see QCA *et al.* 1999) require a percentage of synoptic assessment, i.e. elements of the courses are assessed in a way that prevents the learner from putting to one side any aspects to be covered through course work only. All four foreign language skills must, therefore, be developed and assessed throughout the course. It is this interrelationship with listening and reading that makes the study of speaking and writing so complex.

Evidently, the assessment of speaking and writing must relate to the particular purposes of the activities being used. Criteria and tasks for measuring comprehension through responses in the TL (see Activity 10.1) inevitably differ in emphasis to those designed to appraise standards in speaking and writing as discrete skills. To further complicate the issue, neither the terminology nor the emphasis used by Awarding Bodies is consistent. Aspects such as communication, pronunciation, accuracy, fluency, range (i.e. versatility of the speaker), appropriacy of register, spontaneity of TL use, quality of language or content (including cultural knowledge and awareness), etc. are afforded different weightings by Awarding Bodies. This is one of the reasons why modern foreign languages (mfl) teachers need to select subject specifications (formerly syllabuses) very carefully. For criteria for choosing subject specifications see Chapter 2.

No teaching programme should separate speaking and writing from listening and reading. On the other hand, teachers do need to monitor learners' progress within each skill separately as part of effective formative and diagnostic assessment.

REFLECTION
Activity 10.1 Matching speaking activities to assessment criteria
The grid below represents the assessment criteria for A/AS level speaking.
The categories of criteria are broken down. Insert into the final column
activity types which allow learners to develop appropriate skills. Consult an
experienced colleague and coursebooks to complete this activity.

Category	*Breakdown*	*Activities*
communication	transfer of information	
	transmission of meaning	
	expression of opinions	
pronunciation	accuracy of pronunciation	
	intonation	
	pace	
	expression of mood	
accuracy	grammar	
	syntax	
	register	
range	grammar (e.g. variety of tenses)	
	appropriate use of vocabulary and idiom	
	register (to suit different audiences)	
	topics	
quality of language	fluency	
	independence	
	use of idiom	

Of course, mfl teachers should not teach only to the examination criteria and skill
development should not be entirely assessment-driven. However, assessment criteria will have to be borne in mind and examination tasks be practised throughout

the course in order to maximise the learners' chances of achieving to the best of their abilities in the examination.

For these reasons, the teacher needs to provide a structure and framework to support a coherent process for learning and skill development.

Objectives

By the end of this chapter you should:

- be aware of the expectations of speaking and writing at A/AS level
- be able to discern what makes speaking and writing activities easy or difficult
- recognise the place of speaking and writing activity types in a process of skill development
- be able to link activity types to categories of assessment criteria, and
- understand the need for a process of productive skill development

Productive foreign language skills

Prior to 1988, A level mfl examinations allocated only 10–15 per cent of the total marks available to speaking and, not surprisingly, teachers paid little attention to the development of oral skills. Thorogood and King (see 1991, p. 19) discuss a process-based approach in which oral work is essentially the means by which units of work are introduced. This involves brainstorming, question-and-answer sessions to exploit a text and, occasionally, information-gap activities. The risk of such an approach is that little speaking takes place later in a unit, preventing the development of higher-level skills. Writing, on the other hand, was often introduced later in a unit of work and many learners were expected to produce essays on difficult topics with little preparatory work.

There is no doubt that speaking and writing serve different purposes. Linda Hantrais identifies these by distinguishing the purposes of speaking (see 1989, p. 103) pointing out that through speaking, language users are intending to make an immediate impact. Strategies and techniques include the use of rhetorical questions, intonation and repetition of key points. In contrast to writing, speaking, she notes, is characterised by simplified language forms and the use of first- and second-person verb forms. This is not an argument, though, to cover speaking first and writing later. Hantrais (see 1989, p. 217) could be said to miss the point when noting that professional uses of writing are restricted to drafting and translating documents. For a learner, the chief purpose of writing is to record and practise the expression of linguistic forms, personal ideas and essential cultural details. Hantrais distinguishes different forms of essay writing – descriptive, analytical and argumentative – which can be viewed as the means of rehearsing future interaction (see Hantrais 1989, p. 92).

REFLECTION
Activity 10.2 Categories of essay titles
Below are some essay titles based on A/AS level Specimen (Question) Papers and Mark(ing) Schemes.
Classify the titles according to Hantrais's categories of 'descriptive, analytical and argumentative'.

- *Vous êtes kinésithépeute: Décrivez les exercices que vous conseillez, et expliquez pourquoi vous les conseillez.*
- *Pressefreiheit? Ja, aber in Grenzen. Was meinen Sie?*
- *L'enseignement ou la santé – lequel devrait recevoir la plus grande part du budget national?*
- *Comment expliquez-vous le fait que de plus en plus de couples vivent ensemble sans se marier?*
- *Tiere sollten doch auch Rechte haben.*
- *Un voyage dans l'espace.*
- *'La télévision fait plus de mal que de bien' Partagez-vous ce point de vue?*
- *Mitten in der Nacht läutet bei Ihnen das Telefon. Sie nehmen den Hörer ab. Eine Frauenstimme sagt: 'Bitte, Sie müssen mir unbedingt helfen.' Erzählen Sie weiter.*

Because of the increasing difficulty at A/AS level compared with GCSE, mfl teachers should develop a process-based approach. John Hurman asserts that post GCSE learners are more relaxed and confident and less inhibited using the TL than their O level predecessors and, therefore, more susceptible to learning (see 1992, p. 9). Beyond the pragmatic need to cover the examination requirements, the progressive development of speaking and writing skills in mfl learning leads to the development of transferable skills. Anthony Peck (see 1988b, pp. 146–7) explains that the appeal of advanced level foreign language speakers to employers is that they display good social and interpersonal skills, are able to learn about different cultures and are able to recognise and deploy different modes of expression. Writing in a foreign language requires powers of organisation and precision and an ability to adopt a range of registers – all of which are excellent preparation for professional and adult life. Such qualities must be enshrined in the objectives of a programme of study. One aim for the mfl teacher must be to broaden the range of holistic life skills, not just simply to meet the narrow requirements of an examination syllabus.

Whilst teachers tend not to be short of ideas for classroom activities, it is crucial that activity types are pertinent to course objectives and assessment criteria (see Activity 10.1). At the same time, teachers must be aware of the need to challenge learners without over-stretching them. A well-thought-out process-based approach takes all of this into account. It is important to build up competence step by step, to relate activities to explicit purposes as well as to relate activities to assessment criteria.

Communication

Communication is a 'buzz' word in the world of mfl. For learners of different levels of proficiency it means different things. Communication is, in essence, the conveyance of meaning. For beginners it involves the transmission of facts and information. At advanced level it involves the expression of ideas and a response to the ideas of others. Language development enhances the potential for communication with language being a means to an end, not an end in itself.

Speaking

Anthony Peck articulates clearly that effective communication is a goal for mfl teachers and learners:

> [the] ultimate aim of foreign language teaching and learning is the communication of messages to speakers of the foreign language, which satisfy the speakers' intentions, and which the listener cannot predict.
>
> (Peck 1988a, p. 74)

Contained within this assertion are many variables. Clearly, the level of meaning being conveyed and the level of predictability serve to render a communicative act more or less complex. The complexity is also related to the role of the listener. Teachers need to consider, therefore, whether they, themselves, are always the best audience.

Role plays are a common activity; they require the speaker to convey information and/or express ideas. Information-gap activities provide stimulation and a greater degree of involvement for the listener. If the teacher plays the role of listener, the notion of communication can be nullified as the speaker is aware that the teacher is likely to know the answers.

Communicating factual details to a peer through speaking or writing, as a follow-up to reading and listening, is effective for many reasons. It is a means of reinforcing and extending a learner's knowledge base. The content of the conversation can act as an effective pre-listening/reading exercise for the partner. Learners can be a resource for one another, e.g. one can learn from a presentation given by another. The ready availability of up-to-date news bulletins through satellite television and the internet allows learners to research and provide each other with relevant cultural and socio-political details (see also Chapter 14).

Mfl teachers, therefore, need to take into account the content of messages to be communicated as well as with whom learners (should) communicate.

Writing

In writing, as a means of communication, there is an apparent conflict between conveying the essence of a message and the accuracy of the language used. Hurman comments (1992, p. 9) that '[it] would . . . be counter-productive to sacrifice the desire to put a point of view, for the correctness of its expression.' Other commentators hold differing points of view stressing the importance of accuracy. The stage of learning is an important consideration when judging accuracy (see below).

Successful communication can be motivating. The more realistic and authentic a task is, the easier it is to perform. Authenticity of purpose is an aspect to be considered when developing language learning. Vivian Zamel believes (see 1987, p. 705) that the purposes of writing should transcend the production of a script merely for the purpose of teacher evaluation. Consequently, authentic texts can act as more effective stimuli than those contrived purposefully for teaching and learning activities. For a discussion of authentic material see Chapter 14.

REFLECTION
Activity 10.3 Matching writing activities to professional use
The following are typical writing activities at A/AS level. Alongside each, indicate a purpose for the task which would serve to motivate learners. Discuss this task in the TL with learners.

Activity	Purpose
translation	
note taking	
scripting	
creative writing	
discursive essays	
comprehension questions	
descriptions	
narration	
letter writing (formal)	
letter writing (informal)	

Evidently, at lower levels the purpose of writing is often contained within the task of letter writing, which can gain a far more realistic dimension when learners research topics for themselves by making contact with institutions that can provide the information needed, for instance by letter or e-mail.

Note-taking skills are also an essential part of independent study in that the learner is in fact attempting to communicate with him or herself. This communication with oneself through writing confirms R. Rodrigues's view (see 1985, p. 25) that the writer must believe in what he or she writes and that the structure will emerge from these beliefs and values.

In any classroom, however, the purpose of activities is invariably artificial and situations are inevitably contrived. Improvisation and simulation enable learners to escape the confines of their own beliefs and to learn how to communicate the views of others. This removal from the concrete and personal is an important step towards operating in the abstract. Clearly, an engagement with literature offers opportunities here, as Peck suggests (see 1988a, p. 155).

In the novel L'Etranger by Albert Camus, Meursault does not behave in an expected way. Learners are compelled by the activity in Figure 10.1 to justify his actions by referring to known facts and events. In this way, the communication of ideas, based on facts as they are perceived, represents a shift to abstract thought and expression. The increase in terms of difficulty is obvious and represents a move towards the levels expected at A/AS level. For working with literature see Chapter 11.

Teachers and learners need to develop an understanding of what makes activities/tasks easy or difficult. A common-sense approach in structuring the learning process is to proceed from easier to more difficult activities/tasks. Figure 10.2 shows the component parts of developing communication skills.

Pronunciation

David Nunan comments (see 1991, p. 104) that able learners have little difficulty identifying faults in pronunciation, but fears that a communicative approach does

Objectives:	• to appreciate Meursault's point of view regarding the death of his mother
	• to present Meursault's view point in the TL, drawing on the language forms contained in *L'Etranger*
Activity:	With a partner, prepare a dialogue between Meursault and his (imaginary) father, who criticises his son's attitude and behaviour at the funeral
Organisation:	• weaker learners to prepare in pairs (father and son)
	• more able learners to prepare in groups (all the fathers, separate from all the sons)

Figure 10.1 Using literature to develop writing skills

The following continua illustrate aspects of communication which determine whether a communicative act is easy or difficult to perform.

EASY	AUDIENCE	DIFFICULT
learner	↔	teacher
passive	↔	active
	CONTENT	
factual	↔	ideas
concrete	↔	abstract
	PURPOSE	
communication	↔	accuracy
authentic	↔	simulation

Figure 10.2 The component parts of the development of effective communication

not lend itself to focused attention on the improvement of pronunciation. Certainly, group repetition and chanting is less appealing to older learners. Earl Stevick (see 1982, p. 13) recognises advanced level study to be demanding in all senses and that pronunciation practice can be seen as a relief from the continuous progression through grammar and course content.

Good pronunciation requires effective listening skills and, conversely, close attention to the sound of words is effective practice of listening for detail (see Nunan 1991, p. 109). Reciting texts, poems and songs from memory relieves the learner of the need to concentrate on grammatical accuracy. The study of rhythm supports the process of improvement in pronunciation.

Repetition and recital should not be divorced from meaning. Learners can be required to repeat dialogues and text and can be asked to change the tempo, tone of voice, volume and even mood of the speaker. Such activities also allow for the practice of intonation and stress as well as pronunciation.

REFLECTION
Activity 10.4 Developing pronunciation and intonation
Scan a text to be presented to learners. Extract three or four key phrases. Ask learners to read the phrases aloud in a way that communicates different feelings and emotions.

You, as the teacher, have to guess the emotions expressed. Tape the performances and compare them to a native speaker's efforts (e.g. with the Foreign Language Assistant).

Reading aloud, too, serves a useful purpose, both for speakers and listeners. To hear oneself on tape can be painful at first, but private listening does allow the individual to hone pronunciation skills. Once again, the activity must not be detached from other elements of the course. A concentration on presentation skills through varied forms of repetition can serve to drill and reinforce by content and language structures.

REFLECTION

Activity 10.5 Identifying effective strategies for the development of pronunciation skills

Survey a group of learners asking them to rank the following 'pronunciation activities' in terms of popularity. Add any other relevant activities to the list.

- group chanting
- private repetition
- reading with a cassette playing and keeping pace
- reading aloud
- singing
- taping oneself, or
- reciting texts/poems from memory

Accuracy

More than with any other aspect of language learning and use, the teacher needs to be very sensitive to how much he or she should focus on accuracy at different stages of learning.

Speaking

In general terms, speaking involves the use of simplified language forms and often inaccuracy is only penalised if it renders communication ambiguous or unintelligible. Nevertheless, linguistic accuracy must remain the goal at A/AS level. The teacher's dilemma is to decide when to address the issue. Evelyn Hatch argues (1978, p. 104): '[one] learns how to do conversation, one learns how to interact verbally, and out of this interaction syntactic structures are developed'. The argument is that too great a focus on accuracy too early in the learning process inhibits oral work. Learners are only too aware that teachers notice mistakes, whereas their peers may miss them, or not be so concerned. Regular conversation with peers, therefore, can increase confidence, fluency and independence. The presentation, for example, of book reviews, news items and factual information do need to be interactive. By placing learners in role, they are able to present to peers from the stand point of another. In this way the fear of making errors and of being teased for holding certain opinions are both allayed.

Writing

Writing is the principal means by which accuracy is assessed. Nunan is adamant that teachers must consider 'output' as well as 'input' (see 1991, p. 50). He argues that learners, at any point in time, must be pushed to the limit of their capabilities in order to reinforce what they already know. Written drill exercises must be in context and offer the learner the opportunity to incorporate ever more complicated syntactic structures to their repertoire. In this way, grammar is presented as an aid to communication, rather than as a constraint. Adopting a generative model for grammar teaching, one where new language structures are presented as a means of increasing the language user's powers of expression, enables the learner to develop beyond the use of phrases learnt off by heart. Indeed, rote learning can be the first step in a process for developing accuracy. Learners should, of course, proceed to generating sentences to express ideas of their own. The jump from repetition to free use is enormous and supported substitution exercises serve to bridge this gap.

To encourage accuracy, the teacher also needs to encourage careful checking. Over-correction at an early stage can be disheartening and de-motivating. Consequently, the teacher is not always the best person to mark work. Peers are able to judge if inaccuracy hinders effective communication. The next step is to identify errors and the final stage is to rectify the errors. For such a process, learners must be taught how to check for errors: '[it] is useful to get into the habit of selectively checking, for example, all the verbs, adverbial phrases or adjectives used in a paragraph' (Hantrais 1989, p. 68). (See also Figure 3.5 and Chapters 6 and 13.)

Range

Speaking

To increase range, the teacher has to encourage learners to consider issues from a different angle. This removal of 'the self' from the core of language use is to shift the focus of study towards the abstract. Placing the learner in role to present an argument from a different perspective does introduce alternative view points and, thereby, a need for different language forms. The continuation of a plot by stopping a video and the use of the 'freeze frame' technique to describe activities surrounding the central plot, both oblige the speaker to extend the focus beyond the obvious. The use of literature to stimulate unscripted role plays and improvised drama allows for the personalisation of language forms. The process of developing 'range' concerns firstly the personalisation of language forms and secondly the appreciation that others undergo a similar process. The quality of classroom discussions is dependent, therefore, on careful planning and structuring. Learners need to make use of the language contained within a stimulus, but then learn, through interaction, to use and manipulate language used by others.

Figure 10.3 demonstrates how exposure to different styles of language promotes the development of varying styles and registers of language.

Writing

Increasing the range of vocabulary, grammatical structures and registers available to learners in terms of writing is inevitably linked to reading. Exposure to a full range of text types linked to a single theme is essential. The teacher needs, firstly, to sequence the presentation of texts and, secondly, to develop a sequence of active reading strategies which increase in difficulty. Activities should follow a process: from emulating a text through to the manipulation of texts in order to express personal responses.

Taking notes in the style of a particular text reinforces both the content and register. Substitution exercises facilitate the reproduction of the text in the original style of writing.

However, imaginative and creative tasks release the learner from the constraints of emulating the style and content of the original text, but demand that the learner generates personalised language forms. Tasks contained in Activity 10.6 show that learners can be required to re-write texts in different ways. This procedure demands that the relationship of the learner with any text is challenged and that he or she is obliged to interact with, rather than simply accept the text. This interaction is the first step towards justification, classification and explanation.

Objectives:	• to reinforce facts surrounding a current affairs issue; and • to encourage learners to broaden the range of language to be used.
Activities:	Half the group watches a news bulletin covering a controversial event. They should prepare an oral presentation summarising the key issues.
	Half the group reads a newspaper article covering the same event. They also prepare an oral presentation summarising the key issues.
	The whole group comes together and subgroups give their presentations.
	Following the presentations, the teacher, through question and answer, identifies the key issues.

Figure 10.3 Increasing learners' range

REFLECTION

Activity 10.6 Developing range through register

The following writing tasks are intended to improve learners' range. All are related to the theme of racism. Place the tasks in an order of difficulty. Consider what makes the tasks more or less difficult.

- Write a letter, in the role of an immigrant to her family at home, describing conditions.
- Write a short poem depicting social injustice.
- Write a list of problems faced by an immigrant.
- Write a letter offering advice to a younger relative planning to emigrate.
- Write a newspaper report, accounting for an act of racism.
- Produce a leaflet decrying racism.
- Write an account of how immigrants are harshly treated by the press.

Nunan (see 1991, p. 48) comments that an increase in the level of difficulty relates to the degree of abstraction and the dynamic nature of the relationship between the learner and a text. It is by changing a learner's perspective that increased difficulty can be achieved. Accuracy can be honed as writers maintain a static relationship with the course content. 'Range' increases as the relationship becomes dynamic.

Quality of language

To improve the quality of language, teachers and learners need to focus on fluency, independence and spontaneous use of the TL.

Speaking

It is through rehearsal that existing knowledge and skills are perfected. Learners need to draw on knowledge and skills acquired in one topic area to improve performance in another. Short unprepared presentations demand a quality of language beyond the predictable questions asked of learners. Closed questions tend to demand answers which are right or wrong. Questions which challenge learners' opinions are altogether more demanding. Coping with the unpredictable is to 'put the learner on the spot' and to demand a level of fluency beyond that of normal classroom interaction: 'interaction can be placed on a continuum from relatively predictable to relatively unpredictable' (Nunan 1991, p. 42).

The degree of predictability is, in fact, dependent upon the shared expectations of speaker and listener (see Bygate 1987, p. 8). Bygate claims that speech performs one of two functions: information transfer or interaction. Interaction itself can be divided into two distinct levels: those of transaction and negotiation. Transactional interchanges are predictable – the speaker is aware of the listeners' likely response in advance and, therefore, less likely to lose confidence and motivation. More difficult to cope with is the disagreement between speaker and listener, when language is required for the two to reach a compromise. This is not necessarily to shift to abstract use of language. Indeed, Nunan asserts (see 1991, p. 39) that learners need to recognise the potential uses of language prior to engaging in learning activities.

Writing

In written work, the learner has time to reflect and plan. It is more the selection of an appropriate style and register, the range of vocabulary, accuracy and use of idiom which determines the quality of language and the level of difficulty of a writing task.

Sequencing and structuring units of work

The component parts of the development of productive skills are interwoven and interrelated. A structured process model must take all the factors into account, able to demonstrate how the process contributes to the attainment of assessment criteria and sequenced in a way that the learner is constantly challenged yet is not in danger of losing confidence and motivation.

A regular theme underpinning the arguments in this chapter is that no single language skill develops in isolation from another. Consequently, speaking, reading, listening and writing should not be taught separately. To present a process for the development of oral skills, is not to suggest that the remaining skills are neglected for a period of time. It is for the teacher to develop lesson, unit and long-term plans to enable skills to be practised and developed regularly and continuously (see Activity 10.7).

REFLECTION
Activity 10.7 Structuring teaching and learning
Below are skills which need to be developed at A/AS level. How would you sequence them? Consult an experienced colleague.

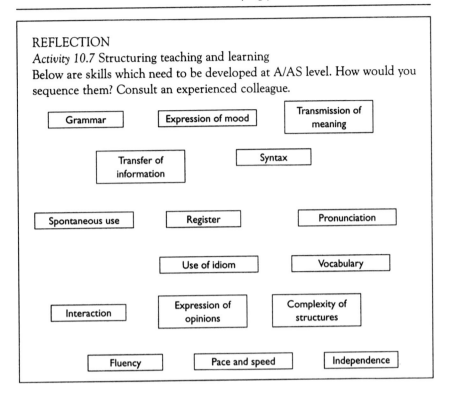

Activity 10.7 is intended to help you structure a unit of work by providing tasks and activities appropriate to the stage of learning. To jump from one activity to the next without giving due consideration to a process of learning is to run the risk of 'losing' the learners.

Despite the obvious integration of skills, what follows is an analysis of how the skills of speaking and writing can be developed. Through careful planning, these will develop hand in hand.

Sequencing and structuring speaking activities

Figure 10.4 represents diagrammatically a process for developing speaking. The 'satellites' represent activity types which suit learners at appropriate phases of development.

These activities are illustrative; it is the principles underpinning the structure of each activity which justify their use.

Presenting a unit

The introduction and presentation of a unit of work has traditionally involved a lot of oral work.

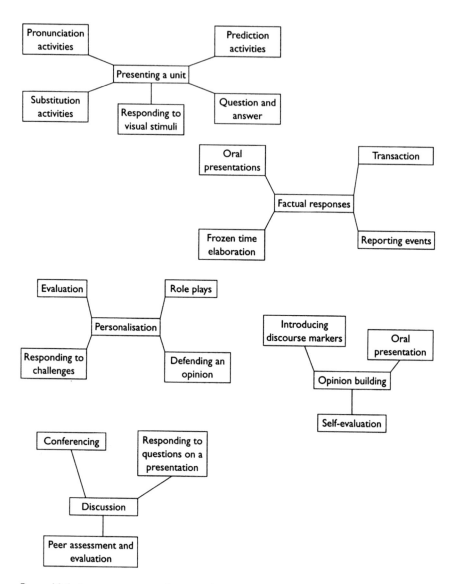

Figure 10.4 A process approach to speaking

First and foremost the teacher will want to activate existing relevant knowledge and linguistic competence. Brainstorming and question and answer (closed questions) provide such an opportunity. Nunan (see 1991, p. 112) commends the reading aloud of a text, enabling a focus on pronunciation whilst the actual content of a text is absorbed, almost as a by-product. This concentration on pronunciation can extend to interaction.

The use of visual aids (posters, photographs, flashcards and video clips) are all useful stimuli for oral work at this stage. The presentation of an image is designed to stimulate a 'stream of consciousness'. As the teacher notes learners' comments, each learner's contribution adds to the range of others. Gradually uncovering a provocative image and encouraging learners to predict the scene depicted is also an effective way to introduce a topic through oral work and simultaneously to assist the development of range.

The presentation of written texts is a very commonly used method of introducing a topic. The written text can be used to develop oral skills. Peck recommends the repetition by learners of key phrases as an effective precursor to substitution and conversion exercises (see 1988a, p. 115). Keith Johnson (see 1989, p. 106) also sees repetition to oneself as a way to drill important phrases. In this way, learners can build up a bank of useful structures and discourse markers (see below) which contribute to joining language and spontaneous use of the TL.

The mention of drills, repetition and habit-forming exercises evoke memories of the rote learning techniques associated with audio-lingual techniques. Johnson (see 1989, p. 106) does not reject repetition methods, but does heed warnings from the past. He recommends that:

- repetition must be of phrases which are understood and in context from the outset
- repetition should begin slowly and subsequently accelerate, and
- the complexity of phrases should not be reduced to short utterances which carry no meaning in isolation

It should also be noted that repetition is recommended as one activity type which leads on to others. This simplified set of rules is not included here so much for the teacher, but more for the benefit of the learner. Effective repetition as a means of introducing topics can be practised outside the classroom.

Factual responses

The relaying of facts through verbal communication is, in fact, transaction. Undoubtedly, the conveyance of essential information is most meaningful when the listener is not already aware of the details being communicated. Reporting events and narrating stories enable the teacher and learners to focus on linguistic accuracy. Early in a unit, the listener fulfils a static role – he or she does not react to what is said, but acts simply as a recipient of facts and information – in that his or her response tends not to provoke further questions demanding clarification and explanation.

Narration activities are an excellent preparation for examination-type presentations. Nunan sees the narrative as 'orientation, complication and resolution' (see

1991, p. 44). Evidently, the speaker should introduce a topic, locate events chronologically and/or thematically and present some form of logical conclusion. As a means of following up independent reading and/or listening, narration permits the active use of language forms encountered. Narration should not be scripted; instead visual prompts could be used. Johnson proposes 'frozen time elaboration' (see 1989, p. 156), when a learner narrates a sequence of images. The video-player is useful here. As the teacher 'freezes' the picture/frame, the narrator is expected to diversify his or her account by providing spontaneous descriptions of scenes contained within the frame. The speaker is not expected to relay ideas and opinions, but to provide factually accurate descriptions. As Peck notes (see 1988a, p. 72), narration is the conveyance of information with a string of sentences. The activity clearly promotes fluency, independence and spontaneity.

The benefits to the listener are obvious. He or she is provided with interesting and useful details related to a topic under scrutiny. News bulletins, cultural events, historical detail can all be reported by learners as a means of developing their narrative skills.

Personalisation

Teenage learners should not be expected to express abstract ideas and opinions without having developed a factual base upon which their ideas will be founded. It is at the 'presentation' and 'factual response' stages that relevant and appropriate information is 'inputted'. Personalisation is the first step from the concrete to the abstract. As the title suggests, the shift represents a move away from being 'in role' to 'speaking for yourself'. Peck notes the need for one-to-one conversations (see 1988b, p. 147). Fluency requires a degree of accuracy (see Johnson 1989, p. 147), particularly as speakers will need to manipulate language to express their own ideas. The listener, therefore, needs to be an authority, yet at the same time sympathetic. The teacher is clearly the best audience in this context.

My recommendation is to organise a schedule of tutorials within lesson time. Other members of the group need to be meaningfully occupied whilst individual tutorials are carried out, of course (see Activity 10.8).

REFLECTION
Activity 10.8 Independent learning in the classroom
Discuss with an experienced colleague activity types which can meaningfully occupy learners while you conduct tutorials. You will need to explain the intended structure for tutorials with individuals to your learners.

The focus for the teacher and learners during tutorials should be range, fluency and accuracy. Johnson (see 1989, p. 148) recommends a process by which teacher and learner should concentrate firstly on range, then on range and

Focus	The teacher should take into consideration . . .
Range	• selection of content/text
	• asking closed questions
Range + Fluency	• challenging learners' viewpoints
	• introducing unpredictability
Range + Fluency + Accuracy	• open questions
	• requiring learners to manipulate tenses

Figure 10.5 Structuring tutorial work

fluency, and finally on range, fluency and accuracy. Figure 10.5 is an adaptation of this recommended process and shows how the teacher needs to take relevant issues into consideration.

The selection of content at the 'range' stage is the responsibility of the teacher. The learner must be familiar with the factual content of the discussion and comfortable with appropriate language forms. The discussion can centre around the learner presenting his or her learner diary (see Chapter 3) and the teacher should ask more demanding evaluative questions. In this way the learner is required to put forward and sustain a point of view.

Range and fluency are encouraged by the teacher asking ever more demanding questions. This corresponds to Barry Jones's recommendation that the teacher challenges the views expressed by the speaker (see 1988, p. 83). The teacher should push the learner to defend his or her point of view. In this way, the conversation replicates a formal, social discussion, when participants do not necessarily agree. The teacher introduces an element of unpredictability by posing questions of the 'what if . . .' type.

Careful and focused questions are the means by which accuracy can be added to the sequence. Teachers should pose very open-ended questions which require the learner to manipulate simple language forms, e.g. changing the tense.

REFLECTION
Activity 10.9 Question-and-answer work
Observe an experienced colleague. Note down every question he or she asks. Afterwards, place the questions into categories:
• closed (a question which demands an answer which is right or wrong, e.g. 'How many . . . ?')
• open (a question which demands an explanation, justification of clarification, e.g. 'Why ?')
• challenging (disagreeing with and/or provoking the learner, e.g. 'You don't mean to say ?')
• requiring manipulation of language forms (through requiring the learner to reform known language, e.g. 'What if ?')
What are the features of particular types of questions?

The one-to-one format of tutorials should be highly structured and not an open discussion. The teacher plays the role of a guide and leader driving the learner towards greater independent language use, not that of an interlocutor of equal status to the learner.

Opinion building

The role of the teacher in the 'personalisation' phase is to encourage the learner to reflect and question beliefs and to take on board what Peck calls 'cultural differences' (see 1988b, p. 147). 'Opinion building' in the form of oral presentations serves the purpose of building competence in independence and fluency. Again, oral presentations should not be scripted, but the learner should be able to draw on visual and verbal prompts. Hantrais notes that able orators draw on particular strategies and techniques: repetition and rephrasing of key points, anecdotes and examples, reference to sources of information and 'verbal signposting' (see 1989, p. 78). These 'verbal signposts' correspond to what Johnson refers to as 'discourse markers' (see 1989, p. 145). The insertion of key phrases at appropriate moments focuses the listener's attention. Peer learners make an ideal audience for presentations, but teachers, too, have a role to play. Peers provide a response and teachers can assess as an observer. The effectiveness of discourse markers can be evaluated and learners may adapt their delivery for future reference.

Discussion

In authentic situations, listeners inevitably demand further clarification through discussion. Peer-group discussions, chaired by the teacher, provide the speaker with the opportunity to expand on the content of a presentation, thereby practising independence, fluency and spontaneity. An active response from an informed audience also leads to the speaker having to deploy more complex language forms. As listeners challenge and the speaker justifies and clarifies, the activity develops into a two-way information-gap activity. This means that both speaker and listener learn from the discussion. The degree of unpredictability also increases as the interactions are not scripted, nor rehearsed.

Indeed, the discussion itself assists with the planning and drafting of essays based on the content of the original presentation. Nunan refers to this type of discussion activity as 'conferencing' (see 1991, p. 87). It is important to stress to teachers and learners that the process is collaborative. Consequently, it is useful to nominate a scribe, who notes the essential points made in the discussion. The notes can then be used to stimulate the production of an essay plan.

Sequencing and structuring writing activities

In sequencing writing activities teachers need to take the difficulty factor into account. It is clear that the assessment criteria demand both a complexity of language through the use of structure and idiom and general accuracy. Not only is it important how a text is written, but the content is important, too. The shift from the concrete to the abstract is both a medium- and long-term issue. Learners need to absorb and retain facts, information and cultural details in order to structure and support arguments and points of view. Different tasks require different levels of support, but it is generally agreed that free expression without the use of verbal and visual prompts is the most difficult. Consequently, a process of developing writing skills also contains the need to develop independence. Such a process is represented by Figure 10.6 and discussed below.

Introducing texts

Sections on the development of receptive skills make reference to pre-reading and pre-listening activities. It is at the earliest stage that writing should be integrated with other skill areas. Brainstorming involves the writing down of key vocabulary and phrases. Prediction activities concern the production of texts from clues as a means of introducing the likely ideas contained within a text to be presented. Johnson refers to this practice as 'flashing headlines' (see 1989, p. 149); clearly, the use of images as opposed to text serves the same purpose.

Language should be kept simple and teachers should insist on accuracy. The goal, at this stage, is not to elicit essays, but lists of simplified sentences which summarise a sequence of events.

The activity can be supported for less able learners. Unjumbling texts and rewriting a sequence of events in order with crucial structures (e.g. verbs, endings, adjectives or conjunctions) missing can serve the same purpose. Mixing and matching halves of sentences to produce a meaningful plot, but requiring some semantic and grammatical analysis will also enable learners to familiarise themselves with the content and also drill basic language structure.

Responding to texts

Structured comprehension questions requiring written responses have always fitted into the traditional textbook learning process. Evidently, there is a sequence of activities leading up to the answering of open questions. Nunan presents

      Introducing texts
   ↓ **Responding to texts**
   ↓ Note taking
   ↓ Planning
   ↓ Drafting
     Redrafting

Figure 10.6 A process for developing writing skills

substitution exercises as a precursor to the answering of comprehension questions (see 1991, p. 50). Rewriting sections of the text substituting phrases and words assists the development of 'range', but also allows for a focus of 'accuracy'. Closed questions requiring simply structured responses allow learners to develop a set of notes and records related to the factual content of a text.

The active use of information as part of a problem solving activity (see Johnson 1989, p. 151) again allows for the reinforcement of key structures. Pupils can be asked to identify which key facts will contribute to an answer to a more open question. Finally, the answering of open questions, such as whether the learner agrees or disagrees with points of view, leads on to the notion of personalisation.

At this point it is crucial not to underestimate the place of evaluation. Gail Ellis and Barbara Sinclair (1989, cited in Nunan 1991, p. 96) recommend a process of reflection by the learner to improve skills. (see Activity 10.10)

REFLECTION
Activity 10.10 Evaluating to improve
Conduct a tutorial with a learner in the TL. Ask him or her evaluative questions along the lines of those suggested by Nunan (see 1991, p. 96). As an outcome of the tutorial, negotiate targets to assist the learner's progress. After the tutorial ask the learner if the experience is valuable.
Questions: How do you feel about writing in the TL?
            What do you know about writing in the TL?
            How well are you progressing?
            How do you practise writing in the TL?
            How can you improve your confidence?
            How can you improve the quality of your writing?

The suggestion that learners maintain a learner diary in the TL is helpful here in that the learner will have, at least partially, prepared answers to questions such as those in Activity 10.10. Such an activity will inevitably involve a degree of reflection, and regular checking by the teacher means that linguistic accuracy and the step-by-step detachment of the learner from the concrete (experiences, facts) to the abstract (attitudes and opinions) can be monitored.

Note taking

Hantrais notes (1989, p. 71): '[research] shows that students who make notes retain more information than those who do not. By making notes, you have a record which you can refer back to at a later stage.'

Hantrais also recommends (see 1989, p. 71) that notes should be taken in the language to which the learner is listening or reading. The assumption is that not only is information retained, but also the forms of language used to express it.

Clearly, note taking is a skill in its own right. When taking notes on a written text, similar skills to abstracting and summarising are demanded. As part of a development process, note taking should clearly follow the 'factual response' as this demands a higher degree of independence. The learner alone should select from the text and represent ideas, facts and views in a suitable format. Successful completion of structured comprehension questions, therefore, serves to develop note-taking skills (see Hantrais 1989, pp. 80–1).

Hantrais (1989, pp. 80–1) gives advice on the production of summaries (see Figure 10.7). Subsequent steps focus on what to do with the notes.

Follow-up activities include rewriting a text from one's notes, providing an oral presentation from the notes and multifarious comprehension activities.

Planning

Nunan notes that commentators have divided writing up into process and product activities (see 1991, p. 86). Indeed, Peck comments (1988a, p. 86):

> time spent by students using the language intensively can be reckoned as credit, while time spent organising the pattern of work deciding what to do and how to do, thinking of what to say and how to say it and correcting mistakes can be reckoned as debit.

This view is open to challenge as teachers focus on greater use of the TL during the planning stages. 'Conferencing' (see above) is an activity where learners can share ideas and plans in the TL. Evidently, planning and experimenting with the content of extended writing contribute to the development of 'quality of language'.

Learners can use notes taken to structure essays. Key points can be planned in this way in the TL. Subsequent discussions will involve justifying, expanding, clarifying and adapting plans. Undoubtedly, planning is a process skill, but one which enhances the product. The process also generates opportunities for TL use itself. This method of planning very much mirrors the process of developing writing skills as a whole. Brainstorming, selecting, prioritising and providing an argument to string ideas together can easily be adopted as a process. Each individual stage is, of course, a product in its own right, requiring the writer to focus on accuracy, range, content and quality of language.

> Isolate key nouns
> ↓ Rank points made in text in order of importance
> ↓ Write a concluding sentence
>   Write a summary

Figure 10.7 A process for developing summary skills

Drafting

One of Zamel's points is that weak writers focus on form from the outset (see 1982, p. 197). Such an obsession with accuracy, he suggests, inhibits expression. Drafting is not about accuracy, it is more a concern with developing a line of argument in the TL drawing on an appropriate style and broad relevant lexis. Drafting written texts relies upon a structured plan. Individual learners clearly require help, and collaborative writing provides this support.

If several learners complete sections of an agreed plan, drawing on the ideas and language contained, the actual writer is able to benefit from the ideas of others. Undoubtedly, the actual writer needs to provide clear guidance in the form of a plan and is free to reject or include contributions at a later date. Able writers tend to use what Hantrais refers to as 'discourse markers'. She lists such markers in categories, but does not claim that her list is exhaustive (see 1989, p. 85). If pupils are able to develop their own bank of markers, their plans for collaborative writing can include the need to deploy particular structures. Scrutiny of the collaboratively written text is then likely to involve a focus on accuracy.

REFLECTION

Activity 10.11 Discourse markers

Below are some discourse markers placed into categories (see Hantrais 1989, pp. 85–9). Discourse markers provide clues to meaning in that they serve a function in a text akin to stage directions in a play.

Add other markers that you can identify in texts you read yourself to the list.

Put all of them into the TL and consider the implications in terms of grammar (e.g. does their use affect word order, tense, etc?).

Devise some drill activities in the context of a unit of work to practise using the structures (e.g. linking two sentences by using expressions of time).

Sequencing
first of all, next, in conclusion

Adding information
and, moreover, incidentally, likewise

Contradicting
though, however, rather, on the other hand, in any case

Re-expressing
to put it another way, in other words

Specifying
namely, that is to say, firstly, secondly

Linking
for, therefore, in order to, so that, as a result, if, unless, otherwise

Referring
as already mentioned, in this connection

Exemplifying
for example, to illustrate this point

Summarising
to sum up, to recap, having shown that

Focusing or signposting
now I want to turn to, I should like to begin by, now I want to move on to look at . . . in more detail

How might you proceed from drill exercises in order that learners are comfortable using these structures as a matter of course?

Redrafting a text

Selecting, rejecting, adapting and amending the contributions of others is a simpler task than redrafting one's own work. The development of useful structures, the development of a structured argument, adequate coverage of the content are all features of good writers (see e.g. Zamel 1982, p. 199). It is at this stage that linguistic accuracy should become the focus. Teachers can provide guidance on how to check (see above), peers can check for accuracy and finally the teacher can mark. An essential part of developmental process is that formative guidance is provided as a matter of course.

Firstly, the exact nature of particular problems should be identified. Secondly, a course of action should be recommended, including leading the learner to appropriate materials and resources. Nunan recognises different levels for checking: lexis, sentence and discourse (see 1991, p. 90). Once again self-evaluation, reflection and, indeed, target setting are key to development and self-refinement.

Summary

The productive language skills of speaking and writing are assessed by applying similar criteria. The exact allocation of marks differs according to activity types. The teaching and learning of speaking and writing are interlinked, just as they are integrated with the receptive skills of listening and reading. The process of development recommended in this chapter is based upon the view that learners should firstly practise what they know and develop more complex skills through ever more demanding activities. Evidently, no teacher could focus purely on one skill to the exclusion of others and careful medium-term planning should serve to balance and sequence appropriate activities. This said, teachers and learners should be fully aware of skill development as well as concentrating on the increase in knowledge and course content. Speaking and writing must be exciting and profitable, communicative and personalised, meaningful and expressive.

References

Bygate, M. (1987) *Speaking.* Oxford: Oxford University Press.

Ellis, G. and Sinclair, B. (1989) *Learning to Teach English.* Cambridge: Cambridge University Press.

Hatch, E. (1978) 'Discourse analysis and second language acquisition'. In Hatch, E. (ed) *Second Language Acquisition: A Book of Readings.* Rowley, MA. Newbury House.

Hantrais, L. (1989) *The Undergraduate's Guide to Studying Languages.* London: CILT.

Hurman, J. (1992) 'Performance in the Advanced level speaking test by candidates with GCSE training: oral examiners' views.' In *Language Learning Journal 5.* Rugby: Association for Language Learning.

Johnson, K. (1989) *Communicative Interaction: A Guide for Language Teachers.* London: CILT.

Jones, B. (1988) 'The four skills'. In Phillips, D. (ed) *Languages in Schools: From Complacency to Conviction.* London: CILT, pp. 70–85.

Nunan, D. (1991) *Language Teaching Methodology: A Text Book for Teachers.* Hemel Hemstead: Prentice Hall.

Peck, A. (1988a) *Language Teachers at Work: A Description of Methods.* New York: Prentice Hall.

Peck, A. (1988b) 'Future reforms at Sixth Form level'. In Phillips, D. (ed) *Languages in Schools: From Complacency to Conviction.* London: CILT, pp. 146–157.

QCA, ACCAC and CCEA (1999) *Subject Criteria for Modern Foreign Languages: GCE Advanced Subsidiary and Advanced Level Specifications.* London.

Rodrigues, R. (1985) 'Moving away from writing process workshop'. In *English Journal 74,* pp. 24–7.

Stevick, E. (1982) *Teaching and Learning Languages.* Cambridge: Cambridge University Press.

Thorogood, J. and King, L. (1991) *Bridging the Gap: GCSE to A Level.* London: CILT.

Zamel, V. (1982) 'Writing the process of discovery meaning'. In *TESOL Quarterly 16,* 2, pp. 195–209.

Zamel, V. (1987) 'Recent research on writing pedagogy'. In *TESOL Quarterly 21,* 4, pp. 697–715.

Chapter 11

Working with literature

Karen Turner

Introduction

In today's syllabuses, the study of literature tends to be optional rather than compulsory. In this chapter I shall argue the case for the inclusion of some literary study in the A/AS level course and for the integration of that literary study with language work. I shall begin by showing why literature tends to be optional and end by outlining in general the approach taken by the Examination Boards.

The past

It is often useful when trying to understand why things are as they are, to know what has happened in the past. This is particularly true in the case of the study of literature at A/AS level where changes in the relatively recent past have been radical.

Up to the early 1980s, the study of literary texts dominated A level modern foreign language courses. Studying at A level was equated with the study of classical texts from the literary canon of the target language country in preparation for study at degree level. As many of these texts dated from the seventeenth and eighteenth centuries, the language tended to be archaic and therefore beyond the experience of learners, particularly at the beginning of the course. A further disadvantage, of course, was that words and phrases could not be transferred into the learners' own active language repertoire, something which compounded the isolation of literature from language work. The favoured approach of the time was to translate the text into English, word for word and to discuss the plot and characters in English too. Examination questions and answers were, for the most part, written in English and examiners were seeking not so much a personal response from examinees but rather 'some critical orthodoxy' or 'ready-made judgements' (Widdowson 1975, pp. 74–5) that had been provided by the teacher and rote learned for regurgitation on the examination paper. This, together with the translation-centred language component, was an approach to A level teaching inherited from the teaching of Latin and Greek and was concerned with the 'great' authors and particular literary movements.

We can identify several factors which changed the above approach, namely:

- the comprehensivisation of secondary schooling in the mid 1970s which led ultimately to a wider ability range of learners at post-16, not all of whom were studying A levels with a view to taking a degree in the foreign language
- growing discontent on the part of A level teachers with the inappropriacy of the 'classical' syllabus
- the move from transmission models of teaching (the teacher/textbook knows all and transmits this knowledge to a passive learner) to learner-centred models of learning. In Piagetian and Vygotskian psychology, learners are actively involved in constructing their own understanding of the world (see Williams and Burden 1997, ch. 1), and
- the paradigm change from grammar-translation methods of modern foreign language teaching to communicative approaches which emphasise practical use of the language and the spoken form in particular (see ch. 12 and Pachler and Field 1997, chs 1 and 3)

Thus, a number of pedagogical and linguistic changes resulted in a review of both the why and the how of literature at A level.

The present

The reorganisation of the A level syllabuses in the 1980s as a result of the above influences led to the downgrading of the literature component to such an extent that the study of literature is no longer a compulsory component. Topics of a non-literary nature (social, economic, cultural, political, geographical, historical) can be studied as alternatives or in addition to literature.

My objectives for this chapter, then, are to consider the *why* and the *how* of including literary texts in the A/AS level course and to provide practical examples of classroom work. The illustrative extracts are taken from French novels but the approach and the activities are appropriate for other languages and for drama as well as for fiction.

Objectives

By the end of the chapter, you will have:

- a rationale for the inclusion of some literary texts in the A/AS level course
- a framework for integrating language studies and literary studies
- some practical ideas and activities for the classroom
- considered some extracts and examples from modern French fiction, and
- a general idea of the requirements concerning literature at A/AS level

REFLECTION
Activity 11.1 Personal experiences of literature
Before you read the next section, think about your own experiences (if any –
you may not have studied literature) of reading literature at A level and/or
degree level:
- how were you introduced to literary texts?
- what sort of texts did you enjoy?
- why do you want your A/AS level learners to read some literature? what
  do you want them to get out of it?
Compare your ideas with those given below.

Studying literature: why?

Since it is possible for a learner to complete an A/AS level course and not to have
studied any literary works, I begin by arguing the case for some literature in A/AS
level studies. Having rejected the idea of studying literature on the grounds of
'tradition', we need to be clear about our reasons for including it in today's
courses. It does not, of course, have to be an examined component of the course.
Figure 11.1 lists the reasons why I believe the reading of literary texts can be a
worthwhile component of A/AS level work.

   If we accept as valid the reasons given in Figure 11.1, then there are implications
for the approach we take. Each of the reasons will shape our teaching and determine the sort of experiences we wish our learners to have. In the following section I
take each reason and suggest what the implications for our teaching might be.

1   At the end of the GCSE course, learners have very little experience of reading.
    They have encountered advertisements, letters, recipes, possibly some short
    stories but they have not, for the most part, read extensively. Their introduc-
    tion to literature, therefore, needs to be graded in just the same way that all
    other aspects of the course are graded. Extracts, short stories, short modern
    novels will make a good starting point, reserving longer novels and concep-
    tually more demanding works for the second year of study. In addition to
    work in class with the teacher, learners also need a programme of personal
    reading on the grounds that 'they only get better at reading by reading'.
       At the end of the GCSE course, learners rarely have well-developed reading
    skills although this may change over time as the effects of the National
    Curriculum Attainment Target 3 (Reading and Responding) are felt. They
    need help to acquire skills such as skimming and scanning and reading
    between the lines. The sort of activities we set must help learners to develop
    these skills. (See examples later in this chapter under 'Supporting independent
    reading'. *Developing Reading Skills* by Françoise Grellet and *Teaching Reading*

1   Our ultimate aim is for learners to handle the foreign language as it is used by native speakers rather than by educational coursebooks; literary texts are examples of authentic foreign language – written for native speakers – in just the same way that newspapers, magazines, letters are.

2   Literary texts exemplify the foreign language 'in use'. Not only can learners see how vocabulary and structures are used to communicative effect (grammar in action) but they can widen their linguistic experience by contrasting the language of literary texts with that of non-literary texts.

3   They make use of a variety of text types – descriptive, narrative, conversational – and registers – formal, informal, colloquial – and they provide a stimulus or springboard for skills development, not only reading but also speaking and writing.

4   They provide insights into the culture of the country – historically, geographically, socially, philosophically.

5   Literature 'speaks to the heart as much as to the mind' (Collie and Slater 1987, p. 3). It invites an emotional involvement, an opportunity to consider the great challenges of life – love, death, betrayal – to step out of one world and enter another without being involved in the consequences.

6   The 'inherent ambiguity' of literature invites a number of personal interpretations according to individual experience, ideas, concepts, beliefs. There is no one 'right' answer in literature.

Figure 11.1 Reasons for the inclusion of literary texts in A/AS level courses

Skills in a Foreign Language by Christine Nuttall are two excellent books for this purpose.)

2   Literature provides examples of language 'in action' but it is important that this language is not too far removed from the experience of the learners, i.e. the vocabulary is not too technical, the sentence structure is not too complex and the ideas are not too obscure for 17- and 18-year-olds. This rules out for me (with the exception of *Thérèse Raquin*) the novels of Emile Zola for example. The technical vocabulary is extensive and off-putting for learners at this level even though there is always a good storyline.

Extract 1 serves to illustrate what I mean by points 1 and 2 above. It is taken from a short novel (some 50 pages) called *La Place* by Annie Ernaux, published in 1983. The book is about a young woman's attempts to reconcile her present middle-class life and her upbringing. The two events which take place at the beginning of the novel – she passes the *Capes* (a highly competitive examination to become a secondary school teacher in France) and her father dies – act as the catalyst for her writing. In this extract, we discover that her background is rooted in the peasant classes.

Extract 1

L'histoire commence quelques mois avant le vingtième siècle, dans un village du pays de Caux, à vingt-cinq kilomètres de la mer. Ceux qui n'avaient pas de terre se louaient chez les gros fermiers de la région. Mon grand-père travaillait donc dans une ferme comme charretier. L'été, il faisait aussi les foins, la moisson. Il n'a rien fait d'autre de toute sa vie, dès l'âge de huit ans. Le samedi soir, il rapportait à sa famme toute sa paye et elle lui donnait son dimanche pour qu'il aille jouer aux dominos, boire son petit verre. Il rentrait saoul, encore plus sombre. Pour un rien, il distribuait des coups de casquette aux enfants. C'était un homme dur, personne n'osait lui chercher des noises. Sa femme ne riait pas tous les jours. Cette méchanceté était son ressort vital, sa force pour résister à la misère et croire qu'il était un homme. Ce qui le rendait violent, surtout, c'était de voir chez lui quelqu'un de la famille plongé dans un livre ou un journal. Il n'avait pas eu le temps d'apprendre à lire et à écrire. Compter, il savait.

Annie Ernaux (1983), La Place

This is a novel that could be attempted relatively early on in the A/AS level course because it meets the requirements set out in points 1 and 2. The vocabulary is not technical, although some terms will need explanation, the sentences are short, the tenses simple. Learners might well be invited to write a similar paragraph about a grandparent, singling out events, characteristics as seen through their eyes and using the familiar imperfect tense. Moreover, the central themes of this novel of family relationships, children and parents growing apart, the death of loved ones, are relevant to the age group.

3   In literary texts, we find a variety of text types and registers which enable us to broaden the linguistic experience of learners. After five years of GCSE work, learners are used to reading and writing descriptions – for example descriptions of themselves, their family, their school – their pets the function of such writing being to impart information. From literary works, they learn how descriptions are shaped to create an atmosphere, to arouse certain responses in the reader.

Extract 2 comes from *L'esprit de famille* by Janine Boissard, published in 1981. In it, the writer prepares us for an act of aggression on the underground which is witnessed by the narrator and her sister. In the lines preceding the extract, the narrator has described the other travellers in the carriage, all travelling in pairs, and here she describes the old lady, travelling alone, who will be the victim. The focus is on the old lady's frailty, her slight stature, her desire to pass unnoticed.

Extract 2

Sur la banquette à côté de la nôtre, une vieille dame. J'aime les personnes âgées, fragiles et neigeuses dont le regard raconte, en pâli, les histoires du passé. J'ai envie de les remercier d'être encore là. Celle-ci est très petite et occupe un minimum de place. Elle porte un tailleur gris, pied-de-poule. Ses chaussures semblent trop grandes pour elle mais ce doit être à cause de la maigreur des chevilles.

Plus tard, tout à l'heure, je me dirai que je l'avais remarquée. Je me souviendrai de détails sur lesquels, pourtant, mon regard passe très vite: les bas gris, opaques, le drôle de chignon retenu par une quantité de peignes alors que vraiment ce n'est pas l'abondance qui règne. Et aussi son sac, d'une autre époque. Plat et haut avec un fermoir qui doit faire 'clac'. Un sac comme en ont certaines filles dans ma classe; et quand elles y cherchent leur peigne ou leur agenda, on dirait qu'elles espèrent y trouver autre chose en plus. N'oublions pas un détail important: une boîte à gâteaux que la vieille dame tient sur ses genoux et qui vient d'une pâtisserie dont on peut lire le nom. *Aux Délicieuses.*
Janine Boissard (1981), *L'esprit de famille*

Learners might well be asked to:

- make a sketch of her (have they understood all the details?)
- provide (or select from a list provided by the teacher) a list of adjectives in the target language (TL) that might be used to describe her (memory work, dictionary work, grammatical work, vocabulary expansion), and
- compare the details provided by the writer with those which would be given on a passport or in a newspaper report of the incident and suggest why each description is different (writing for a purpose/creating an effect). See Figure 11.2 for an extract from a local newspaper reporting a similar incident.

In addition, the text may act as a springboard for creative work which moves between text types and registers and which allows the development of all skill areas. As a follow-up to the reading by Boissard, some learners might be invited to imagine the conversation between the old lady and her daughter as she recounts the incident on the metro and others might be invited to write up the incident for the local paper. This sort of creative work helps learners to understand that there are conventions to writing in different genres, that writing must be appropriate to purpose and audience and that words and structures change accordingly.

4   Literary texts provide insights into cultural aspects of the country. Our definitions of culture have widened considerably in recent years to encompass aspects of everyday life, history, geography, traditions, and are not restricted to 'the greatest and best in art, music and literature'. Moreover, we have much more ambitious aims for our learners; we want them to possess 'intercultural awareness' (see Byram 1989), to see the foreign culture, not as an outsider looking in but as an insider (see also Chapter 5). This is a tall order but it is perhaps through literature that we can experience that insider view and

Le vol de sac à main a tourné à l'agression mortelle

Le procès d'un garçon de 24 ans, Kamel Mohamedi, dans la tête de qui – un jour de janvier 1988 – il est passé l'idée de dérober un sac, histoire de se procurer un peu d'argent pour la drogue ou on ne sait quoi.

Kamel, alors, roulait en compagnie d'un copain Malik Belhachemi, 25 ans, à bord d'une voiture qu'il avait volée. Pour se promener dit-il aujourd'hui ou plus probablement pour commettre quelques larcins comme le laissent penser des objets retrouvés plus tard.

Et puis voilà qu'avenue Leclerc, à Villeurbanne, les deux garçons aperçoivent la silhouette de Joséphine Boucharcot, 75 ans, qui rentre chez elle. La voiture stoppe. L'un des deux descend, s'approche de la vieille dame qui se défend, s'accroche à son sac, écope même des coups, avant de s'effondrer. La voiture disparaît alors que Mme Boucharcot sombre dans le coma. Victime d'une fracture du crâne, la vieille dame décédera dix jours plus tard. Dans son sac . . . 150 francs.

Progrès de Lyon, janvier 1990

Figure 11.2 Le vol de sac à main a tourné à l'agression mortelle

appreciate traditions and beliefs different from our own. Thus we may have a better understanding of why millions of French people deserted the country-side for the towns between the First and Second World War in a huge *exode rural* when we know from *La Place* what life was like.

But let us be wary here! The modern foreign languages A/AS level learner is not part of the intended readership of works of literature, and writers writing for native speakers make all sorts of assumptions about the background knowledge of their readers which learners simply do not have. Learners need, therefore, preparation for reading through maps, travel guides, photographs, postcards, paintings, music, encyclopaedias, the internet, newspapers and magazines, biographical details of the author, etc.

5   Literature speaks to the heart, but only if the writing engages the emotions and imagination of the reader. Texts must therefore be selected on pedagogic grounds, not because they belong to a classical canon. Some of today's Awarding Bodies allow a free choice of texts so that teacher and learners can together decide on what is best suited to the group. Furthermore, literature is 'a dialogue between a text and a reader' (Kramsch 1993, p. 137) and each reader will engage in that dialogue differently according to her socio-cultural background. Each member of the group (teacher and learners) must therefore be open to the views of others. Black female readers will not necessarily interpret and respond to a piece of writing in the same way as a white male

reader. Not everyone will find the same character sympathetic or appreciate the author's stance. This can be challenging for the teacher who comes along to the class with his or her own interpretation.

6   Literature invites a personal response but only if we provide learners with the skills, understanding, confidence and desire to do so. The ability to make a personal response to literature is not innate but must be nurtured. This implies a graded approach where we ensure that learners have first *understood* the text, have answered and asked a number of questions about meaning at a variety of levels – word, sentence, paragraph – have completed written exercises, have been helped, where necessary to read between the lines and have worked independently of the teacher – alone, with a partner and with a group.

In summary, the essential points from the above discussion are that literature is a worthwhile component of an A/AS level modern foreign languages course if:

- the choice of texts and the approach to study are learner-centred
- literature is part of language study, and
- learners are invited to appreciate the particular qualities of literature

---

REFLECTION
Activity 11.2 Choosing texts to suit learners
Think about the sort of learners in your institution. What sort of literature might they enjoy? Look in the stock cupboard (departmental funds are usually limited and you may have to choose from what is there) and decide which texts meet the criteria for choice given in the section above. Do you have any texts at home from which you can take interesting extracts?

Studying literature: how?

In this section, we look in more detail at the sort of activities that can help learners to develop the literary and linguistic skills we think desirable.

Making a start

Learners need some sort of framework into which they can fit the details of their reading – a general idea of what the writing is about – its location in time and place, its themes, some details of the author and in the case of plays, some information on the characters and their relationship with each other. The teacher will provide some of this but learners, too, can be involved in researching background books, the internet, etc. and reporting back to the group. Some of the examination syllabuses provide background reading for topic work which can be useful and, of course, the Foreign Language Assistant and native speaker members of staff are invaluable. The aim of such preparatory work is to provide learners with some of the culturally specific background knowledge possessed by native speakers which writers will take for granted. Of course, the intention is not that we should overwhelm learners with a mass of information and keep them waiting for weeks before they 'get their teeth into' the literature itself. More that, as the reading proceeds, there is a 'filling in' of this necessary information so that the text makes sense.

Some books, novels in particular, have thought-provoking covers in full colour that we can exploit through oral question and answer work before we start reading. There is, for instance, a *livre de poche* edition of *Le Silence de la mer* by Vercors, which has such a cover. *Le Silence de la mer*, first published in 1942, is a short novel set in France during the German occupation. An idealistic German army officer is billetted on a French man and his niece. The front cover portrays a dark, lamp-lit room. We see an elderly man sitting in an armchair, smoking a pipe and looking in the direction of the woman we see seated in the foreground. We see her from the side; a young woman with short dark hair, her hands clasped on her knees, staring ahead, her face expressionless. Between them, standing up, is a man in a *Wehrmacht* army uniform – short blond hair, clean-shaven. He seems to be staring out over the heads of the other two into the distance. This is obviously not a scene of animated conversation! The author's name and the title of the book appear at the top of the page. The front cover allows the teacher to ask a series of questions (or invite a description from learners) which:

- revises the past (what language, what powers of expression do learners already have?)
- provides information about accuracy and fluency
- provides information about learners' background knowledge (Do they know what was happening in France in 1942? Can they imagine why the writer is known only as Vercors?)
- allows learners to hypothesise about the situation portrayed in the picture, and
- allows learners to ask some questions for which the answers will be found in the text. (What is the relationship between the people in the picture? Why is the book called *Le Silence de la mer*?)

Not all books have such rich front covers. My edition of *La Place* is by Twentieth Century Texts. The cover has no pictorial element and is completely uninspiring but on the other hand the text is annotated and there is a very useful introduction for teachers and learners.

Once reading begins, it seems sensible to work together with learners through the first few pages in detail in order to help them 'into' the book. Feeling lost and bewildered at the start of the book does not engender confidence and may lead to misunderstandings. It is a common literary device, for example, to use the third person pronoun when referring to key characters for the first time. Here is the opening line of *Le Silence de la mer*:

Il fut précédé par un grand déploiement d'appareil.

Il here refers to the German officer on the front cover, the key character who will be referred to as *l'immense silhouette* and *l'officier* before the reader discovers on page 4 that his name is Werner von Ebrennac.

The opening of *Le Grand Meaulnes* by Alain-Fournier, first published in 1913, begins in a similar way:

Il arriva chez nous un dimanche de novembre 189 . . .

In order to understand that the first word of the novel refers to the *Grand Meaulnes* of the title, the reader must connect this first sentence with the following sentence which appears one and a half pages further on:

Nous étions pourtant depuis dix ans dans ce pays lorsque Meaulnes arriva.

In Extract 3, the writer uses several other referents to his main characters before the reader can identify them by name. It is the opening sequence from Claude Michelet's *Des grives aux loups*, published in 1979.

Extract 3

Ils abandonnèrent le chemin encaissé et l'abri de ses ronces épaisses. Le vent d'est leur sauta au visage, griffa leurs joues et cingla leurs jambes nues; des larmes froides et piquantes perlèrent entre leurs paupières plissées.

Les trois enfants bifurquèrent vers l'extrémité du plateau et se coulèrent entre les genévriers. La neige couinait sous leurs pas, s'accrochait aux clous de leurs sabots et leur faisait de grosses et lourdes semelles blanches; ils s'arrêtaient souvent, choquaient leurs pieds l'un contre l'autre pour décoller les blocs glacés, puis reprenaient leur trottinement.

L'aîné ouvrait la marche; il allait sans hésitation et aussi vite que le lui permettaient les broussailles, les congères et les rochers. Derrière lui venait un jeune garçon qui tirait, à bout de bras et d'une main ferme, une petite fille au visage rougi par le froid. Elle reniflait bruyamment et devait presque courir pour soutenir l'allure.

Claude Michelet (1979), *Des grives aux loups*

The reader must make the following connections:

Line	Reference
1	Ils
5	les trois enfants

11	l'aîné
13	un jeune garçon
14	une petite fille

Over the next two pages of the novel, readers must link up the name of Léon Dupeuch, 12 years old with *l'aîné*, Pierre-Edouard Vialhe, 10½ with *un jeune garçon* and *sa soeur* Louise, 9 years old with *une petite fille*. In other words, *Ils*, the opening word of the novel, refers to three children: Leon Dupeuch who is 12 and a brother and sister of 10½ and 9 years respectively whose names are Pierre-Edouard and Louise Vialhe. The reader must put together all this information over the first one and a half pages of the book. The presentation of characters is not compact and straightforward as it is in an informal letter between friends at GCSE level. Post-GCSE learners need guidance from the teacher with this (just as they need help with multiple referents in newspaper articles) at a level of understanding in the first instance. Later, they might well be invited to comment on why the writer might want to use this device. What effect does it create?

Finally, with novels, we do not have to begin at the beginning of the book. There are occasions when a more motivating starting point for learners might be a particular incident or phase in the narrative. A novel may, for instance, begin in a reflective or 'stream of consciousness' mode which may appear somewhat abstract for learners to cope with initially. There could be complications with flashback which make it harder to understand at the beginning. We do not want to 'give too much away' but one or two extracts from the complete text, possibly ones that end on a note of suspense or which raise the curiosity of the readers, can be an alternative to starting at the beginning and working sequentially through.

Working through the text

I discussed at the end of the preceding section, the need for learners to be helped through the early pages of a literary work but there is not time and it would be a very long-winded and tedious way of proceeding, even if there was, to work through each page of a novel or a play in this detailed way. There will be sections where events pivotal to the plot, to the development of character, to the understanding of the work are to be found that will need detailed work together. The teacher needs to identify these before reading with the class begins. There will also be chapters, scenes, sections that will be read by the learners on their own. This independent reading will need support and it will need to be followed up in class. Our aims for this personal reading are for learners to sort out the sequence of events, to understand what happens at a surface level, so that the follow-up work in class can flow smoothly, so that learners can contribute to the class review and so that the ground is prepared for discussion at a deeper level.

In the following section I suggest some ways of supporting readers once they get started on the text on their own.

Supporting independent reading

Some learners like to *buy their own texts* because they can then write brief translations and notes on the page where they are immediately visible during
subsequent readings. Where this is financially possible, it is a practice to be
encouraged.

A *glossary* of key vocabulary is very helpful because it reduces the need for
constant dictionary work. Some texts are produced specifically for the educational
market. They have a glossary, explanatory notes and sometimes information about
the author's life and works. The published glossary is rarely enough for first-year
learners, however, and further support with unknown words from the teacher will
be necessary.

When there is a large number of pages to read, *signpost questions* in the TL on a
worksheet produced by the teacher can guide the learner through. Signpost questions point the reader in the direction of the key events and significant actions to be
noted in the chapter. They provide clues about the content of the chapter. Most of
us don't read every single word of every single chapter when we are reading a novel.
Skilled readers will scan the page for significant detail, possibly glancing over
uneventful passages. Providing learners with signpost questions can help them
to do just that. In *Extract 1*, for example, signpost questions might direct readers to
the fact that the narrator's grandfather lived and worked in a small village in
Normandy, that he worked on a farm but did not own it, that he started work at
the age of eight and that he could count but not read. Learners seek out the answers
to the signpost questions and on completion of the exercise, they have not only a
written summary of the chapter in the TL but also the basis of a class discussion in
follow-up lessons. *Multiple choice questions, true/false statements, gaps to fill* and
sentences to complete or *put in order* are alternatives.

As learners become more confident and skilled they can be given more productive tasks. A *written summary in the TL* of the set reading not only challenges
learners linguistically but begins to take them a step beyond the recording of
information into the realm of interpretation. In summarising they must make a
decision about the significant events of the text. In class, pairs or groups may
compare summaries and collectively decide upon a best version which can then be
discussed as a whole class. In presenting its summary orally, a group must *justify its
choice* and *give reasons for omissions*. In this small and supported way, the teacher
builds up the confidence and linguistic skills of learners so that they can express a
personal interpretation and give an opinion.

This development of the personal response can be further encouraged by
prediction activities. When one section of the text has been discussed and written
records are complete, learners can be invited, when it seems appropriate, to predict
what is going to happen in the pages that follow.

Working together

Work in class will take up and develop reading completed at home. It will focus on the literary aspects of the work – development of plot, characterisation, imagery, personal response of the reader – and the linguistic development of learners – speaking and writing skills, knowledge of grammar. In the following, I suggest some activities that will help to develop learners' literary and linguistic understanding. Naturally, those passages in the text which have been identified as highlights or key passages will be exploited intensively through a wide range of activities. Less important passages will be dealt with in less detail.

SNOWBALL SUMMARIES

This is a term used by Collie and Slater (see 1987, p. 52) to refer to collaborative work by learners and teacher where several aspects of the literary work are investigated. A snowball summary grows as time goes by and several snowball summaries might be growing at the same time with different groups of learners being responsible for each. In a novel or play, characterisation will need to be studied. In literary works, characterisation is built up over time and must often be inferred from actions. The writer will not provide the reader with a list of adjectives to describe characters at a first encounter. By writing a snowball summary, learners can record how characters in a book or play develop and then find their own adjectives to describe them. Figure 11.3 shows what the headings for such a summary might look like.

In a similar way, we can record *relationships* between characters or the development of *underlying themes*. Each learner needs to keep an up-to-date record of the snowball summaries or, as Collie and Slater suggest, the record can be kept on the classroom wall for all to see, if this is feasible. When the reading is complete, the class has a detailed record of important aspects of the work which can then be reviewed in its entirety and analysed more closely.

Chapter/ act or scene	Events/actions	What it tells us about character X

Figure 11.3 Snowball summary headings to record development of character

GRIDS AND TABULATIONS

Classifying information in grids or tables can be useful in a number of ways – for getting at underlying meanings and for making comparisons, for example. A grid might juxtapose what someone said with what he or she meant or what the text tells us and what we must infer. A grid might juxtapose a character's good points and his or her bad points or action and description.

Extract 4 is a short passage from *Elise ou la vraie vie* by Claire Etcherelli, published in 1967. The book is set in France in the 1950s during the Algerian War of Independence and relates the love affair of a young French woman from the provinces, Elise, and an Algerian, Arezki. This is a long book and not one to attempt in a first year of study. The extract is taken from a key passage towards the end of the novel where Elise and Arezki go back to his lodgings for the first time with the intention of sleeping together. A police raid on the building puts an end to any romantic plans. The police, looking for illegal Algerian workers, are brutal and racist.

Elise, the narrator, in the dark of Arezki's room, can hear what is going on but cannot see it. In the lines preceding the extract, Etcherelli has created an atmosphere of fear through the use of words that describe loud, piercing or violent noises which invade the quiet of the night.

Extract 4

– Police!

– Police!

Je ne pouvais parler, me détendre. Dans le noir, immobile, j'écoutais et, par les bruits, je suivais le déroulement de la perquisition comme une aveugle. On sifflait maintenant de l'intérieur de l'hôtel. Quelqu'un cria un ordre et les bruits de pas se précipitèrent. Ils avaient atteint notre étage, et couraient aux issues. Les voix prenaient un son étrange, le silence de l'hôtel les amplifiait. Ils avaient de grosses lampes dont le faisceau pénétrait jusqu'à nous par les jointures usées de la porte. L'un, sans doute à la traîne, arriva en courant.

– A la ratonnade, plaisanta-t-il.

Il y eut des rires.

Le plus angoissant était ce silence. Pas de cris, pas de plaintes, aucun éclat de voix, aucun signe de lutte; des policiers dans une maison vide. Puis soudain, il y eut un roulement, un autre, un bruit sourd de chute, de dégringolade. Et le silence par là-dessus. Dans la rue, quelqu'un criait.

–   Allez, allez, allez!

Claire Etcherelli (1967), Elise ou la vraie vie

Readers must infer what is happening from the sounds that Elise describes. To ensure that they understand the physical violence involved in the raid, a grid might juxtapose what Elise could hear with what was happening elsewhere in the building. See Figure 11.4 for some ideas.

This is another passage where learners might be invited to imagine how a report might appear in a national newspaper, perhaps as a short *fait divers* where readers might expect to find some facts but no feelings and emotions.

TIME LINES

Keeping track of the passing of time as learners move through chapter by chapter, act by act will be helpful, as again, the reader must often work out for his- or herself the days, dates, years as the sequence of events unfolds. This will be particularly true where the author uses flashbacks.

Figure 11.5 is an example of a time line which records the events in *La Place*, a novel I mentioned earlier. As I said, the novel begins with the death of the

Ce qu'Elise entendait	Ce qui se passait
Par les bruits, je suivais le déroulement de la perquisition	Les policiers fouillaient dans toutes les chambres
On sifflait . . . quelqu'un cria un ordre et les bruits de pas se précipitèrent	Les policiers sifflaient, criaient les uns aux autres, se précipitaient dans le bâtiment pour faire peur aux habitants
Ils couraient aux issues	Les policiers voulaient empêcher les habitants de s'évader par les sorties de secours et par les portes.
Le plus angoissant était ce silence	Tous les immigrants qui habitaient l'immeuble se taisaient, attendaient en silence, espérant que les policiers ne frapperaient pas à leur porte.
Pas de cris, pas de plaintes, aucun éclat de voix, aucun signe de lutte	Les habitants acceptaient, comme partie de leur vie en France, la descente dans l'immeuble et la violence de la police
Puis soudain, il y eut un roulement, un autre, un bruit sourd de chute, de dégringolade.	Les habitants poussés, bousculés par la police tombaient dans l'escalier, du haut en bas.

Figure 11.4 Descente de police chez Arezki

narrator's father. After some seven pages at the beginning of the novel, she looks back over his life and her own childhood, coming full circle at the end of the novel, to her father's illness and the end of his life.

VISUAL REPRESENTATIONS

Pictorial or diagrammatic representations can be very supportive in helping learners to visualise a theatrical set, the movement of characters, stage instructions by the author, geographical settings, the layout of a room or the scene of action. They also ensure that learners have understood exactly what happens. In Extract 2, for example, a sketch of the arrangement of seats in the French métro (not the same as the London underground) would help learners to understand what the narrator means by the old lady being seated *sur la banquette à côté de la nôtre* and how, later in the chapter, the three thugs who terrorise her are able to surround her and 'lock' her in with their legs.

LANGUAGE DEVELOPMENT

In my rationale for including literature in advanced level modern foreign languages learning, I stated that the study of literary texts can contribute to the development of linguistic knowledge and skills. Many of the activities for non-literary texts that we find in coursebooks such as *Signes du temps: vécu* (Corless *et al.* 1991) are suitable. Our aims when preparing language work are three-fold.

We want learners to:

* *know* the vocabulary (nouns, verbs, adjectives) essential to talking and writing about the text;
* be able to *use* the vocabulary in increasingly complex sentences; to be able to move smoothly between tenses and structures; and
* speak and write *accurately and fluently* and to develop their powers of expression.

Our activities, then, must provide grammar practice, develop powers of expression and improve speaking and writing skills. For some suggestions, see Figure 11.6.

Pulling the threads together

When the reading is over, we shall want to round up all that has been discussed. If literature is an examined component of the course, the follow-up activities will need to prepare learners for the type of tasks required by the examination. Course work titles will have to be identified and content discussed or past examination papers will have to be studied for an idea of the sort of questions favoured by a particular board. Learners will need to be taught how to structure an essay and they will need training in examination techniques – selecting the most appropriate

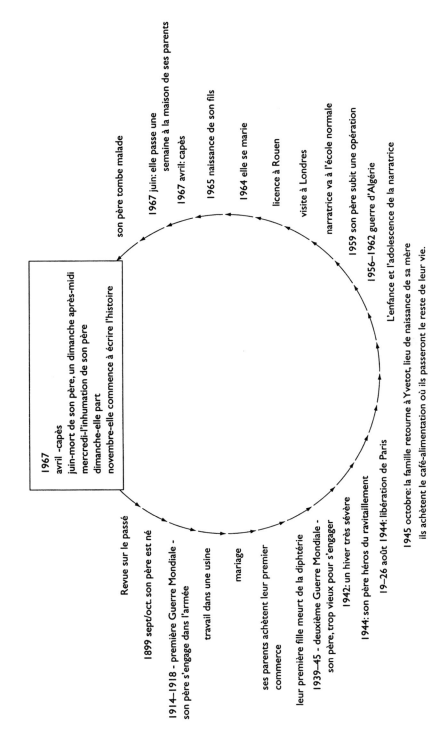

Figure 11.5 Timelines for *La Place*: résumé 1899–1967

Activity	Purpose
classification of nouns, adjectives, verbs used to create particular effects – sounds, images, feelings.	vocabulary expansion
gap-filling sentences with key words	assimilation and accurate use of key vocabulary
rewriting sentences using a different tense	manipulation of verbs
changing first person narrative to third-person	manipulation of verbs, adjectives, pronouns
constructing sentences using new vocabulary accurately	understanding word order and agreements
short paragraphs to translate into English	understanding register
short paragraphs to translate back into foreign language	grammatical accuracy, idiomatic expression
oral questions to ask and answer oral summaries	productive use of foreign language
written questions to answer written summaries	productive use of foreign language, manipulation of language
joining sentences using relative clauses, subordinate and coordinating conjunctions	making more complex sentences
writing paragraphs using connecting words	making personal style more sophisticated
role plays and simulations	creative/imaginative oral work
relating events to characters who were absent from the scene interviews	developing powers of expression
pages of a character's diary recounting events from another's point of view	creative/imaginative written work
reporting events on radio or in newspaper	understanding how language changes according to genre

Figure 11.6 Some suggestions for the development of linguistic knowledge and skills

question from those available, addressing each element of the title, time management, etc. Teachers should attend INSET sessions offered by the Awarding Body and should read the Chief Examiner's report which clarifies expectations for examination performance and provides information about what gains and loses marks.

Other, rather more light-hearted, activities might precede all this, however. Here are some ideas for drawing the work to a close:

- Which character did you like best and why?
- Would you recommend this work to a friend? Why? Why not?
- How else might the work have ended? How would you like it to have ended?
- If this work was turned into a film, which part might make a good trailer?
- How would you illustrate a new front cover for this work?
- What would the 'blurb' on the back cover say?

Using the TL

When working with A/AS level learners, we try, as far as possible to work in the TL. This is the only way we can hope to improve their receptive and productive skills. However, there is a need to be sensitive. Learners in their first year of study can find the leap from GCSE to A/AS level a daunting experience. If we need to use more English at the beginning of the course to put learners at ease and to smooth that transition between the two levels, then we should not feel guilty about it. Certainly when discussing literary works, there will be occasions when use of the mother tongue will be desirable because learners simply do not have the linguistic skills to express their thoughts and emotions in the foreign language. It is frustrating and ultimately de-motivating not to be able to say what you really feel. Like everything else, use of the TL needs to be graded over the length of the course.

REFLECTION
Activity 11.3 Making a start with literary extracts
Preferably working with a colleague/colleagues, put together a selection of literary extracts and prepare some activities to accompany them.

If possible, try them out with a group of A/AS level learners working together as a group with you on one text. (If you are not currently teaching A/AS level, this could still be possible by negotiation with your Head of Department/Curriculum Manager).

Allow the learners to make a personal choice from the remainder. If possible, follow up their reading by inviting them to talk to the whole group about what they have read.

Are any of your extracts appropriate, with some extra support, for a good Year 11 group?

Studying literature: the framework for examinations

I conclude this chapter on working with literature at A/AS level with a brief overview of the place of literature within the framework for examinations. It is not my intention to examine in detail or compare the specifics of individual Awarding Bodies but in Figure 11.7 I list some of the general characteristics of the current examination specifications with the purpose of finding out whether there is a good match between what we would like to do in the classroom, as outlined above, and what the examinations require.

Summary

In conclusion then, if we ask two important questions – do the examination syllabuses exemplify good classroom practice and do they allow us to teach literature as we wish to teach it? – the answer is a qualified yes.

- It tends to be optional, rather than compulsory. Often, learners may omit the study of literature completely from their A/AS level course. Alternatively, they can combine the study of literature with non-literary topics or study literature to the exclusion of non-literary topic work.
- Literature is examined alongside a range of practical skills.
- Literature is seen as integral to language work.
- Where texts are prescribed by the examination board, they contain modern works as well as the well-known classics.
- In some cases, the choice of texts to be studied is left to the institution.
- A wider range of texts is welcomed – Spanish from the Americas, French from the Caribbean, lesser-known writers.
- Study might be organised thematically – for example, 'women in the twentieth century' or 'childhood'.
- In some cases, literature may be submitted as a course work option.
- The texts (with editorial/learner annotations) are allowed in the examination room with some boards.
- Questions and answers on the examination paper and course work are written in the TL.

Figure 11.7 The literature element in the current advanced level examinations

References

Byram, M. (1989) *Cultural Studies in Foreign Language Education*. Clevedon: Multilingual Matters.

Collie, J. and Slater, S. (1987) *Literature in the Language Classroom: A Resource Book of Ideas and activities*. Cambridge: Cambridge University Press.

Corless, F., Corless, H. and Gaskell, R. (1991) *Signes du temps: vécu*. Second edition. London: Hodder and Stoughton.

Grellet, F. (1981) *Developing Reading Skills: A Practical Guide to Reading Comprehension Exercises*. Cambridge: Cambridge University Press.

Kramsch, C. (1993) *Context and Culture in Language Teaching*. Oxford: Oxford University Press.

Nuttall, C. (1982) *Teaching Reading Skills in a Foreign Language*. London: Heinemann.

Pachler, N. and Field, K. (1997) *Learning to Teach Modern Foreign Languages in the Secondary School*. London: Routledge.

Widdowson, H. (1975) *Stylistics and the Teaching of Literature*. London: Longman.

Williams, M. and Burden, R. (1997) *Psychology for Language Teachers. A Social Constructivist Approach*. Cambridge: Cambridge Language Teaching Library.

Chapter 12

Translation in the communicative classroom

Douglas Allford

Introduction

Attitudes towards translation in the modern foreign languages (mfl) classroom are currently so sharply divided as to suggest a fault-line running through foreign language education in the UK. On the one hand, translation is so gravely out of favour that it is viewed almost with hostility under certain interpretations of communicative approaches to foreign language learning at Key Stages 3 and 4. The target language (TL) should be the exclusive medium of instruction, as the OFSTED *Handbook* prescribes: 'Teachers should insist on the use of the target language for all aspects of a lesson' (OFSTED 1993, section 37). And in a classroom where exclusive use of the TL applies, translation can by definition play no part.

On the other hand, in our daily lives we encounter numerous multilingual instruction leaflets, owner's manuals, labels and items of packaging: we are surrounded by the evidence of translation as never before. This reality is reflected in the presence of various types of translation task at A/AS level (as well as in vocational qualifications such as those of the RSA).

Translation is opposed by some proponents of communicative theories of foreign language learning, who hold that it is 'counterproductive to the development of all round proficiency in a foreign language' (Sewell and Higgins 1996, p. 9) and that learners need to practise the four skills of reading, writing, speaking and listening in the TL alone. Yet these theories ignore the ubiquity of translation as a natural and necessary social activity and the fact that learners at every level find translating very helpful. That translation as a foreign language learning device just will not go away both explains the repeated denunciations by its opponents and exposes the futility of trying to ban it entirely from the classroom.

Later in this chapter we shall look at some ways in which translation and related activities, such as paraphrasing between the TL and the mother tongue, can be used in the A/AS classroom. Two important points may be made here. First, we shall consider translation as a *teaching* tool and not as a means of assessment, which is how it tended to be used in the past even if that was not always made explicit. For instance, as we shall see, what is often most useful for teaching, as distinct from testing, are short translation passages that can be discussed in groups. Second, one of the main advantages of translation is to show how the TL conveys or encodes meaning differently from the mother tongue. Translation activities, which require close scrutiny of vocabulary, structures and discourse (i.e. meaningful language as it occurs in coherent units larger than sentences) can sensitise learners to differences between the two languages that may be much less apparent if all work is conducted in the TL. Employing the mother tongue in this way is entirely compatible with extensive use of the TL, which is being complemented, rather than undermined, by cross-lingual comparisons.

However, we shall start by looking at reasons for the *rejection* of translation. The basis of this is complex, but it can be considered under two aspects discussed below, one based on language-learning theory and the other on how translation has been used in foreign language teaching in the past. I shall try to show that many of these objections can be overcome and that, appropriately deployed, translation can play a valuable part in foreign language learning and teaching.

Objectives

By the end of this chapter you should:

- be familiar with some of the arguments against translation in the classroom
- understand that translation has often been excluded on practical, rather than pedagogical grounds
- see that judicious use of translation can be reconciled with extensive TL use in the classroom
- have an insight into ways in which translation can sensitise learners to differences between mother tongue and TL, and
- have some ideas for the use of translation as a teaching tool

The rejection of translation in mfl teaching

The rejection of translation follows inevitably from the assumption that the TL should be taught without reference to the learner's mother tongue, a view that has had an extensive influence (see Stern 1992, pp. 280–2) and currently dominates much thinking about mfl teaching in the UK. In other words, exclusive use of the TL in the classroom is widely regarded as a desirable and realisable ideal. If it is conceded that in practice this may amount to no more than 'virtually' 100 per cent TL use (DES 1990, p. 58), the admission of the mother tongue has nonetheless tended to be undertaken with reluctance and viewed as 'a lapse from the ideal' (Stern 1992, p. 281). Unsurprisingly, within this orthodoxy there has been little discussion of the circumstances under which use of the mother tongue, or indeed of translation, might be legitimate and advantageous.

The grammar-translation method

Historically, the rejection of translation can be seen in part at least as a reaction against the widespread influence of the grammar-translation method, which has become 'the stereotype of the use of translation in language teaching' (Cook 1998, p. 117). In a typical grammar-translation textbook, TL structures are organised according to perceived usefulness and in increasing order of supposed complexity. Each chapter introduces one or two new grammar rules, explained in the mother tongue and exemplified in the TL; there is a short vocabulary list with translations; and there are sentences for translation, both out of and into the TL, employing only vocabulary and structures already encountered.

Obvious weaknesses are the neglect of the spoken language and the artificiality of textbook language composed only to demonstrate particular linguistic features; yet neither weakness is beyond remedy and it is possible to see how grammar-translation started out as a 'simple approach to [foreign] language learning for young school children' (Howatt 1984, p. 136). However, a century or so ago the determination to have mfl study accepted as a serious discipline in British universities led teachers and textbook writers to 'ape the methods of the classics' and in their enthusiasm to show that French or German was as 'intellectually demanding' as Latin or Greek they succumbed to a 'tyrannical obsession with [the] minutiae' of grammatical categories and turned the grammar-translation syllabus into a 'jungle of obscure rules, endless lists of gender classes and gender-class exceptions' (Howatt 1984, pp. 135–6).

The 'natural' method and second language acquisition theory

The most strenuous opposition to grammar-translation comes from approaches to language teaching known variously as the Natural Method, Direct Method, Communicative Approach and so on, all of them based upon the view that:

> learning to speak a new language . . . is not a rational process which can be organized in a step-by-step manner following graded syllabuses of new points to learn, exercises and explanations. It is an intuitive process for which human beings have a natural capacity that can be awakened provided only that [you have] someone to talk to, something to talk about, and a desire to understand and make yourself understood.
>
> (Howatt 1984, p. 192)

These conditions are held to be both necessary and sufficient for language acquisition by some current theorists who believe that learners should attend to the meaning to be conveyed rather than the linguistic forms. Whilst rejecting any formal or analytic syllabus, they argue that learners should focus on communicative activities so that they may acquire the TL system unconsciously, much as infants acquire their mother tongue (see Krashen 1982; Prabhu 1987). These theories have no place for translation, which, as Guy Cook observes (1998, p. 119), 'implies a conscious knowledge of two language systems and the deliberate deployment of both'. However, it may be noted that Krashen's position has been seriously challenged by various commentators (see e.g. Ellis 1994, pp. 652–4), and attempts to draw analogies between infant mother tongue acquisition and adult mfl learning must be viewed with extreme caution.

Nonetheless, the Natural Method has a long history and has been very success-ful under certain circumstances. Foreign language teaching involving near-exclusive use of the TL had been practised for centuries by private tutors to the children of wealthy families, but it was Maximilian Berlitz who applied the Natural Method in schools established for the large numbers of immigrants arriving in the USA from all over Europe at the end of the nineteenth and beginning of the twentieth centuries (see Howatt 1984, pp. 198–204). Plainly, the multiplicity of mother tongues meant that all teaching had to be in the target language and precluded the use of translation in the classroom. An environment of this kind, where learners have little formal education but, because their livelihoods depend upon doing so, are powerfully motivated to learn the language of the host community by which they are surrounded, would seem to be conducive to unconscious language acquisition processes of the kind discussed by Krashen (whose research refers principally to more recent Spanish-speaking immigrants to the USA).

However, the differences between learners in those particular circumstances and A/AS learners in the UK are so great as to make any attempt to generalise from one group to the other quite perilous and to render absurd any suggestion that A/AS groups should abandon their advantages, particularly literacy in the mother tongue and knowledge of language as a system.

REFLECTION
Activity 12.1 Knowledge and motivation
Many immigrants arriving in the USA a century ago had limited formal education but they were powerfully motivated to learn the language of their new country. How do your learners compare?
1   How much formal knowledge of their mother tongue do your learners have? Does knowing about the rules of English help them to understand or use a foreign language any better?
2   What is the motivation of your learners for learning a foreign language? Is it out of interest in the country, perhaps because they want to visit it (again)? Or do they hope that learning a language will give them an advantage on the job market?

The circumstances of British A/AS level learners broadly resemble those of their in mainland Europe, with one striking exception: the status of

~~~nce of English as a foreign language

Given its position as the world's most widely studied second or foreign language and the *lingua franca* of international trade and communication (see e.g. Bryson 1990; Crystal 1997), it is hardly surprising that many influential ideas about foreign language teaching have been developed in relation to teaching English as a Foreign Language (EFL), with a tacit assumption that they also apply to teaching other mfl. Thus there has arisen an 'EFL model' against which mfl teaching in general is measured:

> EFL classes, in which 100% target language is the only possible option, represent an ideal state of affairs which modern language teachers should aspire to recreate in their own classes, despite the handicap of the common language (English) which they share with their students.
>
> (Atkinson 1993, p. 3)

Plainly, the notion that there is an ideal (EFL) approach as opposed to an inferior (mfl) arrangement should not be accepted without question. Integral to the EFL model is the highly dubious assumption that a native speaker teacher is by definition the best (see Phillipson 1992, pp. 193–9), whereas a strong case can be argued for the advantages of having teachers whose mother tongue is that of the learners. Such teachers have already travelled the route from the shared mother tongue towards TL proficiency themselves and should therefore have a detailed grasp of the language-specific problems of their learners.

Another highly influential belief associated with the EFL model is termed by Phillipson the 'monolingual fallacy', which holds (1992, p. 185) that 'English, or by implication any other language, should be taught entirely through the medium of the target language and without reference to other languages'. However, as Ernesto Macaro argues in some detail (see 1997, pp. 55–133), if learners are to assume greater responsibility for their own language learning, there is a strong case for judicious use of the mother tongue, which may also be helpful in explaining the 'exact meaning' of a TL word or idiom (see Macaro 1997, p. 130). Most significantly, in a class where a native speaker is teaching English to a group in which several different nationalities are represented, reference to a 'mother tongue' is impossible and 100 per cent use of the TL is inevitable not because it is pedagogically superior but by sheer force of circumstances, and for similar reasons translation as a pedagogical tool is impracticable.

The 'naturalness' of exclusive TL use

Underlying the case for 100 per cent TL use (and thus for the rejection of translation) is an assumption that it is 'natural' to use the TL as the normal means of communication in the classroom: 'the *natural* use of the target language for virtually all communication is a sure sign of a good modern language course' (DES 1990, p. 58; my emphasis). The phrase 'virtually all' invites attempts to interpret exactly what it may mean and when use of the mother tongue may be permissible – an important question, discussed below – but this may result in its larger significance being overlooked. It clearly implies some recourse to the mother tongue, but if the TL were their 'natural' medium of communication, teachers and learners would simply use it to the full extent of their competence. Yet that is not the case, and use of the TL in the classroom seems not to be 'natural' in any obvious sense.

The instances given in the DES report make it clear that teachers are expected to deploy the TL in ways that are carefully planned in advance and highly conscious in execution. They will 'adapt their use of the target language . . . to introduce words and phrases which learners are going to be using' and, if pupils are to learn from the teacher's TL input, it must be 'skilfully used and combined with judicious checking of pupils' understanding' (DES 1990, pp. 58–9). In other words, the teacher must carefully select TL passages which exemplify given linguistic features, ensure that those features are made perceptually salient and check that the learners have understood what each passage means. Thus, the teacher deploys the TL not primarily in order to communicate but, rather, to provide accessible specimens of language so that the learners may learn from them. Language produced in this way of course has similarities with the TL as used by native speakers for everyday communicative purposes, but it plainly differs from natural language in terms of its context of use and the intention which motivates its production.

The misattribution of 'naturalness' to the teacher's language is matched in the DES report by a questionable representation of part of the foreign language learning process as imitation. Learners will learn 'generally to get their meaning across' – presumably through the use of strategies such as paraphrase when the speaker does not know the exact TL word – and they will learn this by '*imitating* the teacher's own strategies from an early stage' (DES 1990, p. 59; my emphasis). It is not clear, however, that imitation would be of any great value. Teachers are presumably not expected to set themselves tasks to which their TL competence is unequal and then to negotiate these communicative obstacles whilst the learners observe, which would in any case be of limited value.

To illustrate the point, let us assume that the teacher is demonstrating how to respond unprepared to an aural prompt of the kind the learners may expect. She has been asked what her favourite food is and the response runs as follows: *J'aime bien manger les fruits* . . . *et les abricots ou les pêches sont mes fruits préférés* ('I like fruit . . . and apricots or peaches are my favourites'). Now, in truth what she likes most of all is greengages (*reines-claudes*), but the word eludes her for the moment and she opts instead for *abricots* and *pêches*, which more readily spring to mind, being so similar in form to their English counterparts. In a French restaurant or market it might be important to indicate what one really does want, but in the classroom, dissembling of this kind usually makes no practical difference. The sentences are grammatically accurate and otherwise appropriate but literally inconsequential.

Imitation as proposed in the DES report is irrelevant here, but there is none-theless considerable scope for teaching and learning. First, let us assume our teacher is candid and self-confident enough to admit that the word for 'greengages' has slipped his or her mind and to ask the class to look it up with him or her; given the circumstances there is a good chance of the learners remembering it. And it is worth mentioning that it has been highlighted only because there has been a need to translate it. Second, the teacher can point out that he or she employed a communication strategy in order to keep the conversation going. In this case he or she avoided the problem word and substituted others which matched the topic of discussion. Another such strategy of particular help to learners is paraphrase. Thus, if a learner did not know the phrase *de l'eau potable* ('drinking water), he or she might ask instead for *de l'eau qu'on peut boire* ('water which one can drink'). In this way, learners have the chance to learn not just the instances cited (which is imitation) but to learn *from* them and to apply the underlying principle in numerous future contexts. It is worth noting that a cross-lingual strategy (translation) has been easily combined with intralingual communication strategies in the TL (avoidance, paraphrase).

Artificiality of the mfl classroom

In comparison to a natural language acquisition environment, a modern foreign language classroom suffers from a number of disadvantages. There is a shortage of TL input, an absence of uncontrived contextual clues to meaning and a dearth of opportunities for communicative interaction. Even when the teacher appears actually to be communicating in the TL, all may not be entirely as it seems. For instance, classroom management is sometimes cited as an example of authentic language use (see Asher 1993), but when the teacher issues an instruction such as *ouvrez vos livres* it may be the action of opening her own book, as much as her words, that serves as a cue to learners to follow suit. Using actions to complement words is, of course, entirely natural, but it raises an important issue in the particular environment of the mfl classroom. If in the learner's mind an utterance is fused together with a contextual feature, such as an action, the linguistic content may not have been analysed and the expression would not then be available for use in other contexts. Thus it may not be enough for the teacher to produce natur-alistic language resembling native speaker usage; instead she often has to contrive matters so that a given feature is highlighted and analysable by the learner.

Certainly, the creation of tasks and role play requires a degree of artifice: for learners and teachers to collude in the pretence that a classroom in Hackney is a French railway station is a 'self-evidently artificial process' (Hornsey 1994). A key element in this artificiality is the suppression of the knowledge that the learners, and usually the teacher, share a common mother tongue, and even when the teacher is a native speaker of the TL, his or her competence in English is generally such that it would be the natural medium of communication. On the other hand, it is plainly essential for learners to engage in TL use and if possible to initiate TL dialogue, e.g. by asking questions, but such approaches tend to encounter numerous difficulties. These range from: the unpredictable linguistic forms that may figure in answers to non-routine questions, to the very severe constraints upon practising conversation in the TL imposed by having one teacher fronting a class of fifteen or more learners (see Macaro 1997, pp. 111–6). However, when the teacher-dominated classroom is abandoned and, with a view to giving them greater opportunities for TL use, learners are set to work in unsupervised groups, they often revert to natural language behaviour and communicate in their shared mother tongue (see Grenfell and Harris 1993).

Since the TL is not the natural medium of communication, the situations which stimulate its use must be contrived. Teachers and learners cooperate in what Henry Widdowson describes as 'the illusion of reality' (1990, p. 45) but may more accurately be termed 'simulated reality', since the participants need be subject to no illusions as they construct learning situations. For instance, when the teacher poses as a TL speaker with no command of English, the learners are being asked to participate in an overt pretence so as to permit use of the TL in a particular way. What is at issue is not whether they believe in the pretence but whether, as Macaro comments (see 1997, p. 95), they will agree to 'play the game'.

The rationale for engaging in these simulations is that since mfl study in the classroom is itself artificial, subject to immense time constraints and occurs in an acquisition-poor environment, foreign language education must aim to improve upon natural processes (see Widdowson 1990). In the case of older learners literate in their mother tongue, careful selection and presentation of language materials by the teacher, as opposed to 'random linguistic bombardment', can greatly reduce the time and effort needed to induce the grammar of the TL (see Hawkins 1987, pp. 216–8). Indeed, a considerable body of recent theoretical work and empirical research confirms the importance of a focus on grammar in mfl teaching (see Ellis 1994, pp. 611–63; Ellis 1997, pp. 47–75; Spada 1997). And a purposive and systematic approach to language teaching and learning of this kind, that includes scrutiny of linguistic forms, is in principle quite consistent with the use of translation as a pedagogical tool.

It is perhaps worth clarifying one point here: I am most certainly not arguing against extensive use of the TL. The willingness to communicate orally in the TL, which is generally fostered in the years leading up to GCSE, should still be encouraged, even if at A/AS level learners are required to strive for greater linguistic accuracy. Although learners now have to view the TL more analytically than before, this should not be allowed to impair their enthusiasm for *using* it. The aim should be to build upon the foundations of good practice established at 11–16. The process of mfl teaching in the British context has been memorably likened by Hawkins (1987, pp. 97–8) to planting 'a few frail seedlings of . . . the foreign language', which are in constant danger of being destroyed by the 'gale of English' sweeping through the everyday life of the school. Within this hostile environment, maximum TL exposure in the classroom is like creating a micro-climate conducive to the growth of the language, and the close attention to language required by translation is a way of ensuring that the TL 'seedlings' are furnished with strong roots.

REFLECTION

Activity 12.2 'Plausible' activities

When we talk of the mfl classroom not being a 'natural' environment, we generally mean by comparison with everyday contexts of TL use. Can you think of plausible translation activities to help bridge that gap?

1   Is it plausible for learners to discuss a particular point of translation together? Is this what colleagues in an office might do? Or are there circumstances when they might work in isolation, competing against each other?

2   Is it plausible for learners to be given short passages for gist translation to work on in their own time, but to a deadline? If someone were given this kind of task in an office, would they be expected to make use of all available resources? What limitations, e.g. availability of bilingual colleagues or reference works, might they encounter? How might they overcome such limitations?

Use of the mother tongue

There is wide agreement that extensive use of the TL in the classroom helps towards communicative competence and, more specifically, that encouraging TL interaction between learners is of particular value; and much of the current debate centres on just how such approaches can best be implemented (see e.g. Macaro 1997). Nevertheless, there are aspects of classroom discourse where an insistence upon exclusive use of the TL and banning the mother tongue would be perverse.

As learners progress, they learn for example 'how to use the target language to find out what they do not know' (DES 1990, pp. 58–9). Accordingly, when learners are dealing with a French text they will typically frame questions of the type *Comment dit-on x en anglais?* ('How do you say x in English?'). Let us assume that a spoken or written French text has prompted a learner to ask: *Comment dit-on 'falaise' en anglais?* Along communicative lines, the teacher might typically produce an illustration and then confirm that the meaning has been grasped by means of questions and answers in the TL. If the procedure has been successful, the learner will have the equation '*une falaise* = a cliff' firmly fixed in his or her mind. Yet this is an incomplete and potentially misleading picture. *Une falaise* refers only to a seaside cliff, and a cliff inland is denoted, for instance, by *un escarpement*. Trying to explain a distinction of this kind in the TL would certainly provide language exposure but it is not certain that without recourse to the mother tongue everyone in an A/AS class would grasp it. In any event, since an explicit contrast is being drawn between how cliffs are designated in French and English, reference to the latter is inevitable.

The general point is that where the teacher needs to convey the exact meaning of a language item to an A/AS class, time and practicality often favour some use of the mother tongue. For instance, the TL word may have meanings and functions that do not match those of the corresponding English word:

1   *il a descendu les valises* = he brought down the suitcases
2   *te voilà! tu es decendu par l'ascenseur?* = there you are! did you come down in the lift?
3   *il a descendu son verre en deux secondes* = he downed his drink in two seconds flat

Clearly (1) contains a transitive and (2) an intransitive verb, but this does not correspond to the difference between English and French. *Il a descendu l'escalier* can be translated as 'he descended the stairs' but *il a descendu les valises* cannot be rendered by 'descend' since it cannot have 'suitcases' as its direct object. Unlike the French *descendre*, the English 'descend' does not encompass the sense 'bring or fetch down'. The meaning of (3) may not be immediately apparent without a translation, since English focuses on the contents of the glass ('he downed his drink'). It is hard to see how matters of this kind can be fully explained to an A/AS class without some recourse to translation and the mother tongue.

As well as elucidating meaning, cross-lingual comparisons can be used to sensitise learners to subtle but significant differences between the two languages. For example, whilst the English 'self-conscious', associated with embarrassment so acute that it may inhibit action, corresponds literally to *selbstbewusst*, the expression in fact means 'self-confident', suggesting that to the German mind consciousness of oneself and of what one is doing actually facilitates activity. Differing underlying attitudes are likewise implied by *Aussteiger* and its English counterpart 'dropout'. *Aussteigen* ('disembark') suggests a decision to get off a metaphorical vehicle on which society is travelling, whereas a 'dropout' is credited with nothing more than having allowed gravity to pull him downwards. Drawing learners' attention to such features need take up little time, alerts them to myriad differences between the two languages and should help to make the vocabulary items themselves more memorable.

However, rather than assigning a role to the mother tongue, the DES report recommends that, along with the TL, teachers should employ 'a variety of techniques' including 'gestures, mime and visual aids' to 'ensure that learners get the support they need to follow the lesson' (DES 1990, p. 58). While appropriate in many situations at 11–16, this does not help with the type of learner question at 16+ to which the teacher's only logical and natural reply would be in English, e.g. *Wie sagt man 'Vergaser'* (carburettor) *auf Englisch?* Here the 'support' the learner needs is quite clear: nothing other than the English translation of the German word, since it cannot be mimed or, with the exception of specialist groups, illustrated visually with any confidence that the correct meaning will be conveyed.

Indeed, according to a recent survey, teachers most frequently make use of the mother tongue in an unplanned way when they want to convey the 'exact meaning of a word, phrase or idiom' (Macaro 1997, p. 130) and are unable to do so by any other means. Similarly, as a review of surveys from the same source shows, whilst the theoretical case for 100 per cent use of the TL continues to be argued, in practice its exclusive or nearly exclusive use is 'rarely encountered in any learning context' (Macaro 1997, p. 96) apart from the study of English as a second or foreign language. (And, for reasons discussed above, English may be something of an exception.) Teachers typically have recourse to the mother tongue for sound pedagogical reasons such as explaining new and difficult linguistic items or for good practical reasons such as maintaining discipline or conveying information when time is short; moreover the mother tongue may be best suited to establishing the 'essential pupil–teacher relationship' (Macaro 1997, pp. 78 and 82–3).

Some suggestions for using translation as a teaching tool

Foreign language teachers will have experience of working extensively in the TL, and the following suggestions for using translation in the classroom are quite compatible with that approach. In no sense is a return to the grammar-translation methods of old being advocated, but, instead, translation is envisaged here as one in an array of teaching tools. Where A/AS level learners need to grasp particular nuances and cross-cultural dimensions of meaning, these may be thrown into relief by judicious use of translation and the mother tongue.

Material

It is generally sound practice to make clear to the learners exactly what the focus is when a piece is selected to exemplify how the TL differs from the mother tongue, e.g. the different verb tenses in *j'attends depuis deux heures* and 'I have been waiting for two hours'. The extent to which you use metalinguistic terminology (either in the TL or the mother tongue) to explain these matters will depend on the require-ments of the syllabus, your type of learner and your personal preferences. Although some teachers strongly object to the use of such terms, for learners above a certain age there is surely a powerful practical case for working with a basic system of labelling such as '(in)transitive verb' etc. (see also Chapter 6).

Unless there are compelling reasons for doing otherwise, it is generally advisable to avoid 'difficult' literary material (of the type once supposed to establish the academic credentials of mfl study) or nonsensical sentences – of the kind 'I have not seen your father's pen, but I have read the book of your uncle's gardener' (Widdowson 1990, p. 79) – invented so as to illustrate some grammatical feature. Neither type corresponds to everyday use and learners may well see little point in translating such material. Instead, a great array of texts can be drawn from various sources, ranging from those found in coursebooks to road signs, advertisements, short newspaper and magazine cuttings, etc. Short texts made up by the teacher, so long as they are plausible and avoid the type of absurdity mentioned above, can illustrate a particular point very effectively.

It may be useful to divide material as follows:

1 shorter texts intended primarily for in-class translation and discussion; and
2 longer texts, to be translated out of class, but to be discussed later in class.

Context

In translating, it is essential to know the context from which a particular passage has been taken – a business report, a satirical journalistic piece or a personal letter – as this will influence how we read that extract. Therefore, the teacher should normally provide the title or source of the piece with as much of the surrounding context as seems necessary. The translation of even an apparently simple expression such as 'Pleased to meet you' will vary greatly according to who is speaking, to whom and in what circumstances. If a young graduate attending his or her first job interview is being introduced to a personnel director at a formal meeting in which he or she is anxious to make a good impression, he or she might say: *Es freut mich sehr, Ihre Bekanntschaft zu machen* ('I'm very pleased to make your acquaintance'). But if he or she were sitting with friends in a café and was introduced to someone of his or her own age, *angenehm* (literally, 'pleasant') would be appropriate.

Translation entails looking for equivalent meanings in context, of which social appropriateness is one aspect. Examples of the kind just quoted should bring home to learners the fact that searching for literal, word-for-word equivalence between mother tongue and TL is often futile (see also Chapter 5).

Organising the class into groups

A key feature of the approach to using translation for teaching that I am suggesting is discussion of texts in small groups or pairs followed by whole-class discussion. At the first stage you, as the teacher, can explain that it is more useful for learners to develop their ideas and that you will reserve your own translations until later. Nevertheless, do circulate between groups, offering comments on the strengths and weaknesses of learners' work as it progresses and taking notes.

At the class discussion stage, the groups offer their different versions and comment on each other's ideas. You can then indicate your preferences, giving your reasons, but stressing that only rarely is there a single, definitive translation.

Pair/group work

The purpose of these activities is not testing but language learning and practice, which opens up the possibility of learners, rather than working in isolation and competing against each other, benefiting from collaborating with one another. But the approach should also be linguistically rigorous. Learners will examine exactly what a text means and consider various ways in which that meaning, with its various nuances, can be expressed in the other language: all of this lends itself naturally to discussion in groups. Group work gives learners a chance to test out their own ideas, to listen to those of others and make comparisons. Some learners will inevitably contribute more than others, but judicious interventions by the teacher should enable less assertive members to express their ideas in the relatively safe environment of a small group.

Learners will naturally tend to use English in discussion, but this can generally be justified so long as they are making close comparisons between their mother tongue and the TL. To offset any danger of the mother tongue becoming the predominant medium of communication, the teacher may want to intersperse translation activities with communicative tasks on a closely related topic to be conducted solely in the TL, such as finding synonyms, matching words to definitions, etc.

Much of the language correction will be carried out by the learners themselves within their groups. They should be quite receptive to corrections from their peers, with whom they are pooling their ideas; and corrections from the teacher, so long as the reasons are made clear, should be useful rather than inhibiting, since these too can be seen as part of refining draft translations – a joint enterprise in which all are engaged.

Paraphrase and gist translation

Naturally enough, when learners are working in the TL they tend to ask the teacher for words they do not yet know, and one way to reduce their dependence on the teacher (or the dictionary) is to develop their capacity to paraphrase in the TL. In this connection a useful technique is to give topics for group discussion – careers, drug abuse, etc. – during which learners (and teacher) note down several things which they would like to say in the TL but for which they lack the exact words. They can then practise ways of circumventing the problem, employing strategies such as the following:

- using the 'opposite' of the problem word, e.g. *Jean m'a prêté une bicyclette* ('John has lent me a bicycle') instead of *j'ai emprunté une bicyclette à Jean* ('I've borrowed a bicycle from John')
- finding a simpler or less idiomatic expression, e.g. *pas beaucoup de gens* ('not many people') for *peu de monde* ('few people')
- giving a definition or description, e.g. *c'est un truc pour ouvrir des bouteilles de vin* ('a whatsit for opening wine bottles') for *tire-bouchon* ('corkscrew'), or
- using mime or facial expressions or simply pointing, e.g. *j'ai mal ici* ('It hurts here')

REFLECTION

Activity 12.3 Group work

Having learners work in groups is not without problems. How well do your learners respond to working in groups? Are group work and a degree of independent learning compatible with your teaching aims and the types of group you teach?

It may be useful to try the following approaches:

1   start by closely supervising the group activities but gradually relax supervision as the learners become more used to working independently

2   likewise, give the learners very specific instructions at first but gradually allow them to define their tasks for themselves

The use of translation in the classroom

Individual words and phrases

Of course there tends not to be one-to-one correspondence of words or phrases between any two languages, but establishing provisional equivalences between the two languages – at the expense of temporary over-simplification – can be both expedient and pedagogically sound. Indeed, there is considerable evidence that in trying to make sense of the new language learners draw upon the patterns and rules they know from their mother tongue (see Ellis 1994, pp. 299–345). As knowledge of the TL develops and the learner's picture of the relationships between the two languages becomes more complex and accurate, the areas where they do not overlap gradually emerge in greater detail.

The general principle to be followed here would seem to be to progress from what can be easily inferred from the mother tongue to what is less obvious. For instance, given that the learner has got the equation 'foot' = *pied* clearly established in his or her mind there should be no difficulty in encompassing *il était pieds nus* ('he was barefoot/ed') or *partir du bon pied* ('to get off on the right foot'). The image evoked by *avoir toujours un pied en l'air* ('to be always on the go') is sufficiently graphic to be likewise intelligible, perhaps after some prompting from the teacher, despite its misleading verbal similarity to the semantically very different English expression 'he has both feet firmly planted in mid-air'.

Even where there are no such visual equivalences between the mother tongue and the TL, there are advantages to cross-linguistic comparisons. One way of raising awareness of relationships between the two languages is by drawing attention to cognates such as German *Dorf* ('village') and English '–thorpe' as in Scun*thorpe* etc. Given the current widespread obsession with all things relating to the late Princess Diana, a cognate likely to be remembered is the name of her final resting-place, Al*thorp*:

D o r f

```
|        |
|        |
|        |
```

t(h)orp(e)

Examples in context

Using an authentic text on a topic in which it seems reasonable to encourage A/AS level learners' interest, we may take a subheading to an article on the fighting in Kosovo:

> Emissäre Washingtons und Moskaus haben die Pendeldiplomatie . . . intensiviert.
>
> > (*Neue Zürcher Zeitung*, 6 July 1998)
>
> Emissaries from Washington and Moscow have stepped up their shuttle diplomacy.

Working within the TL and starting from the core meaning of *Pendel* ('pendulum'), the teacher might provide a drawing of *eine Penduluhr* ('pendulum clock') and then move on to the transferred sense:

> *Ein Pendler pendelt zwischen seinem Wohnort und dem Büro.*
> A commuter commutes between (his) home and the office.

At this stage, if not before, it is necessary for *Pendeldiplomatie* to be explicitly translated by a learner or the teacher, before the connotations of 'commuting' block out the primary metaphors: on the one hand, of a pendulum swinging back and forth and, on the other, of a weaver's shuttle moving to and fro – although the transferred meaning of 'shuttlecock' may serve better, as learners are likely to be more familiar with badminton than weaving. As examples of current use, the air 'shuttle service' between, say, London and Edinburgh or *le shuttle* under the English Channel are probably known to learners and correspond to *pendeln* in its sense of 'commute'. Once the correspondence between the underlying images has been grasped, related terms in the TL can be mentioned and a translation asked for:

> *der Pendelverkehr* = *der Berufsverkehr* = commuter traffic
> *der Pendelverkehr von Bussen/der Pendelzug* = shuttle service

Thus, a small semantic field has been mapped out and the meaning of the original expression should have been clearly established in the learner's mind. Supplementary examples of this kind are intended to clarify and consolidate the first meaning and in introducing them, the teacher needs to be sensitive to whether the learners understand or indeed see the point of them. Waning learner interest often marks the point beyond which there is a danger of overwhelming with detail.

In contrast to the above examples, there are many TL words and phrases fulfilling a variety of functions whose meaning cannot be clarified by reference to a graphic metaphor and which do not lend themselves to a single rendering. German particles such as *denn, doch, ja, mal*, etc. belong in this category, along with *allerdings*, which twice appears in a text discussing the fiftieth anniversary of the British National Health Service.

Grossbritanniens 'kostenloser' Gesundheitsdienst

Jeder hier Ansässige hat . . . . Anrecht auf die seiner Krankheit angemessene bestmögliche ärztliche Behandlung. Diese ist allerdings [1] nicht mehr völlig kostenlos: Rezeptgebühren wurden eingeführt. . . . Fast nur [die Universitäts- spitäler] besitzen die modernsten hochtechnologischen Apparate, allerdings [2] meistens in ungenügender Zahl . . .

(Neue Zürcher Zeitung, 4–5 July 1998)

Great Britain's 'free' Health Service

Everyone resident here . . . is entitled to the best possible medical treatment appropriate to his illness. This treatment is no longer completely free, however [1]: prescription charges were introduced . . . Almost without exception it is only [the university hospitals] which have the most modern, high-tech equip- ment and even there it is admittedly [2] for the most part in short supply . . .

In both cases *allerdings* has a concessive function, but both translations offered invite alternatives. Where *allerdings* [1] is concerned, 'though' might serve as a less emphatic replacement for 'however'. Alternative renderings of *allerdings* [2] could include 'the university hospitals do have the most modern, high-tech equipment, *albeit* in insufficient quantities . . .' were it not for the powerful constraints imposed by the opening *fast nur* ('almost only'). In fact, given that the translation suggested has 'almost without exception . . .' and 'even there . . .', the concessive 'admittedly' may be superfluous. Its German counterpart, *allerdings* [2], could also be omitted without affecting intelligibility, but the omission would create a blunt and stilted effect.

Redundancy is an integral feature of all language, not merely as a matter of style, but because it is an important aid to clarity and ease of understanding. Particles such as *allerdings* and the others mentioned above (*denn, doch*, etc) generally serve this purpose and belong to natural, colloquial German as used by native speakers. Their 'correct use is a considerable test for the foreigner' (Hammer 1983, p. 145) and it follows that finding equivalents for them in another language can be difficult. Nonetheless, attempts to do so should help to illuminate their functions within German texts, as well as providing valuable points of comparison between the TL and the mother tongue.

Grammar in action in context

A principal weakness of the grammar-translation method is an excessive use of single sentences to exemplify a given grammatical feature or to provide a 'problem' for the learner. Focusing on grammar is an indispensable part of learning an FL, as many researchers and commentators agree (see above), which may entail abstracting the structures in question from their context so as to scrutinise them. Yet it can also be extremely useful to consider the role played by specific language items within a longer passage (or stretch of discourse, as it is often termed). Examining discourse is one way of looking at grammar in action, and translation, rather than being deployed as the sets of mechanical tasks or deliberately problematic texts too often seen in the past, can be used to illuminate aspects of the TL in context.

Attention to discourse is properly part of learning a language from the earliest stages (see Cook 1989), but a more advanced text is required for present purposes. We shall look at the introduction to a longish newspaper article, with at least two aims in mind. A particular grammatical item – the use of the subjunctive in German indirect speech – is examined and its function highlighted partly by considering its discoursal context and partly by comparing it with an English translation. More generally, the passage could be used to elicit TL responses from the learners on a topic on which they are likely to hold views that they will want to express – violence inflicted by men on their women partners.

Detailed suggestions about how such learner discussions might best be organised lie outside the scope of this chapter, but a more general point should become clear. In dealing with such texts, cross-lingual strategies, including translation, and intra-lingual strategies, such as discussions in the TL about the subject matter, can be used quite naturally to supplement each other.

Against the background of the violence committed by English and German hooligans during the 1998 World Cup in France, the article discusses well-publicised cases of English footballers physically assaulting their wives or girlfriends, yet going largely unpunished.

> **Gewalt? Helden zeigen, wie es geht**
> **Englands Fußballstars mißhandeln ihre Frauen – und können mit Nachsicht rechnen**
> Selten wurde eine öffentliche Entschuldigung so kalt aufgenommen. Stan Collymore, Starfußballspieler . . . warf sich mit einem offenen Brief an die *Sun* in den Staub. Am Vorabend hatte Collymore seine Freundin Ulrika Jonsson zusammengeschlagen. Ein einmaliger Wutausbruch, den er bitter *bereue*, hieß es im Brief an die Nation. Niemand war ernsthaft versucht, ihm zu glauben. Am wenigsten Ulrika Jonsson.
>
> (*Die Zeit*, 2 July 1998; my emphasis)

> **Violence? Heroes show how to do it**
> **England's football stars maltreat their women – and can expect leniency**
> Seldom did a public apology get such a frosty reception. Stan Collymore, a

star footballer . . . prostrated himself in an open letter to the *Sun*. On the previous evening Collymore had beaten up his girlfriend, Ulrika Jonsson. A single outburst of fury which he bitterly *regretted*, it said in his letter to the nation. No one was seriously tempted to believe him. Least of all Ulrika Jonsson.

An important pedagogical aim in examining this text is to illuminate the lack of confidence in Collymore's sincerity implied by the use of the subjunctive *bereue*. But other elements in the passage have been chosen by the writer in order to create certain effects and we shall start by looking at larger discourse items. The titles to this article make it clear that we are dealing with a world of distorted values, of which a defining feature is the first word we encounter, *Gewalt* ('violence'). Rather disconcertingly juxtaposed to this is 'heroes' (*Helden*), who are normally thought of, not as perpetrators of violence, but as embodying admirable qualities such as courage or integrity. However, these are 'heroes' only in a very particular sense, for they are revealed to be *Englands Fußballstars*. At the time the article was written, during the 1998 World Cup in France, this phrase could be expected to evoke in the reader's mind two other words borrowed from English, *Fans* and *Hooligans*, and, indeed, there are references later in the piece to the violence and vandalism perpetrated in France by *englische Hooligans*. Some of the 'stars' – other examples are cited further on – far from embodying heroic virtues, inflict violence on their wives and girlfriends and then can expect not punishment but leniency (*Nachsicht*), from the football authorities in Collymore's case, as later becomes apparent.

Further on, the passage reveals that Collymore had earlier assaulted a different girlfriend, a fact which demolishes his excuse that his attack on Jonsson was 'a one-off outburst of fury' (*ein einmaliger Wutausbruch*); and woven into the fabric of the opening paragraph is another compelling reason for doubting the sincerity of his apology. The image of ostentatious self-abasement (*warf sich . . . in den Staub* = 'threw himself into the dust') may be no more than ironic authorial comment, but what is the point of this 'public apology' (*öffentliche Entschuldigung*) offered in the form of a letter to the *Sun* newspaper the day after the assault? It plainly has little or nothing to do with making amends to his victim; how this could be achieved is not entirely clear, but it would surely be a process conducted in private over a considerable period of time. The prompt and public nature of the 'apology' reeks of public relations manoeuvring. Thus, the primary purpose of this posturing seems to be to salvage whatever remains of the footballer's public image – later his sponsorship deals are mentioned – and the dubious character of an apology seen to be motivated by material self-interest is aptly conveyed by the subjunctive *bereue* ('regretted').

At the level of discourse, it should now be clear how the headlines and opening paragraph have been designed so as to make the footballer's apology appear self-serving and hollow. This effect in turn depends on an understanding of the precise grammatical force of *bereue*, the subjunctive in indirect speech being used in German to cast doubt on the veracity of an utterance. English, since it has no subjunctive verb form distinct from the indicative to deploy here, relies on devices such as 'it said in this letter' or 'at least, so he claimed in his letter' to indicate the dubiety of the utterance; in these circumstances English, to a greater extent than German, must rely on the linguistic context or the extra-linguistic context – assumptions about the reader's knowledge of human nature and so on – in order to convey meaning. Here cross-lingual strategies, including translation, provide an opportunity to examine how the two languages deploy their different resources to realise very similar though not identical meanings thereby furnishing insights not accessible if work were conducted exclusively in the TL.

Use of dictionaries

Communicative approaches and working predominantly in the TL should foster the following:

- an ability to avoid problem words by resorting to paraphrase
- a capacity for seeing the gist of a passage rather than getting bogged down with single words, and
- a competence in deducing the meaning of unknown words by reference to contextual clues, such as the title and topic of a passage

Indeed, such skills should assist a learner in using dictionaries, since intelligent guessing as to the meaning of a new word or phrase will generally guide the learner towards a correct entry. Using dictionaries effectively is an essential aspect of work at A/AS level. Learners will be making use of authentic texts, i.e. those written for native speakers in the real world, for which there are no glossaries but which are an indispensable source of material for course-work assignments. Additionally, we hope that learners, as they become more proficient, will be reading for pleasure in the TL. For these various activities, which learners will be conducting with progressively greater independence, dictionaries are a necessity.

Most mfl dictionaries published currently have been carefully designed to help language users and learners perform practical tasks, and the introductions are intended to demonstrate just how to do so. Learners are likely to become much more effective dictionary users if, guided by the teacher, they work through these instructions and then put what they learn into practice.

The Introduction to the *Oxford–Hachette French Dictionary* (1997) covers a range of tasks which a user might wish to undertake, one being to understand the meaning of the acronym SMIC in the phrase *ils sont payés au SMIC* (see p. xxx). Turning to SMIC, the reader will find a cross-reference to *salaire*. Abbreviations and acronyms are always to be found in the compound block at the end of an entry, as the Introduction informs us, and there we find that SMIC stands for *salaire minimum interprofessionnel de croissance*, of which the English equivalent is 'guaranteed minimum wage'. Working through a number of tasks along these lines should help learners to become competent users of bilingual dictionaries, not hunting for word-for-word equivalents but able to exploit the wealth of information available (grammar, idioms, etc, as well as vocabulary).

As learners progress they will also need to use a monolingual TL dictionary. This has a number of uses, one of which is to supplement the bilingual dictionary. The point can be illustrated by considering the start of a passage which discusses a citizens' self-help scheme during the post-war reconstruction of a German spa town.

> Man darf es nicht nur als *das Ei des Kolumbus* beim Wiederaufbau bezeichnen, sondern auch als eines der schönsten Zeugnisse für den Gemeinsinn der Bevölkerung einer kleinen Stadt, daß es Bürgermeister Saam gelang, den Gedanken der Selbsthilfe in die Tat umzusetzen.
>
> (RSA Diploma for Bilingual Secretaries; my emphasis)

> That Mayor Saam succeeded in translating the idea of self-help into action must be seen not only as *Columbus's Egg* in relation to reconstruction but also as fine testimony to the civic spirit of the population of a small town.

Here an understanding of the wider context is essential: the townspeople agreed to pool their assets in a central fund, which provided the capital to start rebuilding the houses destroyed in the Second World War. This initiative is *das Ei des Kolumbus*. An 'inspired discovery', the translation offered by the *Oxford–Duden German Dictionary* (1997), would seem here to be a partial rather than a precise fit. The sense is accurately conveyed by the explanation *eine überraschend einfache Lösung* ('a surprisingly simple solution') to be found in *Duden: Redewendungen und sprichwörtliche Redensarten* (1992). Here the idea of a startlingly simple solution to difficult problems is traced back to an (apocryphal) incident when Columbus supposedly demonstrated that an egg can be made to sit upright if one gently taps and thereby flattens its round end. In English, although we have Archimedes leaping from his bath exclaiming 'Eureka!' or Isaac Newton observing the apple fall or Alexander cutting through the Gordian Knot, we do not seem to possess an exactly equivalent expression.

Thus, one important function of monolingual TL dictionaries is to help learners appreciate such nuances of difference between their mother tongue and the TL.

Conclusion

Extensive use of the TL provides the language exposure and practice essential to mfl learning, but it is also quite consistent with judicious use of the mother tongue and translation. Recourse to the mother tongue may be dictated by practical considerations such as explaining meanings, but translation, being a natural activity, also has a sound pedagogical basis. Using translation for teaching purposes is quite different from the grammar-translation method of old: short passages illustrating particular linguistic features are discussed by learners working in groups so that they can express and compare ideas.

Differences in meaning between the mother tongue and the TL, ranging in scope from single words to stretches of discourse, can be highlighted very effectively by translating.between the two languages. Moreover, an ability to translate is a valuable practical application of mfl knowledge. Finally, we have considered how acquiring dictionary skills both contributes to a greater understanding of the languages in question and is an indispensable feature of becoming an independent language learner and user.

References

Asher, C. (1993) 'Using the target language as the medium for instruction in the communicative classroom: the influence of practice on principles'. In *Studies in Modern Languages in Education 1*, Leeds: University of Leeds, pp. 53–71.

Atkinson, D. (1993) 'Teaching in the target language'. In *Language Learning Journal 8*, pp. 2–5.

Bryson, B. (1990) *Mother Tongue: The English Language*. Harmondsworth: Penguin.

Cook, G. (1989) *Discourse*. Oxford: Oxford University Press.

Cook, G. (1998) 'Use of translation in language teaching'. *Routledge Encyclopaedia of Translation Studies*. London: Routledge, pp. 117–20.

Crystal, D. (1997) *English as a Global Language*. Cambridge: Cambridge University Press.

DES (1990) *Modern Foreign Languages for Ages 11 to 16*. London: HMSO.

Duden (1992) *Redewendungen und sprichwörtliche Redensarten*. Mannheim: Duden.

Ellis, R. (1994) *The Study of Second Language Acquisition*. Oxford: Oxford University Press.

Ellis, R. (1997) *Second Language Acquisition Research and Language Teaching*. Oxford: Oxford University Press.

Grenfell, M. and Harris, V. (1993) 'How do pupils learn?' (Part 1). In *Language Learning Journal 8*, pp 22–5.

Hammer, A. (1983) *German Grammar and Usage*. London: Arnold.

Hawkins, E. (1987) *Modern Languages in the Curriculum*. Revised edn. Cambridge: Cambridge University Press.

Hornsey, A. (1994) 'Authenticity in foreign language learning'. In *Languages Forum 2–3*, pp. 6–7.

Howatt, A. (1984) *A History of English Language Teaching*. Oxford: Oxford University Press.

Krashen, S. (1982) *Principles and Practice in Second Language Acquisition*. Oxford: Pergamon.

Macaro, E. (1997) *Target Language, Collaborative Learning and Autonomy*. Clevedon: Multilingual Matters.

OFSTED (1993) *Handbook: Inspection Schedule*. London: HMSO.

Oxford–Duden German Dictionary (1997) Revised edn. Oxford: Clarendon Press.

Phillipson, R. (1992) *Linguistic Imperialism*. Oxford: Oxford University Press.

Prabhu, N. (1987) *Second Language Pedagogy*. Oxford: Oxford University Press.

Sewell, P. and Higgins, I. (1996) (eds) *Teaching Translation in Universities*. London: CILT.

Spada, N. (1997) 'Form-focussed instruction and second language acquisition', *Language Teaching 3* pp. 73–87.

Stern, H. (1992) *Issues and Options in Language Teaching*, P. Allen and B. Harley (eds) Oxford: Oxford University Press.

Widdowson, H. (1990) *Aspects of Language Teaching*. Oxford: Oxford University Press.

Chapter 13

Assessment

Ann Barnes

Introduction

> Tests should be a help, not a hindrance. They should act as a guide to both student and teacher as to progress made, level of proficiency attained, gaps to be filled, misinterpretations and misconceptions, and the need for further learning or further teaching. We must avoid tests that merely place hurdles or obstacles in the path of our students, upsetting and confusing them with no particular gain from the experience.
>
> (Rivers *et al.* 1988, p. 311)

Written over ten years ago, the above quotation refers to 'tests' rather than assessment, but the authors' message provides a basic outline for this chapter. Assessment can be seen merely as 'tests', which in turn can be seen as something negative and threatening. In fact, the process of assessment should be something positive and forward looking, and is vital to teaching and learning. Wilga Rivers *et al.* conclude their advice on testing by stating that assessment should be part of the developmental process, 'something not to be feared, but to be appreciated for its intrinsic interest and for what can be learned from it' (Rivers *et al.* 1988, p. 332).

Reflecting on the 16–19 curriculum, Jeremy Higham *et al.* (1996, p. 57) comment that A/AS level syllabuses, now known as subject specifications, have been criticised for their narrow assessment methods, in particular terminal written examinations and the preponderance of factual recall. The introduction of course work and modular syllabuses has broadened the range of methods used, but the A/AS level course does tend to be dominated by the assessment methods of the examinations. Indeed, when 'assessment' is mentioned, it is easy to assume that what is meant are solely tests and examinations.

Assessment should not be simply an 'add-on' activity, seen as distinct from the rest of the programme and carried out under formal conditions at the end of a large block of work or at the end of a course. Assessment should be regular and integrated into normal teaching and learning. Caroline Gipps states that assessment has now taken on a high profile and is required to fulfil a wide range of purposes (see Gipps 1994, p. 1). She points out that testing has an effect on teaching in terms of curriculum coverage (i.e. teachers teach what will be tested) and also on the way in which the subject matter is presented (i.e. the tasks and learning activities in class reflect those which are used in examinations) (see Gipps 1994, p. 18). In more didactic models of teaching, assessment was a check on whether what had been 'transmitted' had been 'successfully received' (see Gipps 1994, p. 24). The role of assessment now involves much more than this and is fundamental to the learning process.

The key question is how to use assessment to support teaching and learning whilst also responding to demands for information about learners' progress and achievements (for example, university applications). As Gipps points out, A/AS levels are 'high stakes' examinations (see Gipps 1994, p. 35). They can ensure entry into higher education or employment and are, therefore, very closely observed by a variety of interested parties, not least the media. As these examinations are high stakes, there is an understandable desire to ensure what is tested is taught and that achievement is as high as possible. This aim is not necessarily, of course, at odds with ensuring learners are supported in the learning process.

When reading about assessment, a wide range of purposes and competences becomes apparent: diagnosis, selection, prediction, examination, grading, evaluation, backwash, motivation, research. Gordon Stobart and Caroline Gipps (1997, p. vi) distinguish two *main* purposes of assessment: assessment *for* learning (professional purposes) and assessment *of* learning (managerial purposes). Assessment *for* learning is, they argue, essentially formative (see below). A central difference, then, between the two types is assessment *during* the course and *terminal* assessment at the end of the course. The overriding purpose of assessment is one of supporting the teaching and learning process.

Whatever the purpose, we must be sure *what* exactly is being assessed (for example, recognition of language? ability to manipulate a grammatical structure? creative response to literary material?) and *why* it is being assessed (for example, during the course to help the learner move on? to provide information for outside parties, for example for entry to higher education?). These two questions are fundamental to assessment.

Classroom assessment in foreign language (FL) teaching is not a separate element, it is an integral part of a complex jigsaw in which the aims of classroom assessment are the following:

- 'to motivate pupils and teachers
- to inform the teaching and learning process
- to inform 'relevant others'
- to encourage cooperative styles of work
- to encourage responsibility and involvement, and
- to effect a healthy backwash upon learning and teaching' (Clark 1987, p. 9)

To achieve success in formal examinations, learners need to be assessed and monitored throughout the course and they need to develop the ability to assess and monitor their own progress and therefore to take responsibility for their own learning. Careful assessment and planning of assessment, will help this development. The ability of the teacher to assess learners' progress accurately is vital.

Objectives

By the end of this chapter, you should have:

- gained an understanding of the importance of assessment in FL learning
- familiarised yourself with both formative and summative forms of assessment and understood their different functions
- developed some understanding of teacher assessment and learner self-assessment
- gained an overview of target setting, planning and the use of benchmarks in A/AS level FL courses
- developed an understanding of marking and recording progress at A/AS level
- and learnt about ways in which learners can best be prepared and prepare themselves for examinations

Assessment during the teaching and learning process

Assessment is, then, an integral part of the teaching and learning process. Every learning activity, every task, every response, every lesson is assessed or evaluated in some way, albeit mostly much more informally than through a 'test'. Planning what is to be taught and learnt and then executing those plans is insufficient. It is always necessary for the teacher to ensure that the learning objectives have been met – and this is a continuous process, whether the overall, formal assessment is labelled continuous or not. When teaching, the teacher is continually making decisions as to the extent and type of learning taking place (see Figure 13.1). The teacher's professional judgement is crucial in this ongoing assessment.

- are the learners only at the recognition stage with a linguistic item or is it already part of their productive repertoire?
- is the pronunciation of a particular sound causing problems only for the individual speaking at the moment or is it a more general problem?
- is the learner unable to contribute because of a lack of *language* or a lack of knowledge or opinion?

Figure 13.1 Some assessment questions during the learning process

REFLECTION
Activity 13.1 Observation of assessment in action
Consider a ten-minute phase of a recent lesson you have taught or observed. Referring to Figure 13.1, what sort of questions were being asked by the teacher to assess the learning process?

Questions such as those in Figure 13.1, and many more, are asked by every FL teacher in the course of an activity in class. They are mostly dealt with immediately, perhaps by asking an open question where language manipulation is required or by modelling the pronunciation of a word again. This process is part of assessment, i.e. what exactly is being learnt and how? What needs to happen next to ensure the learning process continues? Planning, progression and assessment are therefore linked.

Effective assessment is more likely to lead to effective learning, greater motivation and higher achievement. It is not only a means of testing *what has been achieved*, as is usually the case with formal tests and examinations, but a process of working out *what should be learnt next*. As learners are moving towards the many goals of their A/AS level course, teachers must assess and monitor their progress and provide information and feedback which enable them to move on.

Suzanne Graham (1997) in her book detailing how A/AS level FL learners can be helped to learn more effectively, stresses that we should not underestimate the complexity of the language learning process A/AS learners go through. She believes we must:

- acknowledge learner anxiety
- help learners develop language learning strategies – more explicitly, and
- help learners become more reflective and self-critical in their approach

She also notes that understanding how learners learn is as important as being aware of what they are learning. In this latter area, and in all three of the points noted above, assessment plays a vital role.

Assessment as part of the teaching and learning process at A/AS level

Moving to the next rung of the learning ladder does not very often only require knowledge of formal content, but the decision-making and problem-solving skills that must be fuelled by that knowledge (see Borich 1995, p. 25). Learners need to be *participants* in the learning process rather than merely *recipients* (see Borich 1995, p. 31). This is certainly true of FL learning. Learners need to know what to do with the linguistic items and structures they are exposed to and how they are to use them. In the following, I shall argue that this learner participation can be furthered by ongoing, constructive assessment.

In his review of research on assessment and evaluation, Terence Crooks finds that assessment appears to be one of the most potent forces influencing education. He describes it as affecting learners in many different ways. Assessment

- 'guides their judgement about what is important to learn
- affects their motivation and their self-perception of their competence
- structures their approaches to and their timing of personal study
- consolidates learning
- and affects the development of evolving learning strategies and skills'

(Crooks 1988, p. 467)

These effects, it can be argued, are contributory to the learner as participant. The effects outlined here are vital in ensuring pupils at A/AS level work and achieve to the best of their potential.

Successful and focused assessment which includes learner training (teaching learners *how* to learn, see below) can enable more learners to follow the more positive route of development (see Figure 13.2). This is, of course, even more important if learners embark on their A/AS level course lacking in confidence. Learners can be given user-friendly information on the course and the assessment involved. This may include advice on how to organise their work (see Figure 13.3) and can contribute to successful goal setting and fewer problems at revision and examination time. It should also include, as Peter Boaks emphasises, 'the destination and purpose of their journey' (Boaks 1991, p. 12), that is the aims of the course. In this vein, the *aims* of an A/AS level syllabus (now specifications) are often more positive as goals than a factual description of the papers. It is vitally important to evaluate how well learners cope with various aspects of the course from an early stage. This is particularly true at the start of an A/AS level programme, in the transition from GCSE to A/AS level, when attitudes and learning habits are formed. An interim assessment of a more formal nature, alongside ongoing monitoring, will help in the transition process, as will an open atmosphere in class where learners feel able to voice their concerns and misunderstandings.

Gipps (1994, p. 27) outlines a Vygotskyan approach to assessment, the 'zone of proximal development' (see also Williams and Burden 1997, p. 65), which involves the gap between the learner's unaided performance and his or her potential level as shown by his or her performance under adult guidance or in collaboration with more capable peers. This support and guidance to help a learner perform at a higher level is labelled 'scaffolding'. This scaffolding is gradually removed. 'Scaffolded assessment' is more interactive, where the focus is on learning potential. It should not be only a memory test. Gipps (1994, p. 30) also points out that current learning theory indicates that what we need in assessment is to be able to assess three elements:

In the first few months of an A/AS level course, learners' progress could be seen according to the following development:

Stage 1

confident, successful and enjoyed GCSE modern foreign languages (therefore chose to continue at A/AS level)

Stage 2

(a) apprehensive about A/AS level (the 'route' has not been mapped out)

or . . .

(b) informed and excited about A/AS level (they have received documentation and information, possibly attended some classes, and have had their queries answered. The 'route' is clear.)

Stage 3

(a) overwhelmed by A/AS level work – 'slog', not progress (they feel lost and see no signposts towards successful achievement)

or . . .

(b) hard but productive work towards A/AS level where progress is noticeable (through feedback, target setting, benchmarks – concrete goals are set and progress is seen.)

Figure 13.2 Learner progress at the beginning of an A/AS level course

- what the pupil already knows
- his or her learning strategies, and
- his or her ability to be aware of and control his or her learning

Reuven Feuerstein (referred to by Williams and Burden 1997, p. 41) considered all learners as capable of becoming fully effective learners, provided they develop the necessary skills and strategies. These strategies include both cognitive (involving the mental processes used when learning a language) and metacognitive (involving the way in which learners go about their learning, for example planning and target-setting) strategies. They can be seen as teaching learners how to learn and are essential in FL learning. A clear definition of learning/learner strategies is not easy to find, but is used here to describe the habits and practices learners adopt to help them learn a language (see Grenfell and Harris 1998, p. 24). It is the role of the

Learners could be given a list such as the following, to provide a framework for the organisation of their work:

- vocabulary (lists, fields)
- how to record vocabulary effectively (e.g. nominative, gender and plural form)
- a learner's 'first aid kit' (see Figure 13.8, and to include evidence of 'corrections')
- texts and articles divided appropriately into topics
- grammar rules/notes/exercises
- work for this week/work in progress
- homework which is mainly listening/reading/speaking/writing, and
- notes on literary/cultural topics

Learners should not be required to stick to the list too prescriptively, but it should be pointed out that whatever approach they adopt, it needs to be clear and easy to follow. You as the teacher can help by checking files occasionally.

Figure 13.3 Organising learners' work

teacher to help learners to find ways of moving into their next level of understanding of the language (see Williams and Burden 1997, p. 66).

All this can be linked to the teacher's own teaching effectiveness. When planning lessons, teachers need to assess where the learners are at present and how they are going to move on. People cannot learn what they are not ready for (see Claxton 1988, p. 26). Learning is essentially a growth, not an accumulation and it must always spring from and return to what is known (see Claxton 1988, p. 27). Ongoing assessment is the key to finding out what learners are ready for and planning how you will assess is crucial in order to have a positive effect.

Formative and summative assessment – definitions and distinctions

Formative and summative assessment can be defined in the following way:

> *Formative assessment:* takes place during the course of teaching and is used essentially to feed back into the teaching/learning process.
>
> *Summative assessment:* takes place at the end of a term or course and is used to provide information about how much students have learned and how well a course has worked.
>
> (Gipps 1994, p. vii)

For linguists, the roots of the two adjectives help clarify the distinction: *formative* concerned with education and shaping and *summative* with a summary of achievements. Assessment is not just restricted to tests, examinations and course work. It is ongoing – teachers assessing the learning process and learners assessing themselves. Whilst A/AS levels as a certification and selection process may indeed be a summative assessment of learners' skills, understanding and knowledge, assessment during the course is aimed at improving learning. Formative assessment helps the learner move forward, increases his or her confidence and motivation and helps the teacher in course development. In the process of guiding each learner and feeding back to him or her, a lot is learnt by the teacher which will effect planning for the following year. At the end of a term or a year, you could also gauge learners' responses to the course with a short questionnaire, which gives them another opportunity to reflect on their learning and enables them to comment on the lessons.

Dylan William and Paul Black (1996, p. 538) stress that the terms 'formative' and 'summative' do not refer to the assessments themselves, but to the *functions* they serve. What is designed as a summative assessment, for example, a test, can be used formatively by the teacher to help learners prepare for an impending examination. The common element in formative assessments, they say, is feedback (see below). William and Black (1996, p. 540) refer to the 'assessment cycle', where evidence of performance or achievement is elicited, interpreted and acted upon (see Figure 13.4). This applies both to summative and formative assessment. When teachers interpret the 'evidence' they are determining the gaps in learning and, to qualify as feedback, the information given must be useful in *closing* the gap between the actual and the desired levels of performance. The feedback must have embedded in it some degree of prescription about what must be done. *All* assessments can be summative, but only some have the *additional* capability of serving formative functions. Feedback and formative assessment are particularly important in FL learning, where learners can feel overwhelmed by the sheer amount of new vocabulary encountered at A/AS level and where comparisons with native speakers can be very demotivating. Learners need to see progress to feel more motivated and for their FL learning self-esteem to grow. FL learning at A/AS level, whilst clearly including content and knowledge, is essentially skills-based, and without formative feedback, these skills will be unlikely to develop positively.

'Evidence' which you could assess in A/AS level FL learning in order to decide on feedback needed could include:

- test results
- homework
- oral presentation in class
- dialogue with another learner, and
- taped homework

Figure 13.4 'Evidence' in assessing foreign languages

REFLECTION
Activity 13.2 Collecting evidence for assessment
Add other examples of 'evidence' you could use when assessing foreign languages to the list provided in Figure 13.4.

Thus the major difference between formative and summative assessment is its function. There can be a tension between the two, when a teacher has to perform both roles (see Gipps 1994, p. 127) – the teacher may be seen as judge rather than facilitator.

The function of formative assessment

This section considers in greater depth the function of formative assessment and the importance of constructive feedback and support. Unlike *normative* assessment, a learner's performance during the learning process should not be judged in relation to others in the group when providing feedback. Formative assessment concentrates on an *individual's* progress. It is asking 'how well' rather than 'how many' and it is personal to the learner (see Gipps 1994, p. 4). Assessment must be used in support of learning rather than just to indicate current or past achievement.

Crooks argues that it might be better for learning to concentrate on useful feedback, and less frequent assessments for summative purposes. Effective feedback:

- 'needs to focus on the individual's progress to mastery
- should take place while still clearly relevant, and
- should be specific and related to need'

(Crooks, 1988, p. 468)

In learning foreign languages, feedback and formative assessment are especially crucial to learners' progress. Individual learners need to understand their errors, to focus on areas where further practice is needed and to feel confident that any feedback is constructive and positive. Williams and Burden (1997, p. 71) show how learners can learn something of more general value than the actual item taught by the task. In FL learning, every task contributes to the learner's overall system of language and understanding of its patterns. In reading, for example, learners can gain much more from a task than the basic comprehension of a target language (TL) text. Constructive feedback can help a learner consider what exactly has been learnt and where effort should be concentrated. If a learner, for example, has failed to use his or her grammatical knowledge to help his or her understanding of a text, this needs to be highlighted and targets set. Paul Lennon (1998, p. 37) emphasises the importance of giving language feedback to learners as soon as possible after an assessment task to aid in their restructuring of their 'interlanguage'. If feedback is delayed when learning a language, the effect of the feedback will be diminished.

There are a number of terms which are used to describe formative assessment, including developmental and evaluative. What is vital, as above, is determining the function of the assessment. Formative assessment is closely linked with the development of learning strategies, leading towards more independent learning, as the feedback helps clarify what exactly the learner needs to do or finds difficult and models, for example, structured checking of work. Williams and Burden (1997, p. 72) state clearly that successful learners tend to be those who feel competent and capable of learning. This involves developing the study skills needed to take control of one's own learning, to become more independent. Learning is a process of knowledge construction and learners learn by actively making sense of new knowledge (Gipps 1994, p. 22). Formative assessment and feedback can help push a learner on to 'deep learning' (see Gipps 1994, p. 24, and Lamb 1998, p. 31), particularly where the feedback stimulates self-awareness processes to help plan, monitor, orchestrate and control one's own learning. Williams and Burden (1997, p. 73) define this 'learner training' as teaching learners *how* to learn languages.

Pat Tunstall and Caroline Gipps (1996, p. 389) note that feedback and formative assessment is the prime requirement for progress in learning. They define formative assessment as 'that process of appraising, judging or evaluating students' work or performance and using this to shape and improve their competence'. Feedback should be used by teachers to unpack the notion of excellence, enabling learners to acquire the standards for themselves. This links closely with target setting and the use of benchmarks.

Formative assessment and feedback as described here allow the teacher to build up a solid and broadly based understanding of the learner's attainment (see Gipps 1994, p. 123). It helps the teacher decide what and how to teach next and helps pupils improve their work and see the next steps in their own learning process. The provision of feedback encourages meaningful interaction between teacher and learner.

Gipps (1994, p. 129) concludes that feedback in the process of teaching is considered to be important for two reasons:

- 'it contributes directly to progress in learning through the process of formative assessment;
- it contributes indirectly through its effect on pupils' self-esteem.'

Formative assessment in foreign languages is, of course, not only based on written work. As Martin Smith (1998) suggests, learners' language work can be recorded on video or cassette tape and used formatively. This can involve them, for example, rehearsing alternatives and improvising corrections.

Benchmarks, models, targets, and 'feedforward'

It is extremely important to be open about assessment objectives with the learners. The goals need to be clear and they need to be shared. This relates back to the models of learner progress in Figure 13.2. Where learners can see the route, they are more likely to be able to structure their learning to achieve their destination. Learners must benefit from knowing what to expect and what is expected of them. Otherwise, the result is mixed messages, vague aims and potential confusion.

A *dialogue* to assess progress is vital. Feuerstein (referred to by Williams and Burden 1997, p. 42) describes this dialogue as 'dynamic assessment', in which both teacher and learner interact. Ways to improve the learner's performance are shared. It is natural that learners will make mistakes when learning languages; learning a FL involves learning through one's mistakes. Learners should be encouraged to discuss these mistakes and work towards specific targets to improve. Learners need to be very clear as to what constitutes good FL learning and what is good performance in the various elements of the course (for example, what is a 'good' summary/literature essay/oral presentation?). They cannot be expected just to know; assuming that learners are aware, for example, of how to argue a point in their own language may be erroneous. It is important that A/AS level achievement is not regarded as some unattainable peak, but that you, as the teacher, make the steps towards the ultimate goal clear and achievable and that you provide the 'route map' (Smith 1998). This implies, of course, that you, as the teacher, must be very clear yourself as to how to get there and the challenges ahead. Graham (1997, p. 18) explains how A/AS level FL tasks often require very different, more cognitively demanding skills than at GCSE. It is therefore crucial that learners are aware of their aims and of the steps involved in reaching them. These aims must be specific to enable learners to work towards aims more independently and with more certainty.

Clearly, A/AS level learners are not going to 'leap' from one set of skills to the next. They will need to work towards them progressively and the explicit stating of criteria and skills required can aid this development and assessment. Learners must be made aware that using language, incorporating new language and 'owning' it as a consequence, is what is expected. It is virtually impossible to assess something which has not been explicitly stated and it is, of course, even more difficult for learners to achieve when they are not aware of the criteria. For example, learners' attention needs to be drawn to the different requirements involved when writing to describe, to compare, to summarise, to analyse and to convince. A/AS level writing, for example, requires precision, a range of vocabulary and structures and expressing yourself well in a limited number of words. These aspects need to be developed carefully.

REFLECTION
Activity 13.3 Making requirements clear
How would you make sure learners understand the different requirements
for the following types of written task?
Avantages/désavantages
'*Citation*' . . . *Vous partagez cet avis?*
Les problèmes (de chômage)
L'influence (de la télévision) est-elle aussi négative comme on le prétend souvent?
Ecrivez une lettre à un journal/à l'éditeur
Comment expliquer . . . ?
Composez un résumé de 40 mots sur la dernière section de l'article

The details and stages involved in providing benchmarks cannot be reduced only
to those elements which make up the terminal examination papers, for example 'a
summary' or 'a business letter'. There is a wide variety of areas in which learners
require feedback and targets; there is a wide variety of skills they need to develop.
Through formative assessment of the steps along the way, of the constituent parts
leading up to this goal, it can be made more achievable (see Figure 13.5).

It should be clear each time an activity is undertaken what is expected:

- do you want the learners to *use* the new structures, for example?
- do you want them to express their own ideas fluently or use a limited range of
  language very accurately? or

What do you want learners to be able to *do* with any piece of language you give them?

Requirement	Prerequisites
summarise in English	they will need practice in summarising skills, selecting key points and language, prioritising content
understand in detail	they will need 'text-cracking' strategies
use the language productively	they will need structured practice and demonstration in how to do this
use new language to communicate facts or opinions	they will need practice in sorting and classifying relevant information

Figure 13.5 Prerequisites of FL activities

- do you want them to imitate a particular style or register and alter the content only slightly?

Learners can benefit from reviewing each other's work and good and poor models of work (see Graham 1997, p. 143). They need to consider writing or speaking from a reader's or listener's point of view (for example, for its clarity and effectiveness) and that these standards of evaluation and monitoring can be demonstrated and practised in class. Assessment should show the learners models of performance that they can imitate and adapt and also indicate the assistance, experience and forms of practice required by the learners as they move towards more competent performance. Learners must have a clear concept of the desired goal, be able to compare their work with the 'model' and to decide how to close the gap between the two. Simple grades or marks, according to Gipps (1994, p. 26), cannot achieve this. These goals must be specific. 'Do your best' is insufficient.

Certainly, learners cannot be expected to read the teacher's mind. Likewise, you need to be very clear what your assessment criteria are. Requirements and criteria should be made very clear before an important task is attempted, to avoid mis-directed effort and increased assessment anxiety (see Gipps 1994, p. 469).

REFLECTION

Activity 13.4 Explicit expectations

1   You set a piece of written homework: a letter to a friend convincing him or her of the benefits of part-time work whilst being a student. A learner asks you: 'What do I have to do to get a really good mark for this?' Could you answer him or her clearly and precisely?

2   How would you answer for a different piece of work? For example, one which expected short answers in the TL?

All skills in FL learning need to be approached in this way as they are progressive and developmental. Listening and reading should not be seen as 'testing' compre-hension; learners need to develop clear strategies just as for writing and speaking. The majority of tasks are now 'mixed skill' and strategies need to be applied flexibly. Listening skills can be developed, for example, by using the transcript when marking work; without this, a 'wrong' answer provides no feedback to the learner. For all skills, marking grids from the syllabuses can be used to set concrete targets and the results can 'feedforward' into what should be done next.

If targets are set in A/AS level FL learning, you need to be specific about their content: are they focusing on linguistic items? content? structure (for example, with essays)? or are they a mixture of targets? For example, are you requiring in a particular piece of work exact grammatical accuracy?

To take one humorous example of a 'benchmark', the following could be used (see Figure 13.6), where definitions of good, bad and 'middling' pieces of work are

Task: Write a letter to a (target language) magazine (approximately 250 words) saying why you think it's important we look after our environment.

A   Write a letter which is set out like a letter and uses lots of impressive phrases and vocabulary which is relevant to the theme of the environment. Argue your case by providing examples of how the environment suffers if we don't look after it, and give suggestions for what we can do to help. Be convincing and interesting. Check your spellings and grammar thoroughly, and write legibly. Write about 250 words. Hand it in on time and work on your errors carefully. Ask about any you don't understand.

C   Write a letter which looks reasonably like a letter although it's not clear you're writing to a magazine. Describe quite a lot of environmental problems and write about a few things you could do to help, but don't make it clear how the two link together. Use some of the phrases you've learnt, but use many of them repeatedly. Check bits of spelling, but don't bother too much with everything. Include some grammar mistakes that you always put in for good measure. Stick basically to sentence structures that you know and love and don't worry if you have written over four sides – it looks impressive after all! Hand it in on time, but don't look at your mistakes too long.

U   Write a couple of short paragraphs that look nothing like a letter and where you've thrown in a couple of words to do with the environment. Don't bother giving an argument, just provide a list, and definitely don't add any subordinate clauses or anything complicated like that. Translate any sentence you think of into the target language without looking anything up, or if you do look anything up, choose the first word given. Make sure whoever reads it won't know what you're talking about. Don't worry about checking the grammar. Hand it in late on a scrap of paper.

(Barnes 1996, p. 25)

Figure 13.6 Example of a benchmark

provided. In this way, the criteria become more obvious. Learners can identify with the description that applies to them and the desired outcome becomes more concrete, without the potential embarrassment of actual pieces of learners' work being presented to the others. Initially, the task alone could be presented and the learners themselves must explain how they would proceed and what criteria may apply. The framework can, of course, be adapted for topic, level of language, etc.

> REFLECTION
> *Activity 13.5* Creating a benchmark
> Take a mixed-skill homework task you have set (or you have observed being
> set) for A/AS level learners. Create a 'benchmark' description such as the
> example in Figure 13.6 which will illustrate to them exactly what is required.

Homework, clearly, also constitutes part of what you assess. As in all teaching, the guidelines, purpose and criteria need to be clear and the resulting feedback prompt and constructive. The purpose of the work needs to be clearly thought out, particularly at a time when more and more A/AS level learners are working part time. Some correlation has been found between homework and achievement at A/AS level (see Tymms and Fitz-Gibbon 1992, p. 5). There was a tendency for learners in those classes which reported receiving more homework to have gained higher than predicted grades (p. 8). It may appear a truism that more effort equals higher achievement, but if the effort is focused and guidelines are clear, then it is more likely to happen. Glenis Shaw and Agnès Anciaux (1996, p. 12) point out that whatever criteria are used in assessment, they must be explicit and clear to the learners and show a regard for their personal achievement and progression.

It is worth noting Tunstall and Gipps's (1996, p. 78) statement:

> effective learning takes place largely as a result of skilful informal assessment, through clear articulation of standards and expectations, and through feedback and encouragement, rather than the 'carrot and stick' of examinations, the knowledge for which is often quickly forgotten.

Self-assessment and the development of study skills

Williams and Burden (1997, p. 75) make it clear that learners themselves need to be fully involved in the process. As they point out, it is virtually impossible to be able to match each learner with the right level of task otherwise. They also note (1997, p. 76) that it is essential to foster the ability to self-evaluate if we are to produce autonomous learners. Grenfell and Harris (1998, p. 25) discuss the potential overlap between learner strategies and self-evaluation. Self-assessment, such as through end-of-unit summary profiles or 'I can' tick lists, is frequently used pre-16 in foreign languages and can be continued post-16.

At A/AS level, learners need to assume responsibility for their own learning from the very start of the course (see Pachler and Field 1997, p. 342). Graham (1997, p. 79) found that effective learners seemed more willing or able to assess their own progress. Indeed, she points out (1997, p. 51) that very good learners use double-check monitoring, for example, they check their own initial interpretation of a word in the light of its use later in the passage. The most effective learners (1997, p. 78) are generally the most active in their approach to reviewing, testing their comprehension of grammar or learning vocabulary. She notes (1997, p. 86) that by monitoring and evaluating their progress, learners learn how to take control of their own learning. (A summary of the strategies used in this way by learners can be found in Graham 1997, pp. 176–9.) Learners should become competent assessors of their own work and, therefore, need sustained experience in ways of questioning and improving the quality of their work (see Gipps 1994, p. 26). This is more likely to increase their intrinsic motivation and positive attitudes to continued learning. A checklist by Graham (1997, pp. 186–188) used with your learners could help you and them pinpoint where they experience problems and provide the basis for specific steps to improvement. Learners at A/AS level need to learn to take criticism positively, so that improvements can be made (see Smalley and Morris 1992, p. 104).

Part of this includes encouraging them to be organised in their learning and to evaluate to what extent they are doing this. To be advised on good study habits just before the main examination period may not be very effective and, indeed, may result in great anxiety! Learners should be made aware of good study habits from the beginning of the course. Learners may not have acquired the study skills pre-GCSE which are necessary for A/AS level work. It certainly cannot be assumed that such skills have been developed and essential basic techniques such as vocabulary learning and checking written work productively need to be incorporated into the course. Some of these are study habits and some are learner strategies specific to FL learning, but all should be made explicit to learners from the start of the course. Learners can, for example, ask themselves the questions in Figure 13.7

Are you doing the following? How often? Be honest!

1   Doing all your homework promptly and planning it carefully?
2   Looking at vocabulary (NOT just the section you're learning for a test) 10–15 minutes daily?
3   Practising new vocabulary via mini-cards and/or reading out loud?
4   Writing out vocabulary and verbs in different ways to practise them?
5   Listening to the TL and watching TL videos outside lessons?
6   Catching up any work immediately the day after being absent?
7   Using the computer in the school library at lunchtimes or after school?
8   Asking your teacher or peers when you don't understand something your teacher has corrected?
9   Reading over notes made in lessons and rewriting them in an organised way?
10   Filing/ordering your notes sensibly and immediately?
11   Speaking the TL whenever you get the chance?
12   Reading TL magazines or newspapers for your own interest?
13   Looking back over work you have done a little while ago: how would you do it differently now? How could you improve it?

Figure 13.7 Study habits questionnaire

and be reminded of them throughout the course. This list contains study skills adapted specifically for learning foreign languages. If they are aware of such strategies and skills from the outset, assessing their own progress and understanding the necessary next steps are more straightforward.

Self-assessment specific to the individual

Self-assessment serves no effective purpose if the teacher only asks generic questions which have no specific relevance for the individual. Checking work, for example, is far more productive if it is specific to the learner. Your feedback as teacher feeds into this. When the learners produce some written work, for example, they should check their own first aid kit (see Figure 13.8). These first aid kits are personalised and additions and deletions are made throughout the course as learners progress. A first aid kit for a learner of German in the first or second term of an A/AS level course may look like the one given in Figure 13.8.

REFLECTION
Activity 13.6 Developing FL first aid kits
Look at the German first aid kit in Figure 13.8.
1   Taking some work completed recently by a group of A/AS level learners, draft a version for the language you teach for one or two of your learners.
2   Develop a similar first aid kit for speaking in the TL with the same learners by discussing their work.

First aid kit for writing in German

(1) CAPITAL LETTERS.
(2) Wie geht's? plus dative!!!!
(3) What's 'to help'? helfen
(4) das Problem/die Probleme; der Grund/die Gründe
(5) Finish one clause before I start another.
(6) *Im Artikel steht, daß* . . .
    der Artikel/der Brief; therefore, in the accusative *den*
(7) 'not a' = *kein*
(8) Spelling using 'ie' and 'ei'.
(9) DATES!
(10) I need no 'ein' or 'eine' with professions.

Figure 13.8 Example of a learner's first aid kit

The kit in Figure 13.8 is personal to a learner and can be used to check work in progress or on completion. As the learner's language develops, items in the kit will no longer be relevant, whereas other items will have taken their place. It certainly should not remain static; items should disappear as they become assimilated into the learner's normal FL habits. Learners can be encouraged to tick off items or queries from their kit when they have been answered and understood and the kit can thus form the basis of an assessment dialogue between the learner and the teacher.

FL learners need to develop the ability to identify their own weaknesses and to pick up on linguistic detail in their work. Learning to see how the FL works and the connections between word, structures and languages is more to do with learning the language than being able to recite long lists of vocabulary. This all links in with learners understanding where they are heading. Strategies for building up their language awareness will be helpful in this area (see Chapter 6). A simple target which can be set for learners of A/AS foreign languages is to encourage them to check how many new linguistic items or how many different tenses or structures they have included: have they written something which consists entirely of GCSE level vocabulary and structures?

Self-assessment involves learners evaluating their own work and, as a result of this, setting new targets. Self-assessment can be aided through the use of a logbook or course guide (see Barnes 1996), which can incorporate targets, goals and a checklist. Such a checklist could include, for example, a simple list of topics to be covered in a term. For each one, learners should assess their progress in a variety of areas, which could include:

- new vocabulary and structures for that topic
- their ability to sustain a conversation on the topic for a specified length of time, and
- a number of new facts (content knowledge) concerned with the topic

This is additional help in understanding the route and the expectations (see also Chapter 7 and 8).

Self-assessment with a whole group

Generic question lists *can* help in self-assessment (see Figure 13.9) to the extent that they can encourage learners to plan and evaluate their own work and check in a more structured way than just 'check'. Additionally, such lists contribute to the models and benchmarks outlined above as they contain information as to what is expected from the learner. These types of questions are a concretisation of the more general 'How am I doing and what do I need to do to improve?' and the answers to them can help a learner decide what exactly is needed.

Questions which might help a learner self-assess whilst writing a TL essay might include those listed in Figure 13.9 and would also include a checklist for gramma-

Which question is best for me?

How long does my response have to be?

How much time have I got?

What about a plan – for each section? for the response as a whole?

Have I mapped my work out clearly?

What do I *know* about this topic?

What do I *think* about this topic?

What might others think (to provide alternative views)?

What relevant language do I know?

What specific terminology do I know?

How should I structure my answer? (What would a 'good' answer look like?)

Is everything I've planned relevant?

Am I oversimplifying or generalising?

Do I contradict myself at all?

Which link phrases can I use?

Do I know a better expression than the one I've used?

Can I add a word or phrase to what I've written?

Can I vary the language structures more?

How can I manipulate any TL provided on the paper?

Am I writing TL I know is correct or am I making up structures to try to say something very complicated?

Figure 13.9 Self-assessment writing questions

tical accuracy (gender, tense, number, adjectival agreement etc. – possibly based on their first aid kit, see Figure 13.8).

On a class basis, a short period of time each week could be set aside for airing any concerns, sharing successful strategies and for clarifying expectations, or a few minutes at the end of a lesson could be used to clear up any immediate worries. This could be as straightforward as asking which elements the learners feel require more explanation or practice. Groups can be encouraged to mark examples of written work by using the assessment grids from the syllabus – now subject specifications – (not necessarily from an accuracy perspective; perhaps from content and range of language) and then explain why they have awarded such marks.

Most textbooks for A/AS level now offer a clear path for progress which sometimes contains material which learners can use to assess their own language learning. Independent learning can additionally be supported by CD-ROMs (see Chapters 4 and 14) and other software, which can enable learners to concentrate on specific weaknesses at their own pace. This latter point illustrates the importance, where possible, of a bank of self-access materials to 'top up' particular areas, for example grammatical points or vocabulary fields. Learners can be encouraged to build up vocabulary on specific topics, for example, on disk, and update as appropriate. Directed self-study can help to plug the gaps which assessment has spotted.

Profiling from self-assessment

Self-assessment can help identify learners' strengths and weaknesses and help build up a profile of the individual learner's progress and achievement. This profile can include linguistic achievement and also the study skills he or she is developing: organisation, using reference materials, time management, research skills. Derek Rowntree (1988, p. 154) makes the point that the qualities and features distinguishing one learner from another are obliterated by 'the baldness of grades'. Learners may 'score' in a test in very different areas, yet end up with the 'same' grade. A number or a letter do not tell the learner or any other interested party exactly what it is the learner can do or understand. As Kathy Wicksteed points out (1995, p. 74), the single final grade achieved at A/AS level does not show attainment even in each language skill, although modular courses may achieve this up to a point. A profile can identify the particular areas of strength and weakness and can feed into the target-setting and self-assessment processes outlined above.

Marking work

Assessment and evaluation of language learners' work must be supportive and thorough. This, of course, applies to marking too. If marking is wholly negative, i.e. only errors are highlighted and no targets are provided for improvement, this is highly unlikely to have a positive effect. Boaks (1991, p. 42) distinguishes between 'correcting' and 'marking'. The point of correcting, he argues, is that learners learn from it. But what is correcting? Does the teacher *indicate*, for example, a grammatical error or stylistic problem or does the teacher 'correct'? Drafting and redrafting, common pre-GCSE, are valuable in the learning process: 'corrections' indicated are used in the redraft. This applies to speaking too: a cassette of a learner's 'draft' presentation can be 'marked'. For tasks requiring more listening or reading ability, marking responses 'right' or 'wrong' with no feedback or comments will not enable the learner to move on.

You will need to ask some fundamental questions about 'marking' learners' work:

- how often are you going to see or hear each learner's work? (Frequent, short and tightly structured pieces of work can provide valuable feedback.)
- which pieces of work are you going to mark intensively and how will you give feedback?
- how will you decide on the criteria for each piece of work to be marked? and
- is there a marking 'code' indicating the problem? (For example, tense, spelling, word order?)

As with all teaching and learning, for marking A/AS level work it helps to have

- a departmental policy, and
- examples of marked work to exemplify standards and help moderate

Benchmarks are particularly useful in small A/AS level groups to exemplify what is possible when role models are perhaps not available within the group.

Criteria, as explained in the section above on benchmarks, need to be explicit. Mostly, for example, written work will be marked for content *and* form, but there will be occasions where one aspect weighs more heavily than the other; similarly with speaking tasks. The learners need to be aware of this. At the beginning of the course, texts and assessment materials from the latter stages of GCSE courses can be used, as much of it can be quite stretching and structurally precise, but it has the advantage of using reasonably familiar language and topics. Such material can serve a useful diagnostic function for you and the learners. Assessment and marking criteria will alter, of course, throughout the course, although the basic descriptions used for A/AS level can form the basis of your standards. Distinctions must be drawn, for example, between structures which have only just been met and practised by the learners and those which they have been using for a long time. Syllabuses now contain a number of assessment grids for each task to be assessed and its constituent elements. These grids clearly vary for the different skills involved.

A discussion of a prepared topic, for example, could be assessed on each of the following aspects: pronunciation and intonation; accuracy; range of structures and vocabulary; spontaneity and fluency; factual knowledge; development of ideas/opinions. Each of these categories has a range of descriptors for the marks to be awarded, so, for example, 'range of structures and vocabulary' in the ORC 2000 Advanced Level Syllabus (p. 43) includes those descriptors given in Figure 13.10.

It is clear from Figure 13.10 that there is still room for some uncertainty with assessment descriptors. For example, how exactly would you define 'some' or la

Range of structures and vocabulary

1–2 points: Struggles to create sentences or use authentic words

3–4 points: Simple sentence structure. Little vocabulary beyond GCSE.

5–6 points: Inconsistent. Some attempt at a wider range of structures. Beginning to use vocabulary for purposes of discussion (stating and describing, reasoning, persuading, reacting).

7–8 points: Some appropriate use of more complex structures and idiom. Good range of vocabulary for purposes of discussion.

9–10 points: Confident and appropriate use of a wide range of structures, idiom and vocabulary for purposes of discussion.

Figure 13.10 Example of assessment descriptors

'good' range? It must be stressed, however, that all A/AS level syllabuses (specifica-tions) now include detailed descriptors for each assessment task and that these should be used alongside specific training from the Awarding Bodies to help improve assessment with your classes.

REFLECTION

Activity 13.7 Using assessment grids

1   Choose an assessment grid with level descriptors from the Awarding Body you are using at A/AS level. Consider how you could apply the descriptors provided to a task you have recently given your learners or which you have observed being carried out.

2   Listen to an oral presentation by an A/AS level learner on tape and allocate marks according to the Awarding Body's assessment grids. Compare your results with those of another teacher or the board's training materials.

Marking work in class

How should you mark or discuss a piece of work in class? Depending on the nature of the task, you could perhaps go over the task on an overhead transparency with an overlay for the correct responses. This could be done before the learners have their work returned to focus attention fully on the particular task or with their own work in front of them, so they can analyse their own responses. The learners could mark their own work from this sort of resource and then ask about any concerns or more open-ended tasks could be marked by the teacher and closed questions altogether. Robin Pickering (1992, p. 161) states that individual marking of all work is not possible. Additionally, the thought process in learners marking some work themselves benefits their learning. Work you mark in detail must therefore be valuable with regard to feedback.

Regular homework at A/AS level is vital and the dates work is due in need to be laid out clearly. Equally, you need to make sure your learners are clear as to when their work will be returned and what they are to do with it once they have it back in their possession. Your feedback should ideally be interactive – it should require the learner to *do* something. This could, for example, involve amending their first aid kit (see Figure 13.8) or rewriting part of the task. Developing their own targets can help in learners' assessment and monitoring of their own learning. If the first aid kit is attached to their file, you can refer to it in your feedback. Graham (1997, p. 68) quotes Cohen, who found that learners pay little attention to corrections, and Leki, who states that correcting written work does little to improve learners' performance. Actively engaging with feedback and comments is therefore crucial and should be checked on.

Research has found that essay-type questions (i.e. questions expecting an extended piece of writing as a response) are less reliably marked than more structured questions (i.e. more 'objective' questions, where specific, short answers are required and there is less room for ambiguity or subjectivity) (see Gipps 1994, p. 69). This is not surprising, as the lack of a subdivided structure does not lead to an immediate mark allocation. Mark schemes need, therefore, to be clear and user-friendly. This is easier to ensure if criteria for the task are explicit in the first place. A mark scheme can also help avoid the marker being influenced by factors cited by Gipps, including neatness, presentation and sex of the learner. Figure 13.11, based on Dale (1988 pp. 144–6), illustrates a possible approach to the marking process.

Betty Hunt outlines how work can be assessed in class:

(a) 'oral and written work can be assessed individually while the rest of the group gets on with the chosen tasks
(b) the group can decide together how some tasks should be assessed: for example, how many marks out of 20 for accuracy, variety of language, intonation, pronunciation?
(c) lists of answers to straightforward written tasks can be available so that learners can mark their own work. They should consult the teacher when they have made mistakes and do not understand why their answers are wrong.
(d) encourage learners to check other learners' work for accuracy.'

(Hunt 1996, p. 34)

Marking written work may involve you as teacher in the following process:
1 Devise a task from the area on which you have been working.
2 Ensure the explanation and instruction for the task are clear.
3 Write a possible model answer and share this with the learners if appropriate.
4 Decide on the necessary criteria for an answer. List them.
5 Allocate marks or weighting to key points (for example, accuracy, range of language, content).
6 Collect in the work and skim read the responses.
7 Mark two or three pieces in detail and decide how well your mark scheme is functioning.
8 Adjust mark scheme if appropriate.
9 Mark the rest of the work, ensuring key feedback is included.
10 Rank them in order if desired and ascertain that you have marked appropriately.
11 Record the marks and comments if appropriate.
12 Return the work and deal with queries.
13 Use what you have learnt from the marking process to evaluate what is now needed.

Figure 13.11 The marking process

Testing

It is recognised that some things are most efficiently learnt by rote (see Stobart and Gipps 1997, p. 15), for example irregular spellings, and that tests requiring the reproduction of rote-learned items are quick and efficient as a way of testing recall of simple facts and basic skills (1997, p. 22). In FL learning this is most clearly exemplified by vocabulary, verb and 'grammar' tests. Such a test may only take a few minutes and only comprise a handful of items, but it is part of the ongoing learning and assessment process. Without such regular 'temperature taking' and 'memory jogging' the task of FL learning would be perhaps too vast and overwhelming. Vocabulary tests can help to reiterate such important elements as accuracy of spelling and gender, particular verbs which take specific prepositions, etc.

Stobart and Gipps (1997, p. 16) point out that there are indications that knowledge acquired through rote learning (in foreign languages, this is usually vocabulary) is difficult to retain in the long term. They argue that learners become competent not by learning more facts and skills but by reconfiguring their knowledge. For FL learning this is indeed crucial. Short, regular tests are not a substitute for language use, but are a step along the way. Learners must then incorporate the language learnt into their active language production and must be encouraged and more importantly shown how to do so. A full mark for a vocabulary test indicates almost nothing about the use to which the learner can put the items included.

Regular tests in class are still necessary at A/AS level. Gipps (1994, pp. 38–9) cites Crooks's benefits of regular testing. They are as follows:

1   'testing makes learners attend to the content a second time (i.e. it gives them 'another practice' and thus enhances retention)
2   testing encourages a student actively to process the content (again, enhancing learning and retention)
3   the test directs attention to the topics and skills tested, which may focus the student's attention more effectively'

REFLECTION
Activity 13.8 The value of 'tests'
When setting the next language test with an A/AS level group, consider how you could explain and then demonstrate to learners *why* they have vocabulary tests, verb tests or tests on specific grammatical structures. Discuss with them how they could apply what they have learnt in a more productive way.

Learners need to see how these elements fit in to the overall picture. Perhaps a visual representation of how everything fits in would help or exemplification of how what they have learnt for a quick test can be used in, for example, a homework task. These short tests do not need to be dry and repetitive to be rigorous; they can be made more interesting and challenging. Vocabulary tests, for example, can be more imaginative than straight translation from and into the TL. They could include definitions, gap fill, categorising or sentence recreation using a 'jigsaw' technique.

Many A/AS level textbooks incorporate advice on learning and retaining vocabulary and books specifically containing A/AS level vocabulary and phrases can also be purchased.

Examination techniques, revision programmes and preparation

Examination techniques and the pressure that goes along with the examination period are well documented, not least in newspapers and magazines. Of course, some pressure is inevitable and probably an advantage when at a reasonable level. But the more a teacher can do to alleviate unnecessary stress by a structured revision programme the better. There is, however, no substitute for learning and practising the skills and knowledge necessary in the first place and throughout the course. This is particularly true with foreign languages, of course. Revision for an A/AS level in a FL does not comprise discrete content areas to be 'swotted' up in an intensive period, but the gradual development of skills and knowledge built up over time. Childline has reported worries about pupils, including A/AS level learners, suffering from examination pressure (see Illman 1998). Childline offers advice on how to beat examination stress on its website available at: http://www.childline.org.uk; revision sites for specific subjects, including foreign languages, can be found at the BBC website available at http://db.bbc.co.uk/education-bitesize/pkg_main.p_home.

Whilst it is clear that courses should not be dominated by formal assessment, it obviously has an inevitable and legitimate influence on the planning and delivery of the programme. The assessment pattern should not be the focus from the start of the course, but it is fair that learners are aware of the major dates and goals. In order to fulfil your role as an A/AS level teacher, you need to be as familiar as possible with the elements listed in Figure 13.12.

Without such detailed knowledge, it is like setting off on a journey unaware of your destination and route. Some factors will have a direct influence on your teaching and revision programme (for example, using texts under examination conditions). Your learners do not need all the details in Figure 13.12 immediately, but you do. In order to be as informed as possible, be systematic in collecting the resources outlined in Figure 13.13.

Once you are informed as to all the requirements, the relevant information should be mapped out in advance, to help learners plan their learning and see an overview of the progression needed. Of course, one of the best ways of learning about standards and assessment involved in the examination is to become an examiner yourself for one of the papers.

- the syllabus (assessment details provided by Awarding Bodies are now very detailed and user-friendly);
- the assessment criteria (particularly, for example, on course work – where feedback may need to be acknowledged, perhaps copied and recorded);
- specific dates and requirements (e.g. course work deadlines – plan carefully!, literary texts); and
- the examination format, e.g. regulations regarding set texts (can they be taken into the examination room?)

Figure 13.12 Information on examinations

- an up-to-date copy of the syllabus for the year the group will be taking the examination (it is unlikely in your first job you will have much influence over the choice of syllabus, but you can still engage in a constructive dialogue with the department on the advantages and disadvantages of a particular syllabus)
- examiners' reports (these are published after each examination and provide information and comment on the particular subject. They are usually very useful and give a good insight into the marking of the examinations and what sort of mistakes and approaches learners are taking. This can provide you with essential help in planning and evaluating your course, and ensuring your learners are fully informed)
- mark schemes
- sample/past papers
- guidance on individual components of the examination (for example, course work, the oral test, etc. Awarding Bodies often publish very clear guidance on how learners can be trained and prepared), and
- any advice from your particular Awarding Body

Figure 13.13 Materials related to examinations

It is unfair to learners and shows a lack of acknowledgement of their understandable anxieties not to devote some time to examination techniques. As Pickering notes (1992, p. 159), giving learners tasks with the same format as in the examination provides them with a sense of security in the approach to 'the real thing'. Mock examinations occur some time before the 'real thing' and modular examinations are spread throughout the course. As the examinations draw closer, learners need to be certain as to what they will be required to do and in what format the tasks will be presented. Examination techniques are clearly bound up with learning strategies and self-assessment and are certainly not to be 'saved' until just before the examination! Strategies and ways of thinking should be incorporated from the beginning of the course into normal class and homework, with the latter stages of the course containing specific details on the examination format and a 'bringing together' of relevant techniques. With the current A/AS level examination tasks, many of the strategies and techniques needed are those used in FL learning throughout the course, but, of course, the pressure associated with examinations can not be ignored. Learners should not meet assessment types in the examination which they have never encountered before. It should not be a trick or a shock. It is true that part of the skill of A/AS FL learning is coping with unfamiliar language, but the skills, strategies and techniques should be taught and practised beforehand and the format made familiar. This has been described as learners being 'test-wise' (see Lennon 1998, p. 33). Learners also need to see examples of examination papers in their entirety before they have to sit the papers. It is vital they become aware, for example, of the *length* of an examination paper (in a literature or culture examination, for example, the examination paper itself may be very long, as it incorporates questions on all the various texts).

Clearly, you will need to be familiar with the examination format, as this will obviously determine the exact strategies to be employed. Most textbooks include sections on essay planning, note taking, reading strategies and some texts are specifically aimed at these areas. Coursebooks obviously vary in the amount of space given to examination techniques and revision practice. In most cases, the teacher can use such sources, together with his or her own knowledge of the learners and his or her own ideas, to collate advice appropriate to the particular group. Some strategies and advice will suit the whole group, others will be more applicable to individuals, but the wider the range discussed and offered the better. These strategies, it must be emphasised, must permeate the course and not be seen as something completely separate. Graham (1997, p. 132), when commenting on essay-planning sessions, found them to be often 'one-off' occasions. These strategies need time to be absorbed and practised by the learners. Advice on using the dictionary as a discrete element, for example, will not be as effective as if learners have incorporated the use of a dictionary into their normal language work. Deciding when to use a dictionary to verify something and how to use one when you require a new word depends on regular practice in these decisions to ensure familiarity with the dictionary conventions. To prepare for speaking tasks must clearly involve learners in speaking practice; the same principle applies to all skills. There is very limited use in talking *about* the tasks in a vacuum. Certain strategies can be practised explicitly (see e.g. Grenfell and Harris 1998), such as communication strategies to sustain spoken discourse, 'fillers' and 'chunks' of language.

Advice on listening, for example, might include the advice in Figure 13.14, ideally devised jointly between you and the learners. This type of advice can be discussed initially in English and summarised in the TL. Extended writing advice might be similar to that in Figure 13.15.

Commercially produced revision guides clearly also have their place and naturally incorporate examination techniques, examples and advice.

- remember there could be peripheral speech, hesitation, repetition, etc. (i.e. like real life!)
- don't forget to use the instructions to orientate yourself
- rehearse the possible key language for the topic in your head
- don't try to grasp every word
- at the first listening – try to gain an overview
- subsequent hearings – confirm your opinions or pick out important phrases
- clear your head between each listening
- practise by listening to radio/cassettes/satellite TV in the TL and by contact with people who speak the language
- expose yourself to a wide variety of voices/accents and speaking styles
- listen to a variety of types of TL – and make judgements accordingly (e.g. different expectations when listening to a political interview and an advert), and
- make sensible use of the playback facility – don't keep playing the whole thing through!

Figure 13.14 Listening advice

Coursework

Coursework, whether written or oral, can be completed as part of an A/AS level in a FL. There is no compulsion at present for candidates to complete coursework. As with all elements of the examination, coursework requirements need to be carefully prepared by the teacher. For example, drafting and redrafting of written work, the acknowledgement of reference sources and prescribed deadlines for submissions of entries and the coursework itself need to be planned out in advance. There are specific regulations laid down by Awarding Bodies. Teachers must ensure they are familiar with all the guidelines regarding choice of topic, word length, procedures for recording oral coursework, etc. Coursework definitely makes different demands on the teacher (and the learner) and this option must be thought through with care.

REFLECTION
Activity 13.9 Departmental decisions on examinations
Discuss with an experienced colleague his or her reasons for:
1   selecting a particular Awarding Body;
2   choosing the coursework option (or not).

Writing an essay
in the TL

Preparation
You cannot produce an essay out of a vacuum like a magician producing a rabbit from a hat . . . reading, listening, practising and learning are all necessary in the build-up, i.e. the whole of your A/AS level course.

Time
Divide up the available time very carefully – and stick to it! You will need:
- time to choose the best essay title for *you*
- time to make a plan
- time to actually write each section
- time to check *everything*
- time to check everything *again*!

Plan/structure
- jot down the main ideas and vocabulary
- short introduction
- points for and against (if appropriate) and stick to your point
- short conclusion

Language
- use varied and interesting vocabulary (e.g. what about *sich bemühen* instead of *versuchen?*);
- vary the linguistic structures (e.g. does every one of your paragraphs begin with 'I think that . . . .' or 'In my opinion . . . .');
- check efficiently (check how you check at the moment – do you just read it through again and tell yourself 'Yes – checked that, looks OK to me' or are you more methodical?).

Figure 13.15 Extended writing advice

Summary

This chapter has attempted to show that effective assessment at A/AS level is crucial for the FL development of the learners. Mfl teachers can, through feedback, provide learners with the information and support they need to move forward and become more autonomous. A teacher who is well informed about the format and nature of the assessment process, both formative and summative, will be in a far better position to provide the appropriate feedback. Where learners are involved in the assessment of their own learning, greater motivation and higher levels of achievement are possible.

References

Barnes, A. (1996) 'Getting them off to a good start: the lead-up to that first A level class'. In Brien, A. (ed) *German Teaching* 14. Rugby: Association of Language Learning, pp. 23–8.

Boaks, P. (1991) *German/Deutsch: Resource Guides for Teachers*. London: CILT.

Borich, G. (1995) *Becoming a Teacher: an Inquiring Dialogue for the Beginning Teacher*. Washington DC: The Falmer Press.

Clark, J. (1987) 'Classroom assessment in a communicative approach'. In *British Journal of Language Teaching* 15, 1, pp. 9–19.

Claxton, G. (1988) 'Teaching and learning'. In Dale, R., Fergusson, R. and Robinson, A. (eds) *Frameworks for Teaching: Readings for the Intending Secondary Teacher*. London: Hodder and Stoughton/Open University, pp. 21–32.

Crooks, T. (1988) 'The impact of classroom evaluation processes on students'. In *Review of Educational Research* 58, 4, pp. 438–81.

Dale, R. (1988) 'Assessment and testing'. In Dale, R., Fergusson, R. and Robinson, A. (eds) *Frameworks for Teaching: Readings for the Intending Secondary Teacher*. London: Hodder and Stoughton/Open University, pp. 136–47.

Gipps, C. (1994) *Beyond Testing: Towards a Theory of Educational Assessment*. London: Falmer Press.

Graham, S. (1997) *Effective Language Learning*. Clevedon: Multilingual Matters.

Grenfell, M. (1995) 'The first foreign language'. In Brumfit, C. (ed) *Language Education in the National Curriculum*. Oxford: Blackwell, pp. 126–49.

Grenfell, M. and Harris, V. (1998) 'Learner strategies and the advanced language learner'. In Chambers, G. (ed) *Language Learning Journal* 17. Rugby: Association of Language Learning, pp. 23–8.

Higham, J., Sharp, P. and Yeomans, D. (1996) *The Emerging 16–19 Curriculum*. London: David Fulton Publishers.

Hunt, B. (1996) 'Grammar into creativity'. In Shaw G. (ed) *Aiming High: Approaches to Teaching A level*. London: CILT, pp. 32–9.

Illman, J. (1998) 'A catch in the question'. In *The Guardian*, 26 May.

Lamb, T. (1998) 'Now you are on your own! Developing independent language learning strategies.' In Gewehr, W. (ed) *Aspects of Modern Language Teaching in Europe*. London: Routledge, pp. 30–47.

Lennon, P. (1998) 'Learner-centred testing: a role for cloze?' In Chambers, G (ed) *Language Learning Journal* 17. Rugby: Association of Language Learning, pp. 33–40.

OCR (1998) *Modern Foreign Languages French, German, Spanish: 2000 Advanced Level Syllabus*. Cambridge: Oxford, Cambridge and RSA Examinations.

Pachler, N. and Field, K. (1997) *Learning to Teach Modern Foreign Languages in the Secondary School: A Companion to School Experience*. London: Routledge.

Pickering, R. (1992) *Planning and Resourcing A level French*. London: CILT.

Rivers, W., Mitchell Dell'Orto, K. and Dell'Orto, V. (1988) *Teaching German: A Practical Guide*. Lincolnwood, Ill: National Textbook Company.

Rowntree, D. (1988) 'The side-effects of assessment'. In Dale, R., Fergusson, R. and Robinson, A. (eds) *Frameworks for Teaching: Readings for the Intending Secondary Teacher.* London: Hodder and Stoughton/Open University, pp. 148–57.

Shaw, G. and Anciaux, A. (1996) 'Bridging the gap between GCSE and A level'. In Shaw G. (ed) *Aiming High: Approaches to Teaching A level.* London: CILT, pp. 8–16.

Smalley, A. and Morris, D. (1992) *The Modern Language Teacher's Handbook.* Cheltenham: Stanley Thornes.

Smith, M. (1998) Teaching mfl in the Sixth Form. Seminar held for Warwick University PGCE mfl students at Solihull Sixth Form College, 4 March.

Stobart, G. and Gipps, C. (1997) *Assessment: A Teacher's Guide to the Issues.* 3rd edition. London: Hodder and Stoughton.

Tunstall, P. and Gipps, C. (1996) 'Teacher feedback to young children in formative assessment: a typology'. In *British Education Research Journal* 22, 4, pp. 389–404.

Tymms P. and Fitz-Gibbon, C. (1992) 'The relationship of homework to A level results'. In *Educational Research* 34, 1, pp. 3–10.

Wicksteed, K. (1995) 'Modern languages 16–19: towards a new curriculum'. In *Studies in Modern Languages Education* 5, pp. 57–81.

William, D. and Black, P. (1996) 'Meanings and consequences: a basis for distinguishing formative and summative functions of assessment?'. In *British Education Research Journal* 22, 5, pp. 537–48.

Williams, M. and Burden, R. (1997) *Psychology for Language Teachers: A Social Constructivist Approach.* Cambridge: Cambridge University Press.

Chapter 14

Reaching beyond the classroom

Norbert Pachler with Thomas Reimann

Introduction

Various chapters in this book highlight an important feature of Advanced (A)/ Advanced Subsidiary (AS) level modern foreign languages (mfl) teaching and learning: the need to supplement classroom-based learning opportunities. Opportunities to extend what happens in the classroom are manifold, as are the reasons for their necessity and desirability.

Clearly, one important reason for reaching beyond the classroom is the recognition that six lessons or so of contact time a week is insufficient to bring the learners up to the level of proficiency required by examinations, particularly since their level at the point of departure can be seen to be limited.

Another equally important reason is the inherently 'acquisition-poor' nature of the classroom environment: exposure to target language (TL) input is invariably limited in scope and variety as are opportunities for learners to use the TL for 'real' purposes. The need to use authentic material for classroom-based learning activities has, therefore, been a central feature of mfl teaching methodology in the various guises of the communicative approach for some time now, albeit at times accompanied by varying degrees of explicit rationale. In this chapter, the issue of authentic material will, therefore, be briefly examined.

Links abroad – penfriend schemes, trips, visits, exchanges, work experience, etc. – have for a long time been a central feature of, often extra-curricular, activities offered by mfl departments up and down the country and have in recent years been documented in some detail (see e.g. Pachler and Field 1997, ch. 12; Byram 1997; Snow and Byram 1997). Rather than repeating and summarising those arguments, this chapter will focus on one particular aspect of links abroad, i.e. their scope for tackling negative stereotypes.

The rapid advance of new technologies of late has opened up a myriad of possibilities for reaching beyond the classroom; these will be the main focus for discussion here.

Objectives

By the end of this chapter you should have an awareness of:

- the role and limitations of the use of authentic material in the communicative classroom
- the potential new technologies, in particular the internet and computer-mediated communication (CMC), afford to mfl teaching at A/AS level, and
- how links abroad can be used to tackle negative stereotypes and contribute to learners' intercultural (communicative) competence

Authentic material and communicative mfl teaching

The use of 'authentic' material, i.e. 'text' produced for a native-speaker audience, to bring the world of real language use into the classroom has become a central methodological tenet of mfl teaching at 11 to 19 and beyond. One important reason for this is the belief that the use of authentic material would go some way to compensating for the invariable artificiality of classroom-based mfl learning. Another is the fact that such material provides ample illustration of the use of words in context (see also Chapter 6). However, Alan Hornsey rightly points out (1994, p. 6) that, given the limit of time available, the learning process does benefit from carefully selected, graded and sequenced input as well as a purely (structurally) random experience characteristic of authentic texts (see also Chapter 6). He views authenticity as a possible goal, 'a point of arrival rather than a point of departure' (Hornsey 1994, p. 7). The means, in other words, do not necessarily have to be the same as the aims of mfl teaching and learning. Authentic material, therefore, needs to be used judiciously by mfl teachers and in the context of a coherent methodological approach as, in themselves, they can be seen to be insufficient to bring about successful foreign language learning.

Access and retrieval of authentic material has become very simple with the considerable growth of the internet. With relative ease and at increasingly affordable cost, TL documents with up-to-date, or indeed up-to-the-minute information (e.g. the latest news and weather reports, etc.) can be accessed, saved, downloaded, printed, used as stimulus material for classroom work, converted into worksheets, etc. For instance, the medium lends itself well to:

- project and research work, with learners, for example, finding relevant material for an aspect of cultural study or for topic or coursework
- the identification of background information about the author and the setting of a novel or play learners are studying
- the collection of data in preparation for a visit abroad, i.e. a virtual visit
- the sharing of experiences/learner diary entries gathered whilst on a visit to the target country, or

- the simulation of real-life tasks, e.g. in the role of a travel agent, the putting together of a travel package to the target country for different client groups including cultural and linguistic background material, etc.

Once authentic material has been collected, assimilated and worked through, learners can be asked to give short presentations to their peers in the TL or they can be asked to publish their work in the form of a webpage, thereby combining a variety of skills.

Research evidence increasingly suggests (see e.g. Cox 1999) that new technologies are a powerful motivator. Computer-based activities seem to engage the attention of learners in ways that printed texts don't. Their pedagogical use can, therefore, be easily justified (see also Chapter 8).

In a short but very useful article (in German) Bruno Frischherz and Peter Lenz (1996) discuss a number of interesting ideas for learning activities using the internet, including:

- reading online TL texts for gist and detail: with the help of grids learners can be encouraged to note key words or phrases and make commentaries about texts. For news bulletins learners can make notes about: who? what? where? when? how? why? what for? (see also Pachler and Field 1997, p. 239)
- fact-finding missions/treasure hunts: learners have to collect web-based information in the TL in order to solve a problem;
- virtual shopping-sprees: learners are given a shopping list and have to access virtual TL shops; for each item learners have to note the place of 'purchase', detailed product description and price in the TL. At the end, products and prices are compared to find out who found the best bargain;
- learners put together a TV/radio schedule for a particular evening using programme pages from the target country which they then discuss with peers in small groups. Through negotiation in the TL a schedule is compiled for the whole group. In a variation of the above activity, learners are asked to come up with a schedule for an interesting night out in a city in the target country; or
- news bulletins and online magazines and newspapers can be used by learners to compare the coverage of certain events in broadsheets and tabloids or in print media and by TV/radio. Alternatively, learners can compile their own 'news reel' for a given week with different groups of learners taking responsibility for different aspects such as politics, culture, economy, sport, entertainment, etc. At the end of the week they present their account of the week to peers.

The increasing 'multimodality' of internet-based material, i.e. the use of words, (moving) pictures and sound – e.g. the ability to listen to and watch news bulletins – as well as their increasing interactivity, i.e. the ability to follow so-called 'hyperlinks' to related pages or the possibility of submitting data – e.g. filling out forms or completing online exercises etc. – allows learners to practise all four skills.

Due to the nature of the medium, electronic texts can, in some respects, be seen to be pedagogically superior to their counterparts from the print media: the display of information on computer screens often means that texts retrieved from the internet tend to be shorter and therefore more manageable for learners; in addition, there are sometimes links to related sources of (background) information or even online discussion fora which allow learners to follow-up their initial reading of the text (see Schlabach 1997, p. 3).

Evidence from colleagues employing internet-based authentic resources suggests that learners, by and large, respond positively to the use of new technologies in the ways described above. However, learners are not always able to find relevant and useful information and there is the problem of wasting time surfing the internet. It is, therefore, advisable to ensure learners have the requisite technical skills and are able to evaluate the usefulness of the material they encounter (see also Schlabach 1997, p. 7; Figure 8.6 in Chapter 8; Pachler 1999a).

Useful strategies in this context are web-based worksheets providing foci for research, concrete activities to be carried out by learners as well as the provision of relevant weblinks as starting points for learners. An example of such links to relevant internet sites in French, German, Spanish and Italian can be accessed, for instance, at http://www.ioe.ac.uk/lie/pgce/, the website of the mfl team at the Institute of Education, University of London. For a detailed discussion of the potential of the internet as a teaching and learning tool, see Pachler 1999b.

CD-ROMs can also be seen to provide easy access to up-to-date information about cultural topics and current issues. Whilst some teachers consider them superior to the internet in a school context as their use is not reliant upon access to a telephone line etc, information stored on CD-ROMs is invariably more ephemeral than that on the internet. There are, however, CD-ROMs such as the Foreign and Commonwealth Office/Auswärtiges Amt/British Council/Goethe-Institut product *Stop Press*, which effectively integrate both technologies. This CD-ROM, distributed free of charge to educational institutions in the UK on request at the time of writing subject to availability, aims to encourage an understanding in learners of the German–British relationship. Material on this CD-ROM is multi-modal: it includes text, audio and video sources combining official and personal accounts. The CD-ROM is interactive: it includes a webeditor which the learner can use to create his or her own webpages including text, audio and video footage all of which can be imported from the CD-ROM; the disc also allows the user to access a website which features regularly updated complementary information available at http://www.britcoun.de/stop/start.htm; and the disk is based on a simulation model which invites the user to explore the culture, society and media of Germany and the UK through the completion of a number of so-called assignments, the setting for which is electronic journalism. Users' research, reporting and editing skills are developed in the process of working through the source material provided with a view to presenting, and publishing, a web-based report on a given topic taken, for example, from education, the environment, the economy, politics, youth culture or pastime (see also Chapter 8). For a general discussion of CD-ROM use, see Bruntlett 1999.

In addition, therefore, to the use of texts featuring language produced for a native-speaker audience, as mfl teachers we need to consider the authenticity of the tasks employed in mfl classrooms, i.e. the extent to which activities simulate real-life language use.

The use of Information and Communications Technology (ICT) for TL communication

It is very important not to view new technologies as supporting only a narrow delivery or transmission model of education and information. Whenever ICT is integrated into classroom-based activities, the importance of the learner's active engagement with new material, both in terms of the construction of meaning via mental processes as well as through the social interaction with others, needs to be borne in mind. New technologies should, therefore, be seen as agents of inter-action and collaboration and, as mfl teachers, we need to ensure that the way in which we plan the use of ICT is conducive to such ways of working. For a more detailed discussion of these issues see Pachler (1999a) and Noss and Pachler (1999).

With the considerable growth of what new technologies are able to offer to mfl teaching and learning, opportunities to reach beyond the classroom and school have increased. It is now easily possible to engage in real-time and delayed-time interaction with TL speakers via e-mail, video conferencing, internet relay chats, etc. through the computer. Research evidence suggests (Osuna and Meskill 1998, p. 66) that the internet 'is a suitable tool to increase language and cultural know-ledge, as well as a means to increase motivation' (see also Cox 1999). A good example of web-based material for culture teaching is a website developed by the Goethe-Institut available at http://www.goethe.de/z/50/alltag/ which explores every-day life in Germany by showing people in ordinary situations, which might – despite their apparent familiarity – seem strange to a learner from a different cultural background, in the form of picture portraits telling the 'stories' of ordinary people, information about customs as well as useful information about how to find one's way around German society.

A webpage entitled 'Language learning activities for the World Wide Web', available at http://polyglot.lss.wisc.edu/lss/lang/nflrc.html and compiled by a number of colleagues in the US, features useful suggestions for internet-based mfl activities with a collaborative orientation. For example, learners are encour-aged, in conjunction with peers in the target country, to create their own so-called 'language learning web pages'; amongst others, the following ideas are suggested: book reviews, interviews, local legends/myths, newspapers, song lyrics, TV reviews, questionnaires, fairy tales, want ads, how-to pages, movie critiques, protest signs or serialised stories.

Other suggestions include the following activities:

- *Talking heads* in which cultural differences and similarities are explored.
  1   Take a class picture and scan the photo.
  2   Mark up the photo as an image map so that each student's head links to a student page with a question about the target language culture and a 'mailto': link to the author.
  3   A collaborating class does the same.
  4   When students click on the heads, they get a question about their culture which they can answer in the e-mail form.
  5   Students can change their questions regularly since it is their page.
  6   Students can share the responses they receive with the class.
                                    (http://polyglot.lss.wisc.edu/lss/lang/nflrc.html)

- *Burning issues* in which learners explore issues that are divisive such as abortion, school prayer/assemblies, gun control, etc.
  1   Have students research both sides of the issue.
  2   For each argument, students prepare pages which link to relevant information on the net.
  3   Link pages to a class e-mail address for further discussion.
                                    (http://polyglot.lss.wisc.edu/lss/lang/nflrc.html)

- *Matching Majors* in which learners share information about the subjects they study.
  1   Students create pages describing the major courses of their [study] plan in both the native and target languages.
  2   Cooperating students do likewise.
  3   'Mailto' links provide students with access to more information.
  4   Possible questions:
      ♦   How much does it cost . . .?
      ♦   How long does it take to complete . . .?
      ♦   What are the hours?
      ♦   How are the teachers?
      ♦   How much homework is required?
                                    (http://polyglot.lss.wisc.edu/lss/lang/nflrc.html)

Working together and learning from each other via the computer, e.g. through e-mail, file sharing, internet relay chats (IRC), Multi-user domains (MUDs), MUDs/object-oriented (MOOs), Multi-user Shared Hallucinations (MUSHes), etc, open up new possibilities for mfl teaching and learning. Computer-mediated communication (CMC) allows mfl learners to use texts as 'thinking devices' (see Warschauer 1997, p. 471) and not just for reading and information retrieval:

the text-mediational view links the concepts of expression, interaction, reflection, problem-solving, critical thinking, and literacy with the various uses of talk, inquiry, and collaboration in the classroom.

(Warschauer 1997, p. 472)

Technological advances mean that more and more the written word, traditionally predominately the medium for reflection and interpretation authored by an individual, can be used for real time (synchronous) or delayed time (asynchronous) communicative interaction, a domain formerly occupied in the main by speech (see Warschauer 1997, p. 472). With the help of new technologies it is now possible for people to collaborate in the construction of texts, thereby linking interaction and reflection.

Increasingly, evidence suggests that CMC is different from face-to-face interaction and that the social dynamics of the process are 'levelling', i.e. encourage participation of those traditionally excluded from discussions. Research also suggests that CMC produces greater learner participation with the teacher *and* other learners; the latter is notoriously difficult to achieve in classroom-based activities. Moreover, asynchronous modes, such as e-mail where the receiver of a message answers in his or her own time, allow for more considered responses and are, therefore, suitable for more complex language production (see Warschauer 1997, pp. 473–4).

For example, a recent study of learners of Spanish as a foreign language at university level (González-Bueno 1998) shows that the use of e-mail can have positive effects on foreign language learning: e-mail use can lead to the use of a greater amount of TL, coverage of a wider variety of topics and TL functions, achievement of a higher level of TL accuracy, more learner-initiated interactions and use of more personal and expressive TL.

Video conferencing allows learners to talk face to face with peers from partner institutions via the computer and an attached camera. Depending on the system used, it also allows users to work collaboratively and in real time with documents on-screen. Even where the requisite equipment is available, video conferencing can be difficult to implement as it must happen synchronously, meaning that interlocutors must be physically present in order for a conference to take place. Given timetable constraints and differences in time-zones this is not always easy. According to one UK pilot study, the benefits to mfl learners' communication skills are considerable in terms of improvement in accent, intonation and pronunciation, self-expression as well as listening skills (see Butler and Kelley 1999).

In a recent paper on intercultural internet writing projects presented at the annual meeting of the American Educational Research Association, Jeff Kuppermann and Raven Wallace (1998) propose an interesting framework consisting of learning outcomes and component activities which offers useful guidance for designing, developing and evaluating internet writing projects. According to this framework, as (mfl) teachers, we should consider whether the project we planned allows the learner to pursue meaningful learning goals such as:

- engagement
- consideration of purpose and audience
- evaluation and synthesis of information
- developing of personal standards for writing
- cultural awareness, and
- participation in a literate community

Furthermore, the authors identify seven activities as being characteristic of potentially successful projects:

- publishing
- friendship exchanges
- data sharing
- collaborative artefact creation
- peer critiquing
- mentoring, and
- question asking

With regard to planning internet-based project work, the above would suggest that clearly delineated learning objectives and collaborative modes of working are particularly important in ensuring successful outcomes.

Thus far, this chapter has identified the use of authentic material and new technologies as important means of reaching beyond the classroom for the benefit, in the main, of learners' linguistic and communicative competence. As Chapter 5 demonstrates, the development of learners' intercultural competence needs to be another important focus of advanced level mfl study. The remainder of this chapter intends to demonstrate how links with the target country can be used to work on negative stereotypes, an aspect of particular relevance to the broader educational aims of A/AS level mfl learning. Whilst the focus here is on Germany, the issues discussed apply equally to other target countries. The discussion of the internet, CD-ROMs and CMC above clearly demonstrates that new technologies have an extremely valuable role to play in supporting the development of learners' intercultural competence. Alas, there is insufficient room here to explore this aspect in detail.

Addressing negative stereotypes through links with Germany
by Thomas Reimann

Definition and introduction of the concept of stereotyping

We all possess, know and use stereotypes. The Greek word 'stereo(s)' means 'solid' as, for example, in 'stereoscopic' meaning 'giving the impression of solidity or depth'. The word 'stereotype' derives from French and refers to a method of printing. In the social sciences the term is used to describe a one-sided, exaggerated and preconceived idea about a particular group or society; the term was coined in 1922 by Walter Lippmann, a US journalist.

Most scientific literature emphasises the negative character of stereotypes because they have a tendency to be based on prejudice rather than fact. By repetition they become fixed in people's minds. This is supported by more recent research, which demonstrates that stereotypes endure, become resistant to change and run through all aspects of life.

It was Lippmann, however, who stressed the unavoidable process of using stereotypes. For him stereotypes are a form of defence everybody needs in a world of overwhelming complexity. We simply do not have the time and inclination to have a good look at everything we create and so rely on reduced and oversimplified pictures of people and their life in other cultures. Considering the fact that Lippmann described this concept in the early 1920s it is apparent that nowadays there is an even bigger demand for ways of coping with mass media, information overload and rapid technological changes.

Nevertheless, stereotypes can prove dangerous in many respects. Some sociologists believe that stereotyping can be used as a form of power structure in which one group in society uses labelling to keep another group in its place. There are attitudes which are immune to reality and endow certain groups with specific negative characteristics. They appear to be frozen into stereotypes and, consequently, become incapable of change. Members of these groups are treated not as individuals but as possessing the same characteristics as each other.

Although stereotypes can work as a means of orientation in a complex world, more often they impede access to the actual reality. (For a discussion of stereotypes see also Schulz and Haerle 1996.)

Stereotypes in Britain

When looking at links between British and German schools it is vital to consider the role stereotypes in general play, and have played, in Britain and to look at and try to explain specific stereotypes which the British hold about Germany and the Germans, and vice versa.

The role of stereotypes in Britain is an essential consideration for any kind of cultural link – a school exchange with France, for instance, or a work-experience programme with Spain or Italy. This will help one to understand the combination of historical, political, social, economic and cultural factors which go to make up the unique relationship between two countries and which may lead to the creation of particular stereotypes.

For a long time stereotypes have played an important role. Since Britain is at the head of the Commonwealth, with numerous states, dependent territories, colonies and protectorates, its contact with various colonial cultures can be seen to have stimulated the disposition to categorise members of different nations as having specific personality attributes. This was not intended to be discriminating but to make the groups more familiar, commonplace and recognisable.

The geographical position of Britain as an island physically isolated from the rest of Europe is also likely to have influenced these opinions and attitudes. For a long time the term 'Continental' was seen as something negative rather than positive. Being far away from the rest of Europe seems to have contributed to some kind of a 'binocular perspective', which made rapid classifications of its European neighbours almost essential. Furthermore, British humour has always been an elemental and indispensable part of the political culture: to joke about others, irrespective of whether they are Irish, French or German, is a welcome way of passing the time. As a result of the Second World War Germany experienced a radical break in its political culture, unlike Britain which has never experienced anything similar.

The mass media, in particular the tabloid press, have been keeping particular attitudes and prejudices alive, ensuring that the public are fed with new stories which reinforce old stereotypes.

Without doubt, the relationship between Britain and Germany is unique. Although there has been a lessening of awareness about the Nazi period – simply because fewer contemporary witnesses are still alive – there remains a large number of people who associate Germany with the Nazi period. This was particularly the case in the early 1990s during the reunification process, when fear of a new, strong, aggressive Germany was growing. In addition, from the British point of view, Germany today is in a position of power, which, despite being defeated twice in wars and having forfeited some of its territory, remains unchanged in comparison to the beginning of the century. Great Britain, on the other hand – despite being twice victorious – has lost its dominant position in Europe and the world. Such developments in Germany have been closely watched by the British. Economic success since the Second World War especially has led to some positive stereotypes about the Germans: they are considered to be hard-working, organised and tidy. Despite this there are many less positive stereotypes: Germans lack imagination, have no sense of humour and are arrogant. (For some of the stereotypes held by US college students about Germany and the Germans see Schulz and Haerle 1996.)

Taking all these factors into consideration, it becomes clearer why the British have a rather uncertain, almost ambiguous attitude towards Europe in general and Germany in particular. There is, on the one hand, the fear of the marginalisation of British influence, being relegated to the fringes of Europe, being politically and economically peripheral and, on the other hand, the anxiety of losing British identity and sovereignty within a Europe driven by European bureaucrats and dominated by a German economy. Both views show to what extent Britain is still attached to the past, trying to deduce the future from historical experience.

Strategies to overcome stereotypes – some theoretical remarks

It is widely accepted that exchange programmes can provide people with incomparable opportunities to experience a foreign country and its people. At a time when European integration is fast becoming a reality, the need for young people in particular to visit other countries and meet their peoples in order 'to see for themselves' is more important than ever. It is, however, not sufficient simply to offer various exchange programmes; these programmes require a great deal of careful forward-planning.

As a result of all this, teachers, lecturers and other organisers of school-exchange and work-experience programmes face an interesting challenge: how to combine and somehow optimise the invaluable advantages of the effects of such programmes on the learning process, with the aim of reducing, or even breaking down, existing negative stereotypes by interaction on a personal, social and cultural level.

One common strategy is an attempt to counter stereotypes by presenting accurate and often favourable information about the group or some individual from the group. With reference to Sherif and Sherif, Scott and Spencer note (see 1998, p. 499) that this method can, however, prove ineffective.

People can hold firm stereotypes about members of other cultural or ethnic groups, even though they have never met such persons. Such attitudes are entirely learned and arise out of general distrust of foreigners and its frequent reinforcement, for instance, at home, by the media, in educational curricula and through the influence of peers and other social groups. The problem is that stereotypes contain a cognitive and an affective element. The affective element can be a deeply rooted, emotionally held attitude. Consequently a person can be convinced intellectually that, for example, not all Germans are arrogant, but it may be very difficult nonetheless for that person to change his or her feelings and, therefore, his or her behaviour.

The self-fulfilling prophecy is another common phenomenon regarding the problem of changing attitudes: a person has certain beliefs or a set of expectations about a country and its people, some of which may be negative stereotypes. These expectations lead to a particular treatment of people from this country which may in turn bring about the expected results. An individual feels that he or she has prophesied the outcome and feels confirmed in his or her beliefs. The individual's stereotype is therefore reinforced, although in reality he or she has caused the outcome rather than predicted it.

There are findings, however, which suggest there are ways to counteract stereotypes. If a person is told to pay close attention to individuals and is motivated to be accurate, then that person relies more on what he or she observes than on what he or she expects.

One major problem, especially on school exchanges, is that of inter-group feelings and conflicts. Although many individuals establish a good relationship with their partners and their partners' families, often the two foreign groups, fuelled by negative experience of single members of the groups, feel as though they are in competition. Although this increases positive feelings within either group it can lead to negative stereotyping of the opposite group and eventually to conflict. A possible solution may be the creation of conditions for inter-dependence between the groups by setting an attractive goal which both groups can only achieve together. By cooperating and working together in this way for a super-ordinate goal, it is hoped that the competitive or conflicting feelings each group has towards the other may dissolve and with them the stereotyping.

There are conditions where a change of attitudes is more likely to happen.

One successful strategy to overcome negative stereotyping is known as the 'concept of integration'. It is based on the 'contact hypothesis' and envisages that when groups get to know each other through face-to-face contact their stereo-types are more likely to be broken down.

According to Weber (see 1992, p. 210) there are conditions for effective contact which have to be met so that those in contact should, for example, have equal status and meet on a level playing field, that the situation should encourage participants to depend on and cooperate with each other and that social norms should promote individual personal relationships among participants.

A few practical examples

Everybody who is involved with setting up exchange programmes has to accept that people hold strong stereotypes about the target country and its people.

One aim must be to raise the awareness of the participants so that they under-stand that visiting the target country does not only mean experiencing a foreign language but also a different culture with a variety of ideas, beliefs, values, manners, traditions, artistic and social pursuits, expressions and tastes. Ideally, the partici-pants should have the chance before the actual visit to reflect upon similarities as well as differences (see also ch. 5 and Pachler and Field 1997, chs 7 and 12). Slide shows, booklets and short talks from people who have taken part in former exchanges may provide a good source of information. Also, information obtained for learners from the internet/CD-ROMs or research carried out by learners themselves using new technologies can play a valuable role in preparing the ground.

Very often participants seem to experience certain problems while staying with their partners. German people, for example, are known for rising early in the morning and consequently going to bed earlier and having their main meal at lunch time. Also, environmental issues like recycling household waste play an important part in the day-to-day-routine and on a Sunday shops tend not to be open. These issues are not problems in themselves but may be perceived as such because of home sickness or difficulty with the experience of new situations. For many learners it may be the first visit to the target country, for some the first experience of being completely away from home and a familiar environment with its everyday routines. Coping with these new circumstances can be difficult, though it is possibly easier in a group situation than for individual participants, having to fit into a different family routine by themselves. Under the best of circumstances the participants will recognise that the differences are part of the diversity of the two countries and will reserve judgement until a later stage – ideally in a group situation where all participants will have an opportunity to exchange their experiences. This will enable them to make a more realistic judgement. Anticipating these problems is common sense. A pre-visit briefing, tact and sensitivity on the part of the exchange leaders in handling any problems that arise, as well as the post-visit meeting, can all be useful ways of tackling these problems head-on, or even preventing them entirely.

As mentioned above, presenting accurate information is a possible way of countering stereotypes. The information should be given out before departure in order to give the participants the opportunity to ask questions and discuss certain issues beforehand. Socialisation does play a vital role in forming stereotypes. Therefore, it makes sense to include parents in the preparation phase before the actual visit so that they also have the opportunity to learn and find out more about the target country.

Motivated observers pay closer attention and rely on what they see rather than expect. Pre-printed materials which structure the observation process during the actual visit – as well as before and after the visit – can be useful tools to counteract stereotypes (see e.g. Pachler and Field 1997, ch. 12, or Herlt et al. 1998).

They can also raise the degree of personal involvement, may motivate the observer to process the new experiences more critically and may encourage participants to interact on an individual level. A survey or interview situation can provide the context in which, for example, a British learner and his or her partner meet. The British learner, acting as the interviewer, concentrates on his or her linguistic intention to question his or her partner. By focusing on obtaining information for the task in hand the learner is also likely to find out about the other person's characteristics, values, opinions, etc. By doing so the learner is likely to rely on how he or she experiences the other person and interprets his or her answers rather than on stereotypic beliefs. The linguistic task necessitates personal involvement, which can influence the affective elements of attitudes held and may result in an actual attitude change. By providing a number of quality contexts in which all participants can interact with their partners, or even other people, the exchange organiser may reduce the likelihood of participants relying on stereotyping.

Unfortunately, there seems to be a lack of appropriate material: 'the teachers deplored the fact that there are not any ready-made structured teaching materials available for use before, during and after the exchange visit to ensure that the pupils' experiences can be better processed' (Herlt et al., 1998, p. ii).

A common issue which seems to cause many problems on exchanges is food and drink – another area where many stereotypes exist. As A. Weber shows (1992), there are favourable conditions where a change of attitudes is more likely. Starting an exchange with a buffet of local/national specialities can be a bad idea, for example, because the British group members are likely not to recognise most of the food. Although the groups have equal status they do not meet on a level playing field. A disco with a mixture of music would provide a far better forum to meet and get to know each other. An example for setting super-ordinate goals could be a quiz with mixed teams and questions in both English and the target language about a variety of topics. The traditional sports competition between British learners and their partners could be transformed into a tournament of teachers against learners, again with mixed teams.

Although some of these practical examples may seem insignificant, they can be very effective in promoting personal relationships among participants in the attempt to break down stereotypes.

Conclusion

'British schoolchildren still don't like the Germans', reported the *Independent* in September 1997. Roger Dobson, the author, explained that children who had never been to Germany or met anyone from the country had still developed a prejudice against Germany by the time they were twelve years old. In war films, comics and tabloid images the German is traditionally portrayed as 'the enemy'.

What do we learn from this? Despite a unified Europe, political correctness, *Vorsprung durch Technik* and Jürgen Klinsmann, national prejudice remains a real issue and many people hold strong negative stereotypes about Germany. It seems that recalling the past is easier than making a fresh start in order to see a Germany in which circumstances have changed. 'Where stereotypes perpetuate an image which no longer applies it may even be subversive. It reveals a complacent hostility that is counterproductive to good relations between allies' (Moyle, 1997, p. 438).

It is wise, however, to see stereotypical treatment of other cultures in a wider frame: to be aware of relevant British historical development, to understand the sociological and psychological impact of attitude changes, to accept the differences between two nations and even sometimes to rise above things, is to do intercultural relationships justice. To find the energy to organise and carry out exchange programmes in order to improve linguistic knowledge, raise cultural awareness and break down stereotypes means going a step further!

Summary

The discussion in this chapter has shown that there are many ways to supplement classroom-based work. ICT allows particularly imaginative and exciting enhancement opportunities. Access to and the retrieval of authentic material through the internet is but one means by which to supplement what goes on in the A/AS level mfl classroom. The evidence presented here suggests that collaborative project work and social interaction are particularly conducive to the construction of meaning. Despite the rapid advances made possible by new technology, face-to-face encounters with native TL speakers remain invaluable, not least in breaking down negative stereotypes.

References

Bruntlett, S. (1999) 'Selecting, using and producing classroom-based multimedia'. In Leask, M. and Pachler, N. (eds) *Teaching and Learning in the Secondary School Using ICT*. London: Routledge.

Butler, M. and Kelley, P. (1999) 'Videoconferencing'. In Leask, M. and Pachler, N. (eds) *Teaching and Learning in the Secondary School Using ICT*. London: Routledge.

Byram, M. (1997) (ed) *Face to Face. Learning 'Language-and-Culture' through Visits and Exchanges*. London: CILT.

Cox, M. (1999) 'Motivating pupils through the use of ICT'. In Leask, M. and Pachler, N. (eds) *Teaching and Learning in the Secondary School Using ICT*. London: Routledge.

Dobson, R. (1997) 'Germans seen as enemy by young'. In *The Independent*, 13 September.

Frischherz, B. and Lenz, P. (1996) 'Deutsch lernen mit dem WWW: 10 Lernideen'. In *Fremdsprache Deutsch*, Sondernummer, München: Ernst Klett, pp. 41–3.

González-Bueno, M. (1998) 'The effects of electronic mail on Spanish L2 discourse'. In *Language Learning and Technology*, 1, 2, pp. 50–65. Online available at: http://polyglot. cal.msu.edu/llt/vol1num2/article3/default.html

Herlt, G. *et al.* (1998) *Spotlight on Going Abroad*. Manchester: Goethe-Institut.

Hornsey, A. (1994) 'Authenticity in foreign language learning'. In Roberts, T. (ed) *Languages Forum 2/3*. London: Institute of Education, pp. 6–7.

Kupperman, J. and Wallace, R. (1998) 'Evaluating an intercultural internet writing project through a framework of activities and goals'. Paper presented at the annual meeting of the American Educational Research Association. Online available at: http://hi-ce.eecs.umich. edu/papers/aera98/

Lippmann, W. (1922) *Public Opinion*. New York.

Moyle, L. 'Once a German – always a German'. In Barfoot, C. (1997) *Beyond Pug's Tour*. Amsterdam/Atlanta.

Noss, R. and Pachler, N. (1999) 'The challenge of new technologies: doing old things in a new way, or doing new things?' In Mortimore, P. (ed) *Understanding Pedagogy and its Impact on Learning*. London: Paul Chapman.

Osuna, M. and Meskill, C. (1998) 'Using the World Wide Web to integrate Spanish language and culture: a pilot study'. In *Language Learning and Technology*. 1, 2, pp. 66–87. Online available at: http://polyglot.cal.msu.edu/llt/vol1num2/article4/ default.html

Pachler, N. (1999a) 'Theories of learning and Information and Communications Technology'. In Leask, M. and Pachler, N. (eds) *Teaching and Learning in the Secondary School Using ICT*. London: Routledge.

Pachler, N. (1999b) 'Using the Internet as a teaching and learning tool'. In Leask, M. and Pachler, N. (eds) *Teaching and Learning in the Secondary School Using ICT*. London: Routledge.

Pachler, N. and Field, K. (1997) *Learning to Teach Modern Foreign Languages in the Secondary School*. London: Routledge.

Schlabach, J. (1997) 'Landeskunde im Web. Werkstattbericht von einem Deutschkurs an 2,1 einer Wirtschaftsuniversität'. In *Zeitschrift für interkulturellen Fremdsprachenunterricht*. Online available at: http://www.ualberta.ca/~german/ejournal/schlabac.htm

Schulz, R. and Haerle, B. (1996) 'Beer, fast cars, and . . .: stereotypes held by U.S. college-level students of German'. In *Zeitschrift für interkulturellen Fremdsprachenunterricht* 1, 2. Online available at: http://www.ualberta.ca/~german/ejournal/archive/schulz1.htm

Scott, P. and Spencer, C. (1998) *Psychology: A Contemporary Introduction.* Sheffield.

Snow, D. and Byram, M. (1997) *Crossing Frontiers: The School Study Visit Abroad.* London: CILT.

Warschauer, M. (1997) 'Computer-mediated collaborative learning: theory and practice'. In *The Modern Language Journal* 81, iv, pp. 471–81. Also available online at: http://www.lll. hawaii.edu/web/faculty/markw/cmcl.html

Weber, A. (1992) *Social Psychology.* Asheville.

Chapter 15

Vocational alternatives

Shirley Lawes

Introduction

The last ten years have been a period of fundamental change in the post-16 curriculum. The main focus of this change in schools and Further Education (FE) colleges has been the introduction of General National Vocational Qualifications (GNVQs) as alternatives to GCSE and GCE Advanced (A)/Advanced Subsidiary (AS) level. Many teachers in schools, when faced with the challenge of introducing vocational courses, have commented that they felt as if they were moving into an entirely new and largely unfamiliar world and that the requirements of the National Curriculum, GCSE and A/AS level were straightforward in comparison with the quite different demands of vocationally orientated courses. However, vocational education in the 14–19 curriculum is gaining much ground and the massive increase in post-16 provision has meant that a significant number of teachers in schools have joined their colleagues in FE in developing the vocational curriculum.

Despite the rhetoric of how important modern foreign languages (mfl) are in the world of work, they are not automatically included in vocational education and training programmes. There are a variety of reasons for this. For example, there is often reluctance on the part of learners embarking on vocational courses to continue with an area of study in which they may not have been successful at GCSE. They may fear 'more of the same' and, rightly or wrongly, do not see the relevance of languages to their future careers. More recently, mfl specialists in schools may not feel confident in teaching languages with a vocational orientation when they do not have experience in a particular area of work. Vocational education is relatively new to the school curriculum and both learners and teachers alike may feel that it is better to concentrate on meeting the requirements of the qualification itself than to take on 'extra' studies which do not contribute directly to that qualification. For it remains the case that mfl are usually an 'optional extra' in vocational education programmes.

However, it is possible to make a very convincing argument for mfl learning to be included in vocational courses as long as foreign language learning is linked to the occupational nature of the course both in terms of content and context. In this way, at the outset, learners see the relevance and value of continuing mfl study, teachers are able to provide interesting, exciting new orientations and approaches to language learning, and this, in turn, increases learner motivation and success.

FE is the traditional 'home' of vocational education and training. Mfl teachers in FE have a long history of experience in vocationally orientated foreign language teaching and learning. In many FE colleges foreign language learning has been included in a variety of vocational courses from business studies to beauty therapy. Mfl teaching and learning have been most successful in FE when the mfl teacher has been fully involved in programme planning and mfl learning is recognised as an integral part of the learner's experience. It has to be said, however, that in both schools and colleges, the inclusion of a foreign language in a vocational course is often a result of the commitment and enthusiasm of mfl teachers who have to make a strong case and offer an interesting new dimension to a vocational course in order to convince programme leaders to hand over precious teaching hours.

If mfl are to sustain a significant place in the post-16 curriculum, it is essential that mfl teachers, particularly in schools, develop their expertise in course design and actively promote vocationally orientated foreign language learning within vocational programmes. The integration of mfl into these programmes offers a unique opportunity for teachers to expand provision throughout the 11–19 phase (see also Pachler 1997) given the ever-greater numbers of young people embarking on vocational courses and the likely increased vocational orientation of the post-16 curriculum in the future.

Objectives

By the end of the chapter you should:

- be aware of the range of vocationally orientated accreditation schemes available
- understand the overall framework and structure of GNVQ and the place of mfl within it
- be familiar with the different approaches to teaching and learning appropriate to vocationally orientated language learning, and
- be aware of the debate around the so-called academic versus vocational divide

What are the vocational alternatives in post-16 mfl learning?

The most recent innovation in the vocational field has been the *Language Units* developed by a variety of Awarding Bodies to accompany National Vocational Qualifications (NVQs) and GNVQs. I shall examine these in more detail later in this chapter. However, several other vocational language qualifications have been in existence for some time and have been run successfully in both school sixth forms and FE colleges either as alternatives to A/AS level or as adjuncts to work-orientated courses.

Foreign Languages at Work (FLAW)

Perhaps the best known of these schemes is the FLAW scheme offered by the London Chamber of Commerce and Industry (LCCI). Aimed at post-16 learners, FLAW offers a very flexible alternative for teachers to plan work-related courses for specific groups of learners. The scheme offers a framework of assessment and certification; it does not specify course content. It is left to the teacher to devise courses that should relate to an area of work, for example, leisure and tourism or working in an office. Such courses may be designed around topic areas or a series of practical assignments. As far as possible, authentic material should be used for teaching: brochures, newspapers, magazines, business correspondence, trade papers, radio and television broadcasts and so on; all selected to promote communicative competence in a vocational field. Courses should be a minimum of fifty hours in duration and it is expected that the teacher combines classroom teaching with independent learning and where possible, arranges contacts in real work situations. Although no previous mfl experience is required so that courses can be designed from beginner's level, it is also possible to meet the needs of learners who have already completed GCSE courses. The teacher is free to choose methods of assessment but must ensure that enough information is collected at the end of the course to complete a *Profile of Performance* of the learner which relates to a minimum of ten and a maximum of seventeen skill areas (see Figure 15.1).

There are five levels of assessment. Each level contains descriptors. For example, at Level 3, in order to demonstrate speaking/interactive skills, candidates must show that they:

> [can] maintain a conversation/exchange, though may need occasional repetition and speech will be halting at times. Can follow the spoken word at normal speed sufficiently to grasp the essentials and make a response.
>
> (LCCIEB 1996, p. 16)

The teacher is also free to choose between continuous assessment of coursework assignments or end-of-unit tests at regular intervals during the course. Learners compile a dossier during the course of their assignments and related work. An overall assessment is made at the end of the course by the teacher based on all the evidence of performance and a *profile of performance* is the summary of the learner's achievement. An LCCI Examinations Board Course Consultant moderates the course and an official certificate is awarded by the LCCI to successful candidates.

FLAW offers great flexibility to the teacher, but also requires a significant amount of planning and preparation. The scheme has the distinctive advantage of being fairly inexpensive, relatively straightforward to assess and the services of the Course Consultant who is appointed at the time of centre registration, is able to

Speaking and listening

1 Giving a talk
2 Giving instructions
3 Interpreting
4 Participating in discussions
5 Obtaining and giving information
6 Using the telephone
7 Informal conversation
8 Listening for detail
9 Listening for gist

Reading

10 Reading for gist
11 Reading for detail
12 Reading faxes, etc
13 Reading correspondence

Writing (optional activities)

14 Form filling
15 Writing faxes, etc
16 Writing letters
17 Summarising and note taking

Figure 15.1 FLAW language activities profile

provide advice and support in setting up and administration. At the time of writing, the FLAW scheme does not conform to NVQ requirements, although this is under review. However, FLAW offers an interesting possibility for the accreditation of mfl learning alongside a GNVQ programme particularly when a broader range of skills and activities is required.

Other alternatives

The LCCI also offers an examination-based scheme called *Foreign Languages in Industry and Commerce* (FLIC). Examination is at four levels: Preliminary, Threshold, Intermediate and Advanced, and is designed to test oral ability in general and business contexts. This scheme provides syllabus guidelines, but again the teacher has a great degree of flexibility and freedom in course planning. The *Certificate of Business Language Competence* offered by the Royal Society of Arts

(RSA), is an assessment scheme only offered in French, German, Spanish and Italian at five levels: Basic, Survival, Threshold, Operational and Advanced. These examinations are available on demand. A separate syllabus is available for Japanese at Basic level. The examinations are specifically business-orientated, reflecting office practice, and are competence-based. Candidates must pass a number of elements, usually four or five depending on the level in order to achieve a pass. *Competence* is interpreted in the strictest sense in that assessments are criterion-referenced. For example, if, during the oral test, a candidate fails to communicate absolutely correctly any aspect of the instructions given (such as a telephone number), competence is not achieved since such information is deemed essential to the competent communication of the message. The element is, there-fore, not awarded, but may be retaken as many times as is necessary to achieve competence. Teachers of learners in post-16 vocational settings may well feel that such apparent rigour and accuracy, while desirable, could make these examinations very costly to run as each element is charged for separately.

The attraction of the vocationally orientated accreditation schemes is that certification can be achieved at a basic level, in the same way as the *Graded Objectives in Modern Languages* in schools sought to accredit achievement in small steps pre-16. This means that a new language can be introduced and a qualification gained, albeit at a basic level, alongside a vocational programme. Also, learners who were not successful at GCSE in a foreign language can still achieve a qualification at a similar or lower level.

At various times, a variety of business language options have been offered by Examination Boards at A and AS level. Most have met with little success, as learners who have achieved this level of language attainment seem to have preferred the standard A level route. However, it is possible that within the context of the new proposals for broadening out A levels more along the lines of a Baccalauréat-style examination, a more vocationally orientated mfl course will be offered.

REFLECTION

Activity 15.1 Why offer a vocational alternative in mfl?

What justifications would you make for offering mfl within vocational programmes at post-16 and how would you argue the case with:

1   a colleague responsible for vocational courses who is reluctant to give time over to a mfl; and

2   a parent of a Year 11 pupil who has chosen a vocational course at post-16?

The national framework for vocational education and training

Before considering how to approach mfl teaching within vocational programmes, it is essential to have an overall understanding of the vocational qualifications framework since it is quite distinctive and has developed out of a different ideology to the traditional school curriculum. Vocational qualifications are competence-based, founded on behaviourist theories of learning. T. Hyland offers an interesting critique of the behaviourist origins of the competence-based approach in education as being conceptually imprecise, confusing and incoherent in its interpretation in the use of the ideas of 'knowledge' and 'understanding' (see 1993, pp. 57–67). However, the competence movement has influenced the entire education and training system in the UK with most professional qualifications, not least Initial Teacher Education, being based on the achievement of standards based on competencies.

The National Council for Vocational Qualifications (NCVQ)

NCVQ was set up by the government in 1986 and, along with the School Curriculum Assessment Authority (SCAA), was incorporated into the Qualifications and Curriculum Authority (QCA) in 1997. Its mission was to promote vocational qualifications for those in work, school or college and to ensure that vocational qualifications meet particular criteria. Over the following five years NCVQ introduced a framework for work-related qualifications which would 'rationalise and simplify the qualifications system and make it both more attractive and accessible to individuals and more relevant to the needs of employers' (see QCA 1997, p. 3). Alongside the traditional A/AS level post-16 qualification route, NCVQ developed two alternatives: National Vocational Qualifications (NVQs) and General National Vocational Qualifications (GNVQs). NVQs and GNVQs are now *the* major vocational qualifications in England, Wales and Northern Ireland.

NVQs, GNVQs and Industry Lead Bodies

NVQs

It is important not to confuse GNVQs and NVQs. NVQs are work-based qualifications, designed to 'set the seal of standards of performance established for specific occupations' (QCA 1997, p. 3), and are primarily intended for people in employment. An NVQ is not in itself a course or programme of study. It is a detailed assessment schedule, which confirms a person's *competence* to carry out a job and is generally administered in the workplace. However, the majority of craft skills courses providing job training for young people such as hairdressing, beauty therapy, engineering, catering, office skills and so on, in various sectors of post-compulsory education, are now also competence-based and lead to an NVQ.

Lead Industry Bodies

NCVQ was *not* set up to award qualifications, but was the organisation which brought together all interested parties including employers and professional bodies from all sectors of industry to form Lead Industry Bodies and to oversee and guide their work. These 'Lead Bodies', as they became known, comprised representatives from occupational areas whose job it was to break down all the tasks, skills and functions that constituted any given occupation and express them as *elements of competence* of that occupation. Thus, standards were set for a whole range of occupational functions. An NVQ can be gained at Levels 1 to 5 according to level of achievement. A set of *performance criteria* indicates what a person has to *do* to achieve each *element of competence* and when all these are achieved in a *range* of situations to confirm transferability of skills, an NVQ is given by an *Awarding Body*. The Awarding Bodies are the Examinations Boards which have traditionally supplied vocational qualifications such as the Business and Technology Education Council (BTEC), the City and Guilds of London Institute (CGLI), the Royal Society of Arts (RSA), Pitman and the London Chamber of Commerce and Industry Education Board (LCCIEB).

The Lead Industry Body for mfl was the *Languages Lead Body* which established the *National Language Standards and Qualifications*, that is the criteria for assessing mfl within the vocational qualifications framework. Lead Bodies were renamed in 1997 and are now known as *National Training Organisations* (NTOs), but they remain the approved bodies for the setting of standards for NVQs in all occupational areas. The *Languages National Training Organisation* (LNTO; details available at http://www.languagesnto.org.uk) is charged with overseeing the development of the National Language Standards and Qualifications which are considered in the next section.

GNVQs

GNVQs on the other hand, are *courses*, which are primarily intended for young people (14–19-year-olds) in full-time education. They were first introduced in 1992 and are designed

> to provide a valued alternative to A level for the increasing number of students staying on in full-time education beyond the age of 16 [and to] . . . provide a broad-based vocational education which continues many aspects of general education. As well as acquiring the basic skills and body of knowledge which underpins a vocational area, all students have to achieve core skills. The attainment of both vocational and core skills provides a foundation from which students can progress either to further and higher education, or into employment and further training.
>
> (NCVQ 1995c, p. 5)

The Dearing *Review of Qualifications for 16–19 Year Olds* (Dearing 1996) confirmed the GNVQ as an important alternative to A/AS level study, suggesting that the focus on evidence of what learners know, understand and are able to do suits learners 'whose approach to learning is by doing and finding out' (Dearing 1996, p. 14). It is the concept of 'applied knowledge' which essentially distinguishes GNVQ from A/AS level. Indeed, it is likely that Advanced GNVQ will be renamed 'Applied A Levels' in the near future. The recent government report, *Qualifying for Success* (DfEE 1998), provides full information of the likely changes in structure of post-16 qualifications following the Dearing Review and is essential reading for the teacher engaged in this area of work. GNVQs are offered currently in fourteen vocational areas at three levels: Foundation, Intermediate and Advanced (see Figure 15.2). Foundation and Intermediate levels are aimed both at 14–16 year olds as part of a learner's Key Stage 4 experience where they are called Part One awards and also at post-16 learners. Within Key Stage 4 they are intended to be studied in conjunction with GCSEs and are both two-year programmes. For post-16 learners, both Foundation and Intermediate qualifications are one-year, full-time programmes. There are no entry requirements for Foundation level, which is equivalent to 2 GCSEs at lower grades or an NVQ Level 1. Entry requirements for Intermediate level post-16 is usually either a Foundation level GNVQ or two or three GCSEs at grades A*–C; at Key Stage 4 entry there are no entry requirements. Intermediate GNVQ is equivalent to 4 GCSEs grades A* to C or a Level 2 NVQ. Advanced GNVQ, which is aimed at 16–19-year-olds, is officially regarded as of equal status and value to two GCE A levels or an NVQ Level 3 and is accepted as an entry qualification to Higher Education. Recommended entry requirements for Advanced GNVQ are four or five GCSEs grades A*–C. In 1996–7, 83,985 candidates registered for Advanced GNVQs. The most popular courses were engineering, business, hospitality and catering, science, health and social care and leisure and tourism (see NCVQ 1997, p. 51).

At the present time the Advanced GNVQ comprises twelve *Vocational units* plus 3 *Key skills units* of communication, application of number and Information Technology, which are a mandatory requirement and are regarded as an integral part of the qualification. The twelve vocational units, the content of which relates to broad occupational areas, comprise eight *Mandatory vocational units* and four *Optional vocational units*. In addition, time permitting, it is possible to offer further *Additional units* which do not form part of the qualification, but are considered useful extra areas of study. In most GNVQs it is in this final category that we find mfl. Only in a small number of Advanced GNVQs are mfl included as optional units. Each unit of an Advanced GNVQ is certificated individually. Although two years is the usual time for the Advanced course to run, the time-scale is open-ended. Candidates are provided with open access to assessment by teachers for some parts of the course together with an externally assessed test, although so called 'externally assessed benchmark assessments' (see QCA 1998) have recently been piloted which are marked by teachers and then moderated by the Awarding Body.

Vocational area	Foundation level	Intermediate level	Advanced level
Art and design	•	•	•
Business	•	•	•
Construction and the built environment	•	•	•
Engineering	•	•	•
Health and social care	•	•	•
Hospitality and catering	•	•	•
Information Technology	•	•	•
Leisure and tourism	•	•	•
Manufacturing	•	•	•
Science	•	•	•
Media: communication and production	Not available	•	•
Retail and distribution services	Not available	•	•
Land and environment	Available 1999	Available 1999	Available 1999
Performing arts and entertainment industries	Available 1999	Available 1999	Available 1999

Figure 15.2 GNVQ vocational areas and levels of certification
Source: QCA 1997, p. 8

GNVQs do not provide vocational training but are designed to develop 'employability' skills. They indicate achievement of general skills, knowledge and understanding related to an occupational area. They also include key skills in communication, application of number and Information Technology. GNVQs are designed for learners in schools and colleges who have limited access to a workplace. However, they are closely related to NVQs in that their defining feature is the achievement of competencies, albeit in a broad sense in GNVQs.

REFLECTION
Activity 15.2 GNVQs in your school
Find out which (if any) GNVQs are offered in your institution and at which level. Discuss with appropriate staff on what basis decisions were made about introducing these courses into the post-16 curriculum.

Then discuss with groups of learners why they decided to take GNVQs as opposed to A/AS level. How far does the course prepare them for gaining employment?

Approaches to teaching and learning – the distinctiveness of GNVQs

A consideration of the distinctiveness of GNVQs, particularly the advanced qualification, necessarily leads to a comparison with A/AS level. A/AS level is shaped by the pursuit of knowledge for its own sake and focuses on what learners know and understand. GNVQs, on the other hand, are concerned with evidence of what learners know, understand and are able *to do*. It is the *application* of knowledge of understanding which distinguishes the GNVQ from A/AS level and as such, it is seen as appealing to learners who 'prefer qualifications which are closely oriented to the requirements of employment' (NCVQ 1994, p. 8). A/AS levels are subject based whereas GNVQs encompass a variety of skills and a body of knowledge in a vocational field with added skills.

Given the contrast in both the interpretation of 'knowledge' and the content of the two sets of qualifications, approaches to teaching and learning are, necessarily, also distinct. The reader will be familiar with the approaches to teaching and learning in A/AS level which are offered as models of good practice throughout this book. In GNVQs, the emphasis on the 'application', 'relevance' and 'usefulness' of knowledge in itself creates a new meaning of the word since not all knowledge is immediately applicable, relevant or useful. For knowledge to be immediately relevant and useful, it has necessarily to be applied to an activity; there has to be immediate evidence of a *learning outcome*. In GNVQs, therefore, learning proceeds through practical investigation and obtaining of information, with an emphasis on developing the skills needed in the workplace. The teacher is required to adopt a *learner-centred* approach, encouraging *active learning*, and learners need to develop a high degree of autonomy. Unit assignments are interdisciplinary in that they may require some research or investigation, perhaps in the form of an enquiry or questionnaire, some basic data analysis and then a drawing together of information into a conclusion or project report. Learners work collaboratively, often on group projects, and the ability to communicate and work as a team is seen as an integral part of the learning experience. Learners are required to show their ability to work independently, to plan and structure their work (through Action Plans), evaluate and justify and present their work (see also Lucas 1997). This style of learning experience is intended to promote the sort of 'flexibility' and 'adaptability' that is said to be needed in the world of work. Here is an example taken from an NCVQ learner's guide of what an assignment for the Advanced Business GNVQ might look like:

Selling Jeans

As part of an assignment on marketing, undertake a study of the Levi Strauss Company's marketing techniques paying special attention to the role of television advertising. What are the intentions behind the methods used? Who are their target audience? Is their marketing effective and, if so, why? Working with other students in groups, devise an advertisement for a new jeans company and analyse its effectiveness.

(NCVQ 1995a, p. 4)

REFLECTION
Activity 15.3 Starting out on a GNVQ assignment
A GNVQ learner would be expected to draw up an action plan for this assignment. What do you think a teacher might expect to see in such an action plan?

Which of the *process skills* identified above would the learner be developing?

Assessment in GNVQ

The fact that assessment is continuous and competence-based is a key feature of GNVQ courses and has a fundamental effect on the way teaching and learning proceeds. The teacher is concerned as much with assessing evidence of process as of outcomes, that is, the finished project. Development of the key skills of communication, application of number and Information Technology are also assessed integrally. The teacher is able to award a pass, merit or distinction depending on how well the work is carried out ('process skills') and on the quality of the work ('outcomes'). The grading criteria are designed to recognise achievement in these two areas. Figure 15.3, which is taken from a guidance booklet, outlines the grading criteria used in Advanced GNVQs.

While NCVQ, and now QCA, have given much guidance and exemplification for the implementation of GNVQ programmes, there remains much contention and even more diversity of approach to teaching and learning amongst teachers. Carol Fitz-Gibbon has conducted some interesting research with GNVQ and A/AS level learners (see 1997) looking at a variety of aspects of their learning experiences. Although she concludes that more research needs to be undertaken regarding the relative effectiveness of teaching and learning activities encouraged in GNVQs compared with those generally used in A/AS level, she suggests that the active

Process skills	Outcomes
Theme 1: Planning	Theme 4: Quality of outcomes
• *draw up plans of action*	• *synthesis*
• *monitoring courses of action*	• *command of 'language'*
Theme 2: Information seeking and information handling	
• *identifying and using sources to obtain information*	
• *establishing the validity of information*	
Theme 3: Evaluation	
• *evaluating outcomes and alternatives*	
• *justifying particular approaches to tasks/ activities*	

Figure 15.3 Grading criteria in GNVQs
Source: NCVQ 1995a, p. 3

learning methods required for the former might work equally effectively in the latter. Fitz-Gibbon, essentially, sees *experiential learning* as the key to success in vocational courses and argues that the tension between the process of acquiring certain skills and the *content* of the course is less problematic in GNVQs, because of the high premium that is placed on learning how to learn, the self-management of learning, problem solving, working in teams, presentation of work to others, research skills and so on. All these skills, it is argued, can only be acquired through practice and must necessarily relate to a 'real world' context.

The OFSTED booklet *Standards of Achievement in Advanced GNVQs in Sixth Forms 1997*, published in 1998, provides some useful insights into the implementation of GNVQs. The examples of good vocationally orientated learning cited reflect all the process skills discussed above while highlighting the tendency in unsatisfactory work towards direct copying of materials from other sources, the exclusive use of textbooks, portfolios containing identical work and inconsistency in marking and grading by teachers. Assessment and grading is in the process of being revised with changes being piloted by the QCA at the time of writing. The new assessment scheme is to be implemented in 2001. In the meantime, OFSTED considered that 80 per cent of the work they inspected was 'broadly equivalent in quality to that of GCE A-level grade E or above' (OFSTED 1998, p. 4).

REFLECTION
Activity 15.4 Learning skills and mfl
Consider the following process skills in turn and think of an example of how the approaches to teaching and learning which infuse GNVQs could be applied to an mfl component of such vocational courses:

- learning how to learn
- self-management of learning
- problem solving
- working in teams
- research skills
- presentation of work to others, and
- key skills: communication, application of number, Information Technology

I have sought to show ways in which GNVQs require a fundamentally different approach to teaching and learning to A/AS level. Clearly, these approaches must be appropriately mirrored and complemented by the mfl component of a GNVQ Advanced programme. Let us now turn specifically to mfl and consider how they can be taught effectively within a GNVQ at advanced level.

Mfl and GNVQs

In GNVQ advanced leisure and tourism, hospitality and catering, business and retail and distributive services the study of a modern foreign language forms an integral part of the qualification as an Optional Unit (that is, mfl can be chosen as one of the twelve units which are required to achieve the qualification). I shall, therefore, refer to these vocational areas for examples of teaching and learning materials and foreign language content. However, the ideas, examples and approaches offered here could equally be adapted for use in other vocational areas. Although mfl are not compulsory and might be regarded as somewhat peripheral in other Advanced GNVQs, they do offer a valuable opportunity to consolidate Key Stage 4 learning but with a vocational orientation. As Additional Units in an Advanced GNVQ, Language Units can be very successfully orientated towards, for example, engineering, health and social care or, indeed, any other area.

The first important distinction to make is between GNVQ Language Units and NVQ Language Units. GNVQ Language Units are approved for use at Key Stage 4 as an alternative to GCSE (short course) as well as for use as Additional Units in Intermediate and Advanced GNVQs. They are also compatible with the National Language Standards. GNVQ Language Units comprise one unit in oral communication and one unit in written communication relating to 1995 National Curriculum Areas of Experience C ('The world around us') and D ('The world of work'). They are offered at *Foundation Level* (aimed at GCSE grades D and G), and

Intermediate Level (aimed at GCSE grades A*–C). GNVQ Language Units, therefore, are appropriate where mfl study is not compulsory within the GNVQ programme. They are available in French, German and Spanish. (See Figure 15.4 for details of what learners must be able to do in a broadly vocational setting.)

NVQ Language Units, on the other hand, are for use in GNVQs only when mfl study is an essential part of the qualification. They are offered within the GNVQ framework as Optional Units for Advanced GNVQs in leisure and tourism, hospitality and catering, business and retail and distributive services. NVQ Language Units are also used to accredit language skills in the workplace. The National Language Standards (see Figure 15.5) provide the assessment criteria.

Both GNVQ and NVQ Language Units are offered by the Royal Society of Arts (RSA), the Business and Technology Education Council (BTEC, details to be obtained through the EDEXCEL Foundation) and the City and Guilds of London Institute (CGLI) with whom institutions need to register as a centre. They are also

ELEMENTS AT FOUNDATION LEVEL	ELEMENTS AT INTERMEDIATE LEVEL
Oral communication: Element FO1 – Take part in simple structured conversations on familiar matters Element FO2 – Give brief instructions and messages **Written communication:** Element FW1 – Read and respond to short texts on familiar matters Element FW2 – Write short sentences using simple, familiar language	**Oral communication:** Element IO1 – Take part in short conversations on familiar matters Element IO2 – Give information, instructions and messages **Written communication:** Element IW1 – Read and respond to a range of texts Element IW2 – Write paragraphs using simple and complex language
Suggested learning activities: Responding to enquiries by phone, producing an audio or video guide to the local area, giving directions to visitors, making a vistor feel welcome, responding to e-mails, faxes and letters, preparing a plan of a hotel, producing a written guide to the local area.	**Suggested learning activities:** Providing details of education and experience by phone, understanding instructions about their daily work routine, writing to arrange and providing an oral audio or written report on work experience, providing details of education and experience by fax, letter or e-mail, responding to conventions in different cultural environments.

Figure 15.4 Assessment of competence in the National Language Standards
Source: RSA 1996, p. 5–23

offered as 'free-standing' units which means that they can be achieved in their own right and outside a GNVQ programme.

The National Language Standards

Having made the distinction between the two types of mfl accreditation possible within GNVQs, we need to look at their composition and the relevant assessment criteria. First of all, the basis of all mfl accreditation within the vocational qualification framework is the *National Language Standards*. These represent the national framework of standards and qualifications for all work-orientated foreign language learning. The National Language Standards provide the criteria for assessment for vocational foreign language qualifications (e.g. the RSA *Business Language Competence* tests as well as NVQ and GNVQ *Language Units*). They are not teaching courses or syllabuses, or in themselves examinations. The National Language Standards consist of five levels of attainment across the four skills of speaking, listening, reading and writing that set out what a person should be able to do using a foreign language. The standards are generic and apply to all languages. Level 1 covers basic language skills, progressing up to levels 4 and 5, which are applicable to interpreters and translators. The National Language Standards are published by the Languages Lead Body, now known as the Languages National Training Organisation (LNTO). Teachers are required to teach to these standards and must therefore become very familiar with them.

Learners must achieve two units, *Listening* and *Speaking*, at Level 2 of the National Language Standards as Optional units in Advanced GNVQs. Figure 15.5 gives an example of some of the standards for Speaking at Level 2. This indicates the level of performance required for an Optional Language Unit in Advanced GNVQs. Besides describing each element of language competence, the National Language Standards set out:

- the *Performance Evidence* required, that is guidance concerning how much work a candidate needs to submit to demonstrate competence
- the *Performance Criteria* which describe in precise detail what constitutes competent performance in each element

Unit 2S1   **Dealing with routine and daily activities by speaking**
            Elements
   2S1.1   **Asking for information to fulfil routine work requirements**
   2S1.2   **Provide information to fulfil routine work requirements by speaking**
   2S1.3   **Establish and maintain spoken contact with others for routine purposes**
   2S1.4   **Express opinions on familiar and routine work and social topics by speaking**

Figure 15.5 The National Language Standards (NLS)

- the *Range Statements* which define the context of the candidate's performance (e.g. face-to-face, telephone and recorded speech), and
- the *Knowledge Evidence* required, that is a list of linguistic features that a competent candidate would be expected to use

Teacher assessment must take account of and record performance in all these areas. Candidates collect evidence for assessment in a portfolio which should include a minimum of five pieces of evidence for each element to be assessed.

The National Language Standards specify that at Level 2 learners should be able to use language to function at a basic level in a work situation and in informal social settings. They should be able to handle both routine and non-routine demands and would use a fairly simple level of language themselves. They should be able to convey routine information with some confidence. We shall return to these standards when we are considering how the teacher might plan activities in a work-orientated context to meet the above assessment requirements.

Planning for mfl learning in GNVQs

The first, most important planning task for the mfl teachers, is to liaise closely with colleagues, particularly the Programme Leader, who are responsible for the occupational content of the course. It will then be possible to build a scheme of work collaboratively ensuring that the mfl content is relevant and relates to learning in the mandatory units. The mfl teacher needs to be familiar with the broad content of each occupational unit although not necessarily an expert in the vocational area. Teacher and Student Guides, together with the unit competencies provided by the Awarding Body, offer ample information to enable mfl planning to relate closely to the context. It is true that every vocational area has technical terms, but these can be easily learned in context by the teacher at the planning stage if necessary. Work-related contexts and some specialist vocabulary are basically all that distinguishes the content of NVQ and GNVQ Language Units. Language structures are universal. As with A/AS level, the teacher should seek to build on existing knowledge and encourage the learner to adapt that knowledge to new contexts. Language learned for asking the way to the cinema as a visitor or writing a postcard from France on a school trip can easily be reorientated to giving directions to visitors in a hotel or tourist office or writing a simple information sheet on the amenities available in a leisure centre. Discussing with a friend on how to spend an evening becomes planning a day's schedule for a business trip (see also Pachler 1997).

REFLECTION

Activity 15.5 Orientating mfl learning to work contexts

Ask yourself the question, 'What sort of things do people do in the office, shop, hotel?' For example *giving and receiving instructions* would feature heavily in all three work contexts.

Consider your list in relation to one of the work contexts. Make a list of situations that arise in a specific work context. For example *giving and receiving instructions* in a hotel (leisure and tourism) context might involve directing guests to their rooms or taking a booking over the telephone.

A learning-needs analysis should also be undertaken, if possible prior to the start of the course. This should be a collaborative exercise between the teacher and the individual learner. As we suggested in Chapter 1, the development of a *learner profile* is a useful way of developing learner autonomy. A learner profile also provides valuable information for the teacher in terms of individual learning needs and is a good starting point for planning.

The distinctiveness of GNVQs with regard to approaches to teaching and learning have already been outlined and should be carried through as far as possible in mfl learning. A key objective is, therefore, to develop learner autonomy. It has also been suggested that for mfl provision within GNVQs to be successful, it should, as far as possible, mirror the teaching and learning strategies adopted in the vocational units. However, it would be a mistake simply to set an assignment and then expect learners form the outset to work autonomously. The skills of independent learning have to be carefully nurtured, they cannot be assumed (see Chapter 4). Learner autonomy is a *goal* that the teacher plans for, no less in GNVQs than in any other course. Mfl learning in a post-16 vocational context is most effective when the teacher is able to adopt a flexible role moving from the didactic to guiding, monitoring and then assessing. The 'communicative classroom' is arguably more important in a work-orientated context since practical competence in the use of a modern foreign language is the absolute measure of success.

GNVQ and NVQ Language Units are perhaps best worked towards through topic-based assignments which create a 'scenario' and therefore allow individual activities to be complementary and to some extent, integrated. Such activities should include possibilities for learners to work independently and collaboratively. It is not really appropriate to rely on a textbook for teaching mfl within GNVQs, although one or two do exist. The teacher needs to draw on a variety of sources for appropriate teaching and learning materials. In particular, the use of authentic materials is preferable, but not always possible. However, various GNVQ work packs are now available which reproduce 'authentic' materials for vocational language learning. A frequent problem with these is often that, in order to attract a large enough market, the content is too generic. The internet is increasingly an excellent resource for mfl teachers and learners (see Chapter 14). The websites of companies, tourist information centres, government departments, to name but a few, provide a rich source of teaching and learning materials for assignment-based work. A word of caution: one of the difficulties with topic-based assignment work which draws on a range of resources is that the sort of systematic progression that a textbook offers may be lost. Planning must proceed, therefore, within a framework of language structures. Fortunately, the National Language Standards offers *Assessment Guidelines* which suggest appropriate language content. In addition, the teacher will find the requirements of GCSE in terms of grammar and language structures a useful point of reference, revision, and departure for NVQ/GNVQ mfl planning.

Figure 15.6 shows the main considerations for planning mfl teaching and learning within Advanced GNVQs. The National Language Standards (or in the case of Additional Units, the unit assessment criteria) are at the centre of the process; achieving those standards is essential although not the only aim of an mfl vocational course. Elements of planning are interrelated. Once a context or 'scenario' for an assignment or series of lessons is established, we can then proceed to planning learning activities which both work towards the assessment requirements which are realistic in terms of the vocational context. The learning activities will progress from, perhaps, a teacher-led presentation of new language content or group planning of the assignment where learners identify for themselves what new language they will need to learn, through to a presentation or performance for assessment. The teaching and learning resources used will also relate closely to the vocational area, the language content and the learning activities. Activity 15.6 will help you get to grips with practical planning issues. This sort of simulated situation would be a substantial topic for a group of learners and would contribute significantly to the achievement of an NVQ/GNVQ Language Unit.

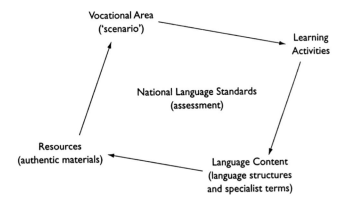

Figure 15.6 Planning GNVQ Language Units

REFLECTION
Activity 15.6 Planning a 'scenario'
One Mandatory Unit of the Advanced Leisure and Tourism course is entitled 'Investigating the leisure and tourism industry'. This topic area is full of exciting possibilities for mfl learning. For example, a 'scenario' could be set for investigating the leisure and tourism industry in an area of the country where the target language is spoken:

> You are working for a travel company as a marketing assistant. You are involved in promotional trade fairs in France and have been asked to research the *Nord/Pas de Calais* region with a view to your company organising a Trade Fair in the area for British companies selling sports equipment . . .

How would you continue this scenario to enable learners to develop their language skills?
Consider specifically, what activities might contribute to the achievement of Unit 2S1 described in Figure 15.5.
What resources might you use?

The kinds of activities you thought of in Activity 15.6 could involve learners working in small groups to plan their assignment collaboratively, using the internet for obtaining information, and could even involve a trip to the *Nord/Pas de Calais* for some 'on the spot' market research. The possibility of expanding on an mfl assignment to be incorporated in the learner's GNVQ portfolio of vocational assignments offers yet another opportunity of integrating mfl learning into the 'mainstream'. Information Technology key skills can also be incorporated into mfl work, particularly the word-processing of assignments, perhaps the production of graphs and spreadsheets or sending e-mails. Nor should we ignore the potential for learners to gain experience of using their foreign language during work experience, either in a UK company or even on a short stay abroad. There are various EU funding projects available to support this sort of initiative and an increasing number of schools and colleges are linking up with similar establishments in Europe to bring together groups of learners on similar vocational courses. The Central Bureau for Educational Visits and Exchanges can supply information and help to set up such contacts. Norbert Pachler notes (1997, p. 18):

> [organising] work experience placements abroad is often treated as a natural extension of [existing] exchange programmes and can help to raise the profile and status of mfl amongst students across the institutions.

There are many similarities between NVQ/GNVQ Language Units and the FLAW scheme. Certainly the approaches to teaching and learning suggested for NVQs/ GNVQs should be applied to FLAW. In many ways FLAW in its present format offers a great deal more flexibility and scope to the teacher as a wider range of skills and activities are included and learning is not confined to the achievement of competencies. This might be seen as a major strength of the scheme.

Does the vocational/academic divide still exist?

The whole issue of the vocationalising of the school curriculum is worthy of serious consideration. Although it is neither appropriate nor possible here to undertake an in-depth analysis of the present context and the likely future developments in post-16 education and training, it is nevertheless important to raise key issues for further reflection and reading.

The debate over the so-called academic/vocational divide has raged for many years with supporters of the traditional classical and liberal humanist curriculum being accused of elitism by their progressive counterparts (see Taylor and Richards 1985 for an account of the various curriculum ideologies). Up until the mid-1970s, and in some quarters up to the present time, education was seen as 'pursuing no ends beyond those set by the educational enquiries themselves' (Pring 1993, p. 65) which 'introduces the learner to the world of ideas, of understanding, of imagination' (Pring 1993, p. 67). This contrasts sharply with the familiar notion of 'training', which is seen as specific preparation for a particular job, such as a fire fighter or a secretary. In a traditional sense, education was what went on principally in schools; training was what took place mainly at work or possibly in Technical Colleges as FE colleges used to be called.

It was the end of the post-war boom years that signalled a more pragmatic and utilitarian view of the role of education in British society. James Callaghan, the then Labour Prime Minister, launched the 'Great Debate on Education' in a speech at Ruskin College, Oxford, in 1976 expressing the concern that there was a need to improve relations between industry and education. Pat Ainley (1988, p. 11) suggests that

> [the] 1976 Great Debate articulated government's concern that education could no longer be left to the educators, but '. . . industry, the trades unions and commerce should now be involved in curriculum planning processes'.

Since then, there have been a number of attempts at vocationalising the post-16 *education* curriculum in schools alongside the traditional *training* curriculum of FE colleges. The Certificate of Pre-Vocational Education (CPVE) and the Technical and Vocational Education Initiative (TVEI) are two examples of this trend. CPVE aimed at offering a more functional, 'relevant' curriculum was introduced into schools and colleges during the 1980s. With an emphasis on core skills and generic 'transferable' skills, this initiative was aimed at the less able, often disaffected learners for whom a work-orientated educational experience was deemed more appropriate. TVEI claimed one of the biggest curriculum expenditures ever made by government. Money was allocated for curriculum innovation with a vocational focus and vast sums were spent on computers, independent learning facilities and the like. These initiatives led to a more generalised vocational orientation in the school curriculum.

'New Vocationalism', as it has been called, of which the GNVQs are the current exemplar, was supported by educationalists critical of government training schemes such as the Youth Opportunities Programmes (YOPS) and the Youth Training Scheme (YTS) who wanted to develop 'programmes which would extend the rights of school leavers and develop all their potential' and which would 'draw on those elements which address the aspirations and destinies of many school leavers' (Finn 1997, p. 190). Finn concludes that a more work-related curriculum is not of necessity 'restricted to an employer-dominated version of work preparation' (Finn 1997, p. 193).

During the late 1980s/early 1990s the youth labour market declined massively, while at the same time social security benefits for the 16–18-year-old age group were cut. Since then, far greater numbers of young people have remained in schools and colleges beyond the age of 16 (75 per cent in 1997). This massive expansion in post-compulsory education is celebrated in most quarters. The fact that young people have no other choice than to continue in education is rarely pointed out, but nevertheless has important implications for the teacher. The general perception built up over a period of time that Britain's economic problems were due to the so-called 'skills gap' means that the vocationalisation of education is readily accepted as the way forward. Education is seen as the key to economic renewal. Edwards (see 1997, p. 3) suggests that the introduction by the government of National Targets for Education and Training (DoE/DfE 1995) for expanding participation in post-16 education 'constitutes a huge break with the tradition of exclusiveness of English post-16 education' and that the achievement of those targets

> is therefore seen as the successful introduction of qualifications offering different kinds of learning to new kinds of 'advanced' students, who would not previously have continued in full-time education. In an especially sharp break with the past, these 'vocational' or applied alternatives to A level have to be both distinctly different in form and content and yet 'equal' (or 'equivalent' or 'comparable', these terms being used almost interchangeably), in the opportunities they make available.
>
> (Edwards 1997, p. 3)

Vocational education should 'provide a bridge between the two previously divided traditions' (Edwards 1997, p. 4). That is, vocational education seeks 'parity of esteem' with traditional academic study. In particular, in post-16 education this means equivalence between the GNVQ Advanced and A level. A key focus of the *Review of Qualifications for 16–19 Year Olds* by Ron Dearing in 1996 was to establish 'parity of esteem' between GNVQ and A level and to promote coherence within post-16 qualifications. The subsequent government consultation document *Qualifying for Success* (DfEE 1998) largely supports the recommendations of the Dearing review and confirms that a 'national framework of qualifications' for 16–19-year-olds is expected to be fully implemented by the year 2002. This would entail revisions of both A/AS and GNVQ Advanced which would mean an alignment of both forms of qualifications. GNVQs would be graded on the same A to E scale as A/AS level and renamed 'Applied A level'. Changes in A/AS level specifications would pull them into line with the unit based certification of GNVQs (see QCA 1998, p. 3). Is this the achievement of 'parity of esteem' or the collapse of academic education into vocationalism? This 'harmonisation' of vocational and academic qualifications has been generally acclaimed as the way forward for post-16 education in the new millennium and is presented (and apparently accepted) as unproblematic. Central government has given its seal of approval in the name of equality of opportunity for all young people (see QCA 1998, p. 1).

However, the vocationalisation of education is not without its critics. In a publication entitled *Teaching People their Place*, Claire Foster suggests that 'new vocationalism actually institutionalises elitism by reducing education for the majority to no more than skill acquisition' (1995, p. 14). Dennis Hayes (see 1998, pp. 19–26) provides an interesting analysis of what he calls the 'triumph of vocationalism' arguing that important conceptual distinctions are being ignored and that complex philosophical distinctions and debates are being resolved as semantic questions. Hayes also points out that 'learning' is used in an undiscriminating way: '[thus] learning to use a lathe, to chop vegetables, learning citizenship, mathematics and ancient languages are given a spurious equality' (Hayes 1998, p. 20). He concludes that 'mainstream education is now dominated by vocational themes of work-related, often competence based curriculum', and that far from providing a 'more democratic, better education for the masses' (Hayes 1998, p. 24) as its advocates claim, vocationalism can only ever be an impoverished form of education.

Summary

In this chapter I have sought to provide an overview of the vocational qualifications framework, from a practical perspective, the wider context of the vocationalisation of education and the place of mfl in it. In the midst of general acceptance, if not approval, of vocational education, I include a dissenting voice to encourage further reading and reflection on the issue. There is much, as yet untapped, potential for mfl learning within vocational programmes and this is an exciting developmental area for the teacher of post-16 learners in schools. However, the scope which NVQ/ GNVQ Language Units currently offer in terms of level of attainment and assessment opportunities might be seen as restrictive. On the other hand, vocational mfl learning can provide new incentives and motivation to learners. For the imaginative, creative and certainly well-motivated teacher, the possibilities for developing mfl learning in a vocational context are enormous. If the achievement of a qualification is seen as a baseline, mfl learning within the vocational framework can provide enriching experiences and valuable knowledge for future foreign language users.

References

Ainley, P. (1988) *From School to YTS: Education and training in England and Wales 1944–1987.* Milton Keynes: Oxford University Press.

DfEE (1998) *Qualifying for Success.* London.

Dearing, R. (1995) *Review of the 16–19 Qualifications Framework: Interim Report and Issues for Consideration.* London: SCAA.

Dearing, R. (1996) *Review of Qualifications for 16–19 Year Olds: Full Report.* London: SCAA.

Department of Employment/Department for Education (1995) *Competitiveness: Forging Ahead.* London.

Edwards, T. (1997) 'Educating leaders and training followers'. In Edwards, T., Fitz-Gibbon, C., Hardman, F., Haywood, R. and Meagher, N. (eds) *Separate but Equal? A Levels and GNVQs.* London: Routledge, pp. 8–28.

Finn, D. (1997) *Training without Jobs, New Deals and Broken Promises.* London: Macmillan.

Fitz-Gibbon, C. (1997) 'Listening to students and the 50 per cent framework'. In Edwards, T., Fitz-Gibbon, C., Hardman, F., Haywood, R. and Meagher, N. (eds) *Separate but Equal? A Levels and GNVQs.* London: Routledge, pp. 29–61.

Foster, C. (1995) 'Teaching People their Place'. In *Living Marxism*, no. 83, London: Junius Publications.

Hales J. and Shaw A. (1997) *Implementation of the Dearing Review of Qualifications: Results of Consultation Surveys.* London: QCA.

Hayes D. (1998) 'Working in post-compulsory Education'. In Armitage, A., Bryant R., Dunnill, R., Hammersley, M., Hayes, D., and Lawes S. (eds) *Teaching and Training in Post-Compulsory Education.* Milton Keynes: Open University Press, pp. 19–26.

Hyland, T. (1993) 'Competence, knowledge and education'. In *Journal of Philosophy of Education*, 27, 1, pp. 57–67.

Languages Lead Body (1997) *The Revised National Languages Standards.* London: CILT.

London Chamber of Commerce and Industry Examinations Board (LCCIEB) (1996) *Foreign Languages at Work: Scheme Booklet.* London.

Lucas, N. (1997) 'The changing sixth form'. In Capel, S., Leask, M. and Turner, T. (eds) *Starting to Teach in the Secondary School: A companion for the Newly Qualified Teacher.* London: Routledge, pp. 211–31.

National Council for Vocational Qualifications (1994) *A Statement by NCVQ on All Our Futures.* London.

National Council for Vocational Qualifications (NCVQ) (1995a) *Grading Advanced Business GNVQ. A Student's Guide.* London.

National Council for Vocational Qualifications (1995b) *Grading Advanced Leisure and Tourism GNVQ: A Guide for Students and Teachers.* London.

National Council for Vocational Qualifications (1995c) *GNVQ Briefing.* London.

National Council for Vocational Qualifications (1997) *Data News.* Issue 4. London.

National Association of Teachers and Lecturers in Further and Higher Education (1996) *GNVQs and Lecturer Workload: A Survey Report.* London.

OFSTED (1998) *Standards of Achievement in Advanced GNVQs in Sixth Forms 1997*. London: Stationery Office.

Pachler, N. (1997) 'Modern foreign languages (mfl) and vocational contexts'. In *Studies in Modern Language Education*, 5, Leeds: University of Leeds, pp. 1–37.

Pring R. (1993) 'Liberal education and vocational preparation'. In Barrow, R. and White, P. (eds) *Beyond Liberal Education: Essays in Honour of Paul Hirst*. London: Routledge, pp. 49–78.

Qualifications and Curriculum Authority (QCA) (1997) *Vocational Qualifications in England, Wales and Northern Ireland*. London.

Qualifications and Curriculum Authority (1998) *On Q*. Issue 2. London.

Royal Society of Arts Examinations Board (1996) *GNVQ Language Units Syllabus*. Coventry.

Taylor, P. and Richards, C. (1985) *An Introduction to Curriculum Studies*. London: NFER-Nelson.

Epilogue

Looking ahead: trends in modern foreign languages in higher education

Jim Coleman

Introduction

University foreign language teaching is extremely diverse. Autonomous institutions with different histories, different missions, different student profiles have developed in unique ways. Under the pressure of funding cuts, student choice and quality assurance, the pace of change is accelerating. However recent teachers' own experience of university language teaching may be, they can know at best a fraction of the picture.

This Epilogue seeks to describe typical trends, and the underlying factors which determine the trends, so that teachers of modern foreign languages at 16–19 can have an accurate, up-to-date factual overview of what happens in the university classroom – and why. Armed with this information, teachers will be able to prepare learners for the transition to higher education where appropriate, to advise them on the choices to be made and how best to approach the choices, and to reflect on their own practice and on how well A/AS level study prepares learners for the undergraduate experience.

Objectives

By the end of this epilogue, you should have some understanding of:

- the history of modern foreign languages in universities
- the types of course and approaches to language teaching currently on offer, including the place of residence abroad, transferable skills, ICT, learner autonomy and assessment
- typical staff and student profiles
- the forces which continue to shape the experience of language students in higher education, and
- where to look for more information

Institutions

To look ahead means first looking backwards: to understand where university language teaching is now, we need to have an idea of where it has come from. Have you ever wondered why university people refer to 'modern languages' rather than 'foreign languages' or simply 'languages'? A century ago, advocates of introducing the study of modern languages to the university syllabus overcame resistance only by modelling their courses on Greek and Latin, prestige subjects which had been taught in universities for centuries. Universities being traditional places, the title 'modern languages' is still widely retained to distinguish them from 'classical languages', although nowadays the latter have disappeared from all but a couple of dozen institutions.

The classical model still weighs heavily on the modern languages syllabus: classical studies embraced literature and associated philosophies, together with the historical evolution of the language. A written competence in the language was acquired essentially through studying the grammatical paradigms and practising them through translation. There was of course no point in acquiring the ability to actually communicate, whether in writing or speech, in Latin or ancient Greek, since the native speakers were all long dead, and Latin's role as a *lingua franca* among European intellectuals had faded out with the Renaissance. The linguistic objective was thus to master the stylistic resources of the target language (TL), in order to read great texts in the original with the fullest understanding and appreciation. Those who graduated in 'modern languages' in the 1960s will recognise the scenario.

The origin of Britain's universities is very diverse, but most share two characteristics: foundation to meet vocational needs – for clerics in the Middle Ages, for industry in the Victorian period, for technology in the 1950s and 1960s – and modest initial status with later promotion to the title 'university'. A handful of medieval and Renaissance institutions – Oxford, Cambridge, Trinity College Dublin and four Scottish universities – survived into the nineteenth century, to be joined by civic and municipal 'redbrick' colleges funded from the fortunes of imperial trade. These colleges, often affiliated to London or another university, received their Royal Charters over the next century, some, such as Nottingham or Southampton, not until after the Second World War. Colleges of Advanced Technology were established in the 1950s, for example at Bradford, Salford and Guildford, to expand the production of trained scientists, engineers and technologists, becoming universities a decade later. The 1963 Robbins Report recommended doubling student numbers within ten years. New 'concrete-and-glass' universities came into being on green-field campuses, while in 1964 the Council for National Academic Awards (CNAA) was created to regulate the polytechnics and colleges, whose role was to promote vocational, professional and industrially based courses in higher education. By the time the polytechnics in their turn became universities in 1992, three decades of focusing on teaching and learning rather than research, of regulation, validation and inspection, had created a 'public sector' of institutions with a view of the education process – objective setting, course design, curriculum planning, quality assurance, documentation – closer to that of schools and education professionals than prevailed in the 'old' or 'traditional' universities. The 'new' universities were thus better prepared for the scrutiny in 1995–6 (see 'Research, teaching and quality assurance' later in this Epilogue).

The 1980s and early 1990s saw very considerable expansion in student numbers, especially in the new universities, accompanied by cuts in resources which continue today under the name of 'efficiency gains'. The ratio of students to academic staff deteriorated substantially, typically rising from around eight to well over twenty, with consequential impact on approaches to teaching. In the 1960s, 6 per cent of eighteen-year-olds attended university. Thirty years later, the figure approaches 40 per cent, while at the same time the majority of those in full-time and part-time higher education are actually not school-leavers but more mature students. The number each university is allowed to recruit is strictly controlled, with severe financial penalties for under- or over-recruitment.

The result of eight centuries of uneven development has been a richly diverse university sector, in which individual institutions have a high degree of autonomy unknown elsewhere in Europe. They set their own aims and objectives, devise their internal structures, decide which courses to offer, define their own syllabuses and levels.

Courses

In UK universities, with their treasured autonomy, there has never been a national curriculum as such. Indeed, the trend has been towards diversification, and I am aware of the many exceptions to the generalisations I make in this epilogue.

My own undergraduate French studies in the late 1960s in a traditional university followed closely the traditional model. There was no history, no contemporary studies, no linguistics. The Part One syllabus (the first two years) comprised seventy-eight set-texts from *Chanson de Roland* to the *nouveau roman* (which still was, then) and history of the language, which concentrated almost exclusively on formal aspects such as diphthongisation and lexical evolution.

But already, in other institutions, changes were afoot. The language departments of many Colleges of Advanced Technology (CATs) began to specialise in career-orientated language skills, particularly translation and interpreting. They also offered new combinations of subjects, such as science and languages. In the polytechnics meanwhile, the literary canon was replaced by 'area studies' – a social science approach focusing on the contemporary culture of countries where the TL was spoken, and embracing politics, geography, economics, sociolinguistics and recent history. As in the CATs, the emphasis shifted from literary competence to a work-orientated spread of skills, including high-level language proficiency. The traditional universities have learnt from such new departures, but the influence has been gradual because of their staffing profile (see 'Staff' later on). Nevertheless, undergraduate choice inexorably leads away from concentration on literature – though students continue to welcome it as light relief.

There has been a concurrent move away from Single Honours degrees, which has accelerated in the 1990s. In the 1960s, Single Honours attracted the brightest students, Combined Honours was spoken of with scorn, and allocated less experienced teachers. By 1994 (see Coleman 1996a and b), better-qualified students were on Joint Honours courses. Now we are seeing an increasingly dramatic transformation: in Portsmouth, for example, in the space of four years to 1997, the proportion of students of French following single honours has dropped from 65 per cent to only 30 per cent. New pathways are devised to optimise recruitment, which is increasingly unstable and unpredictable. 1997, for example, saw a drop in the take-up of German, for which there was no obvious cause.

REFLECTION

Activity E.1 Comparing experiences

Recall your own university experience, and discuss it with your colleagues:

- when did each graduate?
- from what kind of university department?
- which domains did the curriculum emphasise?
- what were the similarities and differences in your university learning experiences?

And for at least five years, the majority of students of languages in British higher education have been *outside* the specialist language departments (see Thomas 1993). They currently represent nearly two-thirds of all language students, with an annual growth rate of 10 per cent. The movement to Institution-Wide Language Programmes (IWLPs) began in the polytechnics in the late 1980s. Language courses for specialists in other disciplines such as economics or engineering, where they existed at all, had until then been scornfully dismissed, with derogatory terminology ('servicing', 'non-specialists') reinforcing the low status of such work. Although some of this snobbery persists, the IWLP movement has become very professional, with an annual conference whose proceedings are published, and codes of good practice. IWLPs offer two or three hours per week of tuition, and work best where there is an explicit institutional commitment to offer a foreign language to every student, and where central support at the highest level ensures genuine opportunity. Languages have a fixed timetable slot across the whole institution, and are a formal part of the student's curriculum, with proper timetable space accorded. Success is certificated on a defined scale, and accredited as part of the student's degree profile. Staffing is by trained full-timers in central, fully equipped accommodation. Needless to say, not all IWLPs meet all the desiderata: too often the position of the IWLP in funding and management structures is precarious, and staff are predominantly part time or hourly paid. French, German,

Spanish and Italian are routinely offered, with less widely taught languages including Russian, Japanese and Chinese also available. The majority of classes are at beginners' or GCSE level.

IWLPs have been helped by a general movement away from a fixed degree course to modularised or unitised degree pathways. Within a 'French' or 'Spanish' degree, students have a much wider choice of options than before, typically taking a total of 120 credits at the appropriate level. Since at the same time nearly all universities have moved from three terms to two semesters, a first-year student might begin with 10-credit introductory units in cultural studies, economics, language awareness and contemporary history, and a compulsory 20-credit unit in language. Prerequisite and co-requisite units ensure some coherence in the individual student's curriculum, although it is argued that the cumulative learning of the past, building to an impressive 'exit velocity' by graduation, may have been diluted.

REFLECTION

Activity E.2 Discuss with learners

Elicit learners' views of university language study:

- do they intend to continue with one or more languages at university level?
- if so – or if not – why?
- what types of courses are on offer?
- what proportion of their degree do they intend to devote to languages?

A further advantage of unitised course structures is their flexibility. Students may opt to move between full-time and part-time modes as family circumstances change, or to take a semester out to earn enough to live on for the next two semesters, or to take their credits to a different university altogether. Few students exploit the flexibility at present, but numbers may grow following the introduction of fees of £1,000 a year for new students from 1998–9.

As employment patterns have changed, as successive governments have sought to link graduate profiles more closely to the needs of British industry, as potential students (and their parents) have become more sophisticated, looking beyond university to subsequent careers, so there has been a move to define, integrate and promote the personal, transferable skills within degree programmes. These days, employers expect graduates to 'hit the ground running' (clichés abound in this domain), i.e. to need a minimum of further training in the skills business requires. As well as the foreign language and intellectual qualities, these include a range of communication skills – written reports, oral presentations, making a persuasive case, researching, analysing and synthesising information from a range of sources – the 'self' skills (self-awareness, self-discipline, self-motivation), and a number of work-related skills (organisation, setting and meeting objectives, project planning, problem solving, time management, working independently and in teams), as well as the numeracy and computer skills (word-processing, spreadsheets, databases, e-mail, internet) which graduate employers take for granted.

These days, thanks to the CNAA legacy and recent quality control initiatives, degree components are documented in considerable detail, including course objectives, approaches to teaching and learning, week-by-week content, form of and criteria for assessment, and indicative bibliography. Unit descriptions will normally indicate the transferable skills acquired as prominently as the knowledge content. Even traditional degrees benefit from making explicit the *transferable* intellectual and other skills their graduates offer, although a proportion of academics, now as in the past, and especially in the humanities, have always mistrusted courses which have too practical an outcome. In a national survey in 1993, a majority of humanities staff, alone of all university disciplines, declared that the purpose of a university degree was *not* to prepare for the world of work.

French and the Enterprise Path (Coleman and Parker 1992) was the first book to describe the impact of the government's Enterprise in Higher Education initiative in foreign languages, and to address the question of integration of foreign language skills with other transferable, work-related skills. Indeed, it is often in foreign language classes that such skills are predominantly developed. Individual and group presentations take a number of forms, as do individual and group projects, often incorporating locating and defining a topic, researching it from TL sources, and putting together a written and oral presentation, perhaps on video. There remains, however, an element of packaging in some cases: 'presentation skills' may mean a clear and structured exposition in good German or Russian, with smiles, eye contact, appropriate OHPs, bullet points and hand-outs, or may disguise the traditional in-class mumbling through a ten-page handwritten essay in English.

REFLECTION
Activity E.3 Employment prospects
Discuss with your learners what else they might gain from a degree course:
- what is the personal employment value of language skills?
- what personal transferable skills, or employment skills, do they expect to develop through a university language course?

A further recent development is the Europeanisation of university courses, through European Commission programmes such as ERASMUS, LINGUA and SOCRATES. Although the EU's target of 10 per cent of European students taking part of their degree in another member state has not yet been attained, and although the UK takes in more students than it can persuade to study abroad, the choice is available on an increasing number of courses. The European Credit Transfer Scheme (ECTS) ensures that students can carry credits internationally.

Virtually all courses with a substantial language component, and an increasing number of others, include an extended period of residence abroad. Even Oxbridge, where until quite recently students were actively discouraged from interrupting intellectual activities with a merely linguistic holiday, has joined the majority. As with other degree components, the objectives, outcomes and skills related to residence abroad are now made more explicit.

Since the earliest assistantships before the First World War, residence abroad has always been intuitively expected to improve language skills and to develop maturity and independence. There is now solid evidence of the substantial improvement in TL proficiency, although the progress is uneven, concentrated in the oral–aural skills, greater for initially weaker learners, and by no means automatic. Enhanced proficiency depends on appropriate attitudes, behaviours and strategies, and seems rarely to extend to grammar.

Where best practice prevails, residence abroad is today expected to contribute also to academic, cultural, personal and professional development; objectives are clearly set out, preparation, support and monitoring are thorough, and the outcomes are assessed, although the grades do not always contribute to the final degree classification. Considerable attention is paid, both in preparation and out-comes, to intercultural competence, which is an amalgam of knowledge, attitudes, beliefs and behaviours which together allow an individual to derive maximum benefit from an extended stay abroad (see also Chapter 5).

Residence abroad is expensive, and will become more so with the disappearance of grants and the advent of fees (currently payable at £500 per annum while abroad, but not within SOCRATES–ERASMUS exchanges). There are fears that univer-sities could offer, and hard-up students take up, 'economy' language degrees with little or no residence abroad. I think this is unlikely: many students opt for languages *because* of the year abroad; and the enhanced employability of graduates who have lived and worked abroad is now well documented and widely recognised.

Figure E.1 shows how students spend the period abroad, which remains a full year in most cases, though often split between two destinations.

	Student	Assistant	Work placement	Combination or other
French	53.4%	26.7%	11.6%	8.3%
German	53.4%	19.7%	17.3%	9.5%
Spanish	72.5%	9.7%	8.9%	8.9%
Russian	91.8%	0.4%	2.9%	4.9%

Figure E.1 How students spend the period abroad

REFLECTION
Activity E.4 Residence abroad
Compare past experience and future expectations with your colleagues and learners:
- recall the main features and outcomes of your own stay in the TL community
- compare these with your colleagues
- did you all take best advantage of the opportunities?
- what is your learners' experience of 'abroad' so far? and
- what do your learners see as the main reasons for residence abroad in a university course?

Staff

Colin Evans used to refer to university modern languages as 'young women being taught by middle-aged men'. There are more women teachers and professors in languages than in almost any other discipline, but men still dominate. The old model of discrete, single-language departments has been largely superseded by larger units, typically schools or faculties, under an umbrella of modern languages, humanities or business studies. A rapid expansion in staff numbers in the 1960s and early 1970s was followed by virtually no recruitment to language departments for nearly twenty years, with the result that the age profile of staff is skewed towards the over-50s. In recent years, carrots and sticks have persuaded many, especially the less committed, to take early retirement. They have been replaced by fewer, younger, cheaper staff: despite the marked deterioration in salaries and working conditions since 1980, there is no problem in recruiting staff. The relevance of their qualifications (typically a PhD near completion and a couple of publications) is, however, more open to question.

The literary culture which university modern language departments inherited from classical studies has from the start been self-perpetuating. The best students on literary courses were encouraged into research and then into a lecturing career (those with a doctorate on imagery in Villon had few alternatives in any case). Even when rival courses came onstream in the 1960s, the literary culture continued: graduates from CATs and polytechnics found better-paid jobs elsewhere, few undertook research, and the profession was restocked with *littéraires*. It continues to be so, as repeated postgraduate surveys show. Whilst literature is often imaginatively taught, and can provide extensive TL input, the tragedy is that what students increasingly demand are not literary courses, but contemporary society and culture, business studies and high-quality language teaching. An annual census of job adverts confirms that these specialisms are what departments themselves seek. Yet from self-interest (research students bring prestige and RAE income – see 'Research, teaching and quality assurance' later on), staff in traditional departments, whose reputation continues to attract well-qualified entrants, encourage their best students into traditional areas. A list of the research topics of research students in French in February 1998 shows 19 in applied linguistics, 36 in other linguistics including translation, 132 in politics, social sciences, cultural studies, cinema, media and feminist theory, and no fewer than 451 in literature. The position is similar in other 'modern' languages. Able and embittered twenty-somethings with PhDs that no one wants leave academia, while departments seeking specialist linguists and sociologists take on staff with inappropriate expertise, or, increasingly, part-timers on temporary contracts.

Already in 1992 (see Thomas 1993), 20 per cent of staff were part-timers, rising to over 50 per cent in some departments. The proportion has increased since. Ironically, the part-timers are often trained language teachers, while the permanent staff are almost wholly untrained as teachers. The universities' resistance to proposals for teaching certificates from the Quality Assurance Agency (QAA) guarantees that this will continue to be the case.

Students

British students of modern languages have been occasionally but never comprehensively studied. In recent years, Thomas (1993) has produced the most reliable account of numbers so far available, and Evans (1988) carried out a fascinating qualitative study of students and staff at three universities in 1985–6. A major investigation was initiated in the mid-1980s, funded by the Nuffield Foundation, and in 1986 collected a good deal of information from a structured sample of 586 students, but the data was left unanalysed until Meara (1993, 1994a, 1994b) pulled out some key findings. More general studies going back twenty years repeatedly lament the lack of reliable statistics. The absence of information was a major reason for conducting my own study in 1994, grandly entitled the European Language Proficiency Survey (see Coleman 1996a).

Women make up 63 per cent of students of Russian, 69 per cent of German, 72 per cent of French, and 75 per cent of Spanish. The average prior language study is eight years for French, six for German, five for Spanish and four for Russian. Over 50 per cent of language students follow joint or combined courses, the most popular combinations being business studies, twin languages or European studies. One in ten students does not have British nationality, and between one-tenth (French, German) and one-quarter (Spanish) of their parents are not native speakers of English. Most of the parents do not themselves speak a foreign language, but they do encourage their offspring, and half have frequent contact with foreign friends. Students from other EU countries now represent 7 per cent of the UK student body.

Virtually all language students have already visited their target country many times, though the circumstances vary according to the language. Their reasons for studying the language are always mixed, with career advantages just shading a liking for the language itself as the most significant reason (though few language graduates today want to become teachers). There is evidence that pleasure and success in learning the language in a classroom environment are more important in motivating continued language study than curiosity and sympathy towards the foreign language community. Women are more anxious about making mistakes than men are – or at least more willing to admit it.

REFLECTION
Activity E.5 Gender imbalance
Explore with your learners possible reasons for the gender imbalance on university modern languages courses. What is the situation in your A/AS level classes?

The survey found that while language learning was effective in virtually every university department in the country (though not as rapid as at school or during residence abroad), there are no national standards: first-year entrants at university X are as proficient as graduates from university Y. The profession as a whole has been slow to address this problem. The data also suggests that, on average, old universities are able to recruit more proficient entrants, but that by graduation there is no systematic difference in level between old and new universities. Graduates offering two languages are typically as proficient in each as those taking only one.

Over the past twenty-five years – and it should never be forgotten that most of those teaching modern languages in today's universities have been in post for the whole of that period – there is widespread anecdotal evidence backed up by a 1996 scientific study (see Alderson *et al.* 1997) that the mastery of TL grammar by incoming students – both explicit knowledge of the terminology and paradigms, and ability to use grammar correctly – has fallen off. This is partly due to schools moving from a grammar-translation to a communicative methodology, from an approach which assumed that all would go on to university to study languages to one which wanted a cash-in value at all levels, from a goal of explicit knowledge to a goal of communicative competence. It is also partly due to the expansion of numbers. There have, of course, been compensating benefits in terms of communicative ability, fluency and learner confidence.

The responses of university teachers to the 'crisis' in the proficiency of school leavers has been diverse. Many blame the 'failure' of school teachers. Some throw in the towel: if school teachers are no longer teaching productive use of the past historic, how can *we* be expected to do so? (Given that the role of university language teachers until quite recently was more one of stylistic refinement and elimination of residual weaknesses than of fundamental teaching of basic principles, and that most have no training to do either, perhaps this is not such a silly response.) Many institutions have 'beefed up' the grammar teaching, especially in year one, not just for 'remedial' streams but for all. Another common response, given the extreme and increasing pressure on contact hours, has been to turn to technology (see 'Language teaching and learning' below).

While 'languages and related disciplines' remain the fourth most popular subject group for university applicants (after social studies, business and administrative studies, and education), applications fell by 20 per cent between 1994 and 1996. Higher acceptance rates have compensated in part, but poor recruitment has led to a reduction in the number of UK Russian departments, and provision for other 'minority' languages may also be under threat.

REFLECTION

Activity E.6 Staff and student profiles

Consider the following questions:

- do you agree that school-leavers have different foreign language skills from those of past decades?
- what do you think should be done to adapt to these changes?
- is it important, at university level, for language teachers to be trained?

Language teaching and learning

The impact of the classical heritage on syllabuses was long-lasting. And I can well remember a generation of literary scholars, now mostly retired, who spoke exquisite *written* French: grammatically correct, drawing on a vocabulary wider than that of most native speakers, it had only one register (very formal), was pronounced in a perfect Oxbridge accent and was largely incomprehensible to the aforementioned native speakers.

The grammar-translation method of language teaching, still very widespread in higher education foreign language teaching today, dominated my own studies, although final year teaching was all in French. We also had rather aimless 'conversation classes' with a native speaker. Our Germanist at Exeter was a charming lady in her seventies who would bathe naked in pools on Dartmoor – or so she told us. Today, many departments no longer have the resources to employ native speakers for conversation classes. Where they are retained, their workload is heavier, more structured and more integrated than in the past, and they tend to be involved in language marking as well as teaching about contemporary society.

New developments in university language teaching have tended to originate in Scotland, where Sam Taylor from the mid-1970s led several initiatives to bring to higher education the insights which were changing language teaching in schools. *Le Français en Faculté*, published in 1980 after national (i.e. Scotland-wide) piloting and currently into its third edition, was the first to provide ready-made materials on the presentation–practice–production model, based on authentic texts (not all of them literary!), focusing on twelve grammar areas which surveys had shown to be problematic for university entrants, with equal emphasis on spoken and written skills and little on translation.

Video was introduced in the late 1970s as a source of authentic spoken texts. A choice of TL satellite channels is now the norm in most university self-access centres, though not quite universal. In *Lyon à la Une* (1986) a Scottish team built a course on authentic video which they filmed themselves, and courses exist which exploit television news items. But in general, video is used off air as required, often for independent student activities. It is still regarded with suspicion by some old and new fogeys, and indeed by many students. Despite widespread language awareness courses, students frequently possess a fresh and naive view of the language-learning process, as untainted by knowledge of second language acquisition research findings as is that of their teachers. Disorientated to have finished the final volume of the school coursebook and to find university teachers working without one, like acrobats without a safety net, they feel insecure, and exhibit an insatiable demand for grammar classes, as if grammar classes alone will solve all their problems, syntactic, linguistic, metaphysical, emotional . . .

The use of the TL in non-language classes is a subject of continuing debate: language proficiency depends on intensive and extensive interaction in the TL, so many institutions have most lectures and seminars in the TL. But financial pressures and the concurrent move to modularisation mean that a course, for example, in French politics, previously reserved for highly proficient French studies students, will first have admitted students on French and Spanish, European studies or international business, who are carrying two foreign languages in addition to demanding core content courses, and may not have such good understanding of the TL; and finally students of politics who have little or no foreign language skills: their presence makes the classes cost-effective but obliges the lecturer to use English throughout.

Within a communicative approach, the received wisdom is that learners derive more benefit from participating in a communicative situation if the focus is on the purpose of the communication rather than on the language used as a vehicle. Hence the value of obliging students to listen to the TL, in a situation where they are very highly motivated to comprehend, such as a formal lecture. But if the linguistic component of the lecture is pitched, as some theoreticians suggest it should be, just above the present level of proficiency of the students, their understanding will be incomplete – to say nothing of their lecture notes. Therefore in literary and other content courses, there is a trade-off between language practice and full comprehension of the material. In some contexts, it is argued successfully that if mere information transfer is the purpose of the lecture, then it could and should be done by hand-out, video or e-mail, and that lecturers who believe that their every word is so important that they dare not put student understanding at risk by using the TL are suffering from excessive vanity. Elsewhere, especially if the lecturer is not primarily a modern linguist, but an economist or medievalist with an uncertain mastery of the language and other priorities than laboriously preparing a lecture in the TL, teaching will be in English.

Autonomy

'All successful language learners progressively dispense with their teacher' (Allford and Pachler 1998, p. 1), and language staff have been at the forefront of university teaching innovation in the introduction of autonomous learning as they have been in the integration of transferable skills. The move from teaching to what is also known as independent learning or resource-based learning has, unfortunately, been driven as often by managerial resource constraints as by academic concerns, but a great deal of work has ensured that the variously named and well-equipped resource centres on which most departments (83 per cent in 1998) now rely for a proportion of their students' language learning are well-used and effective. There is, however, evidence to show that in fact they do *not* save any resources, since staff time previously devoted to teaching is now needed for guidance and counselling. It is always necessary to encourage positive attitudes to independent learning among students, whose 'authority dependency' makes them initially sceptical if not actually hostile. In a few cases, the label 'independent learning' simply means abandoning the student without guidance to learn on his or her own what the lecturer is unwilling or unable to teach: just as Communicative Competence became abbreviated to Co-Co, this is known as the Fo-Fo approach (it stands for Go Away and Find Out). (See also Chapter 4.)

Much autonomous work depends on what was IT and is now ICT (Information and Communications Technology). Satellite television and the internet are routinely exploited in many departments as sources of up-to-date, authentic foreign language materials for students to scan and incorporate in project work, sometimes using computer-mediated conferencing for team interactions outside the classroom. Even chatlines are exploited (see also Chapter 14). In another new initiative, Portsmouth is exploring the 'virtual visit', internet-based video-conferencing in support of students abroad on study or work placement. But perhaps the most influential approach to electronic communication has been tandem learning.

For a long time, departments have brought together their own students with incoming native speakers of the TL, such as ERASMUS exchange students. Whether in joint translation classes, or as 'linguistic partners' carrying out structured tasks together, this is a cost-effective, highly motivating and largely successful approach to language learning. It has been brought up to date in the International E-mail Tandem Network, developed and coordinated since 1992 by Helmut Brammerts in Germany's Bochum University. Individual students (over 6,000 so far) join one of 29 subnets, depending on the two languages involved, and on a basis of autonomy and reciprocity each helps the other to gain insight into the foreign language and culture (Little and Brammerts 1996; further information is available at: http://www.slf.ruhr-uni-bochum.de/email/infen.html).

There is also a good deal of CALL (computer assisted language learning). The government-funded CTI (Computers in Teaching Initiative) Centre for Modern Languages at the University of Hull provides information, advice and training to the sector, including a journal, a newsletter and a software guide. It also led a TLTP (Teaching and Learning Technology Programme) project known as the TELL (Technology Enhanced Language Learning) consortium, which has developed twenty-six commercially available products for learners at all levels. If the take-up of these and other CALL programs has been limited, it is perhaps partly because of the 'not invented here' syndrome, partly because those responsible for language centres lack the time to evaluate complex products, partly because, as in other areas, it can be a career *dis*advantage to spend too much time on teaching-related rather than research-related tasks. The European association EUROCALL maintains a database of current ICT-based language learning projects at http://www.hull.ac.uk/cti/direct.htm.

Since new students are weaker than previous generations especially in the area of grammar, this is where open access, resource-based learning and CALL are often called upon. But the TELL project evaluation suggests we should be cautious in relying too much on technology.

> In most cases, students' knowledge of grammar is poor. This means that it is unreasonable to expect them to make notes on grammar without advice or help. . . In another evaluation, explicit references to grammar were rare; more common was intuition and guesswork, with students judging their answers based on whether or not they were 'feeling' right rather than by analysing the different component parts of words, phrases or sentences. Perhaps because of this intuitive approach, there seemed to be little explicit benefit in terms of rule acquisition and understanding.
>
> (Laurillard 1997, p. 29)

REFLECTION
Activity E.7 New approaches to teaching and learning
How far do the changes in university foreign language teaching described above match recent development at 11 to 19? Also, discuss with your learners their feelings on ICT and learner autonomy.

Assessment

Like language teaching, language exams, both spoken and written, have been defined by tradition rather than any *ante hoc* rationale, and devised and administered by staff with no particular expertise in language testing.

The traditional oral was conducted by one of the most senior members of the department, together with the external examiner. They took turns to ask questions of the candidate. It lasted thirty minutes, had no fixed topic, and no defined criteria. Examiners looked for intellectual as well as linguistic qualities. Often, the oral incorporated a short reading passage, whose presence was sometimes defended on the grounds that it 'put the candidate at ease' while it manifestly did the opposite.

The weight of tradition continues to be manifested in the separate mention of oral proficiency or distinction on degree certificates. Nowadays this is justified on spurious grounds, for example that employers want to know. But in fact employers are less interested in the perfection of accent and total grammatical accuracy than in communicative ability and presentation skills, not to mention intellectual capacity, subject knowledge, memory, teamwork, translation skills and so on. The truth is that the separate certification of oral proficiency goes back to the days when it was an optional add-on, when the actual ability to use the language, in its written but above all its spoken form, was not valued, and often not even achieved, by either staff or student.

In 1993, Swansea's George Evans surveyed written tests used by French departments in the traditional universities. Of 30 respondents, 29 assessed written proficiency by a prose translation, and in half of them written skills were assessed *only* by a prose and general essay. The 'essay' is a literary or journalistic pastiche, of formulaic construction and highly conventional form, whose title is a literary quotation and in which apposite allusions, the structure of the argument, and the intellectual qualities often earn as much or more credit as the language itself. Neither exercise bears any relation to likely real-life uses of the TL. It may, however, be argued that a prose translation obliges students to demonstrate mastery of complex vocabulary and structures which they might otherwise avoid, and an awareness of the stylistic value of near-synonyms; and that an essay illustrates grasp of cohesive devices and an ability to express intellectually demanding concepts in the TL (see also Chapter 12).

I possess the final examination papers for my father's degree, an external University of London degree completed in 1932, with Honours in French and finals in German. The content – and even a large number of the questions – are indistinguishable from my own Exeter degree taken in 1970, and from many finals papers still in evidence today, although if anything there is today less use of the TL in final-year assessed work in the traditional universities – and the prose composition is not so well done.

But in most departments today there is recognition that language proficiency and translation are separate (if related) skills; that translation in the real world is almost never literary, and is never carried out without dictionaries at a rate of three hours per page. There is an attempt to take into account good practice in language testing, i.e. using tests that are valid and reliable as well as practical (see also Chapter 13).

Where a course offers professional skills, the interpreting or translating will closely imitate the professional situation. A translation exam might involve translating a real technical text, for a defined target reader, in a limited time, using appropriate specialised dictionaries and the student's own lexical database built up over a semester. The output will naturally be word-processed. There may also be a commentary on the difficulties thrown up by the translation and on the solutions adopted. Consecutive interpreting will involve two members of staff, one an English native speaker and the other a native speaker of the TL, who will deliver in a natural way a text adapted from, for example, a German politician, interspersed with questions in English of a similar length to the replies. All three participants stick to their roles: the candidate may, for example, ask for clarification from either speaker, and the speakers will appear not to comprehend the other's language.

On general courses, there will mostly be a range of very varied assessments, often incorporating transferable skills. Coursework will count for roughly as much as exams. Much of the 'content' coursework may take place in the TL: in many universities, most lectures, student essays, and student in-class presentations (both individual and small-group) are in the TL from the very start, although curiously, in some traditional universities, once students have survived their year abroad, they are allowed to do all their content work and assessments in English. Institutions are divided as to whether to allow dictionaries in exams: it is more realistic, and tests use of language tools rather than merely memory; but students tend to waste time on nit-picking, and today's dictionaries give perhaps too much help, covering everything from functions to link-words and model CVs.

During a full degree course, a student will typically encounter audio and video comprehension, summary, translation, letter writing, individual and group presentations from notes, role plays, essays, newspaper articles to be written and critical bibliographies to be drawn up. There will be grammar tests (translation, gap-fill) and independent work, e.g. monitoring news broadcasts and reporting back, or reviewing films, books and plays.

Where a candidate is still interviewed individually, it is now common for him or her to be given a topic to prepare for perhaps thirty minutes before the oral. In this way, the oral has a focus, the candidate can demonstrate both presentational and interactive skills, and the examiners can assess the ability to handle intellectually demanding material while disregarding 'content'.

Increasingly, for both validity and economy, departments favour group orals. An agreed topic provides the basis for semi-prepared group interaction including both presentation and discussion, which is followed by questions and discussion involving the examiners. Such exams, if properly conducted, have been shown to be fair to students (however shy, confident, or proficient); to cover a wider range of linguistic functions than a traditional oral – and to take less staff time! There will probably be a grid of criteria (fluency, accuracy of pronunciation, range of vocabulary, appropriacy, structures, etc.) known to both examiners and candidates; marks will be partly for the group and partly for the individual performance.

Many universities have adopted a global policy of anonymity in all assessments. Despite what might intuitively be expected, there is actually little or no solid evidence that any group, such as women, are disadvantaged by having their identity known to examiners. On the other hand, since the majority of courses now incorporate into assessment a substantial element of coursework, one effect of anonymity, in disciplines such as languages where a skill is being developed over a long period of time, is that feedback on coursework is no longer individual. If Edward or Emma is repeatedly failing to address a weakness in verb endings, no one but he or she will know.

REFLECTION

Activity E.8 New approaches to assessment
How far do the changes in university language assessment described above match recent developments at 11 to 19?

Research, teaching and quality assurance

Despite recurrent promises from the funding councils and university management to give equal credit for good teaching, research remains the basis on which academics are appointed and promoted, and on which departments are rewarded. Universities were not exempt from the Thatcherite policy of demanding openness and accountability (from everyone else), and the first Research Assessment Exercise (RAE) was carried out in 1986. It met with howls of indignation and derision, but as the assessment procedure has been refined, and substantial money attached to the results, people have learnt to play the game, and RAEs – the fifth takes place in 2001 – now dominate the professional life of most academics. So important are the funding and status accorded to RAE ratings that star performers share in a transfer market worthy of the Premier League, while under-achievers can expect a 50 per cent higher teaching load. Contact hours – especially language classes – are often sacrificed to the research effort.

Peer assessment of quality in teaching has until recently meant external examiners – senior colleagues from other institutions who take part in the assessment process in order to guarantee compatibility of standards. At worst unsystematic and ineffective, externalling can be a very effective way of sharing best practice and of disseminating new ideas. The networking opportunity, the chance to discuss curriculum and assessment issues with a range of colleagues from other universities is invaluable, especially perhaps for staff in old universities whose other contacts and conferences are limited to research matters. The 'new' universities have always devoted considerable energy to teaching and learning issues, holding workshops and conferences to share expertise. On residence abroad, for example, Working Party reports in 1991 and 1994 complemented the earlier CNAA *Guidelines on Placement Periods Abroad*. There are also some professional associations which take an explicit interest in teaching as well as research. The *Current Issues in University Language Teaching* series, published by the Association for French Language Studies (AFLS) in association with CILT, has published nine titles since 1991 with four more in the pipeline, and epitomises the concern to enhance the quality and status of teaching while providing methodological and empirical support through educational research. A check of the catalogue of any university library will confirm that languages are ahead of all other university disciplines in the research effort devoted to effective teaching and learning.

The new QAA (Quality Assurance Agency for Higher Education) has inherited two contrasting approaches: an *audit* approach, in which an individual institution's quality assurance processes are checked, and the *assessment* approach which is closer to OFSTED practice. In 1995/96, teams of trained language academics conducted Quality Assessments of every language department in the country, evaluating the student learning experience through observation, documentation and discussion, and awarding a grade from one (unacceptable) to four (excellent) on each of six 'Aspects of Provision': Curriculum Design, Content and Organisation; Teaching, Learning and Assessment; Student Progression and Achievement; Student Support and Guidance; Learning Resources; Quality Assurance and Enhancement. In practice, these 'scores' are usually quoted as a mark out of 24. The process was imperfect, but the published reports, by institution and by subject, are an invaluable source of objective information to complement prospectuses.

The Fund for the Development of Teaching and Learning (FDTL) seeks to build on the assessment, to spread best practice and address issues of concern – in particular residence abroad and the proper integration of independent, resource-based learning. In 1997, ten projects in modern languages were allocated three-year funding of over two million pounds. The ten projects address five themes: Residence Abroad, Independent Learning, Staff Development, Assessment and Transferable Skills. They share a website, newsletters and conferences, with the Centre for Information on Language Teaching and Research (CILT) contracted as a central facility for information and dissemination. Through an intensive programme of surveys, workshops, conferences and institutional visits, the projects have been seeking to identify, describe, disseminate and promote best practice in their respective domains. By 2000, all the stake-holders – government, parents, students, employers and institutions themselves – will have checklists against which the procedures and performance of any individual institution can be measured.

Information and admissions

Traditionally, UK universities differ from their Continental counterparts by operating a double system of selection. While the *baccalauréat* or its equivalent gives automatic entitlement to a university place in most European countries, here the university chooses its students, and the students choose their university, through the very efficient UCAS system. A centralised admissions scheme for forty-four universities began in 1963 as UCCA (Universities' Central Council on Admission). PCAS (the Polytechnics and Colleges Admissions System) performed a similar function for the CNAA institutions until the two merged as UCAS (Universities' Central Admissions System) in 1993.

The best general guide to language studies at university (Hantrais 1989) is now sadly out of date, but there is useful guidance in King and Thomas (1997). Maps with lots of supplementary information are on the UCAS site (http://www.ucas.ac.uk) and at the British Council's Virtual Campus (http://www.britcoun.org/eis/index.htm). Institutional websites (http://www.place name.ac.uk) are now universal, but, like prospectuses, may be silent on key issues. Prospective students should read the HEFCE Quality Assessment reports – in full, not just the scores – at http://www.niss.ac.uk/education/hefce/qar, and look at the FDTL project sites, which can all be accessed from http://lang.fdtl.ac.uk. In choosing between departments, they should ask to see course-unit descriptions. Prospective students should look beyond global research ratings to compare staff research expertise with syllabus: do the research specialisations match the subjects you want to study? They should obtain a list of recent staff publications: are they in areas of the curriculum which prospective students regard as important, or are they in areas which are remote from the undergraduate curriculum? Do they have on the permanent staff an expert in language teaching – this is, after all, the only area common to all university modern language courses, but it is often delivered by experts in other domains, or by temporary or part-time staff. Questions could be asked about who teaches what: which courses are delivered by full-time, permanent staff, and which by temporary or part-time staff?

Finally, let me express the hope that choices may be more rational and better informed than in the past. 'Students will judge institutions on "reputation" which is an euphemism for shared fantasy based on minimal and superannuated evidence, augmented by commercial guides and occasional Sunday supplement articles' (Evans 1988, p. 15).

REFLECTION

Activity E.9 Informed choices

Discuss with your learners the choices surrounding language study at university. You may wish to incorporate individual or small-group tasks as preparation:

- what course options including a foreign language are available at UK universities?
- what distinguishes one from another?
- what are the strengths and weaknesses of each?
- what should applicants look out for when choosing a degree course?
- what questions should they ask?

Summary

In this Epilogue I have looked at the historical factors which have given the UK a spread of universities and language courses unique in Europe. I have sketched profiles of today's staff and students. I have reviewed the main features of modern foreign languages teaching, learning and assessment in British higher education, including the roles played by residence abroad, ICT, learner autonomy and new quality-assurance procedures. This Epilogue has also given an idea of the choices facing learners hoping to study languages at university, and how to obtain current and accurate information to help in decision making.

References

Alderson, J., Clapham, C. and Steel, D. (1997) 'Metalinguistic knowledge, language aptitude and language proficiency'. In *Language Teaching Research* 1, pp. 93–121.

Allford, D. and Pachler, N. (1998) 'Learner autonomy, communication and discourse'. In *Proceedings of the Institution-Wide Language Programmes 7th National Conference*, Sheffield Hallam University, pp. 1–24.

Coleman, J. (1996a) *Studying Languages: A Survey of British and European Students. The Proficiency, Background, Attitudes and Motivations of Students of Foreign Languages in the United Kingdom and Europe*. London: Centre for Information on Language Teaching and Research.

Coleman, J. (1996b) 'Languages for specialists in other disciplines in higher education'. In E. W. Hawkins (ed) *30 Years of Language Teaching: Challenge and Response*. London: Centre for Information on Language Teaching and Research, pp. 70–8.

Coleman, J. and Parker, G. (eds) (1992) *French and the Enterprise Path: Developing Transferable and Professional Skills*. London: AFLS/Centre for Information on Language Teaching and Research.

Evans, C. (1988) *Language People*. Milton Keynes: Open University Press.

Hantrais, L. (1989) *The Undergraduate's Guide to Studying Languages*. London: Centre for Information on Language Teaching and Research.

King, A. and Thomas, G. (1997) *The Guide to Languages and Careers: How to Continue your Languages into Further and Higher Education*. London: Centre for Information on Language Teaching and Research.

Laurillard, D. (1997) *The TELL Consortium: Formative Evaluation Report*, University of Hull.

Little, D. and Brammerts, H. (eds) (1996) *A Guide to Language Learning in Tandem via the Internet*. Dublin: Trinity College, Centre for Language and Communication Studies Occasional Paper no. 46.

Meara, P. (1993) 'What do students do on a language course?'. In *Language Learning Journal* 8, pp. 26–31.

Meara, P. (1994a) 'What should language graduates be able to do?'. In *Language Learning Journal* 9, pp. 36–40.

Meara, P. (1994b) 'The year abroad and its effects'. In *Language Learning Journal* 10, pp. 32–8.

Thomas, G. (1993) *Survey of European Languages in the United Kingdom 1992*. London: Council for National Academic Awards.

Index

Printed in the United Kingdom
by Lightning Source UK Ltd.
123566UK00004B/46/A